NEW PERSPECTIVES ON
Adobe® Flash® Professional CS6

INTRODUCTORY

Luis A. Lopez
Robin M. Romer

COURSE TECHNOLOGY
CENGAGE Learning

Australia • Brazil • Japan • Korea • Mexico • Singapore • Spain • United Kingdom • United States

COURSE TECHNOLOGY
CENGAGE Learning·

New Perspectives on Adobe Flash Professional CS6, Introductory

Editor-in-Chief: Marie Lee

Director of Development: Marah Bellegarde

Executive Editor: Donna Gridely

Associate Acquisitions Editor: Amanda Lyons

Senior Product Manager: Kathy Finnegan

Product Manager: Leigh Hefferon

Product Manager: Julia Leroux-Lindsey

Senior Brand Manager: Elinor Gregory

Market Development Manager: Gretchen Swann

Market Development Manager: Kristie Clark

Developmental Editor: Robin M. Romer

Senior Content Project Manager: Jennifer Goguen McGrail

Composition: GEX Publishing Services

Art Director: Marissa Falco

Text Designer: Althea Chen

Cover Designer: Roycroft Design

Cover Art: © Gallo Images/the Agency Collection/ Getty Images

Copyeditor: Karen Annett

Proofreader: Brandy Lilly

Indexer: Alexandra Nickerson

For product information and technology assistance, contact us at
Cengage Learning Customer & Sales Support, 1-800-354-9706
For permission to use material from this text or product, submit all requests online at **www.cengage.com/permissions**
Further permissions questions can be emailed to
permissionrequest@cengage.com

Some of the product names and company names used in this book have been used for identification purposes only and may be trademarks or registered trademarks of their respective manufacturers and sellers.

Adobe®, Dreamweaver®, Flash®, InDesign®, Illustrator®, and Photoshop® are either registered trademarks or trademarks of Adobe Systems Incorporated in the United States and/or other countries. THIS PRODUCT IS NOT ENDORSED OR SPONSORED BY ADOBE SYSTEMS INCORPORATED, PUBLISHER OF ADOBE® DREAMWEAVER®, FLASH®, INDESIGN®, ILLUSTRATOR®, AND PHOTOSHOP®.

Disclaimer: Any fictional data related to persons or companies or URLs used throughout this book is intended for instructional purposes only. At the time this book was printed, any such data was fictional and not belonging to any real persons or companies.

Library of Congress Control Number: 2012946960

ISBN-13: 978-1-133-59298-3

ISBN-10: 1-133-59298-8

Course Technology
20 Channel Center Street
Boston, MA 02210
USA

Cengage Learning is a leading provider of customized learning solutions with office locations around the globe, including Singapore, the United Kingdom, Australia, Mexico, Brazil, and Japan. Locate your local office at:
international.cengage.com/global

Cengage Learning products are represented in Canada by Nelson Education, Ltd.

To learn more about Course Technology, visit **www.cengage.com/course technology**

To learn more about Cengage Learning, visit **www.cengage.com**

Purchase any of our products at your local college store or at our preferred online store **www.cengagebrain.com**

Printed in the United States of America
1 2 3 4 5 6 7 8 9 16 15 14 13 12

Preface

The New Perspectives Series' critical-thinking, problem-solving approach is the ideal way to prepare students to transcend point-and-click skills and take advantage of all that Adobe Flash Professional CS6 has to offer.

In developing the New Perspectives Series, our goal was to create books that give students the software concepts and practical skills they need to succeed beyond the classroom. We've updated our proven case-based pedagogy with more practical content to make learning skills more meaningful to students.

With the New Perspectives Series, students understand *why* they are learning *what* they are learning, and are fully prepared to apply their skills to real-life situations.

About This Book

This book provides complete coverage of the new Adobe Flash Professional CS6 software, and includes the following:

- Hands-on instruction of the most commonly used features of Flash Professional CS6, including the new Timeline controls, improved features of the Code Snippets panel, auto-save option, Text Layout Framework (TLF) text engine, Motion Editor, motion presets, Bone tool, 3D transformations, and Adobe Media Encoder CS6
- Expanded coverage of ActionScript 3.0 programming that incorporates the use of ActionScript, code snippets, preloaders, components, and video
- Tutorials are reorganized for a better introduction of concepts and skills of how to draw shapes, add text, create symbols, create animations, add interactive elements, and program with ActionScript 3.0, including an earlier introduction of layers, bitmaps, and gradients
- New running case scenario for the Tutorial and Review Assignments, new scenarios for Case Problems 1 and 4, and updated case scenarios for Case Problems 2 and 3

New for this edition!
- Featuring expanded coverage on programming with ActionScript 3.0
- New organization for better introduction of concepts and skills

System Requirements

This book assumes that students have a default installation of Adobe Flash Professional CS6, Adobe Flash Player 11, Adobe Media Encoder CS6, and a current Web browser. The screen shots in this book were produced on a computer running Windows 7 with Aero turned on and, for a browser, Internet Explorer 9. If students use a different operating system or browser, their screens might differ from those in the book.

The New Perspectives Approach

Context

Each tutorial begins with a problem presented in a "real-world" case that is meaningful to students. The case sets the scene to help students understand what they will do in the tutorial.

Hands-on Approach

Each tutorial is divided into manageable sessions that combine reading and hands-on, step-by-step work. Colorful screenshots help guide students through the steps. **Trouble?** tips anticipate common mistakes or problems to help students stay on track and continue with the tutorial.

VISUAL OVERVIEW

Visual Overviews

New for this edition! Each session begins with a Visual Overview, a new two-page spread that includes colorful, enlarged screenshots with numerous callouts and key term definitions, giving students a comprehensive preview of the topics covered in the session, as well as a handy study guide.

PROSKILLS

ProSkills Boxes and Exercises

New for this edition! ProSkills boxes provide guidance for how to use the software in real-world, professional situations, and related ProSkills exercises integrate the technology skills students learn with one or more of the following soft skills: decision making, problem solving, teamwork, verbal communication, and written communication.

KEY STEP

Key Steps

New for this edition! Important steps are highlighted in yellow with attached margin notes to help students pay close attention to completing the steps correctly and avoid time-consuming rework.

INSIGHT

InSight Boxes

InSight boxes offer expert advice and best practices to help students achieve a deeper understanding of the concepts behind the software features and skills.

TIP

Margin Tips

Margin Tips provide helpful hints and shortcuts for more efficient use of the software. The Tips appear in the margin at key points throughout each tutorial, giving students extra information when and where they need it.

REVIEW

APPLY

Assessment

Retention is a key component to learning. At the end of each session, a series of Quick Check questions helps students test their understanding of the material before moving on. Engaging end-of-tutorial Review Assignments and Case Problems have always been a hallmark feature of the New Perspectives Series. Colorful bars and brief descriptions accompany the exercises, making it easy to understand both the goal and level of challenge a particular assignment holds.

REFERENCE

TASK REFERENCE

GLOSSARY/INDEX

Reference

Within each tutorial, Reference boxes appear before a set of steps to provide a succinct summary and preview of how to perform a task. In addition, a complete Task Reference at the back of the book provides quick access to information on how to carry out common tasks. Finally, each book includes a combination Glossary/Index to promote easy reference of material.

Our Complete System of Instruction

Coverage To Meet Your Needs

Whether you're looking for just a small amount of coverage or enough to fill a semester-long class, we can provide you with a textbook that meets your needs.

- Brief books typically cover the essential skills in just 2 to 4 tutorials.
- Introductory books build and expand on those skills and contain an average of 5 to 8 tutorials.
- Comprehensive books are great for a full-semester class, and contain 9 to 12+ tutorials.

So if the book you're holding does not provide the right amount of coverage for you, there's probably another offering available. Go to our Web site or contact your Course Technology sales representative to find out what else we offer.

CourseCasts – Learning on the Go. Always available…always relevant.

Want to keep up with the latest technology trends relevant to you? Visit our site to find a library of podcasts, CourseCasts, featuring a "CourseCast of the Week," and download them to your mp3 player at http://coursecasts.course.com.

Ken Baldauf, host of CourseCasts, is a faculty member of the Florida State University Computer Science Department where he is responsible for teaching technology classes to thousands of FSU students each year. Ken is an expert in the latest technology trends; he gathers and sorts through the most pertinent news and information for CourseCasts so your students can spend their time enjoying technology, rather than trying to figure it out. Open or close your lecture with a discussion based on the latest CourseCast.

Instructor Resources

We offer more than just a book. We have all the tools you need to enhance your lectures, check students' work, and generate exams in a new, easier-to-use and completely revised package. This book's Instructor's Manual, ExamView testbank, PowerPoint presentations, data files, solution files, figure files, and a sample syllabus are all available on a single CD-ROM or for downloading at http://www.cengage.com/coursetechnology.

Acknowledgments

Many thanks to the New Perspectives Team, especially Leigh Hefferon, Jennifer Goguen McGrail, Harmony Wilson, Christian Kunciw, Susan Whalen and Susan Pedicini. Special thanks to Robin M. Romer, co-author and Developmental Editor. As always, it has been a pleasure to work with you. To my wife, Gloria, thank you for your love and support. And to our daughter, Alyssandra, your accomplishments make us so proud and your love keeps me going. As you embark on your new journey in college, remember to stay true to yourself and to make your dreams come true.

– Luis A. Lopez

A very special thank you to Luis A. Lopez. As always, it's a joy to work with you. Much love to my family for their constant support. A huge thank you to my husband, Brian, and our children, Jake and Lily, for their patience and endurance.

– Robin M. Romer

TABLE OF CONTENTS

FLASH

Getting Started with Adobe Flash Professional CS6

Exploring the Basic Features of Flash

Case | *Katie's Pet Shop*

Katie's Pet Shop, founded in 2004, is a growing full-service pet supplies store for all types of pets and a boarding facility for cats and dogs. The shop's services include a pet grooming salon, a pet hospital, and supplies for a wide variety of pets. The shop also offers training classes to teach customers how to train their pets. Various community activities, such as pet adoptions, are held on weekends in coordination with local animal shelters.

Katie's Pet Shop is owned by Katie Summers and is staffed by full-time employees, Aly Garcia, Mike Silvers, and Richard Thompson. Katie handles the bulk of the business decisions, Mike oversees the store's marketing efforts, and Richard is responsible for managing the boarding facility. Aly is the graphic designer and is responsible for designing and developing the content for marketing campaigns as well as the store's Web site. You will help Aly develop graphics and animations using Flash.

STARTING DATA FILES

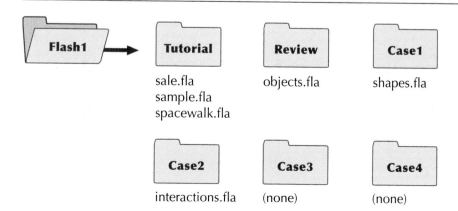

Flash1 → Tutorial

Tutorial
sale.fla
sample.fla
spacewalk.fla

Review
objects.fla

Case1
shapes.fla

Case2
interactions.fla

Case3
(none)

Case4
(none)

SESSION 1.1 VISUAL OVERVIEW

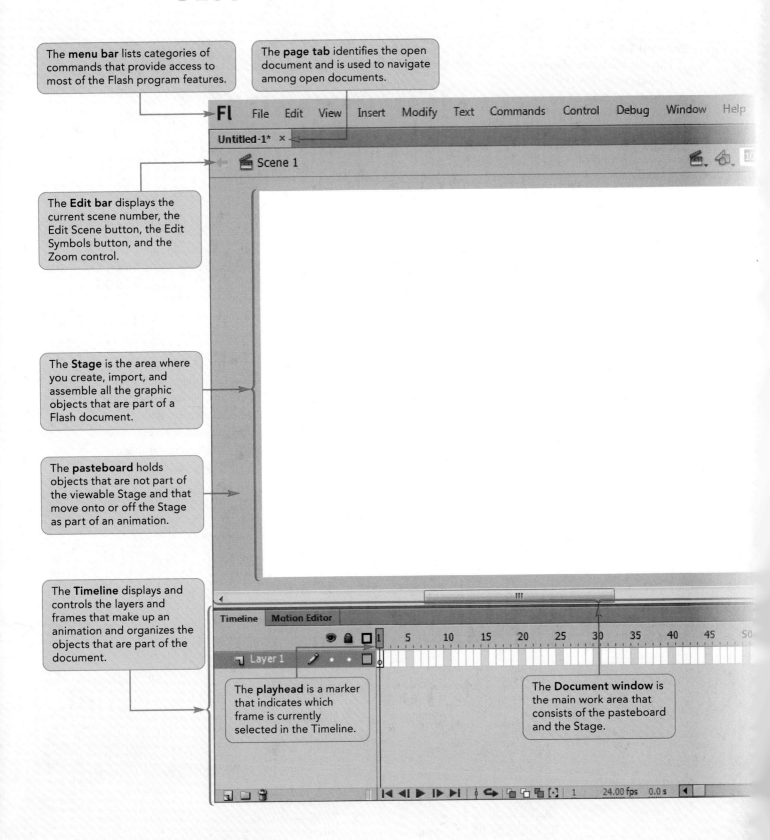

The **menu bar** lists categories of commands that provide access to most of the Flash program features.

The **page tab** identifies the open document and is used to navigate among open documents.

The **Edit bar** displays the current scene number, the Edit Scene button, the Edit Symbols button, and the Zoom control.

The **Stage** is the area where you create, import, and assemble all the graphic objects that are part of a Flash document.

The **pasteboard** holds objects that are not part of the viewable Stage and that move onto or off the Stage as part of an animation.

The **Timeline** displays and controls the layers and frames that make up an animation and organizes the objects that are part of the document.

The **playhead** is a marker that indicates which frame is currently selected in the Timeline.

The **Document window** is the main work area that consists of the pasteboard and the Stage.

FLASH WORKSPACE

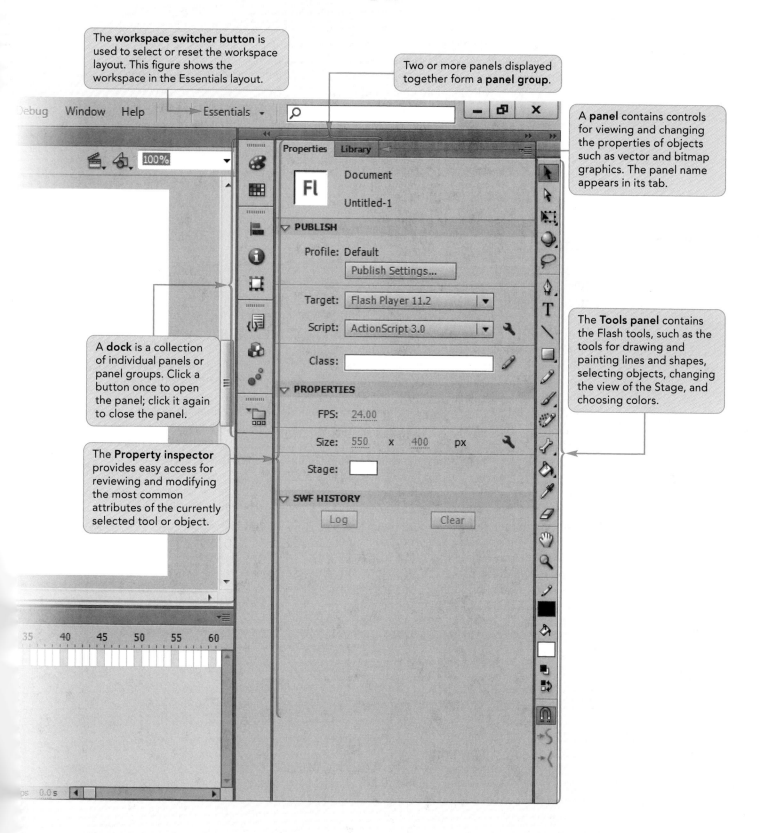

The **workspace switcher button** is used to select or reset the workspace layout. This figure shows the workspace in the Essentials layout.

Two or more panels displayed together form a **panel group**.

A **panel** contains controls for viewing and changing the properties of objects such as vector and bitmap graphics. The panel name appears in its tab.

A **dock** is a collection of individual panels or panel groups. Click a button once to open the panel; click it again to close the panel.

The Tools panel contains the Flash tools, such as the tools for drawing and painting lines and shapes, selecting objects, changing the view of the Stage, and choosing colors.

The **Property inspector** provides easy access for reviewing and modifying the most common attributes of the currently selected tool or object.

Reviewing Types of Web Media

Web pages are made up of text, graphics, animations, sounds, and videos. These elements are referred to as **Web media**. The different types of Web media are created by a variety of programs, and then pulled together to work as a cohesive whole on a Web page through **HTML (Hypertext Markup Language)**, the underlying code used in creating Web pages. The most common types of Web media besides text are graphics and animations, which can be created in Flash.

Adobe Flash Professional CS6 (Flash) is a software program used to create visually exciting and interactive components, such as animated logos and online interactive advertising, that can be used to enhance Web sites. Flash was originally designed to create small, fast-loading animations that could be used in Web pages. Over the years, Flash has evolved into an advanced authoring tool for creating interactive Web media that range from animated logos to Web site navigational controls and interactive Web sites. Flash can also be used to develop engaging content for mobile devices.

Bitmap and Vector Graphics

A **bitmap graphic** is a row-by-row representation of every pixel in the graphic along with each pixel's color. A **pixel** is the smallest picture element on the monitor screen that can be controlled by the computer. A 100×100-pixel bitmap graphic is simply a grid containing 10,000 colored pixels. Bitmap graphics provide blending and subtle variations in colors and textures. You can create and edit bitmap graphics using imaging software such as Adobe Photoshop. An example of a bitmap graphic is a digital photograph. The most common file formats for bitmap graphics used in Web pages are JPEG (Joint Photographic Experts Group), GIF (Graphics Interchange Format), and PNG (Portable Network Graphics).

A **vector graphic** is a set of mathematical instructions that describes the color, outline, and position of all the shapes of the image. Each shape is defined by numbers that represent the shape's position in the window in which it is being displayed. Other numbers represent the points that establish the shape's outline. As a result, vector graphics scale well, which means you can resize a vector image proportionally and the quality remains the same. Vector graphics excel at sharp lines, smooth colors, and precise details. Vector graphic files are generally smaller than bitmap graphic files and take less time to download. Common examples of vector graphics are images created in drawing programs such as Adobe Illustrator as well as images created in Flash.

Figure 1-1 shows an image of a fish as a bitmap graphic (top) and as a vector graphic (bottom). The bitmap graphic becomes distorted when enlarged because it consists of a set number of pixels, whereas the vector graphic retains its quality because its lines and curves are redrawn as it's enlarged.

INSIGHT

Combining Bitmap and Vector Graphics

Designers often import bitmap graphics into Flash and combine them with vector graphics. For example, bitmap images such as photographs often appear as the background to Flash vector graphics and animations. They tend to soften the overall effect and add realism to Flash graphics. Using a bitmap graphic in a Flash document is best when you are developing an advertisement or banner for a business's or professional organization's Web site. You should also edit the bitmap graphic in an image-editing program such as Adobe Photoshop to reduce its size to match the size of the Flash document. Using large bitmap graphics will cause the resulting Flash graphic to download very slowly.

Figure 1-1   **Comparison of bitmap and vector graphics**

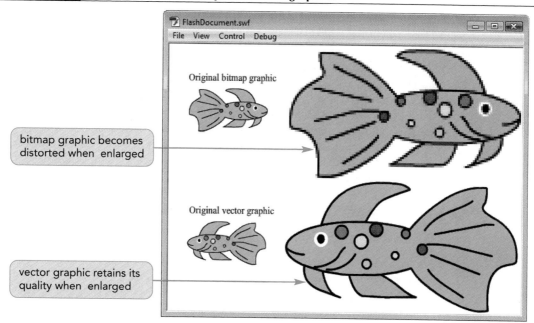

Bitmap and Vector Animation

Animation is a series of still images displayed in sequence to give the illusion of motion. Think of a flip book. Each page shows the same image with a slight alteration. When the pages are fanned or flipped quickly, the image appears to move. Animation can be accomplished with both bitmap and vector images.

Bitmap animation is created by putting a sequence of bitmap images into one file and playing back the sequence. The playback of the bitmap images produces a perception of motion. Each change the viewer sees requires changing the colors of pixels in the frame. A lot of information is required to keep track of all of the pixel changes even for small images of short duration.

Vector animation lists shapes and their transformations that are played back in sequence to produce the perception of motion. The information required to describe the modification of shapes in a vector animation is usually less than the information required to describe the pixel changes in a bitmap animation. Also, vector graphics are resolution independent, which means that they always appear with the optimum on-screen quality regardless of image size or the screen resolution.

Developing Web Media in Flash

Flash allows developers to create media-rich elements that integrate with Web pages and that download quickly. Flash graphics also have streaming capability, which allows animations to start playing even before they download completely. Web media created in Flash are called **documents** and can include text, static images, sound, video, and animations. Flash animations are created from a series of graphic objects such as lines, shapes, and text that are then sequenced. The graphics created in Flash are primarily vector graphics but can include bitmap graphics. Flash supports many import formats so that developers can include media from a broad range of sources, including Photoshop and Illustrator files. In addition, you can export Flash graphics and then reference them in HTML files created with Web site development software such as Adobe Dreamweaver.

PROSKILLS

Decision Making: Using Media in Flash Documents

As you develop Flash documents, you'll have to make many decisions about what media elements to include. A completed Flash document can include many types of media: from silent, still imagery to motion graphics with sound and interactivity as well as elements that incorporate video. You can also add sound—as sound effects, voice-overs, or music—to any element within a Flash document. You can choose to have sound play all the time, be activated by a mouse click, be turned on and off by the user, or be synchronized with events in your document. You can also incorporate video into a Web page as part of a graphic or animation and add controls to the video elements to enable the viewer to manage the video playback. Keep in mind the document's purpose and its intended audience as you decide which media to include in a Flash document. Making good decisions about what to include will help to ensure that the Flash documents you create effectively accomplish your intended goals.

Like other media files, a Flash file must be referenced in an HTML page file to be viewed in a Web page. You can publish the HTML files and references automatically from within the Flash program. You can also insert the reference manually or create your own HTML file to reference and control the Flash file.

While developing content using Flash, you work with a Flash authoring document, referred to as an **FLA file**, which has the .fla file extension. When you're ready to deliver that content for viewing by end users, you publish the Flash document as a **SWF file** (often pronounced "swiff file"), which has the .swf file extension and can be displayed in a Web page. For example, if the Flash document in which you create and develop an animation for the Katie's Pet Shop Web site is named kpsBanner.fla, the published file with the finished animation would be named kpsBanner.swf. The SWF file is also called a **Flash movie**.

The SWF file plays in an HTML file in a Web browser using the **Flash Player plug-in**. All current versions of the major Web browsers come with the Flash Player plug-in installed. Besides allowing Flash documents to be viewed in your browser, the Flash Player plug-in provides controls for zooming in and out of the document, changing the document's quality, printing the document, and other functions depending on settings selected by the document's developer.

Another element of Flash is ActionScript, a scripting programming language that enables you to add interactivity to buttons and other Web media that users can click or select to control the Flash graphics or animation they are viewing. You will learn more about ActionScript in later tutorials.

Starting Flash

When you first start Flash, or when the program is running but no documents are opened, the Welcome screen appears. The Welcome screen provides access to the most commonly used actions such as opening a recently used file, creating a new Flash document, or creating a document using a template. After you open a document or create a new one, the Flash program window appears.

To start Flash and open a new Flash file:

▶ **1.** Click the **Start** button 🕮 on the taskbar, click **All Programs** on the Start menu, click the **Adobe** folder, and then click **Adobe Flash Professional CS6**. The Flash program window opens and displays the Welcome screen.

Trouble? If you don't see the Adobe folder or Adobe Flash Professional CS6 on the All Programs menu, type Adobe Flash in the Search programs and files box, and then click Adobe Flash Professional CS6 in the search results that appear. If you still don't see Adobe Flash Professional CS6, press the Esc key until the Start menu closes, and then ask your instructor or technical support person for help.

Trouble? If the Adobe Product Activation dialog box opens, this is probably the first time Flash was started on this computer. Click the appropriate option button, click the Continue button, enter the information requested, and then click the Register button. If you do not know your serial number or need further assistance, ask your instructor or technical support person.

▶ **2.** If necessary, on the menu bar, click the **Maximize** button 🔲 to maximize the Flash program window.

▶ **3.** In the Create New section of the Welcome screen, click **ActionScript 3.0**. An untitled Flash file window opens.

Trouble? If the Welcome screen is hidden, click File on the menu bar, click New to open the New Document dialog box, click ActionScript 3.0 in the Type box on the General tab of the New Document dialog box, and then click the OK button.

The Flash program window, called the **workspace**, contains elements such as toolbars, windows, and panels that you can arrange to suit your work style and needs. Flash has several preset workspace layouts, including Designer, Developer, and Essentials. Each preset workspace reflects a different way of working with Flash based on the type of project you are creating or your preferred organization. The default arrangement of the Flash elements is the Essentials workspace. The workspace can be customized, which means you can rearrange the elements. The figures in these tutorials show the Flash workspace in the Essentials layout. You'll reset the workspace to the Essentials layout.

To reset the Essentials workspace:

▶ **1.** On the menu bar, click the **workspace switcher** button, and then click **Reset 'Essentials'**. The Flash workspace resets to the default Essentials layout.

   Trouble? If Reset 'Essentials' does not appear as an option, you need to select the Essentials workspace. On the menu bar, click the workspace switcher button, click Essentials, and then repeat Step 1.

▶ **2.** On the menu bar, click **Window**, and then point to **Toolbars**. The menu of available toolbars opens.

▶ **3.** Verify that **Main** and **Controller** do not have check marks next to them and that **Edit Bar** has a check mark next to it. If necessary, click a command to add or remove the check mark; otherwise, press the Esc key twice to close the menu.

Previewing Documents

As you develop a Flash document, you should preview it to check the results of your changes. You can preview your work in Flash in several ways. You can preview or play the document's animation within the Flash workspace, publish the file to play in a separate Flash Player window, or publish it to play in a Web page in your default Web browser. Previewing the document in the Flash workspace is the quickest method, although some animation effects and interactive functions work only in the published format.

   You will open Aly's spacewalk.fla document, and then preview the simple animation from the Flash workspace.

To preview the spacewalk.fla document in the workspace:

▶ **1.** On the menu bar, click **File**, and then click **Close**. If a dialog box prompts you to save changes, click the **No** button. The document closes and the Welcome screen appears.

▶ **2.** On the menu bar, click **File**, and then click **Open**. The Open dialog box opens.

▶ **3.** Navigate to the **Flash1\Tutorial** folder included with your Data Files, click **spacewalk.fla** in the file list, and then click the **Open** button. The spacewalk.fla document opens on the Stage, and its name appears in the page tab.

   Trouble? If the spacewalk.fla file does not include the .fla extension in its filename, your computer's operating system is not configured to display file extensions. Click spacewalk in the file list.

   Trouble? If you don't have the starting Data Files, you need to get them before you can proceed. Your instructor will either give you the Data Files or ask you to obtain them from a specified location (such as a network drive). In either case, make a backup copy of the Data Files before you start so that you have the original files available in case you need to start over. If you have any questions about the Data Files, see your instructor or technical support person for assistance.

▶ **4.** On the menu bar, click **File**, and then click **Save As**. The Save As dialog box opens.

5. Navigate to the **Flash1\Tutorial** folder included with your Data Files if necessary, type **spacewalkNew** in the File name box, and then click the **Save** button. The document is saved with the new name, which appears in the page tab.

6. On the menu bar, click **View**, point to **Magnification**, and then click **Show Frame**. The entire document is visible. See Figure 1-2.

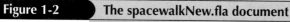

Figure 1-2	The spacewalkNew.fla document

new filename appears in the page tab

Stage and pasteboard display the entire document

playhead moves through the Timeline as the animation plays

you might see different colors

Courtesy of NASA

7. On the menu bar, click **Control**, and then click **Play**. As the animation plays, notice that the Timeline tracks the animation's progress. You will learn more about the elements in the Timeline in the next session.

Another way to preview the animation in the Flash window is to play the animation manually by **scrubbing**, or dragging the playhead back and forth through the frames. Scrubbing is useful when testing an animation during development. You can also preview the published file in a separate Flash Player window or in a browser window.

To preview the published file in Flash Player and a browser:

1. On the menu bar, click **Control**, point to **Test Movie**, and then click **in Flash Professional**. Flash creates a file in the SWF format, opens it in a separate window, and then plays it with Flash Player. See Figure 1-3.

TIP

You can also test the movie by pressing the Ctrl+Enter keys.

Figure 1-3   The spacewalkNew.swf document in Flash Player

SWF file plays in a separate Flash Player window

Courtesy of NASA

2. On the Flash Player window title bar, click the **Close** button [X]. Flash Player closes and you return to the Flash document.

   Trouble? If the Flash program closes, you probably clicked the Close button on the Flash menu bar. Restart Flash and reopen the spacewalkNew.fla file.

3. On the menu bar, click **File**, point to **Publish Preview**, and then click **HTML**. The default browser on your computer opens and the SWF file plays in the browser window. See Figure 1-4.

Figure 1-4   The spacewalkNew.swf file playing in the Internet Explorer Web browser

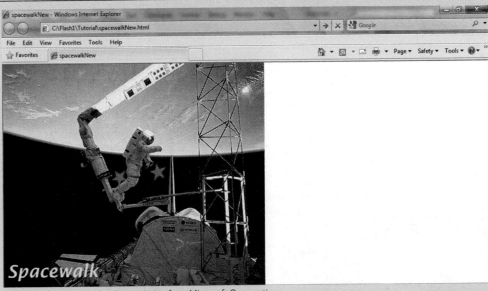

Courtesy of NASA; Used with permission from Microsoft Corporation

> **Trouble?** If a dialog box opens stating that Internet Explorer needs to open a new window to display the Web page, click the OK button.
>
> **Trouble?** If a message appears at the bottom of the window that Internet Explorer restricted the Web page from running, you need to allow blocked content in this instance and whenever you open a Web page in these tutorials. Click the Allow blocked content button, and then click the Yes button in the Security Warning dialog box.
>
> **Trouble?** If the animation still doesn't play, start your Web browser, and then open the spacewalkNew.html file located in the Flash1\Tutorial folder.

4. Right-click the spacewalk animation on the page. A context menu with the controls for the Flash file opens.

5. On the context menu, click **Play** to remove the check mark. The command is deselected and the animation stops.

6. Right-click the spacewalk animation, and then, on the context menu, click **Zoom In**. The graphic's magnification level increases.

7. Use the context menu controls to rewind, zoom out, and step forward and back through the animation.

8. On the browser title bar, click the **Close** button ![X] to close the browser and return to Flash.

TIP

When the graphic is magnified, the pointer shape is a hand and you can drag the graphic to see different areas.

Exploring the Workspace Components

The main components of the Flash workspace are the Stage, pasteboard, Timeline, Tools panel, and other panels.

Stage

A graphic object must be on the Stage to appear in the final document, whether that object is static or animated. The Stage shows only the objects that are visible at a particular point in an animation. In fact, the Stage in Flash is just like the stage in a dramatic production. As the production progresses, actors appear and disappear, and move around from place to place on the Stage. In Flash, different objects are visible on the Stage at different times during playback. As the animation plays, objects might appear or disappear, change position, or change appearance.

Pasteboard

When you complete a Flash document and publish it to view it on a Web page, only the objects and portions of objects on the Stage appear. Objects and portions of objects on the pasteboard are not shown. You can place a graphic on the pasteboard and then animate it to move onto the Stage.

Teamwork: Using the Pasteboard

Creating a Flash document is often a collaborative process involving the client, designers, artists, writers, and others. This group approach can lead to ideas, questions, and eventually decisions that need to be recorded and communicated to the entire team. During development, the pasteboard is a convenient storage area for notes like this. You can use the pasteboard to place instructions or comments that you and team members can use as a reference or guide while working with the Flash document. These notes are visible only in Flash and will not appear in the published document. However, you should still use clear and concise writing; correct grammar, spelling, and punctuation; and appropriate and professional language so that team members easily understand your intended meaning. The pasteboard is also a good place to store graphic objects until you are ready to add them to the Stage. For example, you might display an alternate version of a graphic on the pasteboard for other team members to review. Effective communication among team members can prevent having to rework parts of the Flash document. Strong teamwork is one key to a successful project.

Timeline

Flash documents are divided into frames similar to a motion picture film. Frames represent units of time, and appear in rows along the Timeline. Every column represents one frame. Each frame can contain different images or different states of the same image. The Timeline is used to coordinate and control the timing of the animation by determining how and when frames are displayed. As the animation is played over time, the playhead moves from frame to frame and the contents of each frame appear in succession, achieving the perception of motion. The animation in the spacewalkNew.fla document contains 60 frames, as you can see by the numbers in the Timeline header.

The Timeline also controls **layers**, which are used to organize the content of a Flash document. A new document in Flash contains one layer. As you create an animation, you add more layers to the document. A lengthy or complex animation could have many layers. The layers are listed in a column on the left side of the Timeline. Each row represents one layer. The frames for that layer are shown to the right of the layer name. You can place different objects in the different layers. You select a layer to edit its contents. The selected layer is highlighted and a pencil icon appears to the right of the layer's name. When you draw or change something in a layer, only the contents of the active layer are changed. The objects in the other layers are not affected. As you add layers to the Timeline, it is a good idea to rename each layer with a meaningful name that corresponds to its contents. Then you or anyone else who needs to edit the document can easily locate a layer. Layers don't add to the overall size of the finished file, so you can use as many layers as you need to create an organized structure for a document's content. The animation in the spacewalkNew.fla document contains four layers.

> **TIP**
>
> Although layer names can include spaces and punctuation marks, these are often omitted for simplicity.

To explore the Timeline in the spacewalkNew.fla document:

1. Scrub the playhead by dragging it back and forth along the Timeline header. The animation on the Stage changes based on the content of the different frames. See Figure 1-5.

Figure 1-5   Animation played by scrubbing

animation as it appears in Frame 45

animation has four layers

drag the playhead to manually play the animation

animation has 60 frames, as shown in the Timeline header

Courtesy of NASA

2. In the Timeline header, click **Frame 35**. Frame 35 is the current frame, and its contents appear on the Stage. See Figure 1-6.

Figure 1-6   Frame selected in the Timeline header

animation as it appears in Frame 35

playhead on Frame 35 in the Timeline header

Courtesy of NASA

Tools Panel

The Tools panel includes a variety of tools that you use to create graphics and animations in a Flash document. The first area of the Tools panel contains tools to select and modify graphic images in a Flash document. The second area contains tools to create and modify lines both straight and curved, shapes such as rectangles and ovals, and text that make up the graphic images of a Flash document. The third area contains tools to fill in shapes with color, to copy color from one object to another, and to erase parts of an object. The fourth area contains tools for moving and magnifying the view of the Stage, neither of which affects the way the Flash graphic is displayed to the end user. The default tools and their corresponding button and shortcut are described in Figure 1-7.

TIP

To access additional tools, click and hold a tool button with an arrow to open a menu listing hidden tools, and then click the tool you want to select.

Figure 1-7   Tools panel

Tool Name	Button	Shortcut Key	Function
Selection		V	Selects objects in the Document window; you must select an object to modify it
Subselection		A	Modifies specific anchor points in a line or curve
Free Transform		Q	Moves, scales, rotates, skews, or distorts objects
3D Rotation		W	Rotates movie clips in three-dimensional space
Lasso		L	Selects individual objects or a group of objects
Pen		P	Draws lines or curves by creating anchor points that connect them; clicking draws points for straight lines; clicking and dragging draws points for smooth, curved lines
Text		T	Creates and edits text
Line		N	Draws straight lines (strokes) of varying lengths, widths, and colors
Rectangle		R	Draws rectangles of different sizes and colors
Pencil		Y	Draws lines and shapes in a free-form mode
Brush		B	Paints fills with brush strokes
Deco		U	Applies a pattern, such as a grid or vine fill, to an area or fill
Bone		M	Links objects so that animations applied to one object also affect the linked objects
Paint Bucket		K	Fills enclosed areas of a drawing with color
Eyedropper		I	Picks up styles of existing lines, fills, and text and applies them to other objects
Eraser		E	Erases lines and fills
Hand		H	Moves the view of the Stage and pasteboard
Zoom		Z	Enlarges or reduces the view of the Stage and pasteboard
Stroke Color control			Sets the stroke color from the color palette

Figure 1-7	Tools panel (continued)

Tool Name	Button	Shortcut Key	Function
Fill Color control			Sets the fill color from the color palette
Black and white button			Sets the stroke color to black and the fill color to white
Swap colors button			Swaps the current stroke and fill colors

© 2013 Cengage Learning

Some tools have modifiers that change the way a specific tool functions. The modifiers appear at the bottom of the Tools panel when the tool is selected. For example, when you select the Zoom tool, the Enlarge and Reduce modifier buttons appear so you can choose whether the Zoom tool magnifies or shrinks the view of the Stage.

INSIGHT

Using the Tools Panel Effectively

As you create documents in Flash, you will frequently use the tools in the Tools panel. Always double-check which tool is selected before you click an object on the Stage to ensure that you'll be making the changes you intend. The pointer changes to reflect the function of the tool that is currently selected, providing a visual cue or reminder of which tool is active. For example, when the Zoom tool is selected, the pointer shape is a magnifying glass. A good practice to prevent unintended changes is to click the Selection tool after you use any of the other tools in the Tools panel.

You'll use some of the tools in the Tools panel to modify the spacewalkNew.fla document.

To use the Tools panel to modify the spacewalkNew.fla document:

1. On the menu bar, click **Control**, and then click **Rewind**. Frame 1 is again the current frame.

2. In the Tools panel, click the **Selection Tool** button to select it, if necessary.

3. On the pasteboard to the lower left of the Stage, click the star. The star is selected and the path of the star's animation is displayed. See Figure 1-8.

Figure 1-8   **Star selected on the pasteboard**

pink dotted line
indicates the path
of the star's
animation

light blue box
surrounds the star
to indicate that it
is selected

animation rewound
to Frame 1

Courtesy of NASA

Trouble? If the rest of the document fades, you probably double-clicked the star and entered a different editing mode. On the Edit bar, click the Scene 1 link.

4. Drag the selected star up toward the top of the pasteboard just to the left of the Stage. This new location is now the starting point for the star animation. The star's animation path is modified based on the animation's starting point. See Figure 1-9.

Tutorial 1 Getting Started with Adobe Flash Professional CS6 | Flash

Figure 1-9 ▶ Star's new animation path

selected star in new
location on the
pasteboard

star's animation path
shifts to reflect the
new starting point

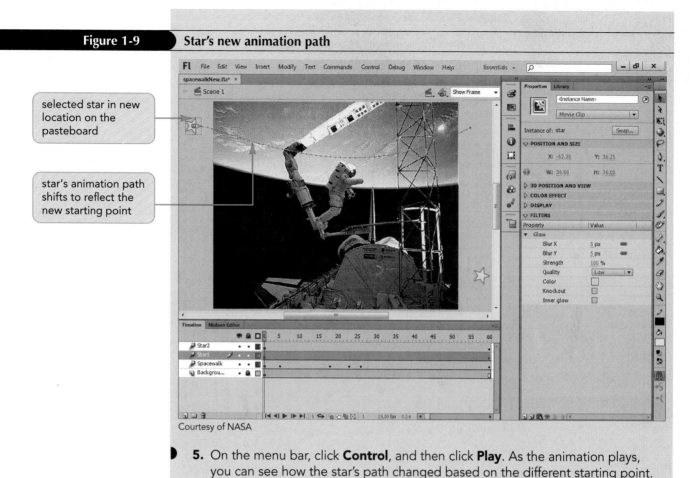

Courtesy of NASA

▶ **5.** On the menu bar, click **Control**, and then click **Play**. As the animation plays,
you can see how the star's path changed based on the different starting point.

Panels

Flash puts most of the controls you need into panels that are available as you work. Flash
includes panels for aligning objects, transforming objects, and mixing and selecting colors.
The Window menu lists all of the available panels. Any panel with a check mark next to
its name appears in the workspace.

You can organize the panels according to your preference. You can close a panel
you don't use often, reposition panels to better fit how you work, and minimize or
collapse panels to icons to minimize the space they occupy in the workspace. You can
also move a panel into another dock or panel group or create a free-floating panel by
moving it onto the workspace.

You work with panel groups in much the same way. You can close, reposition,
minimize, or collapse a panel group. You can move a panel group to a new location
in a dock or create a free-floating panel group. You can also stack free-floating panels
as one unit. A minimized panel group has only its panel tabs visible. In a collapsed
panel group, each panel appears in the dock as a button, which you click to expand or
collapse that panel.

Commonly used panels can be accessed using the docked panel bar on the workspace. You click a panel's icon to open the panel, and then you click the icon again or
the Stage to close the panel.

Organizing Panels and Panel Groups

- To display or hide a panel, on the menu bar, click Window, and then click the panel name.
- To move a panel, drag and drop its tab into another dock or panel group or the workspace.
- To collapse or expand a panel group, click its title bar.
- To move a panel group, drag its title bar to another location in a dock or in the workspace.
- To minimize or maximize a dock, click the Collapse to Icons button or Expand Panels button in the upper-right corner of the dock.
- To select a preset panel arrangement, on the menu bar, click the workspace switcher button, and then click a preset workspace.

You will work with the panels in the spacewalkNew.fla document.

To collapse, expand, and reposition panels:

1. Click the **Library** panel tab. The Library panel moves to the front of the panel group. See Figure 1-10.

| Figure 1-10 | Library panel |

Property inspector moves to the back

Library panel is the active tab

Courtesy of NASA

2. On the menu bar, click **Window**, and then click **Movie Explorer**. The Movie Explorer opens as a free-floating panel.

3. Drag the **Library** panel tab to the Movie Explorer panel title bar and drop the panel when the blue highlighted line appears around the Movie Explorer. The Movie Explorer and the Library panel are now grouped as a free-floating panel group. See Figure 1-11.

Figure 1-11   **Free-floating panel group**

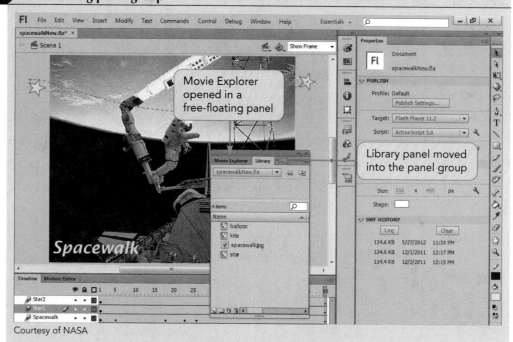

Courtesy of NASA

> **4.** In the upper-right corner of the dock above the Tools panel, click the **Collapse to Icons** button . The Tools panel collapses to a single icon. Panels collapsed to icons minimize the amount of occupied space.

> **5.** In the dock, click the **Tools** button . The Tools panel expands temporarily so that you can select a tool. See Figure 1-12.

Figure 1-12   **Tools panel expanded**

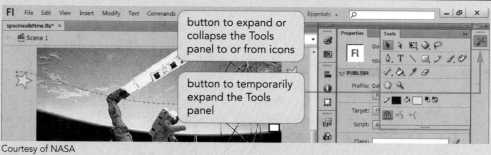

Courtesy of NASA

TIP

After you customize the panels, you can save the workspace layout to quickly rearrange the panels to that layout.

> **6.** In the dock, click the **Tools** button again. The panel collapses to an icon.

> **7.** On the menu bar, click the **workspace switcher** button (labeled Essentials), and then click **Designer**. The panels are docked along the right and left sides of the workspace with the Timeline and Document window at the center. See Figure 1-13.

Figure 1-13   **Workspace in the Designer layout**

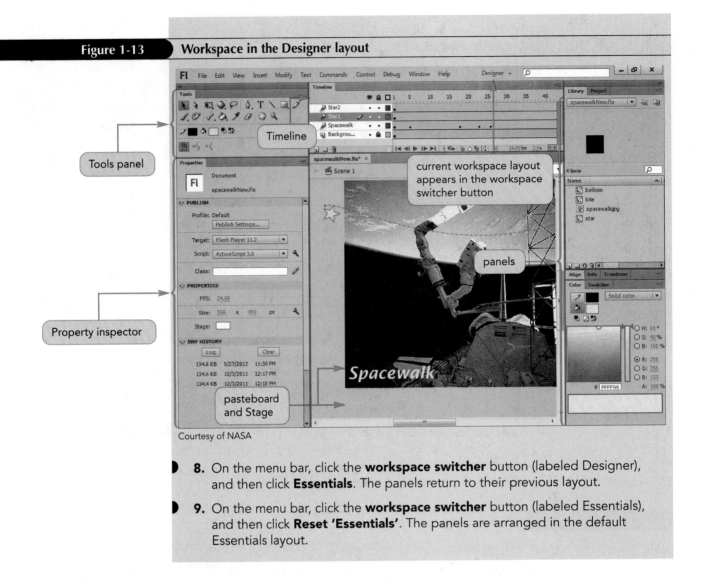

Courtesy of NASA

▶ 8. On the menu bar, click the **workspace switcher** button (labeled Designer), and then click **Essentials**. The panels return to their previous layout.

▶ 9. On the menu bar, click the **workspace switcher** button (labeled Essentials), and then click **Reset 'Essentials'**. The panels are arranged in the default Essentials layout.

Property Inspector

The contents of the Property inspector change to reflect the selected tool. When you click the Selection Tool button in the Tools panel, the Property inspector displays information about the document such as its Publish settings, the background color, or the frame rate. When you select an object on the Stage, such as the star, the Property inspector displays properties specific to that object, such as the object's name, its horizontal and vertical location on the Stage, and its width and height.

You'll use the Property inspector to view the star's properties.

To view information about the star in the Property inspector:

1. On the menu bar, click **Control**, and then click **Rewind**. Frame 1 is the current frame.

2. In the Tools panel, click the **Selection Tool** button ⬚, if necessary. The Property inspector displays information about the spacewalkNew.fla document. See Figure 1-14.

Be sure to select the Selection Tool so you don't make unintended changes to an object.

Figure 1-14   Property inspector for the Selection tool

when selected, information about the star will appear in the Property inspector

Selection tool selected

information about the spacewalkNew.fla document

Courtesy of NASA

3. In the pasteboard, click the star located to the left of the Stage. The star is selected, and information about the star appears in the Property inspector.

You can also use the Property inspector to reposition the star as well as change its dimensions. The values in the X and Y boxes in the Property inspector represent the horizontal (X) and vertical (Y) positions of the star relative to the upper-left corner of the Stage. The W and H values represent the star's width and height dimensions.

To use the Property inspector to reposition and resize the star:

1. In the Position and Size section of the Property inspector, click the value in the X box to select it, type **50**, and then press the **Enter** key. The star is repositioned horizontally.

2. In the Position and Size section of the Property inspector, click the value in the Y box to select it, type **200**, and then press the **Enter** key. The star is repositioned vertically. See Figure 1-15.

TIP

If only the section names are visible in the Property inspector, you need to expand the sections. Click the section name to expand a collapsed section or collapse an expanded section.

Figure 1-15 **Star repositioned on the Stage**

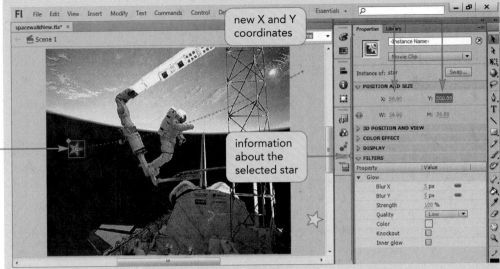

new X and Y coordinates

selected star in its new position

information about the selected star

Courtesy of NASA

▶ **3.** In the Position and Size section of the Property inspector, click the **Lock width and height values together** icon 🈲, if necessary, to change it to locked 🔗.

▶ **4.** In the Position and Size section of the Property inspector, point to the value in the H box. The pointer changes to 🖑.

▶ **5.** Drag the hand pointer to the left to change the height value to **15.00**. The width (W) value adjusts proportionally to the new height value and the star gets smaller. See Figure 1-16.

Figure 1-16 **Pointer used to set object's size**

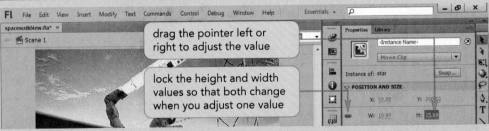

drag the pointer left or right to adjust the value

lock the height and width values so that both change when you adjust one value

Courtesy of NASA

Trouble? If you have trouble setting the exact height value, click in the H box to select the value, type 15.00, and then press the Enter key.

▶ **6.** On the menu bar, click **Control**, and then click **Go To End**. Frame 60 is now the current frame.

▶ **7.** Click the star located to the right of the Stage to select it.

▶ **8.** In the Position and Size section of the Property inspector, point to the value in the W box, and then drag the hand pointer to the right to change the width value to **60.00**. The H (height) value adjusts proportionally to the new width value and the star gets bigger.

Trouble? If you do not see the Position and Size section in the Property inspector, you might have selected the animation's path instead of the star. Click the star again to select it and repeat Step 8.

▶ **9.** On the menu bar, click **Control**, and then click **Play**. The animation plays and you can see the effect of the changes you made to the star's properties.

During the animation, the star starts in its new position and moves to its end position as before. The star gradually changes dimensions. Because you changed the dimensions of the star only in Frame 1 and Frame 60, Flash adjusted the rest of the frames to change the star to its larger dimensions in the final frame.

You are done with the spacewalkNew.fla file. You will save and then close it.

To save and close the spacewalkNew.fla file:

▶ **1.** On the menu bar, click **File**, and then click **Save**. The changes you made to the spacewalkNew.fla file are saved.

▶ **2.** On the menu bar, click **File**, and then click **Close**. The file closes and the Welcome screen appears.

So far, you have learned about Web media and viewed a sample Flash document. You also learned about the main components of the Flash workspace and how to work with panels. In the next session, you will change the view of the Stage, learn how graphic objects drawn in Flash interact, and select and group objects.

REVIEW

Session 1.1 Quick Check

1. What are the two basic types of graphics?
2. How does a bitmap graphic store image data?
3. Vector graphics store information as a set of _____ instructions that describes the color, outline, and position of all the shapes of the image.
4. What type of graphic becomes distorted when enlarged?
5. What is animation?
6. True or False. A completed Flash document can include anything from silent, still imagery to motion graphics with sound and interactivity as well as elements that incorporate video.
7. While developing content in Flash, what is the file extension of the Flash authoring file?
8. Where do you position the objects that will appear in the document?
9. Which panel changes to display different options depending on the tool or object selected?

SESSION 1.2 VISUAL OVERVIEW

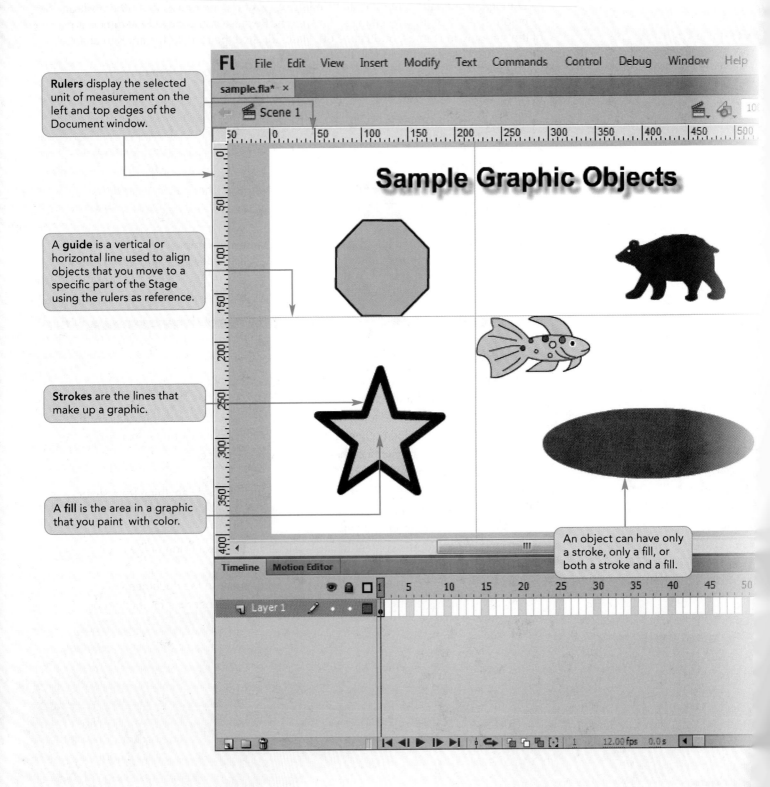

Rulers display the selected unit of measurement on the left and top edges of the Document window.

A **guide** is a vertical or horizontal line used to align objects that you move to a specific part of the Stage using the rulers as reference.

Strokes are the lines that make up a graphic.

A **fill** is the area in a graphic that you paint with color.

An object can have only a stroke, only a fill, or both a stroke and a fill.

GRAPHIC OBJECTS AND COLORS

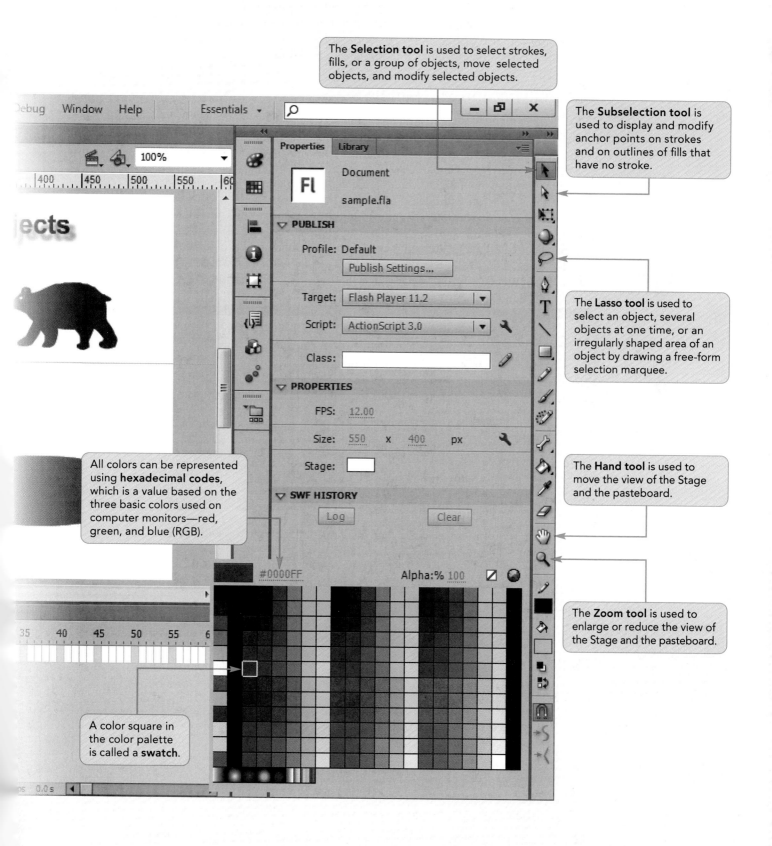

The **Selection tool** is used to select strokes, fills, or a group of objects, move selected objects, and modify selected objects.

The **Subselection tool** is used to display and modify anchor points on strokes and on outlines of fills that have no stroke.

The **Lasso tool** is used to select an object, several objects at one time, or an irregularly shaped area of an object by drawing a free-form selection marquee.

The **Hand tool** is used to move the view of the Stage and the pasteboard.

The **Zoom tool** is used to enlarge or reduce the view of the Stage and the pasteboard.

All colors can be represented using **hexadecimal codes**, which is a value based on the three basic colors used on computer monitors—red, green, and blue (RGB).

A color square in the color palette is called a **swatch**.

Changing the View of the Stage

As you develop graphics on the Stage, you will need to change the view of the Stage. You can adjust the magnification level and move different parts of the Stage into view. You can also display the rulers and guides to assist you as you draw or align graphics, and you can change a document's properties.

Magnifying and Moving the Stage

The Zoom tool adjusts the magnification level of the Stage and pasteboard. The Zoom tool includes the Enlarge and Reduce modifiers, which set the Zoom tool to increase and decrease the magnification level, respectively. You can click the Zoom tool on the part of the Stage or pasteboard you want to enlarge or reduce. You can also select an area by dragging the pointer over an area of the Stage to draw a selection marquee around it. A **selection marquee** is an outline that encloses an area to be selected.

Another way to adjust the magnification level is with the View menu. It has commands to zoom in and out, set the magnification to a specific percentage level, fit the Stage to fill the Document window, show all the contents of the current frame (Stage and pasteboard), and show frame to make the entire Stage visible. A quick way to select these magnification settings is with the Zoom control on the Edit bar.

REFERENCE

Changing the View of the Stage

- In the Tools panel, click the Zoom Tool button.
- In the Tools panel, click the Enlarge or Reduce modifier button.
- Click a part of the Stage (or drag the pointer to draw a selection marquee around the part of the Stage to enlarge or reduce).

or

- On the menu bar, click View, and then click the appropriate command (or on the Edit bar, click the Zoom control, and then click the appropriate command).

or

- In the Tools panel, double-click the Hand Tool button.

You will try various ways to change the view of the Stage. You will use a document that contains objects Aly has drawn in Flash.

TIP

You can also click the Open button on the Welcome screen to open the Open dialog box.

To open the sample.fla document and change the magnification:

1. On the menu bar, click **File**, and then click **Open**. The Open dialog box opens.

2. Navigate to the **Flash1\Tutorial** folder included with your Data Files if necessary, click **sample.fla** in the file list, and then click the **Open** button. The sample document opens in the workspace.

3. On the menu bar, click **File**, and then click **Save As**. The Save As dialog box opens.

4. Navigate to the **Flash1\Tutorial** folder included with your Data Files, type **mySample** in the File name box, and then click the **Save** button. The document saves with the new name. You do not need to type the .fla extension when saving a document; Flash enters the file extension for you.

5. On the Timeline's title bar, click the **panel menu** button ⬛, and then click **Close Group**. The Timeline panel group closes.

TIP

You can also press the Ctrl++ keys and the Ctrl+– keys to set the Zoom tool to enlarge or reduce the magnification level of the Stage.

6. On the Edit bar, click the **Zoom control arrow**, and then click **50%**. The view of the Stage changes.

7. In the Tools panel, click the **Zoom Tool** button 🔍, and then, if necessary, click the **Enlarge** modifier button 🔍. The pointer changes to ⊕ and will magnify any object you click.

8. On the Stage, click the middle of the bear object twice. The magnification level increases each time you click. The bear is centered in the Document window each time you click it. See Figure 1-17.

Figure 1-17   **Magnified bear shape**

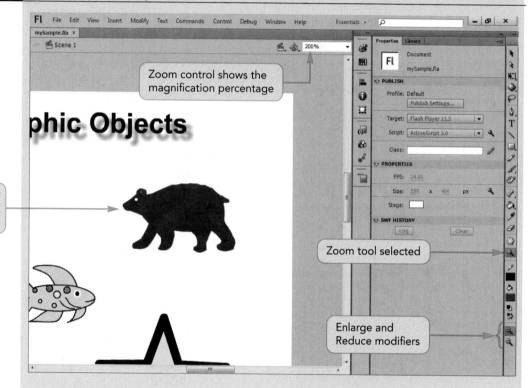

bear shape enlarged and centered in the Document window

Zoom control shows the magnification percentage

Zoom tool selected

Enlarge and Reduce modifiers

After you magnify the view of the Stage, some graphic objects shift out of sight. You can move the Stage without changing the magnification level by using the Hand tool to drag the part of the Stage you want to see into view. You'll shift the oval graphic into view.

To use the Hand tool to view the oval graphic on the Stage:

1. In the Tools panel, click the **Hand Tool** button ✋. The pointer changes to ✋ as you move it over the Stage.

2. Drag the Stage to the right and up until you see the oval in the middle of the Document window. See Figure 1-18.

Figure 1-18 **Stage view shifted**

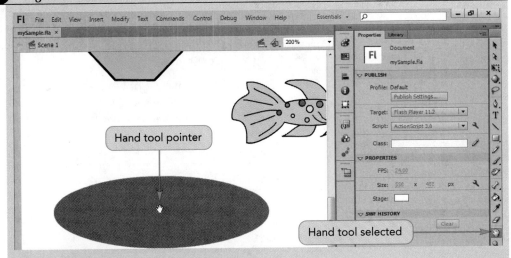

3. In the Tools panel, click the **Zoom Tool** button 🔍, and then click the **Reduce** modifier button 🔍. The pointer changes to 🔍.

4. Click the center of the oval, and then click the center of the fish. The magnification level of the Stage reduces each time you click.

5. In the Tools panel, double-click the **Hand Tool** button 🖐. The magnification level of the Stage is enlarged to show all of its contents centered in the Document window.

Displaying the Rulers and Guides

The Stage includes rulers and guides, which help position objects as you create documents. As you develop graphics, you might want to display rulers. Rulers are useful in placing objects on the Stage according to specific coordinates. The unit of measurement indicated on the rulers, such as pixels, is specified in the Document Settings dialog box.

INSIGHT

Measuring in Pixels

You can use various units of measurement in Flash, including inches, points, and centimeters. Because most elements in Web pages are measured in pixels, you should also use pixels to express the width and height values of Web graphics. A pixel, short for picture element, is the Flash default unit of measurement. Pixels represent the smallest picture element on the monitor that can be controlled by the computer. Each pixel is composed of three colors, red, green, and blue.

When the rulers are displayed, you can create vertical or horizontal guides. To create a guide, click a ruler and drag a line onto the Stage. If you drag from the top ruler, a horizontal guide is created. If you drag from the left ruler, a vertical guide is created. You can edit the guides to change their color to make them easier to see against the background, snap objects to them, and lock them into place. Guides are visible only while you are working with the document.

You will create guides in the mySample.fla document. You need to display the rulers first.

To use rulers and guides in the mySample.fla document:

▶ **1.** On the menu bar, click **View**, and then click **Rulers**. The rulers appear along the left and top sides of the pasteboard.

▶ **2.** In the Tools panel, click the **Selection Tool** button to select it.

▶ **3.** At the top of the pasteboard, click the **horizontal ruler**. The pointer changes to.

▶ **4.** Drag the pointer down to approximately **150** pixels on the vertical ruler. See Figure 1-19.

Figure 1-19	Horizontal guide added to the Stage

click and drag from the ruler to create a guide

horizontal guide at 150 pixels

▶ **5.** Click the vertical ruler and drag the pointer to the right to approximately **250** pixels on the horizontal ruler.

▶ **6.** On the menu bar, click **View**, point to **Guides**, and then click **Edit Guides**. The Guides dialog box opens, so you can modify the guides, such as by changing the guide color. See Figure 1-20.

Figure 1-20	Guides dialog box

color selected for the guides

guides are displayed when checked

objects snap to the guides when checked

guides are locked in place when checked

how close an object must be to snap to a guide

makes the current guide settings the default

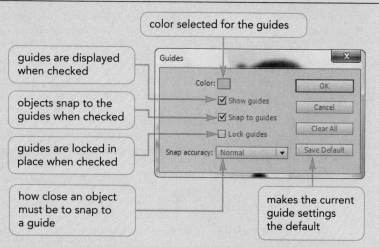

▶ **7.** Click the **Color** control. The color palette opens and the pointer changes to.

> **8.** Click the **red** color swatch located in the first column, seventh row of the color palette. The guide changes to red.

> **9.** Click the **OK** button. The Guides dialog box closes.

Changing the Document Settings

Every document in Flash has certain properties such as title, description, Stage size, background color, frame rate, and ruler unit. Title and description are embedded within the SWF file and can be used by search engines to categorize Flash content on the Web. The other document settings are set at default values when you open a new document. For example, by default, the Stage size is 550 pixels wide by 400 pixels high, the Stage background color is white, the frame rate is 24 frames per second, and the ruler units is pixels. (The frame rate specifies how many frames in an animation are displayed in one second.) You change these default properties in the Document Settings dialog box. Changes you make in the dialog box are reflected on the Stage.

Aly wants you to modify the mySample.fla document's settings by changing its background color. The dimensions, frame rate, and ruler units are fine with the defaults.

TIP

You can also open the Document Settings dialog box by clicking the Edit document properties button in the Property inspector.

To change the mySample.fla document's background color:

> **1.** On the menu bar, click **Modify**, and then click **Document**. The Document Settings dialog box opens. See Figure 1-21.

Figure 1-21   **Document Settings dialog box**

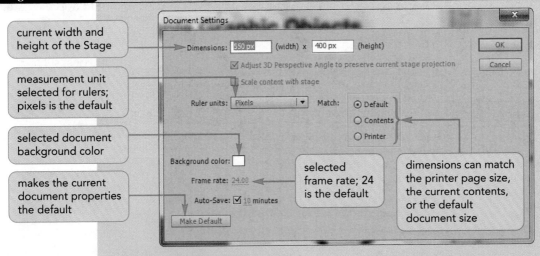

- current width and height of the Stage
- measurement unit selected for rulers; pixels is the default
- selected document background color
- makes the current document properties the default

Document Settings

Dimensions: 550 px (width) x 400 px (height)

☑ Adjust 3D Perspective Angle to preserve current stage projection

☐ Scale content with stage

Ruler units: Pixels ▾   Match: ⊙ Default ○ Contents ○ Printer

Background color: ☐

Frame rate: 24.00

Auto-Save: ☑ 10 minutes

Make Default

OK   Cancel

- selected frame rate; 24 is the default
- dimensions can match the printer page size, the current contents, or the default document size

> **2.** Click the **Background color** control. The color palette opens and the pointer changes to 🖊.

> **3.** Click the **gray** color swatch located in the first swatches column, third row of the color palette.

> **4.** Click the **OK** button. The Document Settings dialog box closes, and the Stage now has a gray background color.

> **5.** Click the pasteboard, if necessary, to display the document settings in the Property inspector. You can also change the document's background color in the Property inspector.

6. In the Property inspector, click the **Stage** control, and then click the **white** color swatch located in the first column, sixth row of the color palette. The Stage returns to a white background.

You no longer need the rulers or the guides. You'll hide them for now. Hiding the guides removes them from view but doesn't delete them; the guides will appear in the same place when you show the guides again. Clearing the guides deletes any guides that are on the Stage.

To hide the rulers and guides:

1. On the menu bar, click **View**, and then click **Rulers** to hide the rulers.

2. On the menu bar, click **View**, point to **Guides**, and then click **Show Guides** to hide the guides.

Working with Objects in Flash

The drawing and painting tools available in the Tools panel include the Line, Pen, Pencil, Oval, Rectangle, Brush, and Deco. These tools allow you to create the lines, shapes, and patterns that make up the images in a Flash document. Before using these tools, it's important to understand how the objects you draw behave and how you can change their basic characteristics, such as their color. In particular, you need to be aware of how shapes or lines you draw interact with existing shapes or lines.

Creating Strokes and Fills

When drawing objects in Flash, you create strokes and fills. Strokes can be straight or curved. They can be individual line segments or they can be connected together to form shapes. The Flash drawing tools provide a great deal of flexibility so you can draw almost any type of line you need. Fills can be enclosed by strokes.

Before you draw a shape, such as an oval or a rectangle, you can specify whether you want the shape to have a stroke, a fill, or both, as shown in Figure 1-22. For example, you can draw a circle that has both a fill and a stroke. You can draw a circle that has a stroke but no fill. Or, you can draw a circle that has a fill but has no stroke.

| Figure 1-22 | Sample shapes with strokes and fills |

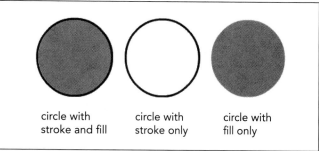

circle with stroke and fill   circle with stroke only   circle with fill only

© 2013 Cengage Learning

Drawing and Grouping Objects

Flash provides two modes for how objects created with the drawing tools such as the Pencil, Line, Oval, and Rectangle tools interact: the Merge Drawing mode and the Object Drawing mode. By default, Flash uses the Merge Drawing mode. The drawing mode you use depends on how you want the objects to interact.

With the **Merge Drawing mode**, objects drawn or moved on top of other objects merge with or segment the existing objects. (Objects in the same layer are not considered to be on top of or below one another.) For example, when you draw a line through an existing shape such as a circle, the line is split into line segments at the points where it intersects the circle. The circle is also split into separate shapes. These line segments and split shapes can be moved individually. If you draw or move a fill on top of another fill of the same color, the two fills merge and become one shape. If you draw a fill of one color on top of another fill of a different color, the new fill cuts away the existing fill.

With the **Object Drawing mode**, the drawn shapes are treated as separate objects and do not merge with or alter other objects in the same layer. When you draw an object using the Object Drawing mode, a blue outline appears around the object on the Stage. Figure 1-23 shows how drawn objects interact in each mode.

Figure 1-23   **Comparison of the drawing modes**

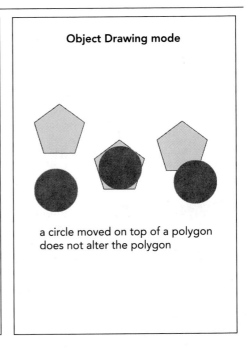

Merge Drawing mode	Object Drawing mode
a rectangle moved on top of a circle with a different color cuts away the circle when moved	a line drawn to intersect a circle splits the line and the circle into separate elements that can be moved independently

a circle moved on top of a polygon does not alter the polygon

© 2013 Cengage Learning

To prevent objects drawn in the Merge Drawing mode from impacting each other, you can **group** them, which treats two or more elements such as a stroke and a fill as one entity. A thin blue rectangle outlines the grouped object when it is selected. Grouped objects are on top of nongrouped objects so they do not alter or merge with other objects. To modify a grouped object, you must enter group-editing mode. You can then edit the individual objects within the group. When editing the objects within a group, the rest of the objects on the Stage are dimmed, indicating they are not accessible, as shown in Figure 1-24. After you finish modifying the individual objects, you exit group-editing mode.

Figure 1-24   Grouped object in group-editing mode

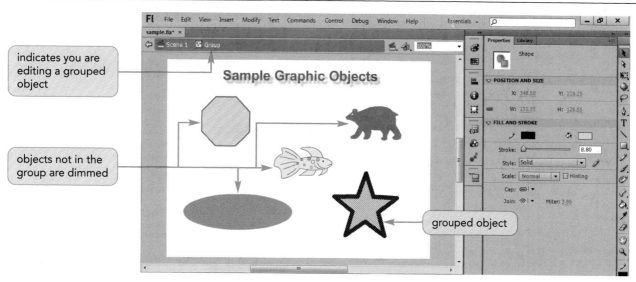

indicates you are editing a grouped object

objects not in the group are dimmed

grouped object

PROSKILLS

Problem Solving: Grouping Fills and Strokes

Objects created in Flash can become quite complex, involving multiple strokes and fills. After you finish creating an object, it is easy to inadvertently shift a line or fill. This problem is especially prevalent when you want to move or resize the object. You must be sure to select all the strokes and fills that make up that object. One way to avoid the problem of accidentally changing one part of the object is by grouping the strokes and fills together. When grouped, you can easily resize or move a complex object at any time without having to modify or select the strokes and fills within the object individually.

You'll group the objects that make up the fish in the mySample.fla document.

To group the fish in the mySample.fla document:

1. In the Tools panel, click the **Selection Tool** button , if necessary.

2. Draw a selection marquee around the fish graphic, refer to Figure 1-25, and then release the mouse button.

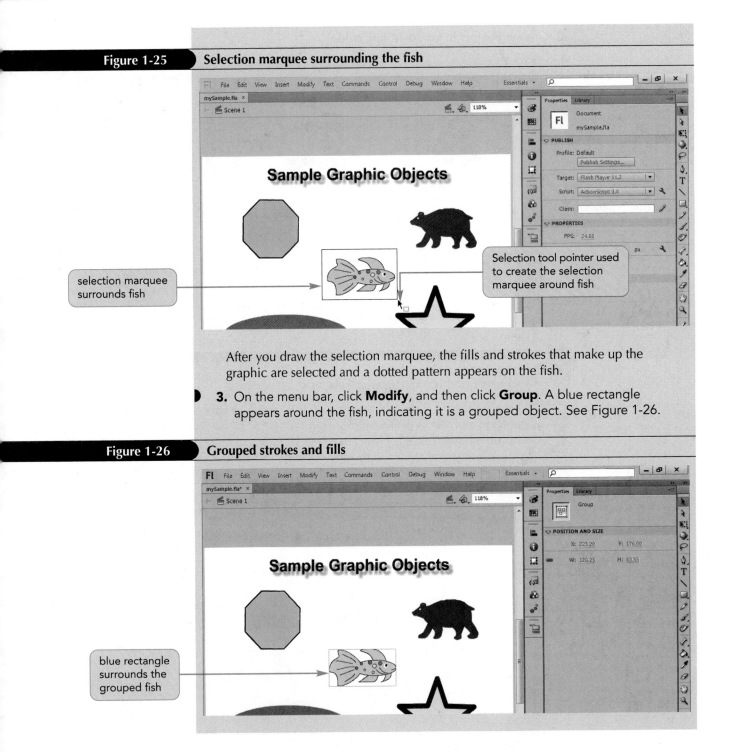

Figure 1-25   Selection marquee surrounding the fish

selection marquee surrounds fish

Selection tool pointer used to create the selection marquee around fish

After you draw the selection marquee, the fills and strokes that make up the graphic are selected and a dotted pattern appears on the fish.

3. On the menu bar, click **Modify**, and then click **Group**. A blue rectangle appears around the fish, indicating it is a grouped object. See Figure 1-26.

Figure 1-26   Grouped strokes and fills

blue rectangle surrounds the grouped fish

Using the Color Controls and the Color Panel

All strokes and fills can be drawn with different colors. You can specify the colors before you draw strokes and fills or you can change the colors of existing strokes and fills. The simplest way to change the color of a stroke or fill is by using the Stroke Color or Fill Color control in the Tools panel. Each of these controls opens a color palette from which you can select a particular color. By default, the color swatches in the color palette are the 216 **Web-safe colors**. These colors were developed to display the same on both Internet Explorer and Netscape Navigator browsers as well as on both Windows and Macintosh operating systems. Today's computer monitors can display many more than the 216 Web-safe colors, so most graphic programs still use the Web-safe colors but aren't limited to only those 216 colors.

INSIGHT

Using Hexadecimal Codes

Every color has its own hexadecimal code. The hexadecimal code (such as #00FF00 for green) is based on the three basic colors used on computer monitors: red, green, and blue, referred to as RGB. The first two digits represent the amount of red, the next two digits represent the amount of green, and the last two digits represent the amount of blue. Values for each two-digit pair range from 00 to FF, which are numbers based on the hexadecimal numbering system. These three color values combine to form the color. If you know the hexadecimal code for the color you want to use, you can enter its value in the box above the color swatches in the color palette.

You can also select colors using the Property inspector. When a stroke or fill tool is selected in the Tools panel or an existing stroke or fill is selected on the Stage, its color controls appear in the Property inspector. These controls work the same way as the Stroke Color and Fill Color controls in the Tools panel.

Finally, you can select colors using the Color panel. In this panel, you can use the panel's color controls to open the color palette, you can enter a color's hexadecimal value, or you can create custom colors.

You'll change the color of the strokes in the fish.

To change the stroke color for the grouped fish object:

1. Double-click the fish graphic. The contents on the Stage are dimmed except for the fish, indicating you are in group-editing mode.

2. Draw a selection marquee around the fish graphic to select it, if necessary. The strokes and fills of the fish are selected.

3. In the Property inspector, click the **Stroke color** control to open the color palette, and then point to the **blue** color swatch located in the first column, ninth row of the color palette. See Figure 1-27.

Figure 1-27 | Stroke color control in the Property inspector

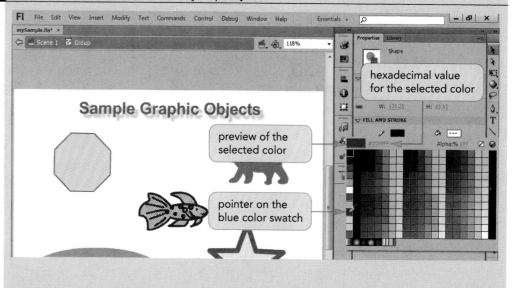

4. Click the **blue** color swatch. The strokes on the fish are blue. See Figure 1-28.

| Figure 1-28 | Fish stroke color changed |

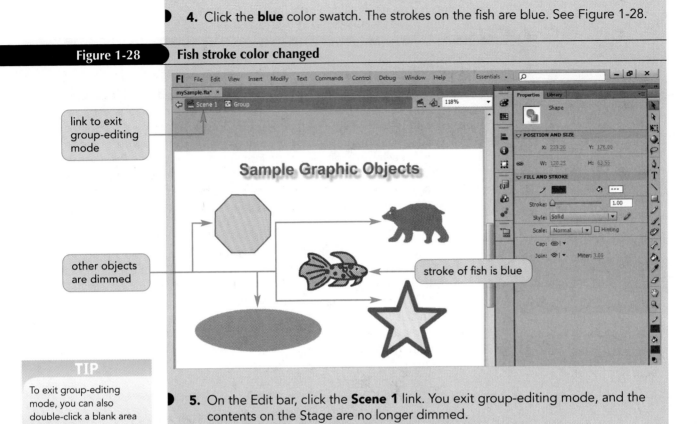

link to exit group-editing mode

other objects are dimmed

stroke of fish is blue

TIP

To exit group-editing mode, you can also double-click a blank area of the Stage.

5. On the Edit bar, click the **Scene 1** link. You exit group-editing mode, and the contents on the Stage are no longer dimmed.

Selecting Objects

Before you can change the characteristics of a graphic object on the Stage, you must select the object. You can use the Selection, Subselection, and Lasso tools in the Tools panel to select part of an object, the entire object, or several objects at one time. You'll use these tools, especially the Selection tool, frequently as you create graphics.

Selection Tool

With the Selection tool, you select an object by clicking it and you select an object's stroke and fill by double-clicking or by dragging the pointer to draw a selection marquee around the object, which is also useful for selecting more than one object at a time. When you select a graphic object, a dot pattern covers it to indicate the object is selected. Some selected objects, such as text blocks, have a rectangular outline instead of a dot pattern. You can move a selected object to a new position by dragging it with the Selection tool. To change an object's shape with the Selection tool, deselect the object, move the pointer to one of the object's edges or corners, and then drag to reshape the object. The pointer changes based on the object you are modifying. If you move the pointer to a corner of an octagon shape, for example, the pointer changes to ▸₎, as shown in Figure 1-29.

Figure 1-29   Selection tool modifying an object

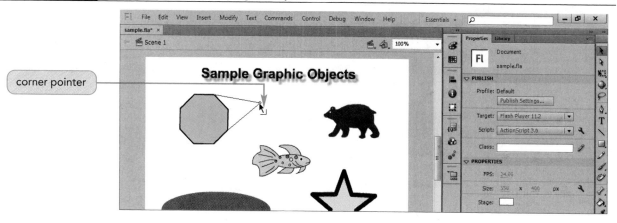

corner pointer

The Selection tool, like many of the tools in the Tools panel, has modifiers that change the way it works. The Selection tool includes the Snap to Objects, Smooth, and Straighten modifiers, which are shown in Figure 1-30.

Figure 1-30   Selection tool modifiers

Modifier Icon	Modifier	Description
	Snap to Objects	Snaps selected objects to other objects when they are moved close together
	Smooth	Smoothes the selected line or shape outline
	Straighten	Straightens the selected line or shape outline

© 2013 Cengage Learning

You will use the Selection tool to select and modify the graphics in Aly's sample document.

To select and modify objects with the Selection tool:

1. In the Tools panel, click the **Zoom Tool** button 🔍 and then click the **Enlarge** modifier button 🔍, if necessary.

2. On the Stage, click the green octagon. The octagon is enlarged and centered in the Document window.

3. In the Tools panel, click the **Selection Tool** button ▶.

4. Click the center of the green octagon and drag it slightly to the right. The octagon's fill is separated from its stroke and the dot pattern indicates the fill is selected. See Figure 1-31.

Figure 1-31	Octagon's fill and stroke separated

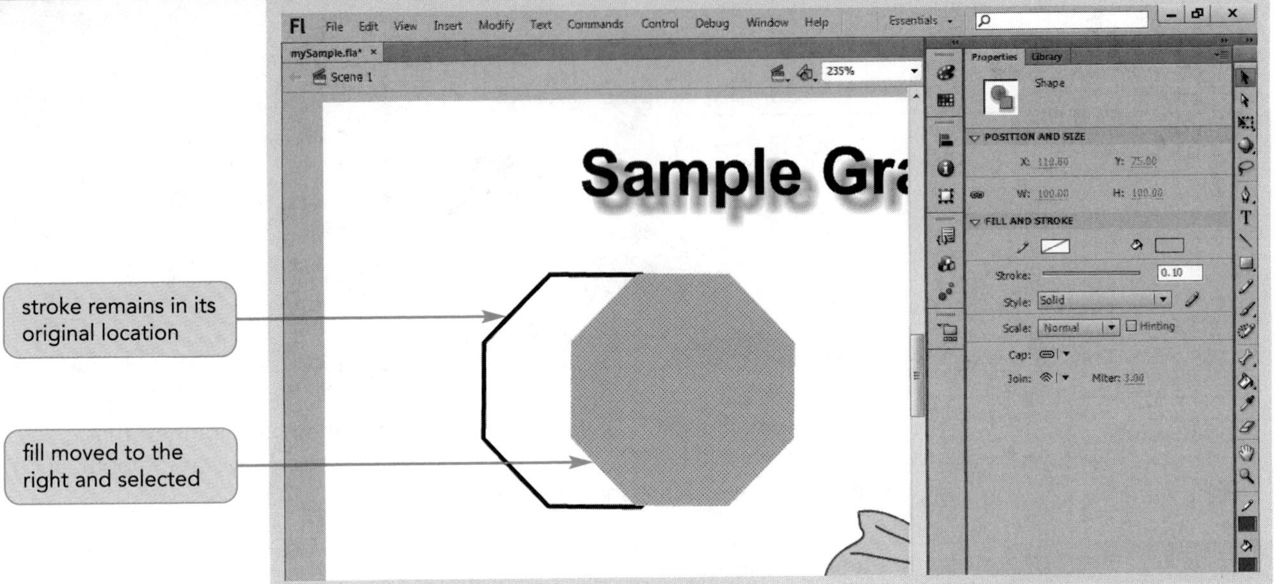

stroke remains in its original location

fill moved to the right and selected

5. On the menu bar, click **Edit**, and then click **Undo Move**. The octagon's fill moves back to its original location.

6. Click a blank area of the Stage to deselect the octagon's fill.

7. Double-click the green octagon. Both the fill and stroke of the octagon are selected.

8. Drag the selected octagon to the right. The stroke and the fill move together.

9. Click a blank area of the Stage to deselect the octagon. Next, you'll use the Selection tool to change the shape of the octagon.

10. Move the pointer over the top stroke of the octagon until the pointer changes to ⬈. You'll use the Selection tool to change the shape of the octagon.

11. Drag the stroke of the octagon away from the center of the octagon to change its shape (but do not release the mouse button). See Figure 1-32.

Figure 1-32   Octagon's shape being changed

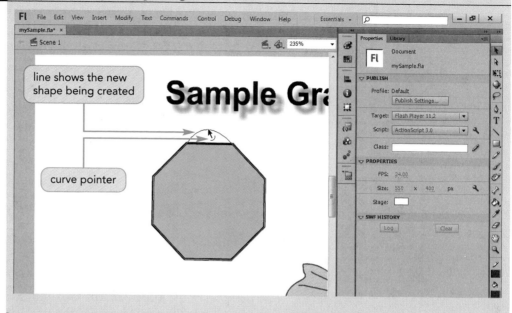

12. Release the mouse button. The fill expands to the new shape.

Subselection Tool

The Subselection tool is used to display and modify points, referred to as **anchor points**, on strokes and on the outlines of fills that have no stroke. The strokes and fills can then be modified by adjusting these points. If you click and drag an anchor point on a straight line segment, you can change the angle or the length of the line. If you click an anchor point on a curved line, **tangent handles** appear next to the selected point, as shown in Figure 1-33. You can change the curve by dragging the tangent handles.

Figure 1-33   Curve's anchor points and tangent handles

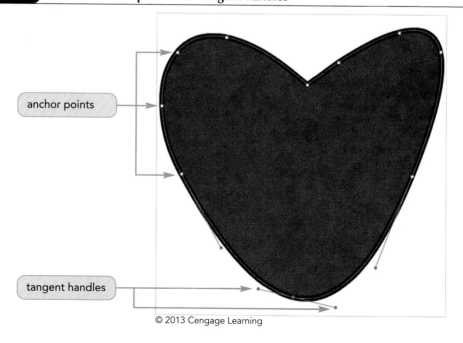

Using the Subselection Tool

- In the Tools panel, click the Subselection Tool button.
- On the Stage, click an object's stroke or its fill outline to display its anchor points.
- Drag the anchor points or tangent handles to modify the stroke or fill outline.

You'll use the Subselection tool to select and modify objects in the mySample.fla document.

To use the Subselection tool to modify the star and oval:

1. In the Tools panel, click the **Hand Tool** button 🖑 to change the pointer to 🖑, and then drag the view of the Stage until the star is in the middle of the Document window.

2. In the Tools panel, click the **Subselection Tool** button ▲. The pointer changes to ▲. You'll use this tool to display the star's stroke anchor points.

3. On the Stage, click the stroke of the star. A thin blue outline overlays the star's stroke, and square anchor points appear on the star's corners and points.

4. Drag the anchor point in the star's top point away from the center of the star (but do not release the mouse button). See Figure 1-34.

Figure 1-34 | **Star's shape being changed**

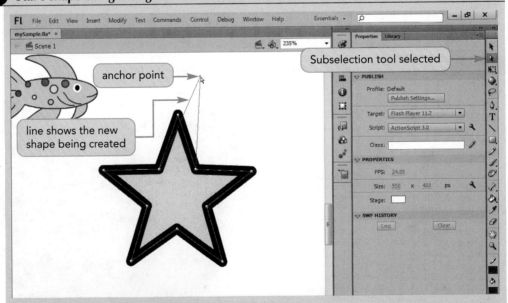

5. Release the mouse button. The star's fill expands to fill the new shape.

6. In the Tools panel, click the **Hand Tool** button 🖑 to change the pointer to 🖑, and then drag the view of the Stage until the orange oval is in the middle of the Document window.

7. In the Tools panel, click the **Subselection Tool** button, and then click the oval's outline. Anchor points appear along the oval's outline.

8. On the Stage, click the anchor point at the bottom of the oval's outline. Because this is a curved outline, tangent handles appear. You use a tangent handle to modify the oval.

9. Drag the left tangent handle of the bottom anchor point down to change the oval's shape. The fill changes to fit the new shape. See Figure 1-35.

Figure 1-35   **Modified oval with tangent handles**

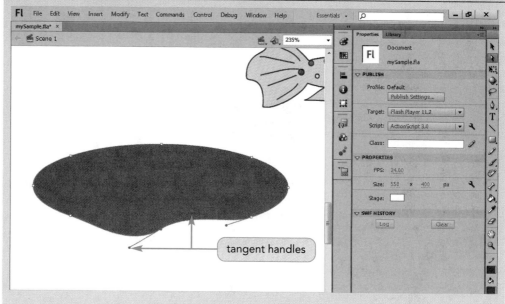

tangent handles

Lasso Tool

If you need to select part of a fill or a stroke, which you cannot do with the Selection or Subselection tools, you can use the Lasso tool. The Lasso tool is used to select an object, to select several objects at one time, or to select an irregularly shaped area of an object by drawing a free-form marquee. You can move the selection or apply other effects to it such as changing the color of all the selected fills at one time.

You will use the Lasso tool with the objects in the mySample.fla document.

To select objects with the Lasso tool:

1. In the Tools panel, double-click the **Hand Tool** button. The entire Stage becomes visible.

2. In the Tools panel, click the **Lasso Tool** button. The pointer changes to when moved over the Stage. You use this tool to select multiple objects at once.

3. Drag the pointer to create a free-form selection marquee that includes parts of the modified star and the bear (but do not release the mouse button). See Figure 1-36.

Figure 1-36   **Free-form selection marquee**

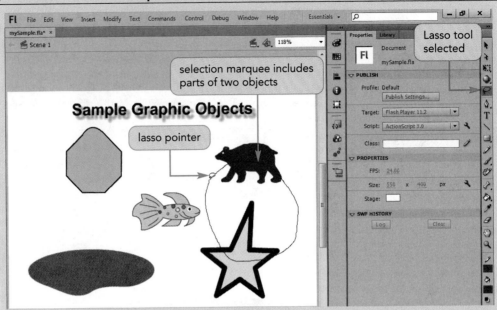

Trouble? If you cannot create a free-form selection marquee, the Polygon Mode modifier is probably selected in the Tools panel. Click the Polygon Mode modifier button in the Tools panel to deselect it, and then repeat Step 3.

4. Release the mouse button. All of the selected areas appear with a dot pattern.

5. In the Tools panel, click the **Fill Color** control to open the color palette, and then click the **green** color swatch in the first column, eighth row of the color palette. The fill color of the selected areas in the star and bear change to green. The strokes are not affected because they are not fills. See Figure 1-37.

Figure 1-37   **New fill color for the selected areas**

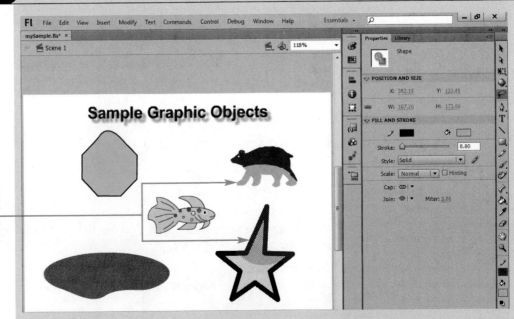

▶ **6.** On the menu bar, click **File**, and then click **Save**. The mySample.fla document is saved with all the changes.

In this session, you learned how objects interact when they are drawn or moved over each other on the Stage. You selected and grouped objects, and you worked with the strokes, fills, and colors of objects.

REVIEW

Session 1.2 Quick Check

1. True or False. Rulers display the selected unit of measurement on the left and bottom edges of the Document window.
2. How do you change the background color of the Stage?
3. What is the difference between strokes and fills?
4. True or False. If you draw a blue oval on top of an ungrouped red rectangle drawn in Merge Drawing mode, the rectangle will not be modified.
5. True or False. Grouped objects cannot be edited.
6. What are two ways to use the Selection tool to select the stroke and the fill of an oval at the same time?
7. What tool do you use to select parts of several objects at the same time?

SESSION 1.3 VISUAL OVERVIEW

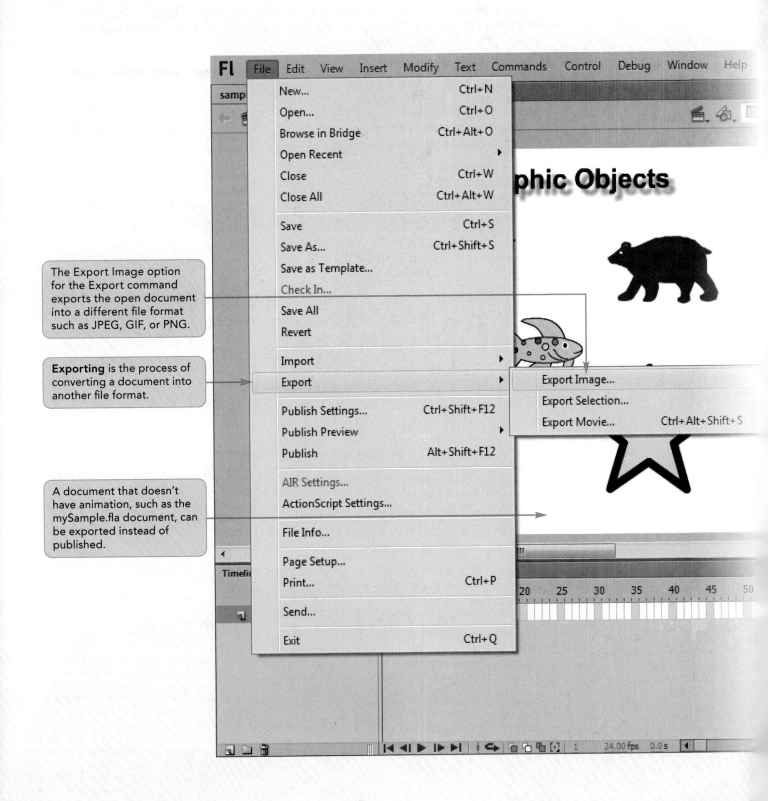

The Export Image option for the Export command exports the open document into a different file format such as JPEG, GIF, or PNG.

Exporting is the process of converting a document into another file format.

A document that doesn't have animation, such as the mySample.fla document, can be exported instead of published.

Fl   File   Edit   View   Insert   Modify   Text   Commands   Control   Debug   Window   Help

New...	Ctrl+N
Open...	Ctrl+O
Browse in Bridge	Ctrl+Alt+O
Open Recent	▶
Close	Ctrl+W
Close All	Ctrl+Alt+W
Save	Ctrl+S
Save As...	Ctrl+Shift+S
Save as Template...	
Check In...	
Save All	
Revert	
Import	▶
Export	▶
Publish Settings...	Ctrl+Shift+F12
Publish Preview	▶
Publish	Alt+Shift+F12
AIR Settings...	
ActionScript Settings...	
File Info...	
Page Setup...	
Print...	Ctrl+P
Send...	
Exit	Ctrl+Q

Export Image...	
Export Selection...	
Export Movie...	Ctrl+Alt+Shift+S

phic Objects

Timeline   20   25   30   35   40   45   50

1   24.00 fps   0.0 s

EXPORTING GRAPHIC OBJECTS

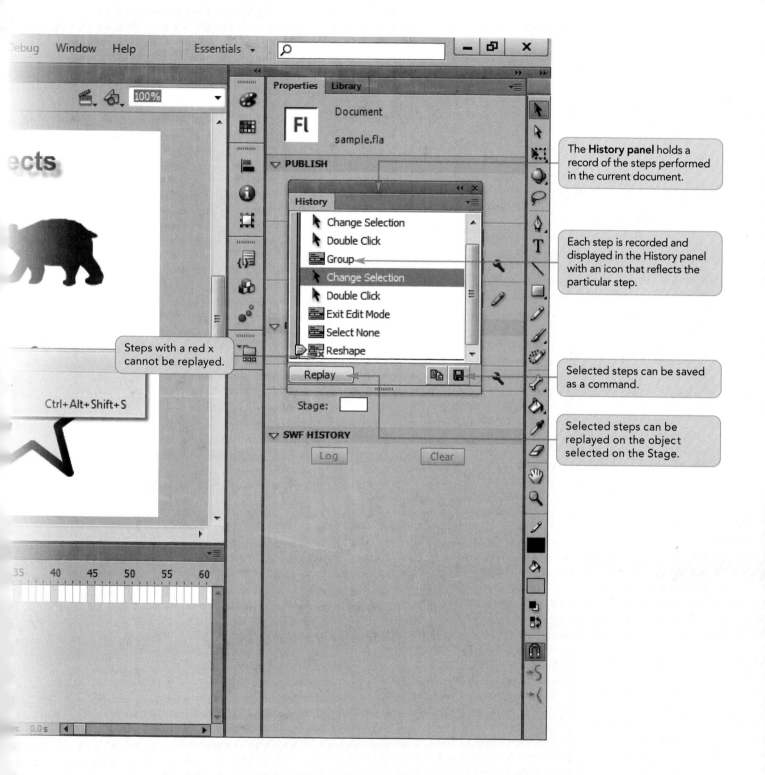

The **History panel** holds a record of the steps performed in the current document.

Each step is recorded and displayed in the History panel with an icon that reflects the particular step.

Steps with a red x cannot be replayed.

Ctrl+Alt+Shift+S

Selected steps can be saved as a command.

Selected steps can be replayed on the object selected on the Stage.

Exporting a Graphic

A document you create in Flash is saved in the FLA format. This format contains all of the different elements you create in Flash. To revise the document, you open the FLA file. To place the image in a Web page, however, it needs to be published or exported.

Publishing a document will be covered in more detail in Tutorial 3 when you add animations to documents. A published document is in the SWF file format and is called a Flash movie. It requires the Flash Player plug-in to play in a Web browser.

When you create a graphic that doesn't have animation, such as the mySample.fla document, you can export it instead of publishing it. Exporting is the process of converting a document into another file format. For example, you can export the mySample.fla document into GIF, JPG, or PNG files, which do not require a plug-in to display in a Web page. Exporting also combines all the individual elements of a document into one graphic. You cannot edit the individual elements of the image in an exported file. To edit the image's elements, you must work in the original FLA file and then export it again when you are finished. After you export a document into the GIF, JPG, or PNG file format, it can be placed in a Web page or a word-processing document, or used in an image-editing program such as Adobe Photoshop.

You'll export the sample graphic document into the JPG file format.

To export the graphic to the JPG file format:

▶ **1.** On the menu bar, click **File**, point to **Export**, and then click **Export Image**. The Export Image dialog box opens.

▶ **2.** Navigate to the **Flash1\Tutorial** folder included with your Data Files, if necessary. The graphic will be saved in that location with the name mySample.jpg.

▶ **3.** Click the **Save as type** button to open a menu of file formats, and then click **JPEG Image (*.jpg, *.jpeg)**. The graphic will be saved in the JPG file format.

▶ **4.** Click the **Save** button. The Export JPEG dialog box opens with additional options and settings, including the document's dimensions and resolution.

▶ **5.** Click the **Include** button, and then click **Full Document Size**, if necessary. This option makes the exported JPG image the same size as the Flash document. The Minimum Image Area option might reduce the size of the exported JPG image based on the content on the Stage.

▶ **6.** In the Quality box, enter **80** for the quality of the exported image. You'll accept the rest of the default settings. See Figure 1-38.

Figure 1-38   Export JPEG dialog box settings

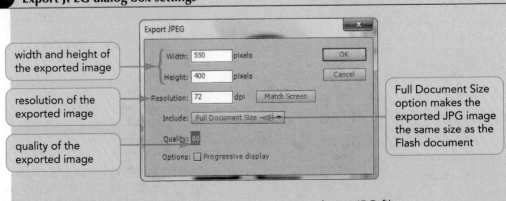

width and height of the exported image

resolution of the exported image

quality of the exported image

Full Document Size option makes the exported JPG image the same size as the Flash document

▶ **7.** Click the **OK** button. The document is exported as a JPG file.

Using the History Panel

The History panel holds a record of the steps performed in the current document. After you open or create a document, each step is recorded and displayed in the History panel with an icon that reflects the particular step. The History panel displays only the steps for the current document. If you switch to another document, the History panel shows the steps taken in creating or editing that document. A document's history is maintained until you close the document or clear its history. You can also save selected steps by creating a command based on those steps. The command can then be used in the same document or in another document and is available each time you use Flash. From the History panel, you can replay, undo, and save the recorded steps.

You will use the History panel as you work with a document Aly created for an upcoming sale.

To use the History panel with the sale.fla document:

1. On the menu bar, click **File**, and then click **Open**. The Open dialog box opens.

2. Navigate to the **Flash1\Tutorial** folder included with your Data Files, if necessary, and then double-click the **sale.fla** file. The Katie's Pet Shop sale document opens.

3. Reset the **Essentials** workspace, make sure the magnification level is set to **100%**, and then, if necessary, scroll the Document window to center the document.

> **TIP**
>
> You can also press the Ctrl+F10 keys to open and close the History panel.

4. On the menu bar, click **Window**, point to **Other Panels**, and then click **History**. The History panel opens.

5. If the History panel appears on top of the document, drag the History panel by its title bar to the lower-right side of the document.

   Before you can work with the document, you need to unlock the layers in the document. You do this by using the Timeline.

6. In the Timeline, click the **Lock or Unlock All Layers** icon 🔒 to unlock all the layers. A step labeled "Lock Layers" appears in the History panel.

7. In the Tools panel, click the **Selection Tool** button ▶, and then click the **Katie's Pet Shop** text block to select it. The Change Selection step appears in the History panel.

8. In the Property inspector, change the Text (fill) color to **blue** (#0000FF) in the first swatches column, ninth row of the color palette. The letters in the text block change color, and this step appears in the History panel. See Figure 1-39.

Figure 1-39   History panel with the current session's steps

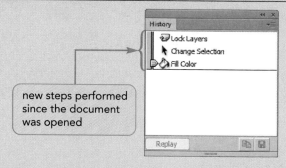

new steps performed since the document was opened

9. In the Tools panel, click the **Free Transform Tool** button , and then click the **Scale** modifier button to select it.

10. Drag the lower-right corner handle on the text block slightly down and to the right to make the text block slightly larger. The Scale step appears in the History panel.

Replaying Steps

You can replay one or more selected steps in the History panel. For example, after you create a shape, you can select the steps in the History panel that you took to create the shape, and then replay the steps to create a duplicate of the shape. If you select steps in the History panel that you used to format an object on the Stage, you can replay the steps to apply the same formatting to another object on the Stage. The steps you select in the History panel are applied to the selected object in the order shown in the panel. The replayed steps can be consecutive or nonconsecutive. Steps displayed with an icon that includes a small, red X cannot be replayed.

You will replay the steps you performed previously from the History panel to further modify the sale document.

To replay steps from the History panel:

1. In the History panel, drag over the **Fill Color** and **Scale** steps to select them. The two consecutive steps are selected. See Figure 1-40.

Figure 1-40   **Steps selected in the History panel**

selected text block with blue fill color and enlarged

last two steps selected by dragging

Trouble? If the last steps performed are undone, you probably dragged the slider on the left side of the History panel instead of the actual steps. Drag the slider down to the last step you performed, and then repeat Step 1, being careful to select the steps in the History panel and not the slider.

2. In the center of the Stage, click the **Columbus Day Sale!** text block to select it. The new step is added at the end of the History panel.

3. In the History panel, click the **Replay** button. The two selected steps are replayed: The Columbus Day Sale! text block increases in size and its text color changes to blue. The History panel records the Replay Steps step.

4. In the Tools panel, click the **Selection Tool** button ![Selection tool icon], and then drag the left dog bone to the bottom of the Stage. The dog bone is repositioned, and the Change Selection and Move steps appear in the History panel.

5. Press and hold the **Ctrl** key, and then, in the History panel, click the **Move** step to select it, click the **Fill Color** step to deselect it, and then release the **Ctrl** key. The nonconsecutive Scale and Move steps are selected in the History panel.

6. On the Stage, click the right dog bone to select it, and then, in the History panel, click the **Replay** button. The nonconsecutive steps are replayed, and the dog bone becomes slightly larger and moves to the bottom of the Stage. The History panel shows the last two steps you performed. See Figure 1-41.

Figure 1-41	Steps replayed and applied to dog bone

Undoing Steps

As you create and modify objects, you might want to undo one or more steps within a document. This might occur if you make a mistake and you want to return to the previous step. You can undo one step or as many as 100 steps. This lets you backtrack though a series of steps until the document returns to the particular state at which you want to start over. You can change the default maximum number of steps that can be undone in the Preferences dialog box.

Flash provides two types of undo. In **document-level undo**, the steps you undo affect the entire document. In **object-level undo**, you can undo steps performed on individual objects without affecting the steps performed on other objects. You change from one type of undo to another in the Preferences dialog box. When you change the type of undo, the steps currently recorded in the History panel are deleted. In this tutorial, you work with the default mode, document-level undo.

You can use the History panel to change the document back to how it was before you performed a series of steps. The slider in the History panel initially points to the last step performed. As you drag the slider to a previous step, any subsequent step is undone and is reflected in the document on the Stage. Undone steps appear dimmed in the History panel.

You will use the History panel to undo some of the steps you have performed.

To undo steps in the sale.fla document:

1. In the History panel, drag the slider up to the **Scale** step. The steps below the Scale step are dimmed, indicating that they have been undone. The objects on the Stage also change to reflect that the steps were undone. See Figure 1-42.

Figure 1-42   Steps in the History panel that were undone

text block and graphics return to their original states

slider dragged to the Scale step

undone steps are dimmed

2. Close the History panel and the Timeline, and then close the sale.fla document without saving changes.

Getting Help in Flash

The Flash Help system is useful for finding information about features in Flash as you work with a document. The Help system is organized topically. The left pane of the Adobe Community Help window contains a search option. The Help content is displayed in the right pane of the window.

The left column of the Help system's content pane shows the list of available categories. The first category is Using Flash Professional CS6, which contains the Help information for most of the features of Flash. The rest of the categories contain information about more advanced features. Clicking one of these initial categories displays subcategories in the right column of the content pane, which, when clicked, display additional Help categories in the left column. When a category in the left column is clicked, a list of topics is displayed. Each topic can be clicked to display a table of contents for the topic, as well as its associated Help information. You can navigate the Help system by clicking any of the categories or topics. You can also use the Previous and Next buttons to navigate between topics.

A Search feature is available in the left pane of the Help window. You can search by a keyword or phrase to display a list of related topics. The search can be limited to the Flash Help system or can include other resources from the Adobe Web site.

REFERENCE

Using the Flash Help System

- On the menu bar, click Help, and then click Flash Help (or click a panel menu button, and then click Help).
- Click a main topic category, and then click a subcategory to display.
- In the left column of the content pane, click a category to display its associated topics, and then click the desired topic.
- In the right column, read the topic information.
- Close the Flash Professional Help window to close the Help system.

You'll use the Flash Help system to obtain more information about the drawing tools.

To use the Flash Help system to get more information about the drawing tools:

1. On the menu bar, click **Help**, and then click **Flash Help**. The Help system opens in the Flash Professional Help window.

   Trouble? If the Adobe AIR setup dialog box opens, click the Cancel button.

   Trouble? If the Updating: Adobe Help dialog box opens indicating an update is available, click the Download later button.

   Trouble? If the Local Content Update dialog box opens indicating an update is available, click the Cancel button.

   Trouble? If the Flash Help system doesn't open, you probably need to update the Help support files that provide access to online Help from within Flash. Go to *www.adobe.com/support/flash/downloads.html#flashCS6* to download and install the update.

2. If necessary, on the Flash Professional Help window title bar, click the **Maximize** button 🔲 to maximize the window.

3. On the Help page, click the **Drawing and painting** topic to display a list of subtopics.

4. Under Drawing and painting, click **Draw simple lines and shapes**. A new Help page is displayed. See Figure 1-43.

Figure 1-43	Draw simple lines and shapes topics in the Flash Help system

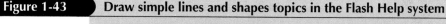

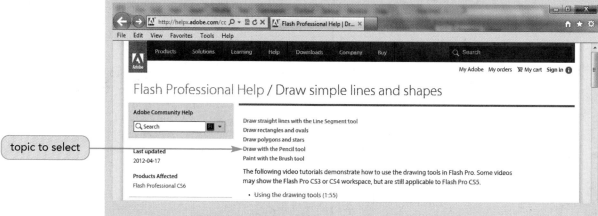

topic to select

5. In the list of topics, click the **Draw with the Pencil tool** topic. The Help topic for drawing lines and shapes with the Pencil tool appears. See Figure 1-44.

Figure 1-44	Help topic selected

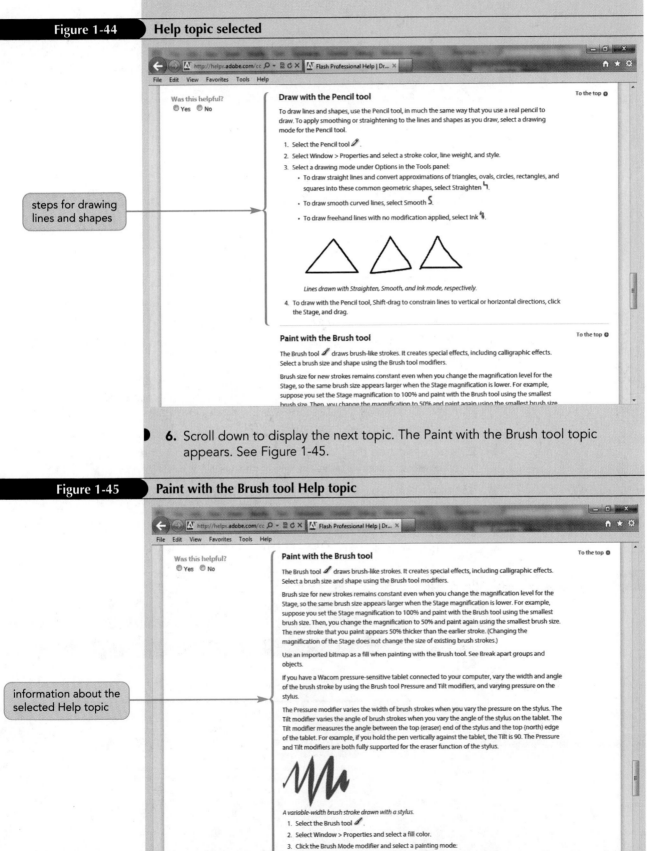

steps for drawing lines and shapes

6. Scroll down to display the next topic. The Paint with the Brush tool topic appears. See Figure 1-45.

Figure 1-45	Paint with the Brush tool Help topic

information about the selected Help topic

▶ **7.** Read the information, and then, on the Help window's title bar, click the **Close** button ▮ X ▮. The Help window closes.

Closing a Document and Exiting Flash

After you finish working with a document in Flash, you should close it. If you haven't already saved the document before you try to close it, Flash prompts you to save the file.

To close the mySample.fla document and exit Flash:

▶ **1.** On the menu bar, click **File**, and then click **Close**. The mySample.fla document closes and the Welcome screen appears.

   Trouble? If you are prompted to save the file, you might have inadvertently made changes since the last time you saved. Click the No button.

▶ **2.** On the menu bar, click **File**, and then click **Exit**. The Flash program exits.

In this session, you learned how graphics created in Flash can be exported in different formats for display in a Web page or to use in another software program. You learned how to use the History panel to undo one or more steps, replay steps, or save steps as a command. You also used the Help system.

REVIEW

Session 1.3 Quick Check

1. _____ is the process that Flash uses to convert a document into another file format, such as GIF, JPG, or PNG.
2. What is the History panel?
3. True or False. A document's history is maintained until you close the document or clear its history.
4. True or False. Steps displayed in the History panel with an icon that includes a small, red X cannot be replayed.
5. What are the two types of undo available in Flash?
6. How can you find topics containing an exact phrase in the Help system?

Practice the skills you learned in the tutorial using the same case scenario.

PRACTICE

Review Assignments

Data File needed for the Review Assignments: objects.fla

Aly wants you to work with some of the tools in Flash and to change the document settings by modifying the document properties. You will use these skills to develop graphics for Katie's Pet Shop Web site.

1. Open the **objects.fla** file located in the Flash1\Review folder included with your Data Files and then save the document as **objectsNew.fla** in the same folder. Reset the Essentials workspace. Hide the Timeline, display the rulers, and, if necessary, change the magnification level to 100%.

2. Click the vertical ruler and drag the pointer to the right to approximately 400 pixels on the horizontal ruler to create a vertical guide. Click the horizontal ruler and drag the pointer down to approximately 200 pixels on the vertical ruler to create a horizontal guide.

3. In the Tools panel, click the Selection Tool button. Double-click the blue circle to select both its fill and stroke, and then move the blue circle to the right side of the Stage onto the pasteboard.

4. Double-click the red heart to select both its fill and stroke, and then move the heart to the upper-right side of the Stage so that its left side aligns with the vertical guide 400 pixels from the left of the Stage and its top aligns with top of the orange rectangle.

5. Double-click the blue circle on the pasteboard to select both its fill and stroke, and then move the blue circle to the lower-right side of the Stage so that its left side aligns with the vertical guide and its top aligns with the top of the tree.

6. In the Tools panel, click the Lasso Tool button. Drag around the beach ball and the green oval to select both shapes. Make sure no other shapes are selected. Click the Fill Color control in the Property inspector, and then click a light pink color in the color palette. The fill color in the beach ball and the oval change to light pink.

7. With the Lasso tool, draw a marquee around the tree to select both its leaves and its trunk. Group the tree's strokes and fills.

8. In the Tools panel, click the Selection Tool button, click the grouped tree to select it, if necessary, and then move it between the kite and the rectangle so that the bottom of its trunk aligns with the horizontal guide.

9. In the Tools panel, click the Zoom Tool button and, if necessary, click the Enlarge modifier button. Click the kite twice to increase the magnification level.

10. In the Tools panel, click the Selection Tool button, and then click the stroke representing the kite's tail to select it. Click the Stroke color control in the Property inspector, and then click the red color in the color palette. The kite's tail color changes to red.

11. Change the magnification level of the Stage to Show Frame.

12. Move the pointer to the top stroke of the orange rectangle. Use the curve pointer to drag the stroke slightly down toward the center of the rectangle to create a curved edge. Repeat to curve each of the other three sides of the rectangle toward its center.

13. Click the pink oval to select it and then move it so that its right edge aligns with the vertical guide and its top edge aligns with the horizontal guide.

14. In the Tools panel, click the Subselection Tool button, and then click the heart shape's stroke to display its anchor points. Drag any anchor points to reshape the heart. Click an empty area of the Stage to deselect the modified shape.

15. In the Property inspector, click the Background color control, and then click a light yellow color in the color palette to change the background color of the Stage.

16. Save and close the document. Submit the finished document to your instructor.

Use the skills
you learned to
modify a Flash
document for a
sports store.

APPLY

Case Problem 1

Data File needed for this Case Problem: shapes.fla

Jackson's Sports Store Dan Jackson is the owner of Jackson's Sports, a local sports equipment and supply company that provides discounted equipment, team uniforms, and player trophies to youth basketball, baseball, softball, volleyball, and soccer teams. Dan hired Chris Jones to develop a Web site that will include graphics and animations in addition to text to promote services the company provides to local youth sports. Chris asks you to explore a sample Flash document to become more familiar with the program.

1. Open the **shapes.fla** file located in the Flash1\Case1 folder included with your Data Files, and then save the document as **shapesRevised.fla** in the same folder. Reset the Essentials workspace and change the zoom magnification to Show All.

2. Display the rulers and drag a horizontal guide from the top ruler to about 200 pixels from the top of the Stage.

3. Use the Selection tool to move both the fill and stroke of the triangle to the center of the Stage. The bottom side of the triangle should rest on the guide.

4. Select all of the baseball, group its strokes and fills, and move the grouped baseball to the right of the triangle. The baseball's bottom edge should rest on the guide.

5. Select all of the basketball, group its strokes and fills, and then place the grouped basketball below the triangle. The basketball's top edge should rest below the guide.

6. Move the cube to the right of the baseball and place it so that its center is on the guide.

7. Select the yellow pentagon shape (both its fill and stroke), and then move the pentagon to the left of the triangle so that its bottom side rests on the guide.

8. With the pentagon still selected, use the Stroke color control in the Property inspector to change the pentagon's stroke color to red.

9. Deselect the pentagon and then use the Selection pointer to curve its top sides toward its center.

10. Change the fill color of the triangle to brown and its stroke color to white.

11. Change the fill color of the baseball to green and its stroke color to blue. (*Hint*: Edit the baseball in group-editing mode.)

12. Change the fill color of the basketball to red.

13. Save and close the document. Submit the finished document to your instructor.

Use the skills
you learned to
modify a Flash
document for a
local zoo.

APPLY

Case Problem 2

Data File needed for this Case Problem: interactions.fla

Alamo City Zoo The Alamo City Zoo, established in 1965, provides animal exhibits for San Antonio and the surrounding area. The zoo is open year-round and has special exhibits throughout the year. Alamo City Zoo staff also work with local schools to arrange field trips and guided tours for students. Janet Meyers, zoo director, commissioned Alex Smith to develop Flash graphics for the Alamo City Zoo Web site. Alex asks you to explore how objects interact with each other in Flash.

1. Open the **interactions.fla** file located in the Flash1\Case2 folder included with your Data Files, and then save the document as **interactionsNew.fla** in the same folder. Reset the Essentials workspace and change the zoom magnification to Show All.

2. Using the Selection tool, drag the orange circle on the lower-right side of the Stage to overlay the right side of the blue circle to its left. Click a blank area of the Stage

to deselect the circle. Select the orange circle again, and then move the circle back to the lower-right side of the Stage. Part of the blue circle has been cut away.

3. Drag the blue circle on the upper-right side of the Stage and place it on the maroon circle to its left. Click a blank area of the Stage to deselect the circle. The blue circle is behind the maroon circle. Move the maroon circle to the upper-right side, and then deselect it. Neither circle changes.

4. Point to the bottom of the maroon circle on the upper-right side of the Stage, and then use the curve pointer to drag the line up slightly to curve it. Repeat this step to modify the bottom of the orange circle. Both objects are modified in the same manner with the Selection tool.

5. Select the fill of the star on the upper-left side of the Stage. Then select the star on the lower-left side of the Stage. Each star's selection is displayed differently.

6. Deselect the star, point to the left point of the star on the lower-left side of the Stage, and then use the corner pointer to drag the star's point to the left slightly. Repeat this step to move the left point of the star on the upper-left side of the Stage. Both objects are modified in the same manner with the Selection tool.

7. Record what you think are the differences and similarities between the two star objects. Also record why you think the circle shapes interact differently with each other.

8. Save and close the document. Submit your answers from Step 7 and the finished document to your instructor.

Customize the Flash workspace for a gardening store.

CHALLENGE

Case Problem 3

There are no Data Files needed for this Case Problem.

G&L Nursery   Gloria Lexington is the owner of G&L Nursery, a specialty store providing a variety of trees, plants, flowers, and gardening accessories. Gloria attributes her success over the last 10 years to her focus on customer service. Customers can look through the nursery's inventory in a relaxing and inviting environment. Friendly and knowledgeable staff provide expert advice and answers to customers' gardening questions.

Gloria contracted Amanda Lester to update the store's Web site. As other local nurseries have developed Web sites, Gloria wants to make sure her store's Web site stays current and remains an effective marketing tool. You'll help Amanda develop Flash graphics for the Web site. She wants you to customize the Flash workspace and arrange the panels you will use regularly. You will also look for information in the Flash Help system.

1. Create a new Flash document, and then reset the Essentials workspace.

2. On the menu bar, click Window, and then click Behaviors to open the Behaviors panel as a free-floating window. Move this window slightly to the left by dragging the panel's tab or title bar. Open the Movie Explorer.

✛ EXPLORE   3. Group the Movie Explorer and Behaviors panel into one window. (*Hint*: Drag the Movie Explorer from its window and into the Behaviors panel's window.)

4. Open the Align panel, and then drag it into the window with the Behaviors panel and Movie Explorer. All three panels are grouped.

✛ EXPLORE   5. Click the Collapse to Icons button above the Property inspector and Library panel. Drag the left edge of the panel dock to the right to reduce the width of the dock and display the panels as icons only.

✛ EXPLORE   6. On the menu bar, click the workspace switcher button, and then click New Workspace. Type **newLayout** in the Name box, and then click the OK button.

7. Switch the workspace to the Essentials layout.

8. On the menu bar, click the workspace switcher button, and then click newLayout, which appears in the list of panel layouts. The panel arrangement reflects the changes you made.

9. Close the free-floating panel group with the three panels.

⊕ EXPLORE   10. Delete the saved layout by clicking the workspace switcher button on the menu bar, and then clicking Manage Workspaces. In the Manage Workspaces dialog box, click newLayout, and then click the Delete button. Click the Yes button to confirm you want to delete the workspace layout, and then click the OK button.

11. Find out more about the Align panel. Open the Flash Help system, type **Align panel** in the search box in the left column of the page, and then press the Enter key.

12. On the Search Community Help page, click the Adobe Flash Professional * Arranging objects link.

13. In the Arranging objects Help page, click Align objects to display the Help information about using the Align panel to align objects. Read the information for aligning objects. Record the basic steps for aligning objects. Close the Help window.

14. Close the document without saving it. Submit your answers to your instructor.

Explore drawing in Flash and Web Media for a nonprofit organization.

RESEARCH

Case Problem 4

There are no Data Files needed for this Case Problem.

River City Conservation Society   Brittany Hill is the current president of the River City Conservation Society, a nonprofit organization of citizens in the San Antonio and South Texas area. The purpose of the organization is to encourage the preservation of historic buildings relating to the history of San Antonio and South Texas. The society provides a forum for its members to volunteer time in support of its preservation efforts, to bring awareness to the community of the history of these buildings, and to meet and learn about the history of the region.

Brittany hired Anissa Ellison to improve and maintain the society's Web site. She wants to add new graphics and animation to the site to improve its appeal to the organization's members. Anissa plans to use Flash to develop the new elements for the site. She wants you to review information about drawing shapes and some of the tools used to draw graphics and then view examples of Web media.

1. In the Flash Help system, type **Drawing in Flash** in the search box in the left column of the page, and then press the Enter key.

2. On the Search Community Help page, click the Adobe Flash Professional * Drawing in Flash link.

3. On the Drawing in Flash page, under Vector and bitmap graphics, read the information about vector graphics and bitmap graphics. Record the definitions found in the Help topics for vector graphics and for bitmap graphics.

4. Scroll to the top of the page, and then click Drawing modes and graphic objects. Read the information about the Merge Drawing mode and the Object Drawing mode.

5. Scroll to the bottom of the page to the Overlapping shapes topic. Read the information about overlapping shapes.

6. Scroll to the top of the page, type **Draw simple lines and shapes** in the search box in the left column of the page, and then press the Enter key. On the Search Community Help page, click the Flash Professional Help * Draw simple lines and shapes link. In the Draw simple lines and shapes page, click the Draw with the Pencil tool topic and read its associated information.

7. Scroll to the top of the page, type **Reshaping objects** in the search box in the left column of the page, and then press the Enter key. On the Search Community Help page, click the Adobe Flash Professional * Reshape lines and shapes link, and then

click the Reshape a line or shape topic. Read the information displayed. Record the difference between reshaping an endpoint and a corner. Switch to Flash.

✥ EXPLORE

8. On the menu bar, click Help, and then click Flash Support Center. The Flash Help page opens. In the Learning section of the page, click Learn Flash Professional CS6. In the Adobe TV Web site, view at least one of the videos under the Getting Started heading. To view a video, click its link. View, listen, or read the information provided, and for the samples, experiment with any interactive components, if available. To return to the center's home page, use the browser's Back button. As you navigate to some of the samples, study and compare the animation effects you see. Listen for sound effects, music, and voice-overs. See if you can distinguish between bitmap and vector graphics.

9. In your browser, open the home page for the Flash Kit site at *www.flashkit.com*. Review the various examples of Flash graphics and animations displayed on the home page. Look for a list of hyperlinks, usually located at the top of page. In this list of hyperlinks, explore several of the categories such as Movies, Tutorials, and Gallery. Note how the various examples make use of animation, colors, sound, and pictures.

10. Close any open files without saving. Submit your answers to your instructor.

ENDING DATA FILES

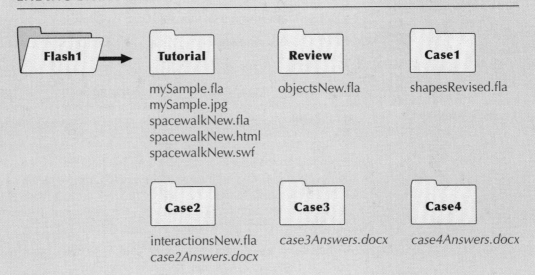

Flash1 → **Tutorial**

mySample.fla
mySample.jpg
spacewalkNew.fla
spacewalkNew.html
spacewalkNew.swf

Review

objectsNew.fla

Case1

shapesRevised.fla

Case2

interactionsNew.fla
case2Answers.docx

Case3

case3Answers.docx

Case4

case4Answers.docx

OBJECTIVES

Session 2.1
- Draw lines, curves, ovals, and rectangles
- Apply stroke and fill colors
- Modify strokes and fills
- Transform graphic objects
- Import a bitmap graphic
- Change a bitmap graphic's properties

Session 2.2
- Create text blocks
- Create symbols and instances of symbols
- Organize symbols in the Library panel
- Apply filters to symbol instances and text
- Apply and transform a gradient

Drawing Shapes, Adding Text, and Creating Symbols

Creating a Banner

Case | *Katie's Pet Shop*

Katie's Pet Shop staff members take pride in providing outstanding customer service and developing informative and educational marketing campaigns. The pet shop has won numerous local and national awards for its special educational programs, customer satisfaction, and contributions to the community. A new initiative is under way to promote the shop's tropical fish supplies while providing educational materials and classes to its customers. Owner Katie Summers wants Aly to develop a new banner for the shop's Web site that promotes the shop's aquarium and tropical fish supplies to promote the new initiative. You will work on this banner with Aly and Mike.

During the planning meeting, Katie said that she wants a colorful banner with graphic images depicting a scene related to tropical fish. Aly suggested that the banner include graphics of an aquarium with several fish, a background image, and several lines of text. Mike agreed that this banner will blend well with the current design of the shop's home page. Katie liked the idea and approved Aly's final sketch of the new banner. You will use Flash to create the banner according to Aly's sketch.

STARTING DATA FILES

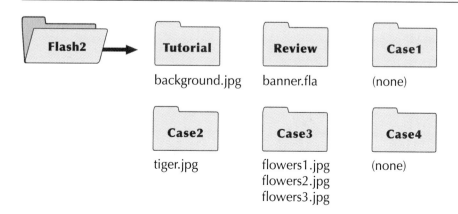

Flash2 → Tutorial — background.jpg Review — banner.fla Case1 — (none)

Case2 — tiger.jpg Case3 — flowers1.jpg flowers2.jpg flowers3.jpg Case4 — (none)

SESSION 2.1 VISUAL OVERVIEW

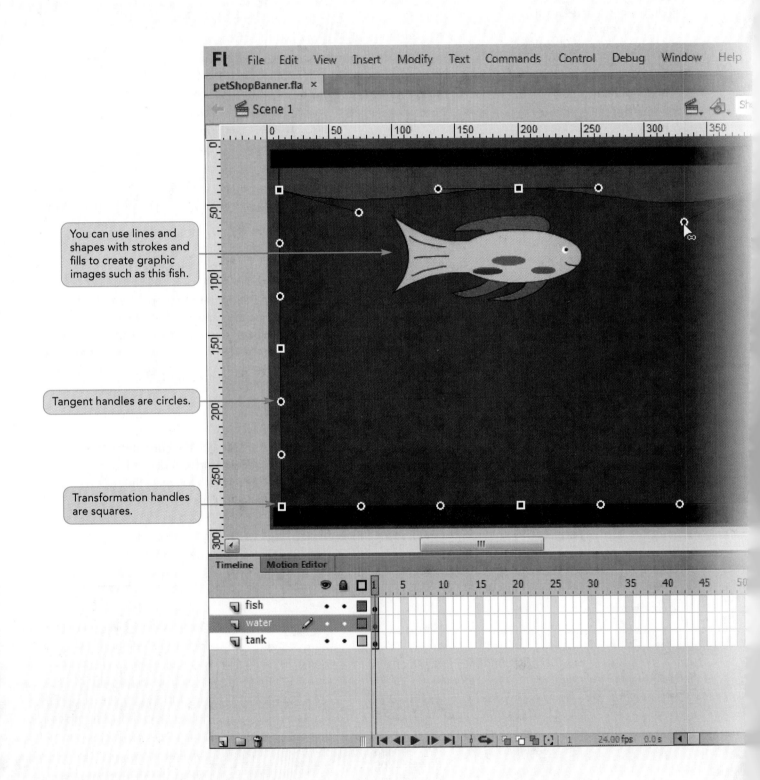

You can use lines and shapes with strokes and fills to create graphic images such as this fish.

Tangent handles are circles.

Transformation handles are squares.

THE DRAWING TOOLS

The **Free Transform tool** moves, rotates, scales, skews, and distorts objects.

The **Line tool** draws straight lines (strokes) of varying lengths, widths, and colors.

The **Rectangle tool** and **Oval tool** draw rectangles and ovals of different sizes and colors. The **Rectangle Primitive tool** and **Oval Primitive tool** create rectangles and ovals that are treated as separate objects whose characteristics can be modified without having to redraw the shapes from scratch.

The **Pen tool** draws lines or curves.

The **Pencil tool** draws free-form lines and shapes, like using an actual pencil to draw on paper.

The **Paint Bucket tool** fills enclosed areas of a drawing with color or changes the color of an existing fill.

The **Eyedropper tool** picks up properties of existing strokes, fills, and text and applies them to other objects.

The **Stroke Color control** sets the stroke color for drawn objects from the color palette.

The **Fill Color control** sets the fill color for drawn objects from the color palette.

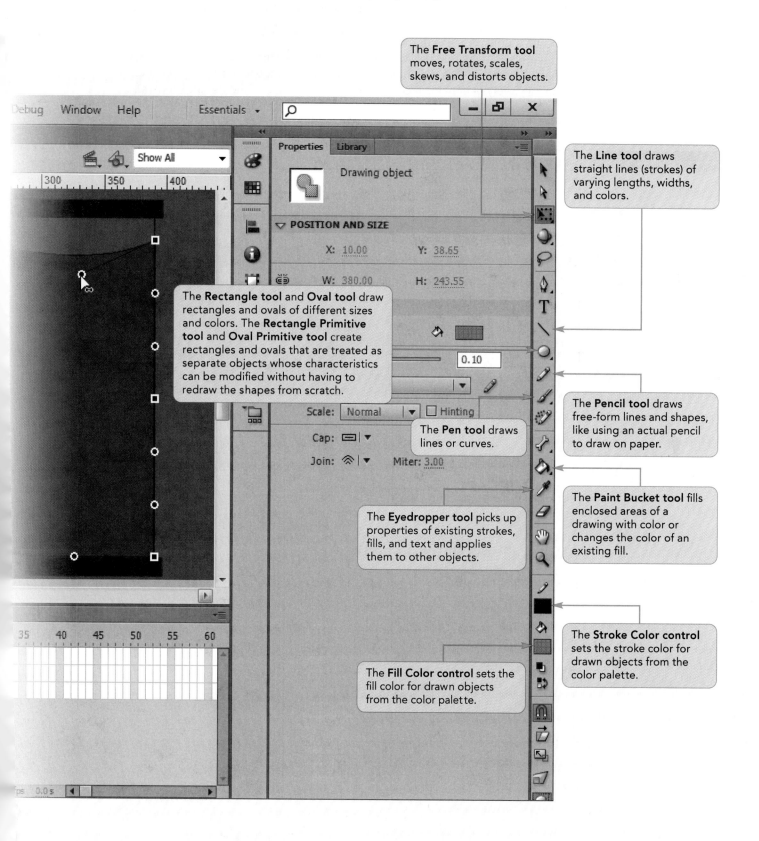

Drawing Lines and Shapes

When working with Flash, you will often create graphic images from scratch. You can draw lines and curves as well as free-form shapes. Enclosed areas of shapes can be filled with a color. You can draw shapes of various sizes and colors. Ovals, rectangles, and polygons can include strokes, fills, or both strokes and fills.

Figure 2-1 shows Aly's sketch of the banner you will create for Katie's Pet Shop. You will use a variety of drawing tools as you create and modify the fish and aquarium. You will use the guides to help you draw and align objects on the Stage. You will also apply a drop shadow effect to graphic objects and text.

Figure 2-1	Sketch of the banner for Katie's Pet Shop Web site

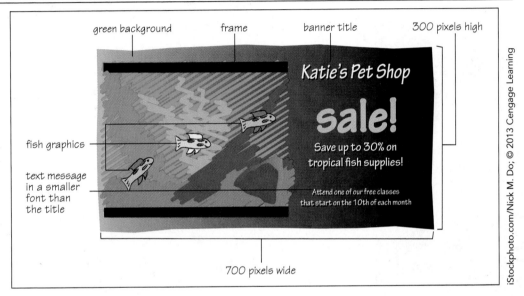

You are ready to begin creating the banner. You will set the document properties, display the rulers, and then save the banner file.

To set the document properties, show the rulers, and save the document:

1. On the menu bar, click **File**, and then click **New**. The New Document dialog box opens with the General tab active.

2. Click **ActionScript 3.0**, if necessary, and then click the **OK** button. The new document opens.

3. Reset Flash to the **Essentials** workspace.

4. On the menu bar, click **Modify**, and then click **Document**. The Document Settings dialog box opens.

5. In the Dimensions area, type **700** in the width box, press the **Tab** key to select the value in the height box, and then type **300**. The document dimensions are set according to the banner sketch.

6. Click the **Background color** control to open the color palette, and then click the **green** color swatch (#006633) in the sixth column, second row of the color palette. The background color is set to green, as shown in the sketch. You will leave the frame rate at 24 frames per second and the ruler units at pixels.

7. Click the **Auto-Save** check box to select it and leave the time setting at 10 minutes. Flash will automatically save the document every 10 minutes.

8. Click the **OK** button. The dialog box closes and the document changes to match the document settings.

9. Change the zoom magnification to **Fit in Window**, and then display the rulers. The document changes to fit within the Document window and the rulers appear along the top and left of the Stage. See Figure 2-2.

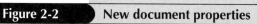

Figure 2-2   New document properties

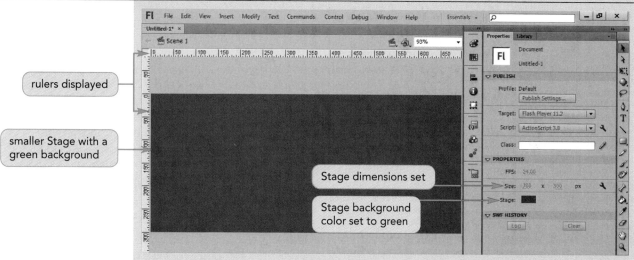

rulers displayed

smaller Stage with a green background

Stage dimensions set

Stage background color set to green

10. Save the document as **petShopBanner.fla** in the Flash2\Tutorial folder included with your Data Files.

Using the Oval, Rectangle, and PolyStar Tools

Drawing simple shapes is easy with the Oval, Rectangle, and PolyStar tools. These tools all work in a similar manner. As you drag the pointer for the selected tool on the Stage, the size of the drawn shape changes until you release the mouse button. When you use the PolyStar tool, you choose whether to draw a polygon or a star. You can also indicate the number of sides the shape will have, which can range from 3 to 32. For star shapes, you can also specify the value of the star point size, which can range from 0 to 1. A number closer to 0 results in narrower star points, and a number closer to 1 results in wider star points, as shown in Figure 2-3.

Figure 2-3   Star shapes with different point sizes

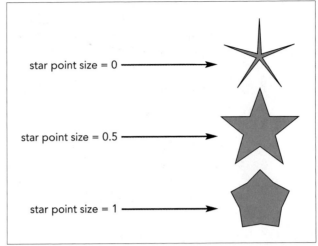

star point size = 0

star point size = 0.5

star point size = 1

© 2013 Cengage Learning

You can use the Oval and Rectangle tools to draw a perfect circle or a perfect square when the Snap to Objects modifier is selected. As you draw with the Oval or Rectangle tool, a small solid ring appears next to the pointer to let you know when you have drawn a perfect circle or a perfect square.

When you select the Rectangle tool, the Rectangle Options appear in the Property inspector. The Rectangle corner radius boxes represent the number of pixels by which to round the corners of the rectangle shape. You can enter a value for one or more corners of the rectangle. The Lock corner radius button locks all corner values to be the same as the value entered in the upper-left corner radius box. A negative value creates an inward corner, a 0 value results in a squared corner, and a higher value produces a more rounded corner, as shown in Figure 2-4.

TIP

To create a rectangle with specific dimensions and corner radii, press the Alt key as you click the Rectangle tool pointer on the Stage, enter values in the Rectangle Settings dialog box, and then click the OK button.

Figure 2-4   Rectangles with different corner radii

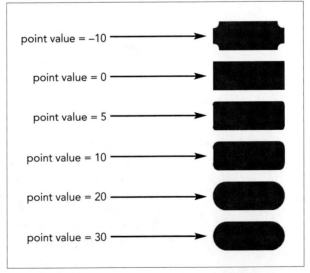

point value = −10

point value = 0

point value = 5

point value = 10

point value = 20

point value = 30

© 2013 Cengage Learning

PROSKILLS

Problem Solving: Selecting a Drawing Mode to Create Graphics

Creating graphics is like solving a puzzle. You need to define how you want the graphic objects you draw to interact with each other. Then, you must determine the appropriate drawing mode based on the results you want to achieve. If you want to create graphic shapes that combine to form one shape, draw them using the Merge Drawing mode. If you want to keep the shapes you draw separate from each other, use the Object Drawing mode. You can also switch between drawing modes as you draw the graphics.

As you draw graphics, you might find that the various shapes and lines you draw interact with each other in undesirable ways. For example, you might need to draw a complex logo consisting of shapes of various colors. As you draw and rearrange these shapes, overlapping shapes can cut away at underlying shapes. To avoid this problem, select the Object Drawing mode before you start to draw. In this mode, you can easily arrange objects without having them interact with other objects.

Sometimes you need to draw a complex logo in which you combine various shapes of the same color into one larger shape, such as a drawing a rectangle, an oval, and a circle to form one final shape. In this case, select the Merge Drawing mode so that the various shapes combine into one shape.

Another problem you might encounter is when you need to draw a shape other than a standard rectangle, oval, star, or other polygon. For example, you might need to draw a rectangle with a circular area cutout from one side of the rectangular shape. In this situation, select Merge Drawing mode. Draw the rectangle, and then draw a circle of a different color overlaid on the side of the rectangle. When you select the circle and delete it, the area on the rectangle covered by the circle will be cut out leaving the desired shape.

So, before you begin drawing, think about how the parts of the graphic work together and the results you want to achieve. Then determine the drawing mode you need to use. This up-front planning helps you to avoid unexpected results and eliminates the need to spend extra time redrawing a graphic.

You will draw a rectangle for the aquarium tank and a rectangle that will represent the water. As indicated in Aly's sketch, the aquarium rectangle will have a stroke and no fill. You will draw the aquarium graphics using the Object Drawing mode so that they won't merge other objects you will create.

To draw the aquarium tank rectangle:

▶ 1. In the Tools panel, click the **Rectangle Tool** button 🔲 and then click the **Object Drawing** button 🔘, if necessary, to select it. The rectangle you draw will not merge with other shapes.

▶ 2. In the Rectangle Options section of the Property inspector, click the **Reset** button to set the Rectangle corner radius values to 0, if necessary. The rectangle you draw will have square corners.

▶ 3. In the Property inspector, click the **Fill color** control ⬧■ to open the color palette, and then click the **no color** button ⊘. The rectangle you draw will not have a fill.

▶ 4. In the Property inspector, click the **Stroke color** control ✐■ to open the color palette, and then click the **black** color swatch (#000000) in the first column, first row of the color palette. The rectangle you draw will have a black outline.

5. Draw a rectangle for the tank by dragging the pointer from the upper-left corner of the Stage to the bottom-center of the Stage. A black rectangle without a fill occupies the left side of the Stage.

6. In the Property inspector, change the rectangle's width to **380**, its height to **275**, its X placement value to **10**, and its Y placement value to **15**. See Figure 2-5.

Figure 2-5   **Rectangle for the aquarium tank**

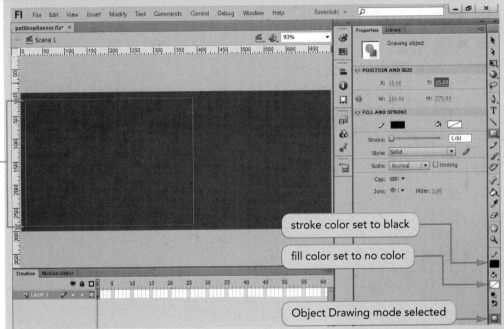

rectangle has
square corners

stroke color set to black

fill color set to no color

Object Drawing mode selected

Trouble? If the width and height values both change as you enter one value, click the Lock width and height values together icon to deselect it.

Next, you will modify the top and bottom sides of the rectangle to resemble an aquarium tank. Because the rectangle was drawn in Object Drawing mode, you will need to edit it as a drawing object.

To modify the aquarium tank rectangle:

1. In the Tools panel, click the **Selection Tool** button ▶.

2. On the Stage, double-click one side of the black rectangle. The rectangle is now in Object Drawing mode.

3. Click the top of the rectangle to select it. Make sure none of the other sides of the rectangle are selected. You will modify the selected side by increasing its width.

4. In the Property inspector, change the Stroke height to **14** and change the Cap style for the path's end to **Square**. See Figure 2-6.

Figure 2-6   **Rectangle side modified**

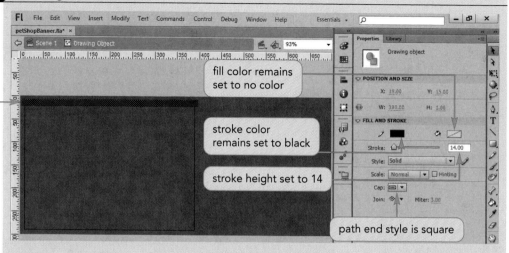

top of rectangle with a larger stroke height

fill color remains set to no color

stroke color remains set to black

stroke height set to 14

path end style is square

▶ **5.** Click the bottom of the rectangle to select it. You will make the same changes to the bottom stroke of the rectangle.

▶ **6.** In the Property inspector, change the Stroke height to **14** and change the Cap style for the path's end to **Square**. The bottom matches the top of the rectangle.

▶ **7.** On the Edit bar, click the **Scene 1** link to exit Object Drawing mode. The modified rectangle better represents an aquarium tank.

Next, you will draw the water for the aquarium tank using the Rectangle tool. Before drawing the rectangle for the water, you will create a new layer in the Timeline. Recall that each layer can contain different objects so you can better organize content. You can also assign a descriptive name to each layer and rearrange the layers in the Timeline. To edit the content of a layer, you select that layer in the Timeline. The selected layer is highlighted in the Timeline and a pencil icon appears to the right of the layer's name. You can also delete layers and add new layers as needed.

To create a rectangle in a new layer:

▶ **1.** In the Timeline, double-click the **Layer 1** name to select it, type **tank** as the new name, and then press the **Enter** key to rename the layer.

▶ **2.** In the Timeline, click the **New Layer** button 🔲 to insert a new layer above the tank layer.

▶ **3.** In the Timeline, double-click the **Layer 2** name, type **water** as the new layer name, and then press the **Enter** key. The Timeline has two layers with descriptive names. See Figure 2-7.

Figure 2-7   **Layers renamed in the Timeline**

Layer 2 renamed

Layer 1 renamed

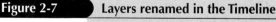
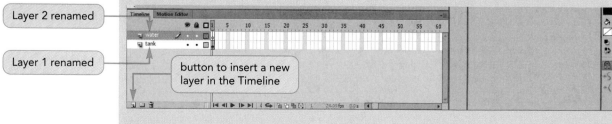

button to insert a new layer in the Timeline

▶ **4.** In the Tools panel, click the **Rectangle Tool** button ▢ to select the Rectangle tool.

▶ **5.** In the Property inspector, click the **Fill color** control ◈ ▱ to open the color palette, and then click the **blue** color swatch (#0000FF) in the fourth column, sixth row of the color palette. The rectangle you draw will be blue.

▶ **6.** In the Property inspector, click the **Fill color** control ◈ ▬ to open the color palette, click the **Alpha** value and drag to the left until the Alpha value is 30. The reduced Alpha value of the fill color will make the rectangle partially transparent.

▶ **7.** In the Property inspector, click the **Stroke color** control ✎ ▬ to open the color palette, and then click the **no color** button ▨. The rectangle you draw will not have an outline.

▶ **8.** Draw a rectangle for the water by dragging the pointer from the left side of the tank rectangle about 40 pixels from the top of the Stage to the lower-right corner of the tank rectangle. A partially transparent, blue rectangle without an outline fills the aquarium tank. See Figure 2-8.

| Figure 2-8 | **Rectangle created for the water** |

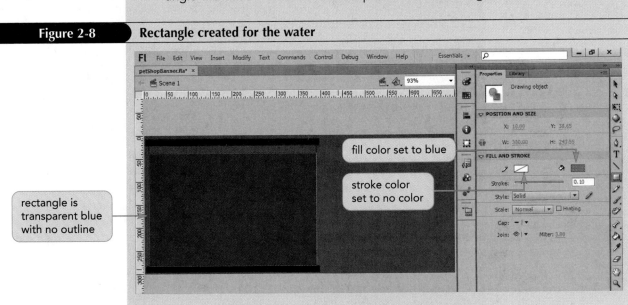

rectangle is transparent blue with no outline

fill color set to blue

stroke color set to no color

Next, you will create the fish in a new layer at the center of the rectangle that Aly sketched. You will draw a large oval for the body of the fish and a rectangle that you will modify to become the fish's tail. You will use the Merge Drawing mode so that the two shapes combine into one. Guides will help you draw these shapes.

To draw the fish:

▶ **1.** In the Timeline, click the **New Layer** button ▣ to insert a new layer above the water layer, double-click the new layer's name, type **fish** as the new layer name, and then press the **Enter** key.

▶ **2.** In the Tools panel, click the **Selection Tool** button ▸ to select it.

▶ **3.** Drag a horizontal guide from the horizontal ruler to approximately 70 pixels from the top of the Stage, and then drag another horizontal guide from the horizontal ruler to approximately 110 pixels from the top of the Stage.

4. Drag a vertical guide from the vertical ruler to approximately 150 pixels from the left of the Stage, and then drag another vertical guide from the vertical ruler to approximately 250 pixels from the left of the Stage. See Figure 2-9.

Figure 2-9   **Guides for creating the fish**

vertical guides at 150 and 250 pixels

horizontal guides at 70 and 110 pixels

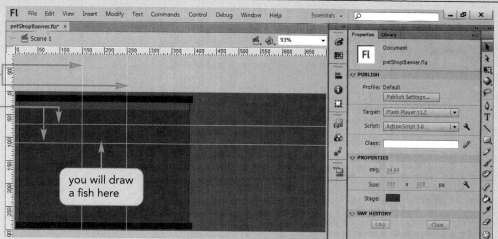

you will draw a fish here

5. In the Tools panel, click the **Zoom Tool** button, click the **Enlarge** modifier button, if necessary, and then, on the Stage, click the center of the rectangle formed by the intersecting guides to increase the magnification level.

6. In the Tools panel, click and hold the **Rectangle Tool** button to open the menu of tools, and then click the **Oval Tool** button. With the Oval tool selected, the pointer changes to ✛.

7. In the Tools panel, click the **Object Drawing** button to deselect it. Merge Drawing mode is now in effect.

8. In the Tools panel, click the **Snap to Objects** button to select this option, if necessary. Objects drawn will snap to the guides.

9. In the Property inspector, click the **Stroke color** control to open the color palette, and then click the **black** color swatch (#000000) in the first column, first row of the color palette.

10. Enter **1** in the Stroke height box, and then make sure the stroke style is set to **Solid**.

11. In the Property inspector, click the **Fill color** control to open the color palette, and then set the fill color's alpha % value to **100**.

12. In the Property inspector, click the **Fill color** control to open the color palette, and then click the **light orange** color swatch (#FFCC00) in the second column from the right, seventh row of the color palette. The fish body you draw will be light orange with a black outline.

13. Draw an oval from the upper-left corner of the rectangular area formed by the guides to the lower-right corner of the rectangular area formed by the guides. See Figure 2-10.

Figure 2-10   Oval for the fish body

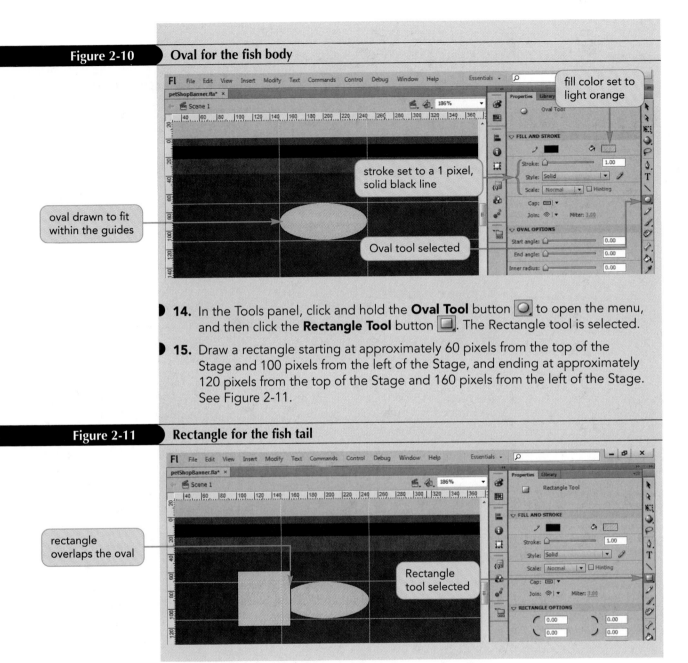

oval drawn to fit
within the guides

stroke set to a 1 pixel,
solid black line

fill color set to
light orange

Oval tool selected

▶ **14.** In the Tools panel, click and hold the **Oval Tool** button ⬤ to open the menu, and then click the **Rectangle Tool** button ▭. The Rectangle tool is selected.

▶ **15.** Draw a rectangle starting at approximately 60 pixels from the top of the Stage and 100 pixels from the left of the Stage, and ending at approximately 120 pixels from the top of the Stage and 160 pixels from the left of the Stage. See Figure 2-11.

Figure 2-11   Rectangle for the fish tail

rectangle
overlaps the oval

Rectangle
tool selected

You will use the Selection tool to modify the two shapes so that they more closely resemble the fish Aly sketched. The right corners of the rectangle will connect to the oval, and the sides of the rectangle will be curved. You will clear the guides because you don't need them anymore.

To modify the oval and rectangle shapes:

▶ **1.** On the menu bar, click **View**, point to **Guides**, and then click **Clear Guides**. The guides are removed from the Stage.

▶ **2.** In the Tools panel, click the **Selection Tool** button ▸, drag the upper-right corner of the rectangle down until it snaps to the upper edge of the oval, and then drag the lower-right corner of the rectangle up until it snaps to the lower edge of the oval. See Figure 2-12.

Figure 2-12   **Modified rectangle**

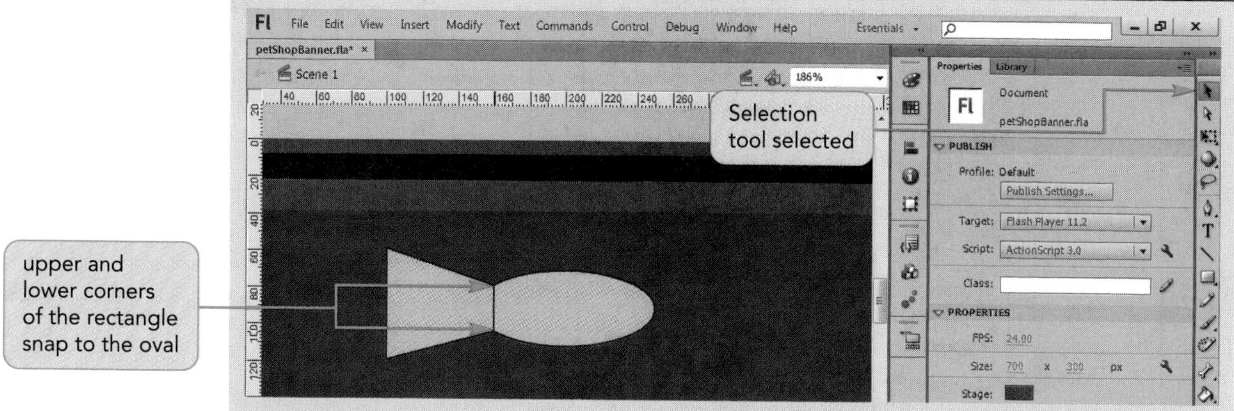

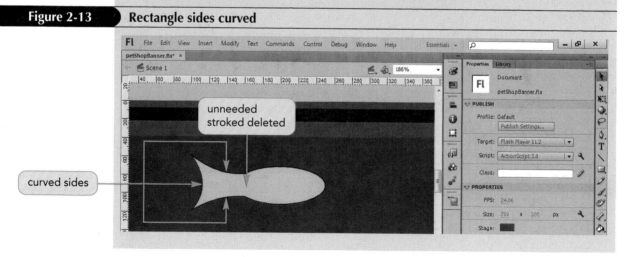

upper and lower corners of the rectangle snap to the oval

3. Move the pointer to the stroke on the left side of the modified rectangle shape until the pointer changes to ↳, and then drag the line slightly to the right to curve the back of the tail.

4. Drag the top line down slightly to curve it; drag the bottom line up slightly to curve it.

5. Click the right side of the modified rectangle to select it, and then press the **Delete** key. The unneeded stroke is removed. See Figure 2-13.

Figure 2-13   **Rectangle sides curved**

unneeded stroked deleted

curved sides

The modified rectangle and oval now resemble a fish shape. You are ready to draw the eye for the fish. You will also draw several oval spots on the fish. To do this, you will use the Oval tool.

To draw the eye and oval spots on the fish:

1. In the Tools panel, click the **Zoom Tool** button 🔍, make sure the **Enlarge** modifier button 🔍 is selected, and then click the right side of the fish shape once to zoom in.

2. In the Tools panel, click and hold the **Rectangle Tool** button ▢ to open the menu, and then click the **Oval Tool** button ◯. The pointer changes to ✛.

3. In the Property inspector, click the **Stroke color** control 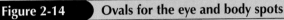 to open the color palette, click the **no color** button ☑, click the **Fill color** control ☒ to open the color palette, and then click the **white** color swatch (#FFFFFF) in the second column, sixth row of the color palette. Any oval you draw will have no stroke and a white fill.

4. Draw a small circle on the upper-right end of the fish shape for the fish eye, and then draw three ovals of different sizes on the fish body. You will change the color of the ovals later in this session. See Figure 2-14.

Figure 2-14	Ovals for the eye and body spots

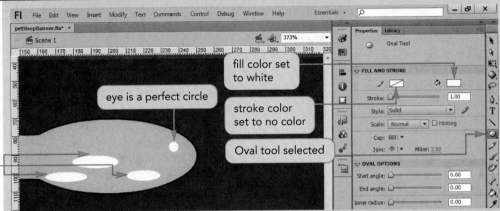

5. In the Tools panel, click the **Snap to Objects** modifier button 🧲 to deselect it. Having the modifier off will make it easier to draw a small circle for the pupil of the fish eye.

6. In the Property inspector, click the **Fill color** control ☒ to open the color palette, and then click the **black** color swatch (#000000) in the first column, first row of the color palette. The next oval you draw will have a black fill.

7. Draw a smaller circle inside the eye to represent the pupil. See Figure 2-15.

Figure 2-15	Pupil added to the fish eye

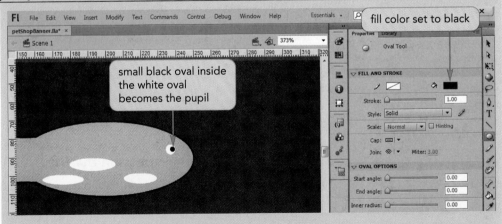

Trouble? If you make a mistake and draw over the orange fill of the fish, click Edit on the menu bar, click Undo Oval, and then repeat Step 7 to redraw the circle for the pupil of the fish eye.

Using the Pencil Tool

The Pencil tool works in a similar way to the Line tool, but it doesn't limit you to drawing straight lines. Instead, you can draw free-form shapes as if you were using an actual pencil to draw on paper. As with the Line tool, you can select a color, height, and style for the lines drawn with the Pencil tool. The Pencil modifier buttons in the Tools panel lets you control the way lines appear as you draw them. Figure 2-16 summarizes the options for this modifier.

Figure 2-16   **Pencil modifier options**

Modifier Button	Option	Description
↳	Straighten	Helps straighten the lines you draw
S	Smooth	Smoothes the lines and curves you draw
✎	Ink	Provides minimal assistance as you draw

© 2013 Cengage Learning

You will use the Pencil tool to add fins, a mouth, and tail lines to the fish.

To add fins, mouth, and lines to the fish:

▶ 1. In the Tools panel, click the **Hand Tool** button 🖐 and use 🖐 to drag the Stage to the right so that all of the fish is visible on the Stage.

▶ 2. In the Tools panel, click the **Pencil Tool** button 🖉 to select it.

▶ 3. In the Tools panel, click the **Pencil** modifier button ↳ to open the menu of options, and then click **Smooth**. The Smooth option for the Pencil Mode modifier ensures that the lines you draw are smooth.

▶ 4. In the Property inspector, make sure the stroke color is **black** (#000000), the stroke height is **1**, and the stroke style is **Solid**. The stroke color, height, and style are set for drawing lines for the fins, mouth, and tail.

▶ 5. Draw a fin on the top side of the fish and two fins on the bottom side. See Figure 2-17.

Figure 2-17 Fins drawn on the fish

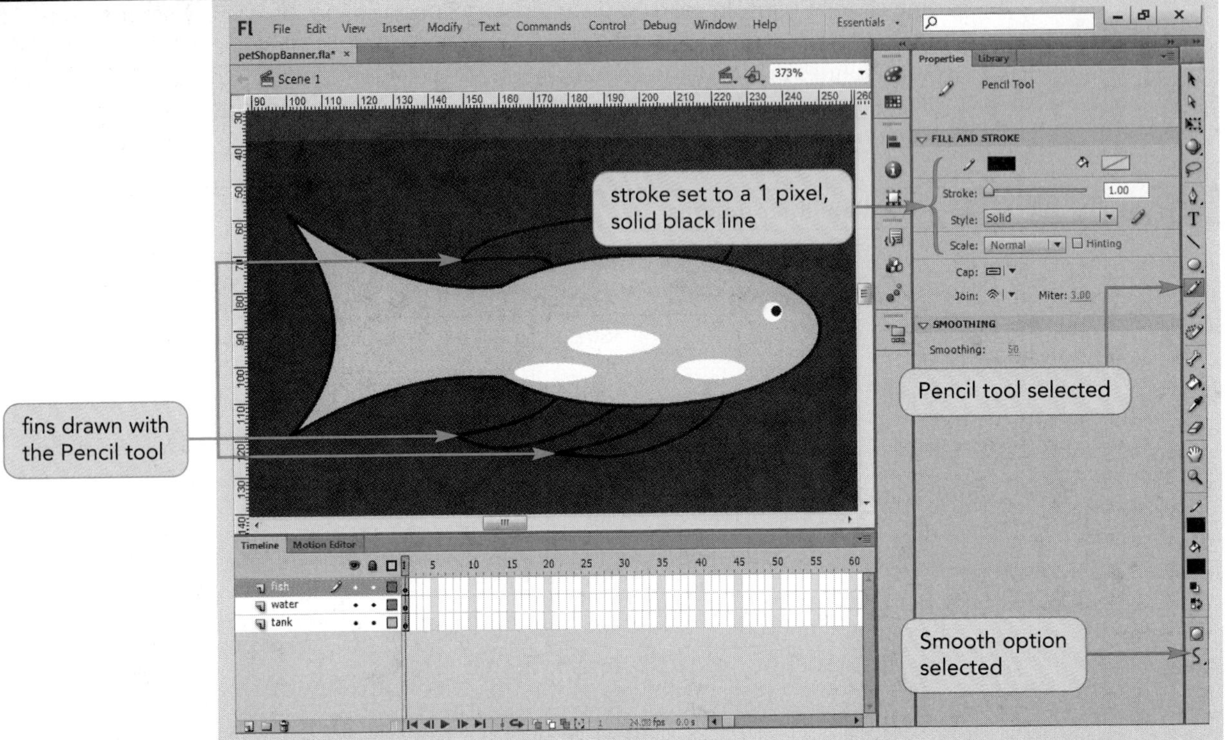
stroke set to a 1 pixel, solid black line
fins drawn with the Pencil tool
Pencil tool selected
Smooth option selected

6. In the Tools panel, click the **Zoom Tool** button, make sure the **Enlarge** modifier button is selected, and then click the center of the fish shape once to zoom in.

7. In the Tools panel, click the **Selection Tool** button, click the **Snap to Objects** modifier button to select it, move the pointer to the left endpoint of the lower-right fin stroke until the pointer changes to, and then drag the endpoint so that it snaps to the stroke representing the body of the fish. See Figure 2-18.

Be sure that the fin strokes connect to the fish body strokes so you can later fill the enclosed fin shapes with color.

Figure 2-18 Endpoints of the fins connected to the fish's body

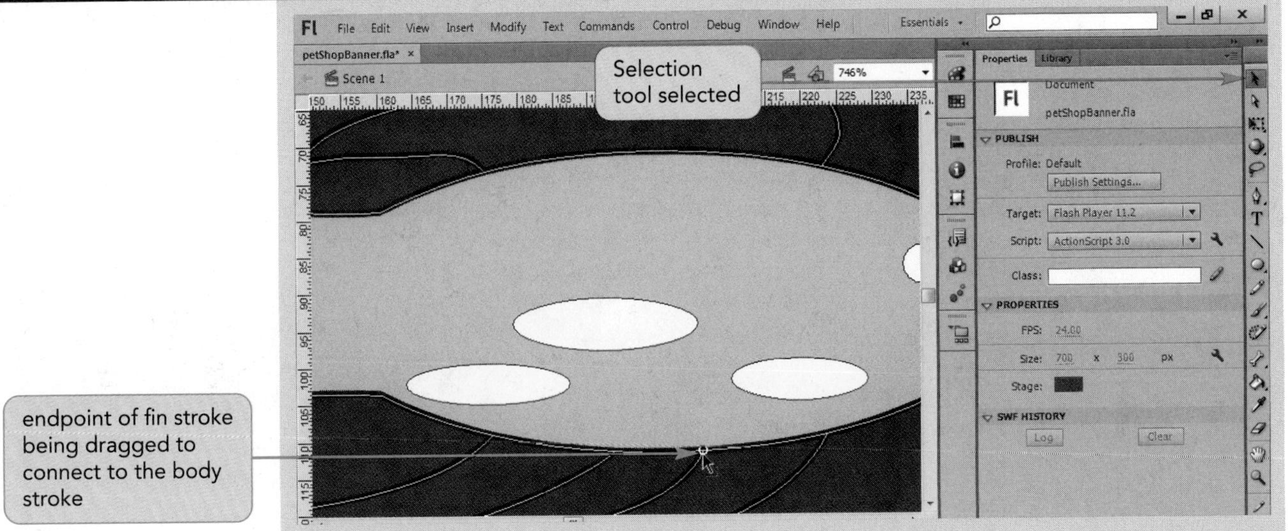
Selection tool selected
endpoint of fin stroke being dragged to connect to the body stroke

8. Repeat Step 7 as necessary to connect the endpoints of the other fins to the fish's body.

Trouble? If you cannot see all of the fins on the Stage, you need to reposition the fish. In the Tools panel, click the Hand Tool button, drag the fish so you can see another fin on the Stage, and then repeat Step 7.

9. On the Edit bar, click the **Zoom control arrow**, and then click **400%** to enlarge the contents of the Stage.

10. In the Tools panel, click the **Pencil Tool** button 🖊 to select it, make sure the **Smooth** modifier option ⑤ is selected, and make sure the stroke is set to a **1** pixel, **solid black** line.

11. Draw a small curved line for the fish's mouth from right below the eye to the stroke in the lower-right side of the fish, and then draw three short lines in the tail section of the fish. See Figure 2-19.

| Figure 2-19 | Fish with fins, mouth, and lines |

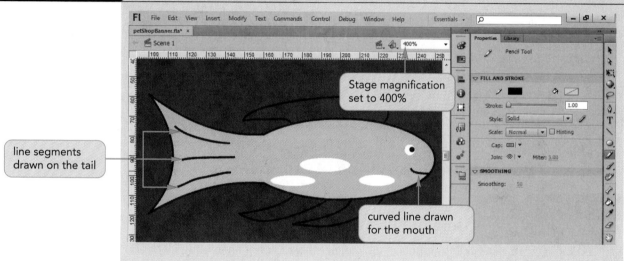

Changing Strokes and Fills

After you draw an object, you can still change its strokes and fill. You can change the stroke's color, height, or style, and you can change a fill's color. You can even add a fill or a stroke to an object that doesn't have one or the other. Based on Aly's sketch of the banner, the oval shapes and the fins on the fish should be areas of color.

To keep the various parts of the fish together, you will group them. This way, you can easily modify or create copies of the fish graphic as a whole. You can still modify individual elements of a grouped object in group-editing mode.

To group the fish graphic:

▶ 1. On the Edit bar, click the **Zoom control arrow**, and then click **200%** to view all of the fish.

▶ 2. In the Timeline, in the water layer, click the **dot** ⬚ in the Lock column (the second dot to the right of the water layer's name) to lock the layer's contents. This ensures that no changes are made to the contents of this layer.

▶ 3. In the Tools panel, click the **Selection Tool** button ▶, and then draw a selection marquee around the entire fish to select all of its parts.

▶ 4. On the menu bar, click **Modify**, and then click **Group**. The graphic elements are grouped. A thin rectangular line surrounds the grouped object to show it is selected. See Figure 2-20.

| Figure 2-20 | Grouped fish graphic |

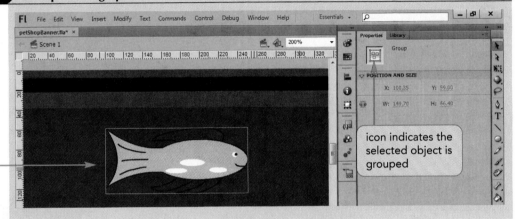

outline indicates a grouped object

icon indicates the selected object is grouped

Using the Paint Bucket Tool

The Paint Bucket tool changes the color of an existing fill or adds a fill to an enclosed area that does not have a fill. The fill color is selected with the Fill Color control. The Paint Bucket tool also has a Gap Size modifier and a Lock Fill modifier. The Gap Size modifiers—Don't Close Gaps, Close Small Gaps, Close Medium Gaps, and Close Large Gaps—determine how the tool will paint areas that are not completely enclosed. The Lock Fill modifier extends gradient and bitmap fills across multiple objects.

You will use the Paint Bucket tool to fill the spots on the fish with bright colors.

To add fills to the fish:

▶ 1. Double-click the grouped fish graphic to enter group-editing mode, and then click another area of the Stage to deselect the fish. In group-editing mode, you can modify each part of the fish independently.

▶ 2. In the Tools panel, click the **Paint Bucket Tool** button 🪣. The pointer changes to 🪣.

▶ 3. In the Tools panel, click the **Gap Size** modifier button ⃝ to open the pop-up menu, and then click **Close Medium Gaps**. With this Gap Size modifier, you can use the Paint Bucket tool to paint areas that are not completely enclosed.

4. In the Property inspector, click the **Fill color** control to open the color palette, and then change the Alpha amount to **100%**.

5. In the Property inspector, click the **Fill color** control, and then click the **blue** color swatch (#0000FF) in the fourth column, sixth row of the color palette.

6. Click inside the white oval at the left side of the fish body to apply the fill color. The fish has a blue spot. See Figure 2-21.

Figure 2-21   **Fill color applied with the Paint Bucket tool**

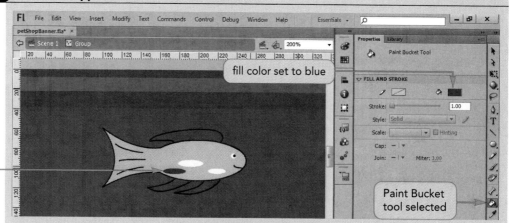

oval shape is blue

Trouble? If a padlock icon appears next to the paint bucket pointer, the Lock Fill modifier is selected. This does not affect the way the Paint Bucket tool works. Continue with Step 7.

7. In the Property inspector, click the **Fill color** control to open the color palette, click the **pink** color swatch (#FF00FF) in the second column, bottom row of the color palette, and then click the middle white oval on the fish body. The spot changes to pink.

8. Repeat Step 7 to apply a **red** color swatch (#FF0000) to the right white oval on the fish body. The spot changes to red.

Using the Eyedropper Tool

The Eyedropper tool copies the properties of a fill or stroke from one object and applies them to the fill or stroke of another object. You can also use the Eyedropper tool to copy the properties of a text block and apply them to another text block. When you select the Eyedropper tool, the pointer changes to . If you move the eyedropper over a stroke, the pointer changes to to indicate that you are about to copy the stroke's attributes. After you click the stroke, the pointer changes to , which indicates that you can apply the copied stroke attributes to another object. If you move the eyedropper over a fill, the pointer changes to , indicating that you are about to copy the fill's attributes. After you click the fill, the pointer changes to , and you can click another object to apply the copied fill attributes. The pointer includes a padlock when the Lock Fill modifier is selected.

Using the Eyedropper Tool

- In the Tools panel, click the Eyedropper Tool button.
- Click the stroke or fill whose attributes you want to copy.
- Click the stroke or fill to which you want to apply the copied attributes.

Based on Aly's sketch, the fins of the fish need to be the same color as the bottom oval spot on the fish. You will use the Eyedropper tool to copy the fill color of the spot to the fins.

To copy the color from the bottom spot to the fins:

1. In the Tools panel, click the **Eyedropper Tool** button . The pointer changes to .

2. Click the red fill color in the lower-right spot of the fish. The pointer changes to or , depending on whether the Lock Fill modifier is selected, to indicate that you can apply the red color to another part of the fish.

3. Click the blank area enclosed by the top fin. The top fin now has the same color as the lower-right spot of the fish. See Figure 2-22.

Figure 2-22   Red oval fill color copied to the top fin

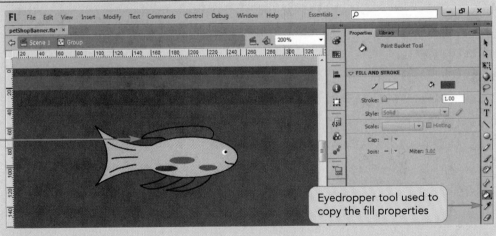

top fin has the same color as lower-right spot

Eyedropper tool used to copy the fill properties

4. Click in the bottom fins. The red fill color is applied to them.

5. On the Edit bar, click the **Scene 1** link to exit group-editing mode.

Using the Free Transform Tool

You can modify the strokes and fills of objects you draw in ways other than just changing their colors. The Free Transform tool allows you to modify objects. You can transform a particular stroke or fill, or you can transform the entire object at once. When you select an object with the Free Transform tool, a bounding box with transformation handles surrounds the object. These handles are different from the anchor points you used with the Subselection tool. The anchor points modify individual curves, lines, or shapes. The transformation handles on the bounding box affect the entire object.

REFERENCE

Transforming an Object Using the Free Transform Tool

- In the Tools panel, click the Free Transform Tool button.
- Select the object to transform.
- In the Tools panel, click a modifier button.
- Drag the transformation handles on the bounding box to modify the object.

As you move the pointer near a transformation handle on a bounding box, the pointer changes to indicate how the object will be modified when you drag that handle. For example, when you point just outside a corner handle, the pointer changes to ⟲, indicating that you can rotate the object by dragging the corner. The Free Transform tool also has several modifiers you can select in the Tools panel, which are described in Figure 2-23.

Figure 2-23   **Free Transform tool modifiers**

Button	Modifier	Description
	Rotate and Skew	Freely rotates an object by dragging a corner handle or skews it to a different angle by dragging an edge handle
	Scale	Changes the size of an object by dragging a corner or edge handle
	Distort	Repositions the corner or edge of an object by dragging its handle
	Envelope	Displays a bounding box with points and tangent handles that you can adjust to warp or distort the object

© 2013 Cengage Learning

Aly's sketch shows a wavy line for the top of the blue rectangle that represents the water. You will use the Free Transform tool to modify the blue rectangle.

To modify the blue rectangle:

1. On the Edit bar, click the **Zoom control arrow**, and then click **Show All** to set the magnification level so you can see all of the objects on the Stage.

2. In the Timeline, in the water layer, click the **lock** icon 🔒 in the Lock column to unlock the layer's contents. You can now make changes in the layer.

3. In the Tools panel, click the **Free Transform Tool** button 🔳, click the blue rectangle on the Stage, and then click the **Envelope** modifier button 🔘 in the Tools panel. The bounding box and transformation handles appear around the rectangle. Tangent handles also appear on the bounding box.

> **Trouble?** If the Envelope modifier button is not visible, click the Collapse to Icons button ⏩ above the Tools panel, click the Tools button 🛠, and then click the Envelope modifier button 🔘. Click the Expand Panels button ◀◀ to expand the Tools panel.

4. Near the upper-left corner of the rectangle, drag the upper-left tangent handle down slightly to create a curve. See Figure 2-24.

Figure 2-24   **Curve created by dragging a tangent handle**

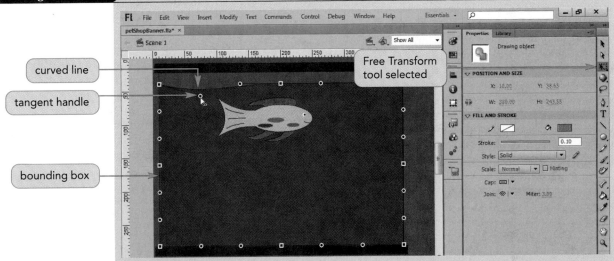

curved line

tangent handle

bounding box

5. Near the upper-right corner of the rectangle, drag the upper-right tangent handle down slightly to create a curve. See Figure 2-25.

Figure 2-25   **Second curve created by dragging a tangent handle**

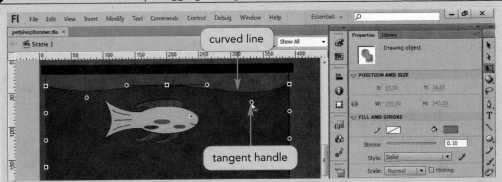

6. In the Timeline, in the water layer, click the **dot** · in the Lock column (the second dot to the right of the water layer's name) to lock the layer's contents.

Aly's sketch shows another fish swimming to the right of the fish you already drew. Instead of drawing a second fish from scratch, you will copy the existing fish, and then use the Free Transform tool to resize and rotate the copied fish. You will also resize and reposition the first fish.

To copy, reposition, resize, and rotate the fish:

1. In the Tools panel, click the **Selection Tool** button ![cursor], and then click the fish. The grouped fish is selected.

2. On the menu bar, click **Edit**, and then click **Copy**. The fish is copied to the Windows Clipboard.

3. On the menu bar, click **Edit**, and then click **Paste in Center**. A copy of the fish appears in the center of the Stage.

4. Drag the copy of the fish to the lower-left side of the Stage and then drag the first fish toward the right side of the aquarium tank. See Figure 2-26.

| Figure 2-26 | Fish copied and repositioned |

5. In the Tools panel, click the **Free Transform Tool** button ![icon]. A bounding box with transformation handles appears around the selected fish. You want to reduce the size of the fish.

6. In the Tools panel, click the **Scale** modifier button ![icon]. When you drag a corner handle, the fish will be resized.

7. Drag a corner handle to reduce the size of the fish to about half its original size.

8. Repeat Step 7 to reduce the size of the left fish.

▶ **9.** In the Tools panel, click the **Rotate and Skew** modifier button 🔄, and then move the pointer near a corner handle. The pointer changes to ↻.

▶ **10.** Drag a corner handle counterclockwise to rotate the fish so that it appears to be swimming up. See Figure 2-27.

Figure 2-27	Scaled and rotated fish

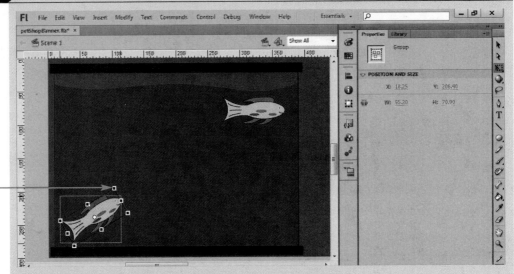

bounding box handles used to rotate the object

Trouble? If the fish in your banner are in a different location than shown in Figure 2-27, you need to reposition them. In the Tools panel, click the Selection Tool button, and then drag the fish as needed to match the locations shown.

The fish in the banner now match the sketch that Aly provided. Next, you will add a background to the aquarium tank.

INSIGHT

Transforming Objects Precisely

When you want to make very specific changes to an object, the Transform panel provides precise control over how you modify the object. In the Transform panel, you can enter specific values in pixels to resize an object. You can also enter values in degrees to rotate an object or skew an object horizontally or vertically. If you want to try different transformations without affecting the original object, you can make a copy of an object and then apply a transformation to the copied object.

Working with Bitmaps

The Katie's Pet Shop banner that you created will use a photograph as a background for the aquarium tank. A photograph is a bitmap graphic. Recall that a bitmap graphic is stored as a row-by-row list of every pixel in the graphic, along with each pixel's color. The most common bitmap file formats for Web graphics are JPEG and GIF. Bitmap graphics are different from vector graphics, which are stored as mathematical instructions that describe the color, outline, and position of all the shapes in the graphic. Bitmap graphics do not resize well, and their file sizes tend to be larger than the vector graphics created in Flash. As a result, using bitmaps in a Flash movie increases the movie's download time. However, file size and download time alone should not keep you from using bitmap graphics in Flash documents. Just make sure that the graphic really is needed in the document's design.

Using Bitmaps in Flash

You cannot easily edit bitmap graphics within Flash, so you should use an image-editing program such as Adobe Photoshop or Adobe Fireworks to edit and resize the bitmaps before importing them into a Flash document. Before using a bitmap graphic in Flash, optimize it by reducing its size while maintaining its quality. Reducing the file size of the bitmap minimizes its impact on the download time of the Flash document. If possible, also consider the target audience and the types of Internet connections they have. Flash documents targeted at users with slower connections should include few, if any, bitmap graphics, even if the bitmap graphics can greatly enhance a document's design.

Importing Bitmaps

You cannot create bitmap graphics in Flash, so you need to import them into Flash. Importing a bitmap into a Flash document places the bitmap in the document's library. The **library** is a storage location for bitmaps and other objects used in a document. You can view, organize, and edit objects stored in the library from the Library panel.

The Library panel displays a list with the names of all the objects in the library for a document. Each item in the Library panel has an icon to the left of its name to show what type of object it is. The Library panel also includes information about each item, including whether it is shared with other documents (Linkage column), the number of times it is used in the document (Use Count column), the date it was last modified (Date Modified column), and its type (Type column). You can sort the items by clicking a column header; for example, to sort the objects by date, click the Date Modified header. The dates range from most recent to oldest. This order can be reversed by clicking the Toggle Sorting Order button. You can access additional Library panel options using the Library panel's menu. This menu includes options to create, rename, edit, delete, or duplicate an object. You can also share bitmaps and other library items with other documents by making them part of a shared library.

Importing a Bitmap

- On the menu bar, click File, point to Import, and then click Import to Stage or Import to Library.
- In the Import or Import to Library dialog box, navigate to the location of the bitmap file, and then click the bitmap file in the files list.
- Click the Open button.

The new Katie's Pet Shop banner uses a bitmap for the aquarium's background that Aly has provided. You need to import this bitmap into the banner's library. You can then copy the bitmap from the library to the Stage.

To import the background bitmap image into the banner document:

▶ **1.** On the menu bar, click **File**, point to **Import**, and then click **Import to Library**. The Import to Library dialog box opens.

▶ **2.** Click the **All Formats** button, and then click **All Image Formats** so that the files list displays any type of image.

▶ **3.** Navigate to the **Flash2\Tutorial** folder, click the **background.jpg** file, and click the **Open** button. The bitmap file is imported into the document's library.

▶ **4.** Click the **Library** tab above the Property inspector to display the Library panel.

▶ **5.** In the Library panel, click the **background.jpg** bitmap. The background.jpg picture appears in the preview area. See Figure 2-28.

Figure 2-28   **Library panel with bitmap**

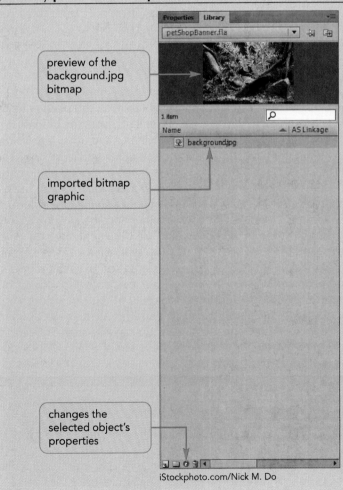

preview of the background.jpg bitmap

imported bitmap graphic

changes the selected object's properties

iStockphoto.com/Nick M. Do

Setting a Bitmap's Properties

After you have imported a bitmap into Flash, you can set its properties, use it in animations, and even convert it into a vector graphic. You can modify a bitmap's properties by changing the bitmap's name, updating the bitmap if the original file has been modified, and even changing its compression settings. These properties are stored with the bitmap in the library.

Compression takes away some of a file's data to reduce its size. You can compress a bitmap yet maintain its quality. **Lossy compression**, used by the JPEG format, removes some of the original data in the image to achieve a smaller file size. **Lossless compression**, used by the GIF format, retains all the original data in the image but is limited to 256 colors. JPEG uses a compression method designed for compressing full-color images such as photographs. Although JPEG removes some of the image data, it stores full-color information, resulting in very good image quality. The GIF and PNG formats are better for images with solid areas of color, such as logos and drawn shapes. The PNG format is not as widely used as the GIF format, but is supported by most current Web browsers.

PROSKILLS

Problem Solving: Finding the Right Compression

A bitmap file in the JPEG file format is already compressed. Compressing it further in Flash can degrade the quality of the picture, so you need to balance how much compression to apply to a bitmap with the picture's quality. This requires some problem solving.

Think about how you plan to use the bitmap. Keep in mind that pictures in a Flash movie don't always have to be of the highest quality, especially if they are small and are used as part of a larger graphic. Applying additional compression to bitmaps in Flash reduces the overall size of the final movie.

Trial and error is a good way to find the right compression for a particular bitmap. Experiment with several quality values and compare how the picture quality is affected. Select the value that maintains the picture quality needed for the particular design while still compressing the bitmap as much as possible.

The bitmap properties available depend on the bitmap's file type. Figure 2-29 describes the different properties, which are available in the Bitmap Properties dialog box.

Figure 2-29	Bitmap properties

Property	Description
Name	Specifies the name of the bitmap in the document's library.
Smoothing	Offers the option to smooth the edges of the bitmap so they do not appear jagged.
Compression	Specifies the type of compression: Lossless (PNG/GIF) is for bitmaps in the PNG or GIF file formats or that have large areas of single colors. Photo (JPEG) is for bitmaps with many colors or many color transitions, such as photographs.
Quality	Specifies the amount of compression to apply to the bitmap, ranging from 0 (most compression) to 100 (least compression). The more compression that is applied, the more data that is lost. You can also keep the quality setting of the original bitmap for JPEGs, or use the quality value set for the whole document for PNGs or GIFs.

© 2013 Cengage Learning

Before placing the bitmap in the banner, Aly wants you to minimize the size of the final movie by changing the compression settings for the bitmap. You will reduce the JPEG quality to decrease the overall size of the final movie, and then check what effect the new JPEG quality value will have on the picture.

To change the background.jpg bitmap properties:

1. In the Library panel, click the **background.jpg** bitmap, if necessary, to select it, and then click the **Properties** button ⓘ at the bottom of the panel. The Bitmap Properties dialog box opens.

2. Right-click the **bitmap preview** in the upper-left corner, and then click **Zoom In** on the context menu. The preview image is larger, so you can more easily see the effects of changes to the bitmap's properties.

3. In the Quality section, click the **Custom** option button. You want to adjust the bitmap's compression rather than use its imported compression data. The Custom box shows the default value of 50.

4. In the Custom box, click **50** to select it, and then type **20** to change the compression value.

5. Click the **Test** button. The preview shows the bitmap with the new compression settings. With the lower quality value, the picture quality is poor. Some colors have changed significantly, and the picture has less detail, as evidenced by the small blocks that appear throughout the picture. See Figure 2-30.

TIP

You can drag the preview image in the Bitmap Properties dialog box to see other areas of the bitmap.

| Figure 2-30 | Bitmap Properties dialog box |

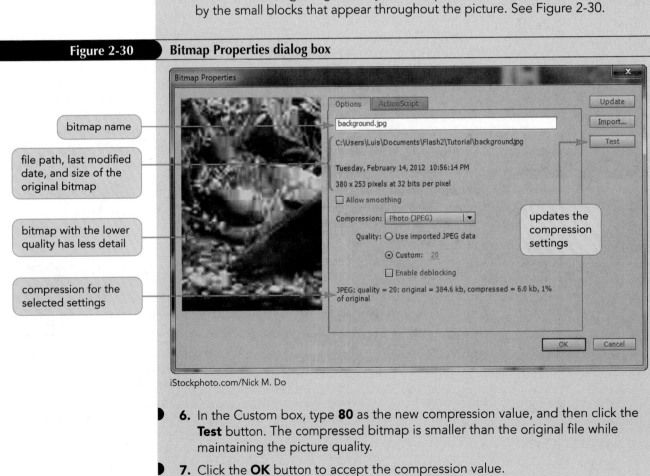

bitmap name

file path, last modified date, and size of the original bitmap

bitmap with the lower quality has less detail

compression for the selected settings

updates the compression settings

iStockphoto.com/Nick M. Do

6. In the Custom box, type **80** as the new compression value, and then click the **Test** button. The compressed bitmap is smaller than the original file while maintaining the picture quality.

7. Click the **OK** button to accept the compression value.

The bitmap will be used as a background in the aquarium. You will insert a new layer, move the layer below all of the other layers, and then place the bitmap in the new layer so that it appears behind the other objects on the Stage.

To add the background.jpg bitmap to the Stage in a new layer:

1. In the Timeline, insert a new layer, rename the layer **background**, and then drag the background layer so that it is below the tank layer. See Figure 2-31.

| Figure 2-31 | New background layer moved below the tank layer |

background layer in the Timeline

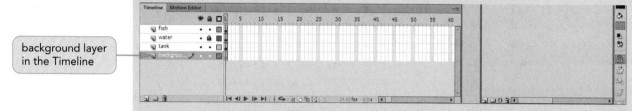

2. In the Timeline, in the water layer, click the **dot** • in the Show or Hide All Layers column (the first dot to the right of the water layer's name) to hide the layer's contents. See Figure 2-32.

| Figure 2-32 | Contents of the water layer hidden |

blue rectangle in the water layer not visible

icon indicates the layer is hidden

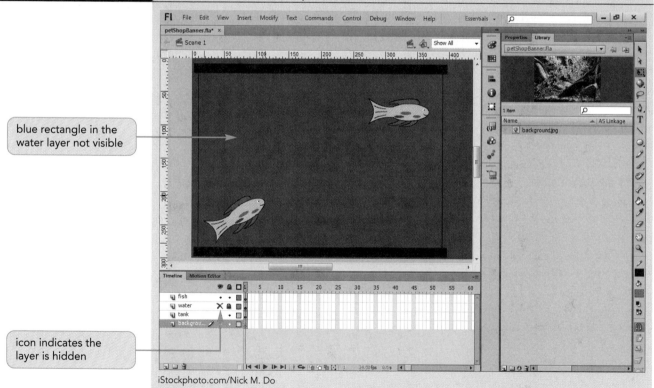

iStockphoto.com/Nick M. Do

3. In the Timeline, in the fish layer, click the **dot** • in the Show or Hide All Layers column (the first dot to the right of the fish layer's name) to hide the layer's contents. Temporarily hiding the layers' contents will make it easier to position the background image.

4. In the Tools panel, click the **Selection Tool** button ⬚ to select it.

▶ **5.** Drag the **background.jpg** from the Library panel preview pane to the Stage and place it inside the aquarium tank. See Figure 2-33.

Figure 2-33	Bitmap added to the banner

background.jpg dragged into the aquarium tank

iStockphoto.com/Nick M. Do

▶ **6.** In the Timeline, in the background layer, click the **dot** • in the Lock column (the second dot to the right of the background layer's name) to lock the contents of the background layer.

▶ **7.** In the Timeline, in the fish row, click **show layer** icon ☒ to unhide the contents of the fish layer.

▶ **8.** Repeat Step 7 to unhide the contents of the water layer.

▶ **9.** Save the banner.

In this session, you used the drawing tools to create and modify the graphics on the new banner for Katie's Pet Shop, including the aquarium tank, the fish, and the background. You modified fill colors, stroke colors, heights, and styles. You also scaled and rotated the fish. You imported a bitmap and modified its properties. Aly is pleased with the aquarium, the fish, and the background bitmap. In the next session, you will add text to the banner.

Session 2.1 Quick Check

1. True or False. When drawing a shape with the Oval tool, you can draw a perfect circle when the Snap to Grid modifier is selected.

2. How can you draw a rectangle with rounded corners?

3. The _____ modifier helps straighten lines you draw with the Pencil tool.

4. Describe how to use the Eyedropper tool to copy a stroke's attributes to another object.

5. Which tool can you use to add a fill to an enclosed area that has no fill?

6. Which modifier can be used with the Free Transform tool to resize a selected object?

7. What is the purpose of the Library panel?

8. Where are bitmap properties stored?

SESSION 2.2 VISUAL OVERVIEW

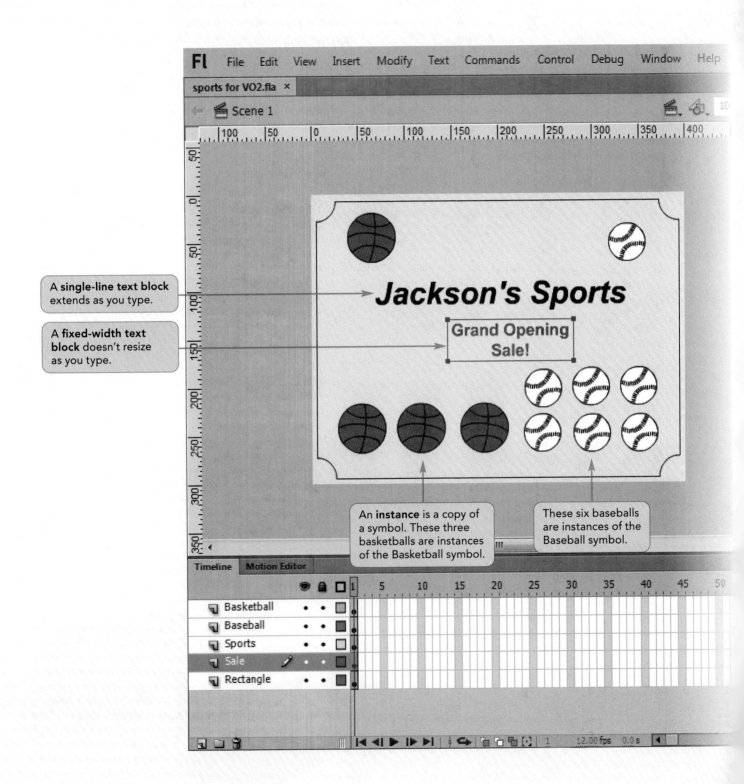

A **single-line text block** extends as you type.

A **fixed-width text block** doesn't resize as you type.

An **instance** is a copy of a symbol. These three basketballs are instances of the Basketball symbol.

These six baseballs are instances of the Baseball symbol.

TEXT BLOCKS AND SYMBOLS

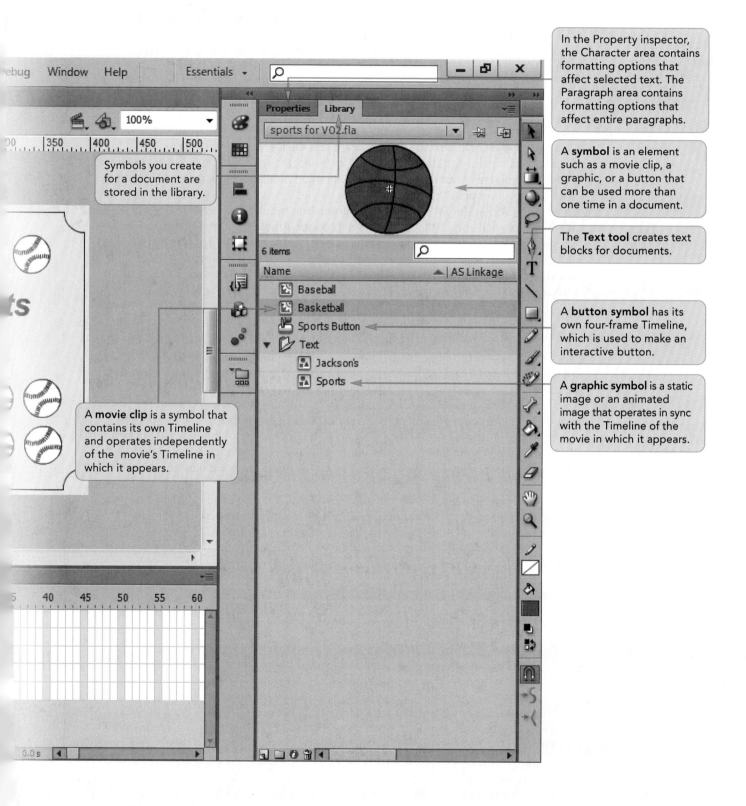

In the Property inspector, the Character area contains formatting options that affect selected text. The Paragraph area contains formatting options that affect entire paragraphs.

Symbols you create for a document are stored in the library.

A **symbol** is an element such as a movie clip, a graphic, or a button that can be used more than one time in a document.

The **Text tool** creates text blocks for documents.

A **button symbol** has its own four-frame Timeline, which is used to make an interactive button.

A **movie clip** is a symbol that contains its own Timeline and operates independently of the movie's Timeline in which it appears.

A **graphic symbol** is a static image or an animated image that operates in sync with the Timeline of the movie in which it appears.

Adding Text

Graphic images do not always communicate the message you are trying to convey. Many images and animations also include text. In Flash, you can create text blocks in a variety of colors, font families, and fonts. A **font family** is a design for a set of fonts. A **font** is a set of text characters in a specific style (such as bold or italic) and size.

TIP

Text blocks can be arranged in columns so that text flows from one column to the next.

By default, Flash uses the **Text Layout Framework (TLF) engine** to create text. The TLF engine provides extensive formatting options, including the ability to create columns of text and to link text blocks. Text created using the TLF engine is called **TLF text**. The TLF engine creates Read Only, Selectable, or Editable text blocks. A **Read Only text block** cannot be selected or changed. The text in a **Selectable text block** can be selected but not changed. The text in an **Editable text block** can be selected and changed by the user. You will work with Read Only text blocks in this tutorial.

You can also create text using the **Classic Text engine**, which creates static, dynamic, or input text blocks. A **static text block** is an object that contains text entered when you create the document but does not change after you publish the document. A **dynamic text field** is an advanced feature where text is updated as a result of programming instructions within the SWF file or with information from a Web server when the document is published and displayed in a Web browser. A **field** is a unit of data such as a person's age or phone number. An example of a dynamic text field is one that displays up-to-the-minute sports scores retrieved from a Web server. Dynamic text fields can also display the results of a calculation based on values entered into input text fields. An **input text field** allows the user to enter text in forms or surveys.

Using the Text Tool

The Text tool can create fixed-width text blocks or single-line text blocks. If the width of the text block is fixed, the text wraps to create new lines as needed. A fixed-width text block has a square handle in its upper-right corner when created as Classic Text, and square handles on both its left and right sides when created as TLF text. The square handles indicate that the width of the text block will remain fixed. As you type, the words wrap to the next line when you reach the right margin of the block. A single-line text block has a round handle on the upper-right corner when created as Classic Text and on the lower-right corner when created as TLF text. The round handles indicate that the width of the text block extends as you type.

TIP

You can drag the round handle of a single-line text block to adjust its width, changing it to a fixed-width text block.

After you create a text block, you can move it using the Selection tool. You can also resize, rotate, and skew the text block using the Free Transform tool. The font, font size, text fill color, text styles, alignment, and other text properties are specified in the Property inspector. You can set these properties before you type the text, or you can select existing text and then change the properties.

INSIGHT

Anti-Aliasing Text

To improve readability, Flash uses a rendering engine that provides high-quality, clear text in Flash documents. **Anti-aliasing**, which is part of the rendering process, smoothes the edges of text displayed on the computer screen. Anti-aliasing is especially effective when using small font sizes. When text is selected on the Stage, the Font rendering method list in the Property inspector provides two methods: Anti-alias for animation and Anti-alias for readability. Select Anti-alias for animation when the text will be animated to create a smoother animation. If the text will not be animated, select Anti-alias for readability, which improves the legibility of the text.

You will use the Text tool and Classic Text engine to add four text blocks to the banner. The text blocks will be placed to the right of the aquarium.

To add a single-line text block to the top of the banner:

1. If you took a break after the previous session, make sure the petShopBanner.fla document is open and Flash is reset to the Essentials workspace.

2. Change the zoom magnification to **Show Frame**.

3. In the Timeline, insert a new layer above the fish layer and name it **text**.

4. In the Tools panel, click the **Text Tool** button ⊤ to select the Text tool. The pointer changes to ⊤, indicating that you are working with text.

5. About 50 pixels from the top of the Stage and 550 pixels from the left of the Stage, click the Stage to create a text block.

6. In the Property inspector, click the **Text engine** button and click **Classic Text**, and then click the **Text type** button and click **Static Text**, if necessary. Before you type the banner text, you will set the text properties.

7. In the Character section of the Property inspector, click the **Family arrow**, and then click **Arial** to select the font family.

8. Click the **Style arrow**, and then click **Bold Italic** to select the font style.

9. Click the **Size value** and drag to change the point size to **32**.

10. Click the **Color** control, click the **white** color swatch (#FFFFFF) in the second column, sixth row of the color palette, and then, if necessary, change the color's alpha value to **100%**.

11. Click the **Anti-alias** button, and then click **Anti-alias for readability** to select that option, if necessary.

12. In the Property inspector, click **PARAGRAPH** to expand the paragraph properties, if necessary, and then click the **Align center** button ≡ to select the center style.

13. Type **Katie's Pet Shop**. The text in the single-line text block in the top area of the Stage to the right of the aquarium displays the properties you selected.

14. In the Tools panel, click the **Selection Tool** button ▸, and then, if necessary, drag the text block to the position shown in Figure 2-34.

> **TIP**
>
> You can also click the Size value, type a point size in the box, and then press the Enter key to change the Size value.

Figure 2-34   Text block for the top of the banner

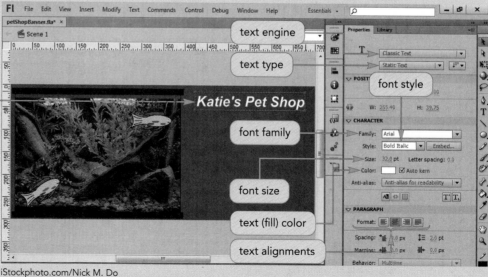

iStockphoto.com/Nick M. Do

15. Click an empty area of the Stage to deselect the text block.

You will create a second text block below the first text block. Before you create the second text block, you will change the text properties in the Property inspector.

To add a single-line text block to the banner:

1. In the Tools panel, click the **Text Tool** button [T] to select it.
2. In the Character section of the Property inspector, click the **Style arrow**, and then click **Bold** to change the font style.
3. Click the **Size value**, and then drag to change the size to **96**.
4. Click the **Color** control, and then click the **orange** color swatch (#FF9933) in the third column from the right, eighth row of the color palette to change the text fill color.
5. Make sure the anti-alias setting is still **Anti-alias for readability**. Center alignment remains selected from the previous settings.
6. Click the Stage below the first text block to create a single-line text block, and then type **sale!** in the text block.
7. In the Tools panel, click the **Selection Tool** button, and then on the Stage, drag the text block so that it is centered below the first text block.
8. In the Property inspector, click the **Letter spacing value** and drag to the left until the value is **–10** to place the letters closer together.
9. Click the Stage to deselect the text block.

TIP

You can also press the V key to select the Selection tool in the Tools panel.

You will create two more text blocks below the sale! text block. Each text block will have different properties.

To add two more single-line text blocks to the banner:

1. In the Tools panel, click the **Text Tool** button [T].
2. In the Character section of the Property inspector, change the font family to **Verdana**, set the style to **Bold**, set the size to **20**, change the letter spacing to **0**, set the text fill color to **white** (#FFFFFF) in the second column, sixth row of the color palette, and make sure the anti-alias setting is **Anti-alias for readability**. Center alignment remains in place from the previous settings.
3. Click the Stage below the second text block to create a single-line text block, and then type **Save up to 30% on** in the text block, press the **Enter** key to create a new line and then type **tropical fish supplies!** as the second line of the text block.
4. In the Tools panel, click the **Selection Tool** button, and then drag the text block so that it is centered below the second text block.
5. Click the Stage to deselect the text block.
6. In the Tools panel, click the **Text Tool** button [T].
7. In the Character section of the Property inspector, set the style to **Regular**, set the size to **14**, make sure the text fill color is **white** (#FFFFFF), and make sure the anti-alias setting is **Anti-alias for readability**. Center alignment remains in place from the previous settings.

8. Click the Stage below the third text block to create a single-line text block, type **Attend one of our free classes**, press the **Enter** key to create a new line in the text block, and then type **that start on the 10th of each month.** as the second line of the text block.

9. In the Tools panel, click the **Selection Tool** button , and then drag the text block so that it is centered below the third text block. See Figure 2-35.

Figure 2-35   **Text blocks aligned on the banner**

text blocks centered below the title text block

iStockphoto.com/Nick M. Do

Checking the Spelling of Text

Flash can check the spelling of text you add to a document. The Check Spelling command verifies the spelling in each text block in the document. It can also check the spelling of text in other parts of the document, such as layer names and symbol names. Symbols are covered in the next section.

Before you use the Check Spelling command, you can specify options in the Spelling Setup dialog box. Under Document options, you specify which text areas to check, such as the content of text fields and the names of layers. You also select which built-in dictionaries to use, such as the Adobe dictionary and the American English language dictionary. The personal dictionary is a file that Flash creates on your hard drive to which you can add words that are not in the Adobe or language dictionaries but are spelled correctly, such as a company name. You can also edit your personal dictionary after it is created. In the Checking options, you specify whether Flash ignores or finds specific character types such as words with numbers or words with all uppercase letters. You can also select options such as Suggest phonetic matches to have Flash provide a list of suggestions when it encounters a misspelled word. You can then choose one of the suggested words to replace the misspelled word.

You will set the spelling checker options before checking the spelling of text in the banner.

To set the spelling checker options:

1. On the menu bar, click **Text**, and then click **Spelling Setup**. The Spelling Setup dialog box opens. See Figure 2-36.

Figure 2-36   Spelling Setup dialog box

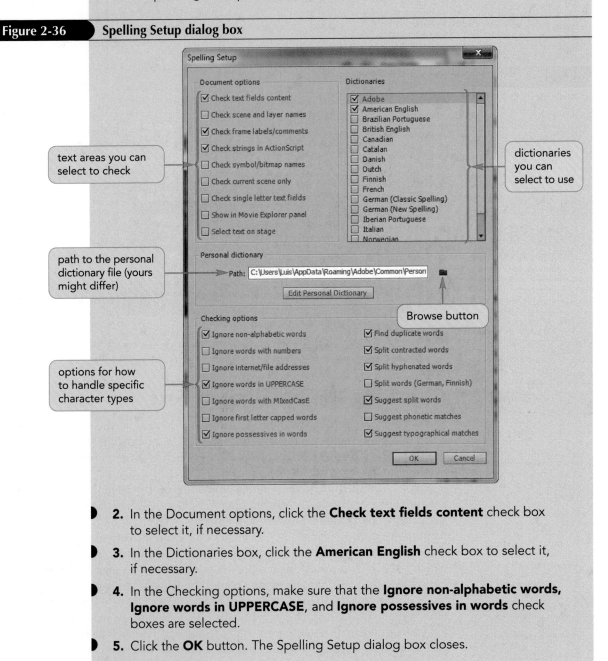

2. In the Document options, click the **Check text fields content** check box to select it, if necessary.

3. In the Dictionaries box, click the **American English** check box to select it, if necessary.

4. In the Checking options, make sure that the **Ignore non-alphabetic words, Ignore words in UPPERCASE**, and **Ignore possessives in words** check boxes are selected.

5. Click the **OK** button. The Spelling Setup dialog box closes.

When you check the spelling in a document, the Check Spelling dialog box opens if Flash finds a word that is misspelled or is not in its dictionaries. Depending on the options you selected in the Spelling Setup dialog box, the Check Spelling dialog box might offer suggestions for replacing the word. You can choose to ignore, change, delete, or add the word to your personal dictionary. The Check Spelling dialog box also shows in what element of the document the word not found is located, such as in a text field, a scene name, or a layer name.

PROSKILLS

Written Communication: The Importance of Correct Spelling

Having a misspelled word in a Flash movie can detract from the message or idea you are trying to promote. So, take advantage of the spelling checker in Flash to ensure that the text in your document uses standard spelling. Keep in mind that the spelling checker only compares words in the document with words in the selected dictionaries. If a word is incorrect in context but is spelled correctly, the spelling checker will not detect it. Think of homonyms such as *they're*, *there*, and *their* or easily mistyped words such as *form* and *from*. Because the spelling checker might not catch every error, be sure to review your work carefully. As a final check, it is a good idea to ask someone who isn't working on the document to proofread the text. This will help to ensure that the finished product is error free, leaving the audience free to focus on the intended message of the Flash movie.

You will check the spelling of the text in the banner.

To check spelling in the banner:

1. On the Stage, click the bottom text block, if necessary. The spelling check will start with this text block.

2. On the menu bar, click **Text**, and then click **Check Spelling**. The Check Spelling dialog box opens, indicating the first word not found in the selected dictionaries. The word not found in the Check Spelling dialog box is 10th. See Figure 2-37.

Figure 2-37 **Check Spelling dialog box**

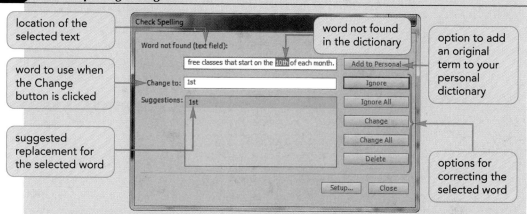

Trouble? If a different word is found, you might have another word spelled incorrectly. If the word is spelled correctly, click the Ignore button. If the word is not spelled correctly, click the correct spelling in the Suggestions box or type the correct spelling in the Change to box, and then click the Change button. Repeat until 10th is the word not found.

3. Click the **Ignore** button. A dialog box opens, asking whether you want to continue checking from the start of the document.

4. Click the **Yes** button. A dialog box opens, indicating that the spelling check is complete.

Trouble? If the Check Spelling dialog box displays another word, it is not in your selected dictionaries. If the word is spelled correctly, click the Ignore button to ignore the suggestion and leave the original spelling. If the word is spelled incorrectly, click the correct spelling in the Suggestions box or type the correct spelling in the Change to box, and then click the Change button to replace the word not found. Continue until the dialog box opens indicating that the spelling check is complete.

▶ **5.** Click the **OK** button.

Working with Symbols

A symbol is an element that can be used more than one time in a document. You can create a symbol from an existing object or you can create a new symbol. You can also use symbols from other Flash documents in the current document.

Comparing Symbol Behavior Types

Symbols can have one of three behavior types: movie clip, graphic, or button. A movie clip operates independently of the movie in which it appears. For example, a movie clip that contains an animation sequence spanning 10 frames within its own Timeline occupies only one frame within the document's Timeline, yet it still plays its own 10-frame animation. Most of the symbols you create will be movie clips. A graphic symbol operates in sync with the Timeline of the movie in which it appears; for example, a Flash document's Timeline. A button symbol has its own four-frame Timeline so you can create an interactive button. You will learn more about buttons in Tutorial 5.

Creating Symbols

To create a symbol, you can either convert an existing graphic into a symbol or create a new symbol. For each symbol you create, you specify its name and its type. When converting an existing graphic into a symbol, you can also specify its registration point, which can be used to control how the symbol is animated.

REFERENCE

Creating a Symbol

- Select an existing graphic, click Modify on the menu bar, and then click Convert to Symbol.
- Type a symbol name in the Name box, click the Type button and select a symbol type, and then click the OK button.

or

- On the menu bar, click Insert, and then click New Symbol.
- Type a symbol name in the Name box, click the Type button and select a symbol type, and then click the OK button.
- In symbol-editing mode, create the graphic(s) for the symbol.
- On the menu bar, click Insert, and then click Edit Document.

You will convert the fish graphic you created for the banner for Katie's Pet Shop Web site into a symbol.

To create a symbol from the fish:

▶ **1.** In the Tools panel, click the **Selection Tool** button ![cursor], if necessary, and then click the fish on the right side of the fish tank. The fish graphic is selected. You will ungroup the graphic before converting it to a symbol.

▶ **2.** On the menu bar, click **Modify**, and then click **Ungroup**. The fish is no longer grouped, but all of its parts are still selected.

▶ **3.** On the menu bar, click **Modify**, and then click **Convert to Symbol**. The Convert to Symbol dialog box opens. In this dialog box, you can specify a name for the symbol and select a behavior type.

▶ **4.** In the Name box, type **Fish1**, and then, if necessary, click the **Type** button, and click **Movie Clip**. See Figure 2-38.

TIP

You can also ungroup a grouped object by pressing the Ctrl+Shift+G keys.

| Figure 2-38 | Convert to Symbol dialog box |

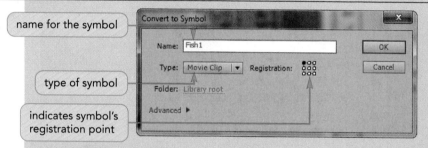

name for the symbol

type of symbol

indicates symbol's registration point

▶ **5.** Click the **OK** button. The dialog box closes. The symbol is created and added to the library for this document.

Exploring Symbols in the Library

As with bitmaps, you view, organize, and edit symbols stored in the library from the Library panel. When you create a symbol for a document, you assign a name to it, and then specify its properties. These properties are stored with the symbol in the library. Symbols created within a document are saved with that document. However, you can share symbols with other documents by making them part of a shared library. You can modify a symbol's properties using the Library panel.

INSIGHT

Organizing Library Items

As you create a document, you will often incorporate many objects, including bitmaps and symbols, in the document. Some objects might be related to a particular graphic in the document. For example, you might have multiple symbols that make up a button on the Stage. As the document gets more complex, the number of symbols and other objects in the library can increase significantly and become unmanageable. To make it easier to manage and organize the items in the Library panel, you can create folders to group and hold related objects. By default, the Library panel contains a **root folder** that contains all the document's objects. All new folders are created within the root folder. Any objects inside a folder are indented under the folder name.

The names you give folders and objects can also help keep your work organized. Assign meaningful names to the folders and symbols you create, especially if you plan to have many symbols in a document. Descriptive names, such as Fish1 and Fish2, make it easier to find the symbol you want in the Library panel without having to preview each symbol. You can also enter an object's name in the Library panel search box to quickly display that object in the panel.

You will explore the petShopBanner.fla document's library to see how symbols are stored.

To explore the petShopBanner.fla document's library:

1. Next to the Property inspector, click the **Library** tab to bring the Library panel to the front of the panel group. The Library panel displays the symbols for this document.

2. In the Name column of the Library panel, click the **Fish1** symbol to select it. A thumbnail of the fish appears in the preview box at the top of the Library panel. The symbol's icon indicates the symbol is a movie clip. See Figure 2-39.

| Figure 2-39 | Library panel for the petShopBanner.fla document |

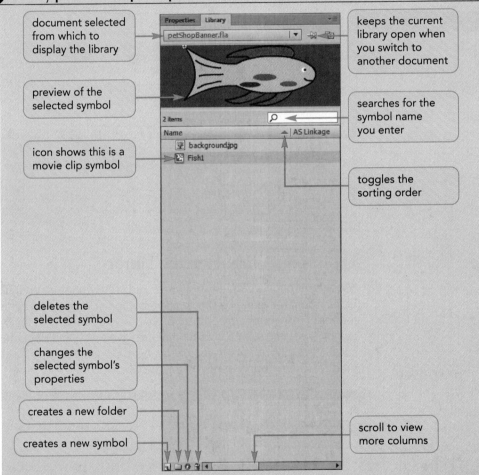

document selected from which to display the library

preview of the selected symbol

icon shows this is a movie clip symbol

deletes the selected symbol

changes the selected symbol's properties

creates a new folder

creates a new symbol

keeps the current library open when you switch to another document

searches for the symbol name you enter

toggles the sorting order

scroll to view more columns

3. In the Library panel, click the **Properties** button. The Symbol Properties dialog box opens for the Fish1 symbol. You will change this symbol's type.

4. Click the **Type** button, click **Graphic**, and then click the **OK** button. The Properties dialog box closes, and the Fish1 symbol's icon reflects the new type. See Figure 2-40.

Figure 2-40   **Changed symbol in the Library panel**

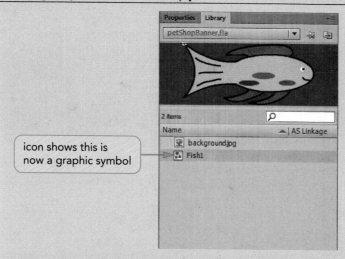

icon shows this is
now a graphic symbol

5. At the bottom of the Library panel, drag the scroll bar to the right to see the rest of the symbol's properties, including Graphic in the Type column, and then drag the scroll bar to the left to display the Name column.

6. In the Library panel, click the **Properties** button 🔘, click the **Type** button, click **Movie Clip**, and then click the **OK** button. The symbol's icon and type change to reflect the movie clip type.

After a symbol is added to a document's library, you can duplicate it and then modify the duplicate copy to create a new symbol. The duplicate symbol must have a different name. You will create a duplicate symbol of the Fish1 symbol that you can then edit to create a second, different fish symbol.

To create a duplicate of the Fish1 symbol:

1. In the Library panel, click the **panel menu** button 🗏 to open the panel menu, and then click **Duplicate**. The Duplicate Symbol dialog box opens.

2. In the Name box, type **Fish2**. This is the name for the duplicated movie clip symbol. The movie clip type is already selected.

3. Click the **OK** button. The Fish2 symbol is added to the library.

Editing a Symbol

You can modify a symbol by placing it in symbol-editing mode. A symbol can be edited by itself in symbol-editing mode or it can be edited in place with the rest of the graphics on the Stage dimmed. When a symbol is in symbol-editing mode, the name of the symbol appears on the Edit bar next to the scene name. Flash documents can be divided into multiple scenes, but every document has at least one scene.

Editing a Symbol

- Select a symbol instance on the Stage.
- Click Edit on the menu bar, and then click Edit Symbols, Edit Selected, or Edit in Place (or double-click a symbol instance on the Stage or select the symbol in the Library panel, click the Library panel menu button, and then click Edit).
- Modify the symbol in symbol-editing mode.
- On the Edit bar, click the Scene 1 link (or double-click an empty area of the Stage or on the menu bar, click Edit, and then click Edit Document).

Aly wants the Fish2 symbol to be unique from the Fish1 symbol. You will edit the Fish2 symbol by changing the fish's body color and resizing the graphic.

To edit the Fish2 symbol:

1. In the Library panel, click the **Fish2** symbol to select it, if necessary.

2. In the Library panel, click the **panel menu** button ▾≡, and then click **Edit**. The symbol opens in symbol-editing mode, and Fish2 appears on the Edit bar.

3. Click an empty area of the Stage to deselect the fish.

4. Change the zoom magnification to **400%**. Use the scroll bar at the bottom of the document window to view the entire fish, if necessary.

5. In the Tools panel, click the **Paint Bucket Tool** button ⬧ to select it, click the **Fill Color** control ⬧ ▮, and then click the **lime green** color swatch (#99FF99) in the ninth column, tenth row of the color palette.

6. On the Stage, click the orange body of the fish to change it to lime green.

7. In the Tools panel, click the **Paint Bucket Tool** button ⬧, if necessary, to select it, click the **Fill Color** control ⬧ ▮, and then click the **yellow** color swatch (#FFFF99) in the last column, tenth row of the color palette.

8. On the Stage, click the areas enclosed by the fins to change the color of the fins to yellow. See Figure 2-41.

Figure 2-41   Fish2 symbol in symbol-editing mode

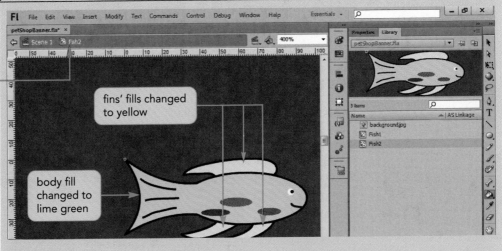

Fish2 symbol being edited

fins' fills changed to yellow

body fill changed to lime green

9. On the Edit bar, click the **Scene 1** link to exit symbol-editing mode. The banner reappears on the Stage.

Creating and Editing Instances of Symbols

Every symbol you create is automatically stored in the document's library. To use the symbols in the document, you create instances. Each time you drag a symbol from the Library panel onto the Stage, you create an instance of the symbol in the document. No matter how many instances of a symbol you create, the symbol is stored in the document only once.

INSIGHT

Using Instances of Symbols

If you want to use a graphic multiple times in a document, you should convert it into a symbol. Then you can insert instances of the symbol wherever that graphic is needed in the document instead of creating the same graphic multiple times. Using instances of a symbol also makes it easier to modify all instances at the same time by just modifying the symbol. In addition, any graphic you convert into a symbol can be copied from one document's library to another. Finally, using instances of a symbol minimizes the document's size, which in turn reduces the download time of the published SWF file.

Each instance in a document can be edited without changing the symbol in the document's library. For example, consider a document that includes several instances of the same symbol. You can make one instance smaller than the others. You can rotate each instance to a different angle. Any changes you make to one instance do not affect the other instances or the symbol. If you modify the symbol, however, all the instances of that symbol are also changed.

You will place an instance of the Fish2 symbol on the banner, and then convert the leftmost fish to a movie clip symbol.

To create a Fish2 symbol instance and convert a graphic to a symbol:

1. In the Tools panel, click the **Selection Tool** button.

2. In the Timeline, click the **fish** layer to select it, if necessary. You will add an instance of the Fish2 symbol to this layer.

3. Drag the **Fish2** symbol from the Library panel to the Stage in the middle of the aquarium to create an instance of the symbol. See Figure 2-42.

Figure 2-42 **Fish2 symbol instance added to the Stage**

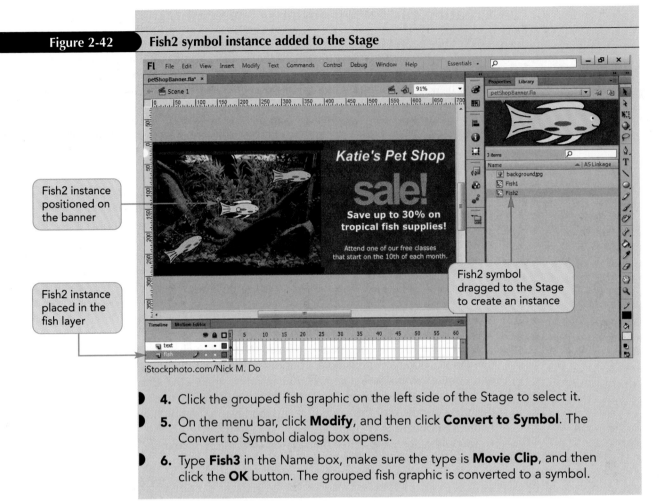

Fish2 instance positioned on the banner

Fish2 instance placed in the fish layer

Fish2 symbol dragged to the Stage to create an instance

iStockphoto.com/Nick M. Do

▶ **4.** Click the grouped fish graphic on the left side of the Stage to select it.

▶ **5.** On the menu bar, click **Modify**, and then click **Convert to Symbol**. The Convert to Symbol dialog box opens.

▶ **6.** Type **Fish3** in the Name box, make sure the type is **Movie Clip**, and then click the **OK** button. The grouped fish graphic is converted to a symbol.

Applying Filters

A **filter** is a special graphic effect, such as a drop shadow, that you can apply to movie clips, buttons, and text. Filters are applied from the Filters section of the Property inspector, which includes preset filters, such as drop shadow, blur, glow, and bevel. Multiple filters can be applied to one object, and each filter has properties you can set to adjust the filter's effect on the object. In the Property inspector, you can enable or disable a filter, reset a filter's properties, and delete a filter. You can also copy the filters and properties that have been applied to one object and apply them to another object. Or, you can save a set of filters and properties as a new preset filter, and then apply the saved preset filter to objects in other Flash documents.

You will apply a drop shadow effect to the movie clip symbols and text on the banner.

To apply a drop shadow filter to objects in the banner:

1. Next to the Library tab click the **Properties** tab to display the Property inspector.

2. In the Filters section of the Property inspector, click the **Add filter** button ⬛ to open a menu of preset filters. See Figure 2-43.

Figure 2-43 ▶ Menu of preset filters

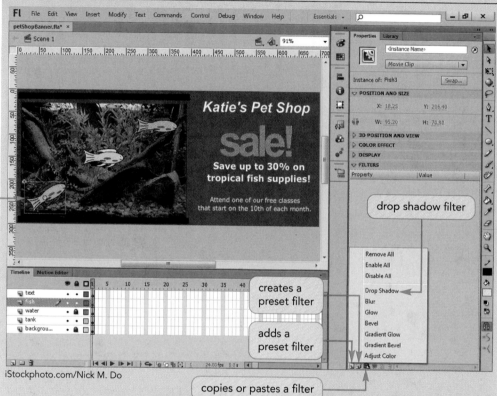

Fish3 instance selected on the Stage

drop shadow filter

creates a preset filter

adds a preset filter

copies or pastes a filter

iStockphoto.com/Nick M. Do

3. Click **Drop Shadow**. A drop shadow effect is applied to the Fish3 instance selected on the Stage.

4. In the Filters section of the Property inspector, drag the **Strength value** to the left to set the filter strength to 80%, and then drag the **Distance value** to the right to increase the filter distance to 10px. The drop shadow strength is reduced and its distance from the instance increased. See Figure 2-44.

Figure 2-44   Drop shadow filter applied to a fish graphic instance

iStockphoto.com/Nick M. Do

Trouble? If you cannot see the distance value, the pointer is probably covering it. Type 10 in the Distance box, and then press the Enter key.

5. In the Filters section of the Property inspector, click the **Clipboard** button 📋, and then click **Copy All**. The filter and properties are stored in the computer's temporary memory so you can apply them to the other two fish instances.

6. On the Stage, click the **Fish2** instance to select it, and then, in the Property inspector, click the **Clipboard** button 📋 and click **Paste**. The drop shadow effect is applied to the Fish2 instance.

7. On the Stage, click the **Fish1** instance to select it, and then, in the Property inspector, click the **Clipboard** button 📋 and click **Paste**. The drop shadow effect is applied to the Fish1 instance.

8. Click the text block at the top of the Stage to select it, and then, in the Property inspector, click the **Clipboard** button 📋 and click **Paste**. The drop shadow effect is applied to the selected text.

9. In the Property inspector, click **PARAGRAPH** to collapse the Paragraph section. You can now more easily access the Filters section and reset the filter's properties.

> **10.** In the Filters section of the Property inspector, click **Drop Shadow** in the Property column, and then click the **Reset Filter** button 🔄. The filter's properties return to their default values. See Figure 2-45.

Figure 2-45 | **Drop shadow effect applied to text**

iStockphoto.com/Nick M. Do

Using Gradients

A **gradient** is a gradual blend or transition from one color to another. Gradients can be used to create special effects and add a professional touch to documents. For example, you can use a gradient for a banner's background, create a gradient to simulate a sunset or a rainbow, or use a gradient as part of an animation. Gradients can be added as fills to any object the same way you add solid color fills.

The two types of gradients you can create in Flash are linear and radial. A **linear gradient** blends the colors from one point to another in a straight line. A **radial gradient** blends the colors from one point outward in a circular pattern. Figure 2-46 shows examples of linear and radial gradients.

Figure 2-46 | **Gradient examples**

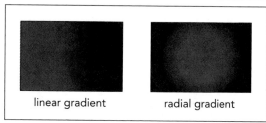

linear gradient   radial gradient

© 2013 Cengage Learning

Flash includes several preset gradients in the color palette and in the Swatches panel. You can use these gradients as fills for any closed shape. You can also create custom gradients using the Color panel.

NSIGHT

Gradients Impact Performance

Although gradients are easy to create and add to a Flash document, they increase the processing requirements of the computer displaying the SWF movie. Because of the greater number of colors in a gradient, a computer's processor might have to work harder to display a gradient compared with displaying solid colors. If you have concerns about a movie's performance when displayed on a user's computer, you can reduce the number of gradients used in the movie or omit them altogether if the SWF movie contains complex graphics or animations. You should always test the movie to ensure its quality is acceptable.

Applying a Gradient Fill

Gradient fills can be applied to shapes such as circles, rectangles, and triangles as well as to text. You apply a gradient fill to an object the same way you apply a solid fill. You can select the gradient fill color before you draw a shape such as a rectangle, or you can use the Paint Bucket tool to apply a gradient to an existing shape. When using the Paint Bucket tool to apply a radial gradient, you specify the gradient's center point, which is where the first color begins. The point you click becomes the gradient's center point, as shown in Figure 2-47. When using the Paint Bucket tool to apply a linear gradient, you draw a straight line with the Paint Bucket pointer ◇. The line you draw determines the direction of the gradient.

| Figure 2-47 | Radial gradient being applied with the Paint Bucket tool |

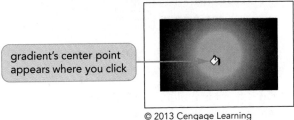

gradient's center point
appears where you click

© 2013 Cengage Learning

You can also use the Paint Bucket tool's Lock Fill modifier when applying gradients. With the Lock Fill modifier selected, the Paint Bucket tool paints one gradient across several objects on the Stage rather than one gradient for each object, as shown in Figure 2-48.

| Figure 2-48 | Effect of the Lock Fill modifier on gradients |

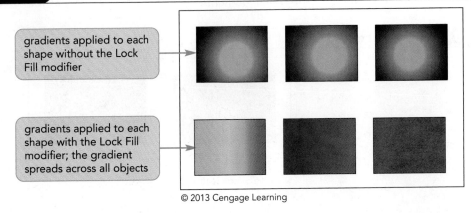

gradients applied to each shape without the Lock Fill modifier

gradients applied to each shape with the Lock Fill modifier; the gradient spreads across all objects

© 2013 Cengage Learning

The background of the new banner for Katie's Pet Shop should be a radial gradient using a blend of a light green color that transitions into a dark green color. You will select the green radial gradient to use as the fill for the banner's background.

To add a rectangle with the green radial gradient to a new layer:

1. In the Timeline, insert a new layer and name it **gradient**. You will draw the rectangle for the banner's background in this layer.

2. In the Tools panel, click the **Rectangle Tool** button to select it.

3. In the Property inspector, click the **Fill color** control , and then click the **green** radial gradient in the bottom row of the color palette. See Figure 2-49. The rectangle will use the green gradient you selected as its fill.

Figure 2-49 Green radial gradient in the color palette

iStockphoto.com/Nick M. Do

4. In the Property inspector, click the **Stroke color** control , and then click the **no color** button . The rectangle you draw will not have a visible stroke.

5. In the Rectangle Options section, click the **Reset** button, if necessary, to set each rectangle corner radius to 0. The rectangle you draw will have square corners.

6. On the Stage, draw a large rectangle the size of the Stage. The rectangle covers the entire Stage and temporarily obscures the text and images. See Figure 2-50.

Figure 2-50 Gradient added to the banner

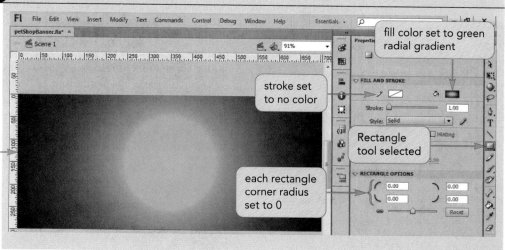

Transforming Gradient Fills

A gradient fill in an object can be modified by using the Gradient Transform tool. You can move a gradient's center, change its size, or change its direction. When you select a linear gradient with the Gradient Transform tool, a bounding box surrounds it. When you select a radial gradient, a bounding circle surrounds it. The gradient's center point also appears along with editing handles, as shown in Figure 2-51. You drag these handles to transform the gradient.

Figure 2-51	Editing handles

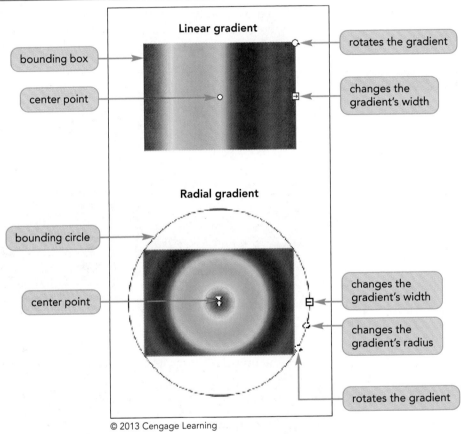

© 2013 Cengage Learning

You drag a gradient's center point to reposition it. The linear gradient has a circular handle to rotate the gradient and a square handle to change the gradient's width. The radial gradient has two circular handles. The middle circular handle changes the gradient's radius, and the bottom circular handle rotates the gradient. It also has a square handle, which changes the gradient's width. A radial gradient also has a focal point, indicated by a small triangle, which is initially in the same position as the center point. You can drag the small triangle to change the gradient's focal point.

Aly wants you to modify the gradient in the banner background so that the lighter color of the gradient is behind the aquarium. To do this, you will move the gradient's center point to the left side of the banner over the aquarium and increase its radius slightly to spread more of the lighter color to the rest of the banner.

To modify the gradient in the banner background:

1. In the Tools panel, click and hold the **Free Transform Tool** button, and then click the **Gradient Transform Tool** button. The Gradient Transform tool is selected.

2. Click the rectangle with the gradient fill. The gradient's bounding circle and editing handles appear.

3. Change the zoom magnification to **50%**. The entire bounding circle is visible, making the rectangle easier to work with. See Figure 2-52.

Figure 2-52   Gradient selected for transformation

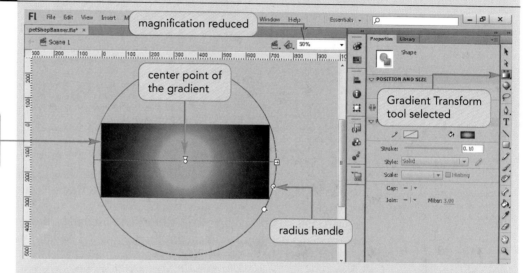

- magnification reduced
- center point of the gradient
- background rectangle selected to display the bounding circle and editing handles
- Gradient Transform tool selected
- radius handle

4. Position the pointer over the center point of the gradient until the pointer changes to ✛ to indicate it is over the center point, and then drag the center point of the gradient to the left side of the Stage. The entire bounding circle moves as you reposition the center point of the gradient.

5. Drag the **radius handle** slightly outward to the right to increase the gradient's radius so that the light green color extends more than halfway across the banner.

6. In the Timeline, drag the **gradient** layer below the background layer.

7. In the Tools panel, click the **Selection Tool** button to select it, and then click an empty area of the Stage.

8. On the Edit bar, change the zoom magnification to **Show Frame**. You can see the entire completed banner on the Stage. See Figure 2-53.

Figure 2-53   **Completed banner**

iStockphoto.com/Nick M. Do

▶ **9.** Save the document, and then close it.

The new banner for Katie's Pet Shop is complete. The new banner effectively encourages sales of the shop's aquarium and tropical fish supplies while promoting the educational materials and classes the shop is providing to its customers. To accomplish this, you added text blocks to the banner for Katie's Pet Shop, set the properties for the text, and checked for spelling errors. Then, you used the Library panel to work with symbols in the petShopBanner.fla document's library. You also applied special graphic effects to movie clips and text. Finally, you completed the banner by adding a gradient background. In the next tutorial, you will learn how to create animations with the symbols in the Katie's Pet Shop banner.

Session 2.2 Quick Check

REVIEW

1. What is a font?
2. What is the difference between a static text block and a dynamic text field?
3. Why is it important to check the spelling in a document?
4. What are the three behavior types for symbols?
5. Why should you convert a graphic you want to use multiple times in a document into a symbol?
6. What is the difference between a symbol and an instance of a symbol?
7. What is a filter?
8. Describe two different kinds of gradients available in Flash.

Practice the skills you learned in the tutorial using the same case scenario.

PRACTICE

Review Assignments

Data File needed for the Review Assignments: banner.fla

Aly is pleased with the banner you created for Katie's Pet Shop Web site. She asks you to modify another banner ad by finishing a fish graphic, adding instances of the fish to the banner, drawing a starfish graphic, adding a text block, and adding a gradient background. She also wants you to add drop shadow effects to the fish and text and to draw lines as underlines for the text.

1. Open the **banner.fla** file located in the Flash2\Review folder, save the document as **newBanner.fla** in the same folder, and reset Flash to the Essentials workspace.

2. Edit the fish symbol in the Library panel. Use the Oval tool to draw a circle that has a white (#FFFFFF) fill color and no stroke color for the fish's eye on the right part of the fish graphic.

3. Change the fill color to black (#000000) and draw a small circle inside the white circle to represent the eye's pupil.

4. Use the Pencil tool to draw a small line that has a black (#000000) stroke color and a stroke height of 1 below the eye to represent the fish's mouth. Draw three short horizontal line segments on the tail of the fish.

5. Create a color band on the fish by drawing a vertical line inside the fish body starting at the top stroke of the fish near the right side of the top fin and ending at the bottom stroke of the fish near the bottom fin. Draw another vertical line to the left of the first line on the fish from the top stroke to the bottom stroke of the fish. Make sure the vertical lines connect to the strokes representing the fish's body.

6. Use the Paint Bucket tool to apply a yellow-orange color (#FFCC33) to the middle band on the fish created by the vertical lines and to apply a green color (#669966) to the areas inside the top and bottom fins. Exit symbol-editing mode.

7. Insert a new layer above the tank layer and name it **fish**. In the fish layer, place an instance of the fish symbol on the water in the center of the fish tank.

8. Place another instance of the fish symbol to the right of the first instance, and then rotate the second instance so that it appears to be swimming in the water in a downward direction.

9. Apply a drop shadow filter effect to each fish instance on the Stage. Use a filter distance of 7px and a filter strength of 90%.

10. In the text layer, add a new single-line text block as Classic Text that reads **Free fish food with purchase of fish tank!**. Use Verdana for the font family, Regular for the style, 16 for the point size, and light yellow (#FFFFCC) for the text color. Center the new text block on the banner above the fish tank.

11. Use the Line tool to draw horizontal lines under each of the two lines of text on the top of the banner. The lines should be maroon (#660000), have a height of 2, a stroke style of solid, and appear as underlines for the text.

12. Add a drop shadow filter to the top text block. Use default settings for the drop shadow, and change its color to gray (#666666).

13. Create a new movie clip symbol named **starfish**. In symbol-editing mode, use the PolyStar tool to draw a star graphic. (*Hint:* In the Property inspector, click the Options button, and then click star in the Style menu to select the graphic shape.) Use the default settings to create a star graphic with five sides. The star should have a light orange (#FFCC66) fill color, a black (#000000) stroke color, a line height of 1, and be approximately 75 pixels in width and 75 pixels in height.

14. Center the star graphic in the symbol-editing window, and then use the Selection tool to curve each side slightly outward to make it look like a starfish. Exit symbol-editing mode.

15. Insert a new layer above the text layer and name it **starfish**. In the starfish layer, place an instance of the starfish symbol on the banner to the left of the title text.

16. Place another instance of the starfish symbol to the right of the title text.

17. Insert a new layer above the background layer and name it **gradient**. In the Timeline, move the gradient layer below the background layer.

18. In the gradient layer, use the Rectangle tool to draw a rectangle with the gray radial gradient for the fill color and no stroke. Make the width of the rectangle 500 pixels and its height 400 pixels. Align the rectangle with the Stage.

19. Submit the finished file to your instructor.

APPLY

Use shapes, text, and symbols to create a grand opening banner.

Case Problem 1

There are no Data Files needed for this Case Problem.

Jackson's Sports Store   Jackson's Sports Store is preparing for a grand opening celebration of a second store. Dan meets with Chris to discuss the development of a banner for the store's Web site. Dan suggests developing a banner that will set a festive tone for the celebration. The banner will help promote the grand opening celebration by including graphics that depict a celebration and text about the grand opening. You will create the banner shown in Figure 2-54.

Figure 2-54   Completed Jackson's Sports Store grand opening banner

© 2013 Cengage Learning

1. Create a new document. Change the document properties so that the width is 600 pixels and the height is 250 pixels. Change the background color to light yellow (#FFFF99).

2. Save the document as **sportsBanner.fla** in the Flash2\Case1 folder included with your Data Files.

3. Create a square with sides of about 45 pixels in length. Use yellow-orange (#FFCC33) for the fill color and a solid black stroke of 1 pixel in height. Place the square near the upper-left side of the stage.

4. Add a text block centered inside the square with the uppercase letter **J**. Use Classic Text, black as the text color, Comic Sans MS or something similar as the font family, bold as the style, and 32 points as the size. (*Hint*: Use the Selection tool and the arrow keys to nudge the text block within the square as needed.)

5. Group the square and the text, being sure to select both the fill and the stroke for the square.

6. Make a copy of the group, paste it on the Stage, and then edit the copy to change the letter to **A** and the fill color of the square to the color of your choice. Move the copy to the right of the square with the letter J.

7. Repeat Step 6 to make six more copies of the group. Change the letters in the copies to **C**, **K**, **S**, **O**, **N**, and **'S**, respectively, and use a different color for each square's fill. Move the copies so that the text blocks and squares spell JACKSON'S.

8. Use the Free Transform tool to rotate and position each letter block, as shown in Figure 2-54.

9. Convert each of the letter blocks into a movie clip symbol, naming each symbol according to the letter in the text block: **J**, **A**, **C**, **K**, **S**, **O**, **N**, and **'S**, respectively. Apply a drop shadow filter effect to each of the letter block instances on the Stage. Use the default settings for the filter.

10. In the Timeline, rename Layer 1 as **blocks**. Insert a new layer and name it **text**.

11. In the text layer, add a text block in the center of the Stage. Use Classic Text and the same text properties as in Step 4, changing the size to 60 points and the format to center align. Type **Sports Store!** in the text block.

12. Add a second text block using dark blue (#000099) as the text color, bold as the style, 18 points as the size, and center align for the format. Type **Grand Opening this Saturday!**, and then on a separate line in the same text block type **Try our new batting cages!**.

13. Use the Selection tool to align the text blocks as shown in Figure 2-54.

14. Check the spelling of the text and make corrections, as needed.

15. Lock the text and blocks layers to prevent accidently changing their content.

16. Insert a new layer and name it **balloons**. Draw two balloons on the left side of the Stage using the Oval tool with different colors for each balloon. Do not include a stroke for the balloons. Draw a string for each balloon using the Pencil tool with a light gray (#999999) color for the stroke.

17. Repeat Step 16 to draw two more balloons on the right side of the Stage with different colors.

⊕ EXPLORE   18. Insert a new layer and name it **confetti**. Use the Brush tool to draw multicolored confetti on the Stage. Select a small brush size from the Brush Size modifier in the Tools panel. Select a brush color of your choice using the Fill Color control in the Tools panel, and then click dots with the tool on the banner to create the confetti. Repeat to create different colored dots throughout the Stage using at least three different colors.

19. Insert a new layer and name it **border**. Create a rectangle as a border around all of the objects on the Stage. The rectangle should have slightly rounded corners, a maroon (#660000) stroke, no fill, a stroke height of 3, and a solid style. Draw the rectangle so that it is just inside the edges of the Stage.

20. Submit the finished file to your instructor.

Use text, shapes, symbols, gradients, and a bitmap to create a banner advertising a zoo.

APPLY

Case Problem 2

Data File needed for this Case Problem: tiger.jpg

Alamo City Zoo   Janet asks Alex to develop a new banner for the Alamo City Zoo's Web site. The new banner will advertise an open house celebration event promoting a new tiger exhibit. The banner will contain text with the zoo's name and event information as well as graphic elements depicting tiger paws and a picture of a tiger. You will create the banner shown in Figure 2-55.

| Figure 2-55 | Completed Alamo City Zoo open house banner |

© 2013 Cengage Learning; iStockphoto.com/Willi Schmitz

1. Create a new document. Change the document properties so that the width is 300 pixels and the height is 200 pixels. Keep the background color as white (#FFFFFF).

2. Save the document as **zooBanner.fla** in the Flash2\Case2 folder included with your Data Files.

3. Create a single-line text block on the top part of the Stage for the name of the zoo. Use Classic Text, light peach (#FFCC99) as the text color, Times New Roman font family, italic as the style, 36 points as the size, and center align as the format. Type **Alamo City Zoo** in the text block.

4. Create a fixed-width text block of about 200 pixels wide on the lower part of the Stage. Use Classic Text, maroon (#660000) as the text color, Monotype Corsiva as the font family, a size of 30 points, and center alignment. Type **TIGER Exhibit Now Open!** in the text block. (*Hint*: The font might be listed with the Cs instead of the Ms in the font list.)

5. Create a single-line text block on the center of the Stage. Use Classic Text, black (#000000) as the text color, Times New Roman as the font family, regular as the style, a size of 18 points, and center alignment. Type **Special Open House!** in the text block.

6. Use the Free Transform tool to rotate the text block so that it is in a vertical position on the left side of the Stage, as shown in Figure 2-55.

7. Check the spelling in the text blocks. Make corrections, if needed.

8. Rename Layer 1 as **banner text**, and then lock the banner text layer.

9. Create a new movie clip symbol named **tigerPaw**. (*Hint*: On the menu bar, click Insert, and then click New Symbol.) In symbol-editing mode, on the center of the Stage, draw a small circle about 40 pixels wide and 40 pixels high. Use brown (#663300) for the fill color, black (#000000) for the stroke color, solid for the stroke style, and 1 for the stroke height.

10. Zoom in on the circle and use the Selection tool to move the upper-left part of the circle's stroke slightly inward and then move the upper-right part of the circle's stroke slightly inward to give the top half of the circle a slightly triangular appearance. Using the same stroke and fill colors as the circle, draw four small ovals equally spaced above the flattened part of the circle, as shown in Figure 2-55. Exit symbol-editing mode.

11. Insert a new layer and name it **tiger paws**. Drag four instances of the tigerPaw symbol from the Library panel to the Stage. Place two instances below the top text block, place one instance to the left of the bottom text block, and place one instance to the right of the bottom text block.

12. Use the Free Transform tool to resize two of the tigerPaw instances to make them slightly smaller. Also, rotate the two left instances on the Stage slightly to the right, and then rotate the two right instances on the Stage slightly to the left.

13. Apply a bevel effect to one of the tigerPaw instances on the Stage. Change the filter strength to 80% and change the highlight color to a light peach (#FFCC99).

14. Copy all of the filter's properties, and then apply the copied filter effect to each of the other tigerPaw instances on the Stage. Lock the tiger paws layer.

15. Insert a new layer and name it **bitmap**. Import the **tiger.jpg** file from the Flash2\Case2 folder included with your Data Files to the document's library. Drag the tiger.jpg bitmap from the library to the Stage. Use the Free Transform tool to resize the bitmap to about 95 pixels in width and 63 pixels in height. Center the bitmap below the top text block, as shown in Figure 2-55.

16. Insert a new layer and name it **background**. Drag the background layer below the banner text layer. Use the Rectangle tool to draw a rectangle on the Stage. Use the green radial fill, no stroke, and square corners for the rectangle and make the rectangle the same size as the Stage.

17. Unlock the banner text layer and change the color of the vertical text block on the left side of the Stage to white (#FFFFFF).

18. Submit the finished file to your instructor.

Extend your skills by using gradients, filters, and the Oval Primitive tool to create a logo for a nursery.

CHALLENGE

Case Problem 3

Data Files needed for this Case Problem: flowers1.jpg, flowers2.jpg, flowers3.jpg

G&L Nursery   Gloria meets with Amanda, who was contracted to update the G&L Nursery Web site. Gloria requests that a new logo be developed for her business. The logo should contain the business name, phone number, and an appropriate slogan, along with some graphics. You will create the logo shown in Figure 2-56.

Figure 2-56   Completed G&L Nursery logo

© 2013 Cengage Learning; iStockphoto.com/PeskyMonkey; iStockphoto.com/Carrie Winegarden; iStockphoto.com/Dan Moore

⊕ EXPLORE

1. Create a new document. Change the document properties so that the width is 450 pixels and the height is 300 pixels. Change the background color to light green by typing **#9ACC9A** in the color palette's hexadecimal box.

2. Save the document as **nurseryLogo.fla** in the Flash2\Case3 folder included with your Data Files.

3. Draw a rectangle about 350 pixels wide and 65 pixels high across the top of the Stage. Use the Rectangle tool and the Merge Drawing mode with a dark green (#006600) stroke, a height of 2, a solid style, no fill color, and a rectangle corner radius of –5 for every corner. Place the rectangle about 40 pixels from the left of the Stage and 20 pixels from the top.

4. Create a single-line text block inside the rectangle. Use Classic Text, white text, Verdana or a similar font family of your choice, bold as the style, a size of 34 points, and left alignment. Type **G&L** in the text block, and then position the text block on the left side of the rectangle.

5. Draw a straight vertical line to the right of the text block to split the rectangle into two sections. One end of the line should snap to the top of the rectangle and the other end should snap to the bottom of the rectangle. Use a dark green (#006600) stroke, a stroke height of 2, and a solid style.

⊕ EXPLORE

6. Use the Paint Bucket tool to apply the green radial gradient fill (fourth gradient from the left on the color palette) to the center of the left section of the rectangle.

7. Create a single-line text block on the right side of the rectangle. Use Classic Text, black text, Verdana or a similar font family of your choice, bold style, a size of 34 points, and left alignment. Type **Nursery** in the text block, and, if necessary, position the text block in the center of the right side of the rectangle.

8. Create a single-line text block centered at the bottom of the Stage. Use Classic Text, white text, the same font family as in Step 7, bold style, a size of 16 points, and center alignment. Type **We Deliver! Call 555-4444!** in the text block. Apply a drop shadow to the text block.

9. Create a single-line text block in the center of the Stage. Use purple (#660099) text, the same font family as Step 7, bold style, a size of 44 points, and left alignment. Type **FLOWERS** in the text block. Use the Free Transform tool to skew the text block so that the letters are slanted to the right.

⊕ EXPLORE

10. Apply a gradient glow filter effect to the FLOWERS text block. In the Gradient Glow properties, click the Gradient box, click the right gradient marker (small triangle in lower-right corner of gradient), and select an orange color (#FF3300) in the color palette.

11. Draw four straight horizontal lines, each about 40 pixels in length, to the left of the letter F in the center text block. Use black for the stroke color, solid for the style, and 1 for the stroke height. Position the lines equally spaced and approximately the same distance from the letter F.

12. Use the Oval Primitive tool to draw a circle with a black fill and no stroke about 25 pixels in diameter on the Stage. If necessary, reset the values for the controls in the Property inspector before drawing the circle.

⊕ EXPLORE

13. In the Property inspector, change the Inner radius value for the circle to 40 to create the image of a car tire.

14. Convert the circle to a movie clip symbol named **tire**. Add a second instance of the tire symbol from the Library panel to the Stage. Move the two tire instances right below the FLOWERS text block. Place one tire right below the L in the FLOWERS text, and place the other tire right below the R.

15. Use the Selection tool to select the four horizontal lines, the FLOWERS text, and the two tire instances at one time. Group the selected objects. If necessary, position the group on the Stage as shown in Figure 2-56. Rename Layer 1 as **text blocks** and lock the layer.

16. Import the **flowers1.jpg**, **flowers2.jpg**, and **flowers3.jpg** files from the Flash2\Case3 folder included with your Data Files to the document's library.

17. Insert a new layer and name it **flowers**. Drag the flowers1.jpg bitmap from the library to the left side of the Stage above the FLOWERS text. Drag the flowers2.jpg bitmap from the library to the right of the flowers1.jpg bitmap. Drag the flowers3.jpg bitmap from the library to the right of the flowers2.jpg bitmap. Position the bitmaps below the top text block as shown in Figure 2-56.

18. Submit the finished file to your instructor.

Use symbols and text blocks to create a banner for an association.

CREATE

Case Problem 4

There are no Data Files needed for this Case Problem.

River City Conservation Society   Brittany meets with Anissa to discuss improving the River City Conservation Society's Web site. They decide to start by developing a new banner for the site's home page, which will include the society's name as well as keywords highlighting the services available to the members. You will create a banner of your design to do this. Figure 2-57 shows one possible solution.

Figure 2-57   **Sample home page banner**

© 2013 Cengage Learning

1. Create a new document with the dimensions and background color of your choice.

2. Save the document as **rccsBanner.fla** in the Flash2\Case4 folder included with your Data Files.

3. Draw two or more small shapes using the fill and stroke colors of your choice on the Stage, and then set the X and Y coordinates in the Property inspector as needed to position the shapes.

4. Draw a large rectangle shape with a gradient fill and then use guides as needed to modify the shape, such as by dragging anchor points to convert the shape to another shape. For example, you could convert the rectangle to a polygon with unequal sides. (*Hint*: You can use the Snap to Objects modifier to make the shape snap to the guides.)

5. Draw a rectangle to frame the banner. Use no fill color but select an appropriate stroke color and stroke height.

6. Modify the frame as needed. For example, you can use the Selection tool to select the bottom frame rectangle that overlaps another shape you drew, and then delete the selected portion.

7. Convert the frame rectangle to a movie clip symbol named **frame**.

8. Apply a filter to the frame instance, changing the filter properties appropriately. For example, you can apply a bevel filter, change the quality to high, and change the shadow color to a light gray.

9. Insert a new layer for text blocks and create a text block using the family, style, size, color, and alignment of your choice, and then type **Helping Preserve History** in the text block. Position the text block attractively on the banner.

10. Create another text block, using the family, style, size, color, and alignment of your choice (for example, you can use a different family, different style, larger point size, and different color), and then type **River City Conservation Society** in the text block. Apply a filter of your choice such as a drop shadow. Position the text block attractively on the banner.

⊕ **EXPLORE**   11. Create a new movie clip symbol named **star**. In symbol-editing mode, use the PolyStar tool to draw a star shape on the Stage that is about 50 pixels wide and 50 pixels high. Use colors of your choice for the fill and the stroke. In the Tool Settings, set the style to star, the number of sides to 5, and the star point size to 0.50. Exit symbol-editing mode.

12. Place at least two instances of the star symbol on the banner in attractive positions.

13. Apply a drop shadow effect to each star instance on the Stage, using the settings of your choice for the filter.

14. Submit the finished file to your instructor.

ENDING DATA FILES

Creating Animations

OBJECTIVES

Session 3.1
- Learn the different elements of animation
- Create frames and layers
- Organize frames and layers using the Timeline
- Work with scenes

Session 3.2
- Create animations
- Create and modify motion tweens
- Apply a motion preset animation
- Test animations

Session 3.3
- Use graphic symbols in animations
- Create a frame-by-frame animation
- Learn about shape tween animations

Developing Tween and Frame-by-Frame Animations

Case | *Katie's Pet Shop*

Katie is interested in incorporating animation into the new Katie's Pet Shop banner to attract more attention to the aquarium and tropical fish specials being promoted. Aly revised the Katie's Pet Shop banner to use as the basis for the animated banner. The new banner will have an initial animation of a fish pulling a sale sign while the words *Aquarium Supplies* and *Tropical Fish* are displayed one after the other. The banner will also include an animated fish swimming as well as an aquarium plant with moving leaves. Before you complete the animation for the Katie's Pet Shop banner, Aly wants you to review and modify a document she created for another promotion.

In this tutorial, you will learn the basics of creating Flash animations and how to coordinate these animations in the Timeline using frames and layers. You will learn how to extend a document using scenes. You will learn how to create motion tweens, frame-by-frame animations, and animations using graphic symbols.

STARTING DATA FILES

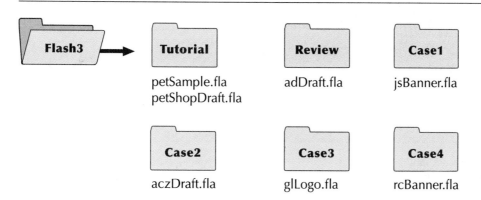

Flash3 → Tutorial
petSample.fla
petShopDraft.fla

Review
adDraft.fla

Case1
jsBanner.fla

Case2
aczDraft.fla

Case3
glLogo.fla

Case4
rcBanner.fla

SESSION 3.1 VISUAL OVERVIEW

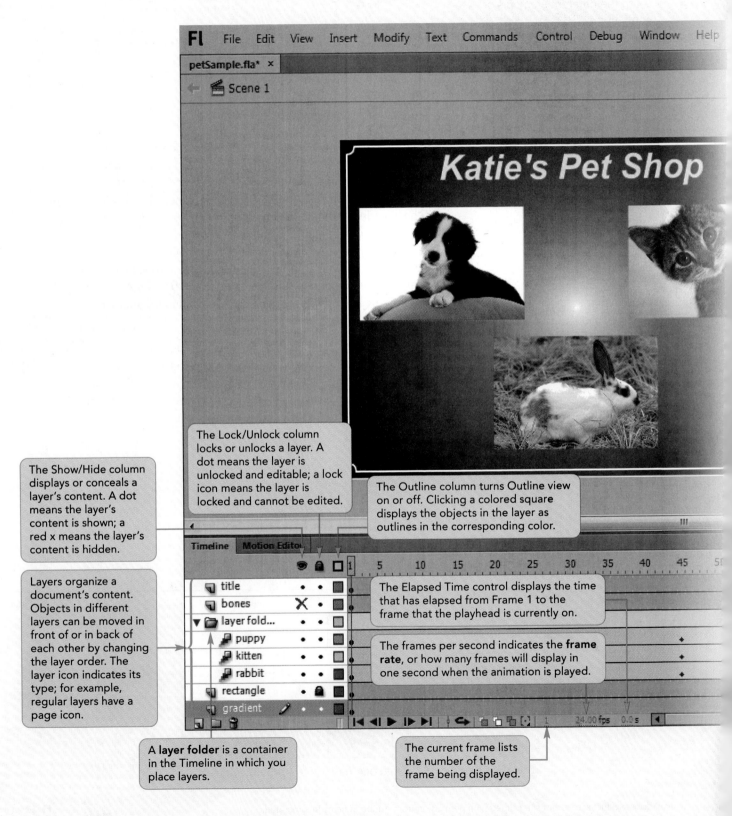

The Show/Hide column displays or conceals a layer's content. A dot means the layer's content is shown; a red x means the layer's content is hidden.

The Lock/Unlock column locks or unlocks a layer. A dot means the layer is unlocked and editable; a lock icon means the layer is locked and cannot be edited.

The Outline column turns Outline view on or off. Clicking a colored square displays the objects in the layer as outlines in the corresponding color.

Layers organize a document's content. Objects in different layers can be moved in front of or in back of each other by changing the layer order. The layer icon indicates its type; for example, regular layers have a page icon.

The Elapsed Time control displays the time that has elapsed from Frame 1 to the frame that the playhead is currently on.

The frames per second indicates the **frame rate**, or how many frames will display in one second when the animation is played.

A **layer folder** is a container in the Timeline in which you place layers.

The current frame lists the number of the frame being displayed.

TIMELINE AND SCENES PANELS

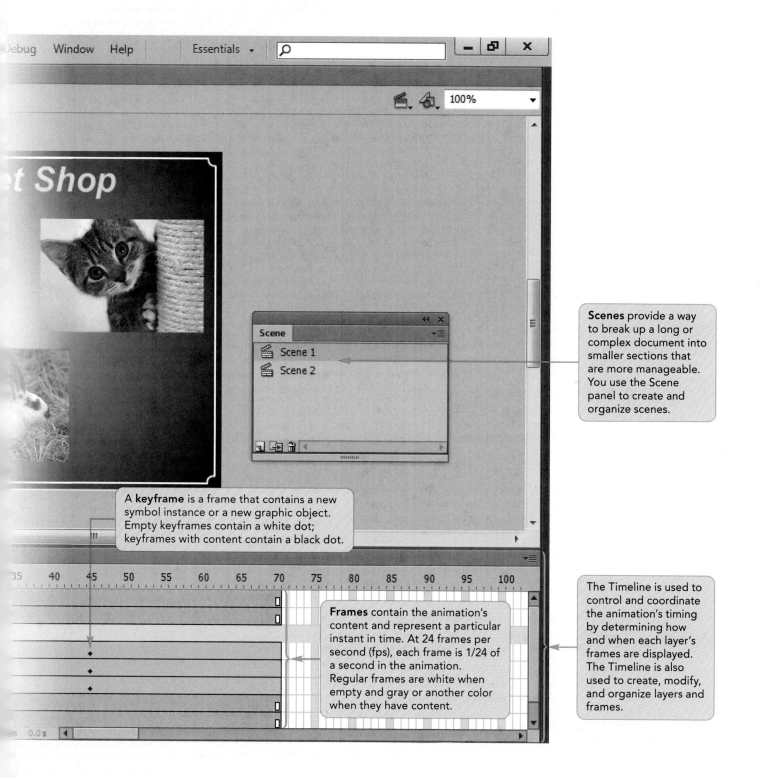

Scenes provide a way to break up a long or complex document into smaller sections that are more manageable. You use the Scene panel to create and organize scenes.

A keyframe is a frame that contains a new symbol instance or a new graphic object. Empty keyframes contain a white dot; keyframes with content contain a black dot.

Frames contain the animation's content and represent a particular instant in time. At 24 frames per second (fps), each frame is 1/24 of a second in the animation. Regular frames are white when empty and gray or another color when they have content.

The Timeline is used to control and coordinate the animation's timing by determining how and when each layer's frames are displayed. The Timeline is also used to create, modify, and organize layers and frames.

Elements of Animation

One of the most powerful features of Flash is its ability to create animation. Animation creates the perception of movement by changing the location or appearance of an object from one moment in time to the next. To do this in Flash, you coordinate the document's layers, frames, and graphic objects (such as symbols on the Stage) from the document's Timeline.

A Flash document starts with one layer. You can insert additional layers and then place graphic objects on different layers. This prevents objects that are drawn or moved on top of other objects from splitting or merging those objects in Merge Drawing mode. It also allows you to overlap the objects on the Stage. Layers are especially useful for animating multiple objects at the same time. For example, an object on one layer can move across the document at the same time as an object on another layer moves down. The animations occur simultaneously but do not impact each other in any way.

Placing different content on each frame or slightly modifying the content from one frame to the next creates the perception of movement that is animation. Initially, a document contains only a keyframe. To create animation, you add frames to a layer and then keep the content the same, change the content from previous frames, or create new content. If you want the content to remain the same in the new frame, you add a regular frame. If you want to modify or create new content, you add a keyframe. As you add more frames, the length of the animation increases.

Working with the Timeline

TIP

When working with a complex animation, turn on Outline view to see how the objects from the various layers overlap.

The Timeline is used to create, modify, and organize layers and frames. The Timeline header contains the frame numbers and the playhead as well as the layer controls. Each row represents one layer. Next to the layer names are three columns: the Show or Hide All Layers column, the Lock or Unlock All Layers column, and the Show All Layers as Outlines column. You can control the column settings for all layers at one time by clicking the column's corresponding icon in the Timeline header.

INSIGHT

Locking Completed Layers

If you have multiple objects on different layers, it might become difficult to select an object in one layer without accidentally selecting another object in a different layer. A good practice when working with objects in multiple layers is to lock a layer after you finish editing its contents. Objects in a locked layer are not selectable. This ensures that you do not inadvertently modify the objects in a finished layer as you work with objects in another layer.

You will explore the Timeline of the sample banner. The banner's Timeline contains several layers. The layers include animations of several bitmaps and a text block. Each layer has a descriptive name and contains 70 frames. You will play the animation and watch the Timeline as it displays the elements of the document. You can control the playback of the frames using commands on the menu bar, the playback controls at the bottom of the Timeline, or the keyboard.

To explore the Timeline of the sample banner:

1. Open the **petSample.fla** file located in the Flash3\Tutorial folder included with your Data Files, save the document as **petSampleNew.fla**, and then reset Flash to the Essentials workspace. See Figure 3-1.

Figure 3-1	Sample Katie's Pet Shop banner

Stage displays the content of Frame 1, the current frame

playhead at Frame 1

each layer has multiple frames

layers with descriptive names

iStockphoto.com/elenaleonova; iStockphoto.com/Sarah Salmela; iStockphoto.com/ChrisAt

TIP

You can also press the Enter key to play the animation.

2. On the menu bar, click **Control**, and then click **Play**. As the playhead moves from Frame 1 to Frame 70 in the Timeline, the two top pictures move across the Stage and the bottom picture rotates. After Frame 45, the contents on the Stage remain stationary through Frame 70.

3. In the Timeline, click the **Play** button ▶. The playhead returns to Frame 1 and plays through Frame 70.

4. In the Timeline, click the **Go to first frame** button ◀. The playhead moves to Frame 1.

5. In the Timeline, click the **Step forward one frame** button ▮▶. The playhead moves to Frame 2.

6. Click the **Step forward one frame** button ▮▶ twice to see the playhead move forward two more frames and observe how the contents on the Stage change as each frame is displayed.

7. In the Timeline, click the **Go to last frame** button ▶▮. The playhead moves to Frame 70 and the final frame of the animation appears on the Stage.

8. Review the Current Frame (70), Frame Rate (24.00 fps), and Elapsed Time (2.9 s) at the bottom of the Timeline. See Figure 3-2.

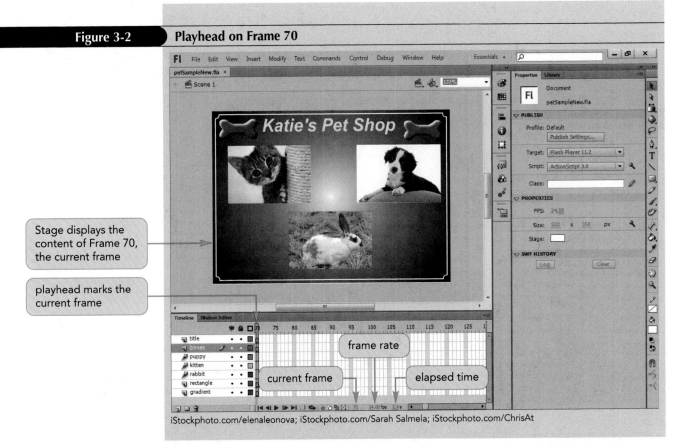

Figure 3-2   Playhead on Frame 70

Stage displays the content of Frame 70, the current frame

playhead marks the current frame

frame rate

current frame

elapsed time

iStockphoto.com/elenaleonova; iStockphoto.com/Sarah Salmela; iStockphoto.com/ChrisAt

The Timeline displays useful information that you might review as you test an animation. The Elapsed Time control displays the time that has elapsed from Frame 1 to the frame that the playhead is currently on. The elapsed time depends on the frame rate. By default, the frame rate is 24 frames per second, which means an animation that spans 24 frames takes one second to play. The length of the sample banner animation you just viewed can be determined by looking at the elapsed time when the playhead is in the last frame. In this case, the length of the animation is 2.9 seconds.

INSIGHT

Checking the Frame Number Before Modifying Content

A document can have many frames, and the contents of the frames often look very similar from one frame to the next. As you work with content on the Stage, be aware of which frame is displayed because that is the frame whose content you are working with. Be careful that you don't change or create the content for the wrong frame. To determine which frame you are working with, check the location of the playhead in the Timeline header or look at the number listed for the current frame.

Changing the Timeline View

As you develop an animation, the number of frames can grow very rapidly, as can the number of layers. At some point, you might need to change the view of the Timeline to work more efficiently with the elements in the animation. You can also modify the dimensions of the frames to see more frames within the Timeline window or to see more of the frame's contents. By default, the frames are tinted different colors based on the type of content they contain, such as a blue tint for a motion tween. You will learn about motion tweens later in this tutorial. You can deselect the Tinted Frames option to remove the color tints on the frames.

Because you will be working extensively with the Timeline, you will practice changing the view of its frames and layers.

To change the view of the Timeline:

▶ **1.** In the Timeline, click the **Go to first frame** button. The playhead moves to Frame 1.

▶ **2.** Press the **F4** key. The panels disappear. You will display the Timeline next.

Trouble? If the Timeline doesn't disappear, the pointer was still over the Timeline. Move the pointer to the Stage, and then repeat Step 2 until all of the panels disappear.

▶ **3.** On the menu bar, click **Window**, and then click **Timeline**. The Timeline appears.

▶ **4.** In the Timeline, click the **Frame View** button to open the panel's menu, and then click **Preview**. The frames increase in size, and the content in Frame 1 is displayed. See Figure 3-3.

Figure 3-3   **Frames in Preview view**

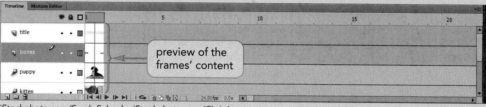

iStockphoto.com/Sarah Salmela; iStockphoto.com/ChrisAt

▶ **5.** In the Timeline, click the **Frame View** button, and then click **Small**. The frames decrease in size.

▶ **6.** In the Timeline, click the **Frame View** button, and then click **Short**. The height of the layers decreases. See Figure 3-4.

Figure 3-4   **Frames in Short view**

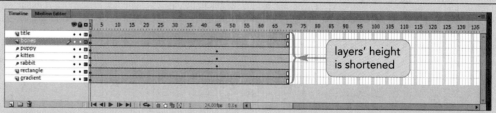

▶ **7.** In the Timeline, click the **Frame View** button, and then click **Short** to turn off Short view.

▶ **8.** In the Timeline, click the **Frame View** button, and then click **Normal**. The frames return to their default, or Normal, view.

▶ **9.** Reset the Essentials workspace.

As you work, you can switch the Timeline view to best fit your needs at any specific moment, depending on the content you are creating.

PROSKILLS

Written Communication: Using Layers to Organize Content

A new document in Flash contains one layer and one frame within that layer. As you add more content or create an animation, you add layers to the document to help organize the document. However, this can lead to many layers, which can become difficult to manage and challenging to find a specific part of the document. So be sure to plan a logical layer structure for each document.

The Timeline is a useful tool for working with the different layers and frames in your document most efficiently. As you add more layers to the Timeline, a good practice is to assign each layer a meaningful name that corresponds to its content. This helps keep the content organized as the complexity of the animation increases. It also ensures you or someone else who needs to edit the document can easily locate a layer based on its name. Although layer names can include spaces and punctuation marks, these are often omitted for simplicity. Layers can also be renamed as needed. Keep in mind that when a document has many layers, you can hide some layers as you work with the content of other layers.

Additional layers don't add to the overall size of the finished file, so you can create an organized structure for the document's content while keeping the size of the final published SWF file as small as possible. This way, the SWF file downloads quickly from the Web server to the viewer's computer.

Adding Layer Folders

When you have multiple layers in the document's Timeline, you can create layer folders to help you work more efficiently. The names of layers in a layer folder are indented under the layer folder in the Timeline.

Using a layer folder is similar to how you use a folder on your computer's hard drive—you place related files into the folder to make the files easier to find and manage. You can use a layer folder to keep related layers together. For example, you can create a folder in which to place all of the layers that contain text. Then you can quickly find the text layers when you need to edit them. You can name a layer folder with a descriptive name the same way you name a layer, making it easier to know what each folder contains. You can collapse the layer folders so that the layers in the folders are not visible. This makes the Timeline less cluttered and makes it easier to work with the other layers in the document. Collapsing the folder's layers doesn't affect the view of the layers' content on the Stage.

You will add a layer folder in the sample banner, and then move the related layers into it.

To insert a layer folder in the sample banner:

1. In the Timeline, click the **puppy** layer. The layer is selected.

2. In the Timeline, click the **New Folder** button 🗀. A layer folder named Folder 1 is inserted above the puppy layer.

3. Double-click **Folder 1** to select the folder name, type **bitmaps** as the new name, and then press the **Enter** key. The folder is renamed.

4. Drag the **rabbit** layer to the bitmaps folder but do not release the mouse. A black line appears below the bitmaps folder, as shown in Figure 3-5.

Figure 3-5 | Layer being moved to the bitmaps layer folder

new bitmaps layer folder

black line indicates that the selected layer will move into the folder

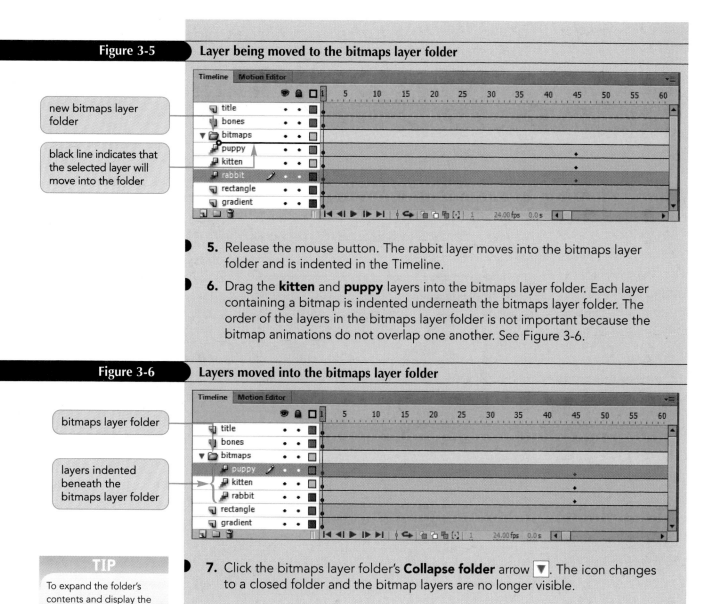

5. Release the mouse button. The rabbit layer moves into the bitmaps layer folder and is indented in the Timeline.

6. Drag the **kitten** and **puppy** layers into the bitmaps layer folder. Each layer containing a bitmap is indented underneath the bitmaps layer folder. The order of the layers in the bitmaps layer folder is not important because the bitmap animations do not overlap one another. See Figure 3-6.

Figure 3-6 | Layers moved into the bitmaps layer folder

bitmaps layer folder

layers indented beneath the bitmaps layer folder

TIP

To expand the folder's contents and display the layers, click the folder's Expand folder arrow.

7. Click the bitmaps layer folder's **Collapse folder** arrow ▼. The icon changes to a closed folder and the bitmap layers are no longer visible.

Selecting and Copying Frames and Layers

A document's frames can be copied or moved within the same layer or from one layer to another. To copy or move frames, you must first select them. You can select individual or multiple frames in the Timeline or you can select frames within one layer or across multiple layers. You can also move, copy, or duplicate layers within the document's Timeline or from one document to another.

You will select and copy a layer in the sample banner.

To select, copy, and paste the bones layer:

1. In the Timeline, right-click the name of the **bones** layer to open the context menu. The layer and all of its frames are selected. You will copy the layer to create a new bones layer within the Timeline.

2. Click **Copy Layers** to copy the layer to the Clipboard.

3. Right-click the name of the **bones** layer, and then click **Paste Layers**. A duplicate of the bones layer is placed above the original bones layer.

▶ 4. Double-click the new **bones** layer's name, type **bones 2**, and then press the **Enter** key. The layer is renamed.

▶ 5. Click the name of the **bones 2** layer to select all of its frames.

▶ 6. In the Tools panel, click the **Selection Tool** button ![tool] to select it, if necessary. The two copied bone instances remain selected.

▶ 7. Drag the bones instances to the bottom of the Stage. Both instances move at the same time. See Figure 3-7.

| Figure 3-7 | **Copied instances moved on the Stage** |

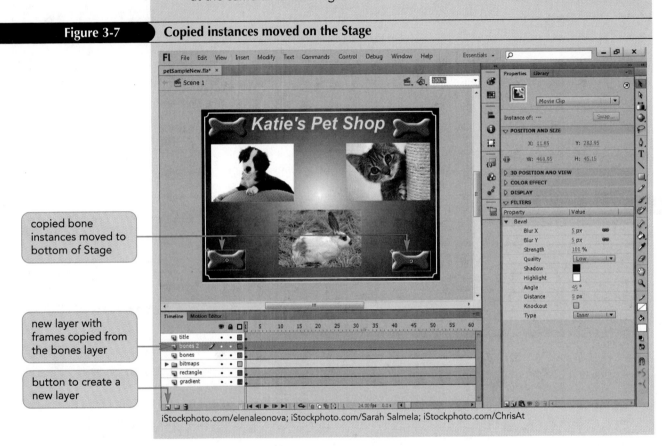

copied bone instances moved to bottom of Stage

new layer with frames copied from the bones layer

button to create a new layer

iStockphoto.com/elenaleonova; iStockphoto.com/Sarah Salmela; iStockphoto.com/ChrisAt

Using Scenes and Multiple Timelines

Every Flash document starts with one scene that contains a Timeline. For more complex animations, a document can have more than one scene, and each scene has its own Timeline, as shown in Figure 3-8. A document's scenes are similar to those of a motion picture. In the same way that the scenes in a motion picture are played in order, the scenes in a Flash document are played one after the other. The content of all layers is displayed one frame at a time within a scene's Timeline. When you add new scenes to a document, you are essentially adding new Timelines that contain their own frames with new content.

| Figure 3-8 | Multiple scenes in one document |

content of Scene 1

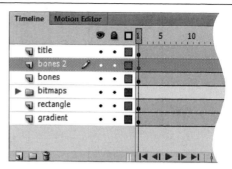
content of Scene 2

After a document with multiple scenes is published, the SWF file plays in a Web page using Flash Player. The player treats all the scenes in a SWF file as one long Timeline. So, if a Flash document has two scenes and each scene has 30 frames, Flash Player treats this as one long Timeline with 60 consecutive frames and plays them according to the order of the scenes in the Scene panel.

Using the Scene Panel

The Scene panel lists the scenes in the current document in the order in which they will play. From the Scene panel, you can change the order the scenes will play as well as duplicate, add, and delete scenes. A duplicate scene has the same name as the original with the word *copy* added to its name, and it has the same contents as the original. Any new scene you add has the name *Scene*, followed by a number that is one higher than the previous scene.

INSIGHT

Naming Scenes

When a document has only a few scenes, using the default scene names such as *Scene 1*, *Scene 2*, and *Scene 3* might be okay. When a document has many scenes, a better practice is to assign more meaningful names to each scene to make it simpler to manage the document. If you have 10 scenes, for example, you might not remember the content of each scene, and someone else working on the document has no idea of what each scene includes. To locate specific content to work with would require searching all of the scenes. By giving each scene a meaningful name, you and others can easily determine what each scene contains. Scene names can include spaces, symbols, and punctuation marks.

When you add a new scene or create a duplicate of a scene, the Stage automatically displays the new scene. You can tell which scene is currently displayed by the scene number in the upper-left corner of the Stage window or by looking at the Scene panel to see which scene is currently selected. You can switch between scenes at any time.

You will rename and reorder the scenes in the sample document.

To rename and play scenes in the sample banner:

TIP

You can also press the Shift+F2 keys to open and close the Scene panel.

▶ **1.** On the menu bar, click **Window**, point to **Other Panels**, and then click **Scene**. The Scene panel opens, showing two scenes named Scene 1 and Scene 2. You will rename these scenes with more meaningful names.

▶ **2.** In the Scene panel, double-click **Scene 1** to select the name, type **Pets in Action** as the new name, and then press the **Enter** key to rename the scene.

▶ **3.** In the Scene panel, double-click **Scene 2**. The Scene 2 scene name appears on the Edit bar, the contents of the Timeline change to that scene, and the view of the Stage switches to the first frame of that scene.

▶ **4.** Type **Pets for Sale**, and then press the **Enter** key. The scene is renamed and the Pets for Sale scene name appears on the Edit bar. See Figure 3-9.

| Figure 3-9 | Renamed scenes in the Scene panel |

Pets for Sale scene is the active scene and its content appears on the Stage

button to add a scene

iStockphoto.com/Sarah Salmela

▶ **5.** Drag the **Scene** panel to the right of the Stage, and then, in the Timeline, click the **Play** button ▶. The animation for the Pets for Sale scene plays, showing the center text block increasing in size.

You will test the animation to see how both scenes play one after the other.

▶ **6.** On the menu bar, click **Control**, point to **Test Movie**, and then click **in Flash Professional**. A new window opens, showing the SWF file as it plays the animation of the Pets in Action scene followed by the animation of the Pets for Sale scene.

▶ **7.** On the Flash Player menu bar, click **File**, and then click **Close**. Flash Player closes and you return to the document.

You can use the Scene panel to reorder the scenes in a document.

To reorder scenes in the sample banner:

1. In the Scene panel, click and drag the **Pets for Sale** scene so that it appears before the Pets in Action scene.

2. On the menu bar, click **Control**, point to **Test Movie**, and then click **in Flash Professional**. The movie plays, but the sequence of the animations changes based on the order of the scenes in the Scene panel. The Pets for Sale scene's increasing text animation plays first, followed by the animation in the Pets in Action scene.

3. On the Flash Player menu bar, click **File**, and then click **Close** to return to the document.

4. On the Edit bar, click the **Edit Scene** button to open a menu that lists all the scenes in the document, and then click **Pets in Action**. The Timeline and Stage for the Pets in Action scene appear.

5. On the Edit bar, click the **Edit Scene** button, and then click **Pets for Sale** to return to the Pets for Sale scene.

6. Save and close the petSampleNew.fla document.

Adding a Duplicate Scene

Based on the planning instructions and Aly's sketch shown in Figure 3-10, the new animated banner for Katie's Pet Shop will have two animation sequences. The first sequence will show a fish swimming across the Stage pulling a sign advertising aquarium specials. It will also show an animation of phrases being displayed one after the other. The second animation sequence will show a fish swimming back and forth in the aquarium tank and plant leaves moving.

| Figure 3-10 | Animation instructions for the Katie's Pet Shop banner |

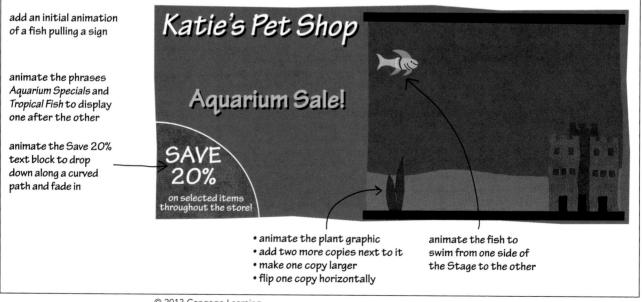

© 2013 Cengage Learning

To make it easier to manage the two animation sequences, you will create each in a separate scene. You will add a new scene to the banner by duplicating the initial scene and then renaming both scenes with more meaningful names.

To duplicate and rename scenes in the Katie's Pet Shop banner:

▶ 1. Open the **petShopDraft.fla** file located in the Flash3\Tutorial folder included with your Data Files, and then save the document as **petShopBanner.fla** in the same folder.

▶ 2. In the Scene panel, click the **Duplicate Scene** button 🔲. The duplicate scene appears in the Scene panel with the name "Scene 1 copy."

▶ 3. In the Scene panel, double-click **Scene 1** to select its name, type **Specials Sign** as the new name, and then press the **Enter** key to rename the scene.

▶ 4. In the Scene panel, double-click **Scene 1 copy** to select its name, type **Fish and Plant**, and then press the **Enter** key. The new scene name appears in the Scene panel.

▶ 5. Close the Scene panel, and then save the document.

In this session, you learned about the basic elements of Flash that are used in creating animations—layers and frames. You worked with these elements using the Timeline. You also learned how scenes can help you manage a longer or more complex document. In the next session, you will create animations.

Session 3.1 Quick Check

1. What is the purpose of the Timeline?
2. How can you tell which is the current frame in the Timeline?
3. What is the default frame rate for a Flash document?
4. What is the difference between frames and layers?
5. What is a layer folder and what is its purpose?
6. What is a scene?
7. When you have more than one scene, how can you tell in what order the scenes will play?
8. Why would you rename a scene from its default name?

SESSION 3.2 VISUAL OVERVIEW

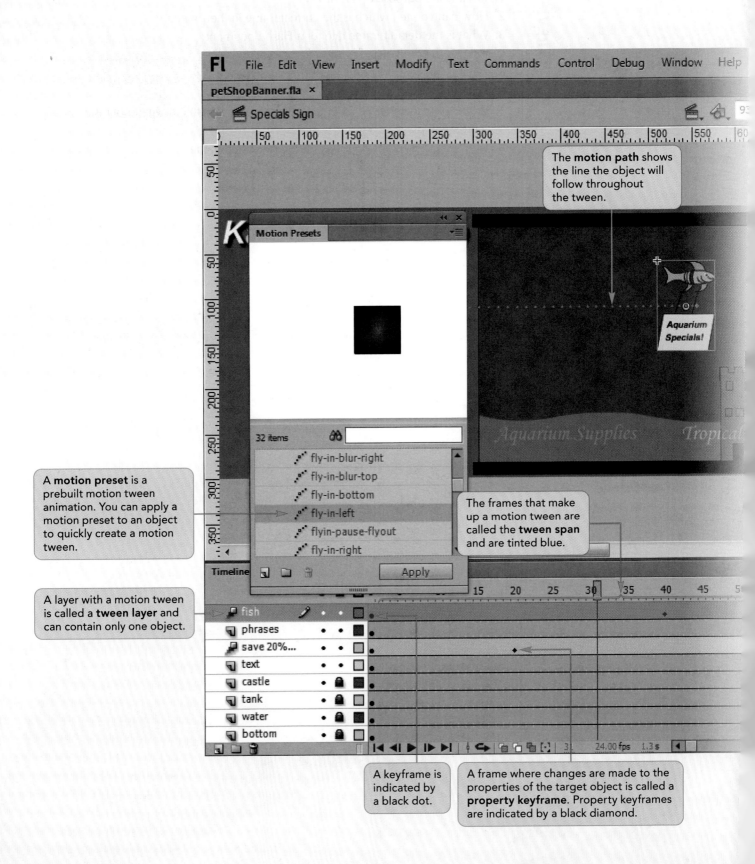

The **motion path** shows the line the object will follow throughout the tween.

A **motion preset** is a prebuilt motion tween animation. You can apply a motion preset to an object to quickly create a motion tween.

The frames that make up a motion tween are called the **tween span** and are tinted blue.

A layer with a motion tween is called a **tween layer** and can contain only one object.

A keyframe is indicated by a black dot.

A frame where changes are made to the properties of the target object is called a **property keyframe**. Property keyframes are indicated by a black diamond.

MOTION TWEENS

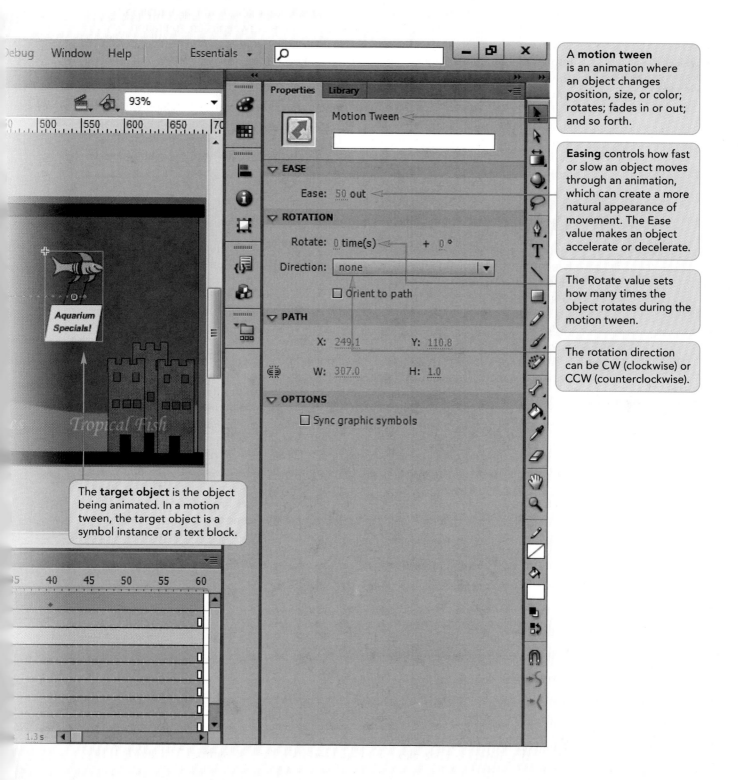

A **motion tween** is an animation where an object changes position, size, or color; rotates; fades in or out; and so forth.

Easing controls how fast or slow an object moves through an animation, which can create a more natural appearance of movement. The Ease value makes an object accelerate or decelerate.

The Rotate value sets how many times the object rotates during the motion tween.

The rotation direction can be CW (clockwise) or CCW (counterclockwise).

The **target object** is the object being animated. In a motion tween, the target object is a symbol instance or a text block.

Creating Animation

Animation is accomplished by displaying the content of different frames one after another. Each frame contains some graphic element that is displayed for a short instant in time. As the content of each frame is displayed in succession, the graphic elements appear to be moving. You can create several types of animations in Flash: motion tweens, shape tweens, and frame-by-frame animations. A **tween** is an animation where you create the beginning content and the ending content, and Flash creates the in-between frames, varying the content evenly in each frame to achieve the animation. The word *tween* comes from the words *in-between*. In a frame-by-frame animation, you create or modify the content in each frame of the animation.

The animations of the fish in the new animated banner for Katie's Pet Shop will be created with motion tweens. In the second scene, the plant leaves will be animated so that the leaves' tips appear to be moving. This movement will be created with a frame-by-frame animation because you need to specify the positions of the leaves at different moments in time.

TIP

If a frame is part of a tween, it is called a **tweened frame**; otherwise, it is called a **static frame**.

Creating a Motion Tween

Motion tweens in Flash are **object-based animations** because after you create a motion tween, you can easily modify the tween as one entity, similar to the way you would modify any other object. You can change the motion tween's duration, change the target object's direction, or move the motion tween within the Timeline. When you make changes to the motion tween, Flash adjusts the contents of all the frames in the tween span. A target object in a tween can be replaced by a different instance without having to re-create the tween.

The process for creating a motion tween animation is relatively simple. You add a symbol instance or a text block in one frame at the start of the animation and then apply a motion tween to the object. Flash creates a tween span in the Timeline that extends for one second, which is 24 frames when the frame rate is set to its default value. At any point in the tween span, you can modify the object by moving it to a different position or changing its properties, such as its size, color tint, or color brightness. A property keyframe is created at each point where you modify the object's properties. Flash varies the content in each intermediate frame to change the object's position or properties slightly from one frame to the next. You can also adjust the settings for the motion tween such as by adding rotation to the target object in the Property inspector.

You will use two motion tweens in the Fish and Plant scene to create an animation of a fish swimming from one side of the aquarium tank to the other. One motion tween will move the fish across the tank from left to right, and the other motion tween will move the fish from right to left.

TIP

If you have more than one object in the layer in which you create a motion tween, Flash places the other objects into a separate layer.

To create a motion tween with an instance of the fish symbol:

1. If you took a break after the previous session, make sure the petShopBanner.fla file is open, Flash is reset to the Essentials workspace, and the Fish and Plant scene is displayed.

2. Change the zoom magnification to **Fit in Window**. The magnification level of the Stage is changed to fit all the contents within the Document window.

3. In the Timeline, click the **fish** layer to select it, and then convert the fish graphic to a movie clip symbol named **fish**. The fish symbol is created.

TIP

You can press the F8 key on the keyboard to open the Convert to Symbol dialog box.

4. Right-click the **fish** instance, and then click **Create Motion Tween**. A tween span is created from Frame 1 through Frame 24 in the Timeline and the playhead moves to Frame 24. See Figure 3-11. The rest of the graphics disappeared when you added the motion tween because these graphics exist only in Frame 1.

Figure 3-11   Motion tween created

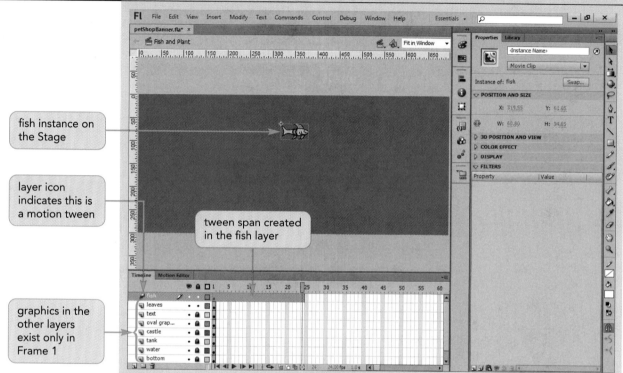

fish instance on the Stage

layer icon indicates this is a motion tween

tween span created in the fish layer

graphics in the other layers exist only in Frame 1

5. In the Timeline, drag the right edge of the tween span in the fish layer to Frame 50, as shown in Figure 3-12, and then release the mouse button to extend the motion tween through Frame 50. For the other graphics in Frame 1 to exist through Frame 50, you need to add frames to their respective layers.

Figure 3-12   Tween span extended in the Timeline

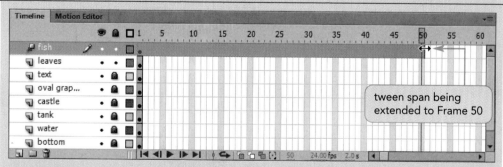

tween span being extended to Frame 50

6. In the Timeline, click and drag from **Frame 50** of the leaves layer to **Frame 50** of the bottom layer. Each Frame 50 of the layers is selected at the same time.

7. On the menu bar, click **Insert**, point to **Timeline**, and click **Frame**. A regular frame is added at Frame 50 of each selected layer. Regular frames are also automatically added between Frames 1 and 50 to fill the empty intervening frames in each layer.

8. Drag the **fish** instance from the left side of the tank to the right side of the tank, placing it in the same relative vertical position. A motion path for the motion tween is created and displayed on the Stage. See Figure 3-13.

Figure 3-13   Motion path displayed on the Stage

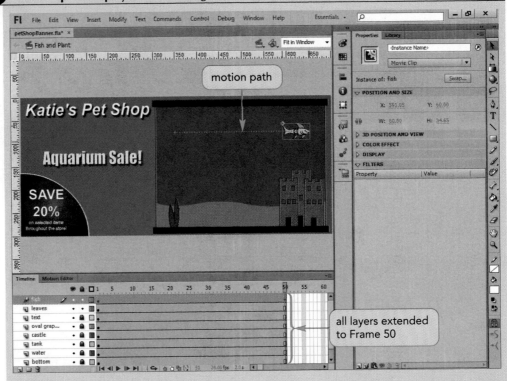

9. Press the **Enter** key to play the motion tween. The fish moves across the tank from left to right following the motion path.

The fish is animated to move across the aquarium tank. The fish also needs to move from the right side of the tank to the left. To do this, you will create another motion tween of a fish moving from right to left in a new layer. You will use another instance of the fish symbol and flip the instance so that it faces to the left.

To create a motion tween for a second fish instance:

1. In the Timeline, in the Show/Hide column of the fish layer, click the **dot** · to hide its contents temporarily.

2. In the Timeline, click the **New Layer** button. A new layer is inserted in the Timeline above the fish layer.

3. Double-click the name of the new layer to select it, type **second fish**, and then press the **Enter** key to rename the layer.

4. Click the **Library** tab to display the Library panel, and then drag an instance of the **fish** symbol from the Library panel to the Stage on the right side of the tank at the same relative location as the fish instance in the fish layer.

5. On the menu bar, click **Modify**, point to **Transform**, and then click **Flip Horizontal**. The fish flips so that it faces to the left.

6. Right-click the **fish** instance, and then click **Create Motion Tween**. A tween span is created from Frame 1 through Frame 50 in the Timeline.

7. Drag the **fish** instance from the right side of the tank to the left side of the tank, placing it in the same relative vertical position. A motion path is created. See Figure 3-14.

Figure 3-14	Second motion tween with motion path

fish flipped to face left

motion path of the second fish

motion tween in the second fish layer

8. In the Timeline, in the Show/Hide column, click the **red X** ⊠ for the fish layer to unhide that layer.

9. In the Timeline, click the **Play** button ▶. The first fish instance moves across the Stage from left to right while the second fish instance moves from right to left.

Modifying a Motion Tween

A motion tween animates an object to move from one part of the Stage to another, following along a motion path. The default motion path is a straight line. For many objects, you will want to modify the motion path to animate the objects to move in a more natural way. For example, you can make a ball appear to bounce up and down while gradually coming to a stop, you can make a car move along a curved road, you can make a bird fly in a circular pattern, or you can make a fish swim along a curved path. You can modify a motion tween by changing the properties of the target object anywhere within the tween span or by changing the curve of the motion path. When you make changes to the target object or to the motion path, Flash automatically adjusts the rest of the motion tween. If the target object's properties change, Flash adds property keyframes where the change is made.

You can modify a motion path with the Selection tool by dragging any segment of the path using the Selection tool pointer the same way you modify a stroke. You can also extend a motion path's length by dragging either of its endpoints. You can move a selected motion path to a different location on the Stage. As you adjust the motion path, the target object stays attached to the path and the motion tween automatically changes based on your adjustments.

You can also modify a motion path by using the Free Transform tool to rotate, skew, or scale the path, as shown in Figure 3-15.

Figure 3-15   **Motion path modified with the Free Transform tool**

© 2013 Cengage Learning

Finally, you can modify a motion path by selecting it and then making changes to its properties in the Property inspector or in the Transform panel.

You will modify the motion paths of the fish in the banner so that the fish will swim along a curved path. Each motion path guides the fish across the Stage.

Controlling an Object's Speed in an Animation

Objects do not usually move at a constant rate of speed. They might start slowly and then accelerate, or they might start quickly and then decelerate. For example, a kicked ball starts moving quickly but then slows toward the end of its movement. To simulate this natural movement, you can adjust a motion tween's Ease value in the Property inspector. A negative value causes the object to begin slowly and accelerate toward the end of the animation. A positive value causes the object to begin rapidly and decelerate toward the end of the animation. For more control over a motion tween, you can use the Motion Editor, which is covered in a later tutorial.

You will modify the properties of the motion tweens.

To modify the properties of the motion tweens:

1. In the Timeline, hide the second fish layer, and then click the **fish** layer to select it. The tween span is selected.

2. Click the **Properties** tab to display the Property inspector. You will change the motion tween's properties.

3. In the Property inspector, drag the **Ease** value to the right to change the value to **50**. The fish instance will slow down toward the end of the motion tween.

4. In the Tools panel, click the **Selection Tool** button ![cursor] to select the Selection tool, if necessary.

5. On the Stage, point to the center of the motion path to change the pointer to ![pointer], and then drag the pointer up slightly to curve the motion path, as shown in Figure 3-16. The fish instance will follow a curved path.

| Figure 3-16 | Motion path being changed |

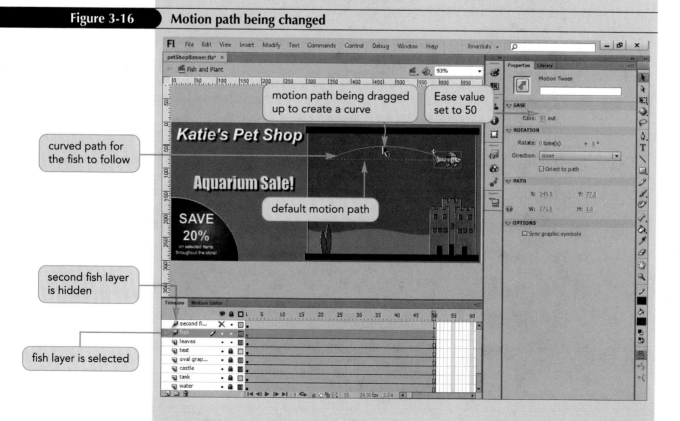

curved path for the fish to follow

second fish layer is hidden

fish layer is selected

motion path being dragged up to create a curve

Ease value set to 50

default motion path

6. In the Timeline, hide the contents of the fish layer, display the contents of the second fish layer, and then select the **second fish** layer.

7. In the Property inspector, drag the **Ease** value to the left to change it to **–50**. The fish instance will move faster toward the end of the motion tween.

8. Point to the center of the motion path on the Stage and drag it up slightly to curve it. The fish instance will follow a curved path.

Because you don't want both fish animations to occur at the same time, you will move the tween span for the second fish so that its animation occurs after the first fish animation.

To move the tween span for the second fish:

1. In the Timeline, click **Frame 1** of the tween span in the second fish layer, and then drag the span to the right so that its first frame starts on Frame 51. See Figure 3-17.

Figure 3-17 **Tween span moved in the Timeline**

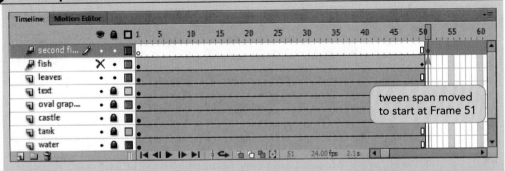

tween span moved to start at Frame 51

2. In the Timeline, move the playhead to the right to Frame 100.

3. In the Timeline, add regular frames at Frame 100 to all of the other layers, except the fish layer. The fish layer animation will end at Frame 50 and the second fish layer animation will start at Frame 51. The entire movie now occupies 100 frames.

4. In the Timeline, display the **fish** layer. Its contents appear on the Stage again.

5. In the Timeline, click the **Play** button ▶. The first fish moves across the tank from left to right, moving slightly up at the center of its path, and then the second fish moves across the tank from right to left. It also moves slightly up at the center of its path.

When you animate an object to follow a curved path, the object stays in a horizontal position as it moves along the path. You will usually want the object to move in a more natural way, which you can do by selecting the Orient to path option in the Property inspector. The Orient to path option works best with curves that have gentle slopes.

You will orient the fish to follow the slope of the path.

To orient the fish to the curved paths:

▶ **1.** In the Timeline, click the **Go to first frame** button ⏮, and then click **Frame 1** of the fish layer.

▶ **2.** In the Property inspector, in the Rotation section, click the **Orient to path** check box to check it. Property keyframes are added in Frame 2 through Frame 50, representing how the fish is slightly rotated in each frame of the tween span. The fish will have a more natural movement during the animation. See Figure 3-18.

Figure 3-18	Orient to path applied to the motion tween

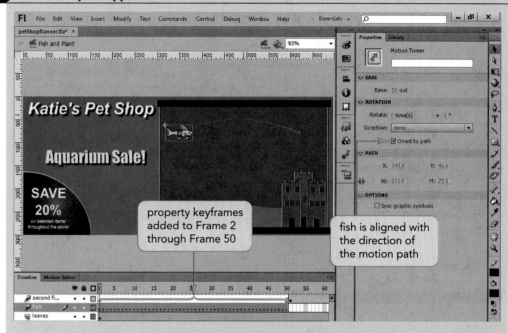

▶ **3.** In the Timeline, click **Frame 51** of the second fish layer.

▶ **4.** In the Property inspector, in the Rotation section, click the **Orient to path** check box to check it. Property keyframes are added to the tween span.

▶ **5.** In the Timeline, move the playhead to **Frame 1**, and then press the **Enter** key to play the animation again. The fish orients itself to the slope of the motion paths.

▶ **6.** Save the banner.

Using Motion Presets

The simplest and quickest way to create a motion tween is to apply a motion preset to an object selected on the Stage and let Flash create the necessary elements for the animation. A motion preset is a prebuilt motion tween animation. Each motion preset you apply is created in its own layer, and the new frames added to the Timeline are based on that motion preset. Figure 3-19 describes some of the default motion preset animations available in the Motion Presets panel. After you select a motion preset, the preview window in the Motion Presets panel displays a preview of the effect.

Figure 3-19	Default motion presets

Motion Preset	Description
bounce-smoosh	Animates an object to simulate bouncing on a surface
fly-in-blur-bottom	Animates an object to fly in from the bottom up; a blurring effect is applied to the object to simulate a rate of speed
fly-in-left	Animates an object to fade in and move from the left to the right
med-bounce	Animates an object to bounce across the Stage
pulse	Animates an object to create a pulsating effect

© 2013 Cengage Learning

Applying a Motion Preset Animation

When you apply a motion preset to an object, Flash converts the layer in which the object resides into a motion tween layer and creates frames with the appropriate content for the animation. If the selected object is not a symbol, Flash prompts you to create a new symbol before applying the motion preset animation.

One of the animation sequences for the Katie's Pet Shop banner is of a fish moving across the Stage while pulling a specials sign. You will create this animation in the Specials Sign scene using the fly-in-left motion preset. Before you apply the motion preset, you'll draw the sign graphic.

To draw the sign graphic for the animation:

1. On the Edit bar, click the **Edit Scene** button [icon], and then click **Specials Sign** to make it the current scene. The plant leaves will not be used in this scene, so you will delete the leaves layer.

2. In the Timeline, select the **leaves** layer, and then click the **Delete** button [icon]. The leaves layer is deleted.

3. Change the zoom magnification to **200%**. The contents of the Stage are magnified, making it easier to draw the sign. If necessary, use the scroll bars to move the view of the Stage so that the fish is centered at the top of the Document window.

4. Display the rulers, if necessary, and then create horizontal guides at approximately **120 pixels** and **160 pixels** from the top of the Stage and create vertical guides at approximately **320 pixels** and **380 pixels** from the left of the Stage.

5. In the Tools panel, click the **Rectangle Tool** button [icon], click the **Black and white** button [icon] to change the stroke color to black and the fill color to white, and then, if necessary, click the **Object Drawing** button [icon] to deselect it.

6. In the Property inspector, if necessary, set the Rectangle corner radius to **0**, the stroke height to **1**, and the stroke style to **Solid**.

7. In the Timeline, select the **fish** layer, and then, on the Stage, draw a rectangle that is approximately **60 pixels** wide and **40 pixels** high below the fish inside the rectangular area formed by the guides. The rectangle will be the sign the fish pulls across the banner. See Figure 3-20.

Figure 3-20 ▶ **Rectangle created for the sign**

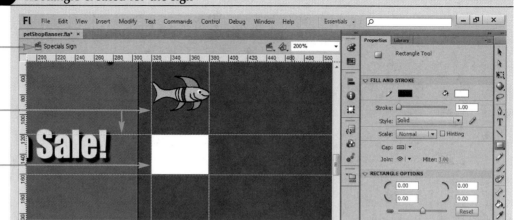

Specials Sign scene is the current scene

guides for drawing the rectangle

rectangle for the sign

You will add the words to the sign next.

▶ 8. In the Tools panel, click the **Text Tool** button $\boxed{T}$, and then, in the Property inspector, if necessary, change the Text engine to **Classic Text**, the Text type to **Static Text**, the font family to **Arial**, the font style to **Bold**, the point size to **10**, the text (fill) color to **black** (#000000), the format to **Align center**, and the font rendering method to **Anti-alias for animation**. This setting of the font rendering method will enhance how the text block is displayed when animated.

▶ 9. Create a text block inside the rectangle you drew in Step 8, type **Aquarium** in the text block, press the **Enter** key, and then type **Specials!**.

▶ 10. In the Tools panel, click the **Selection Tool** button $\boxed{\text{\k}}$, reposition the text block on the Stage so that it is centered within the rectangle, and then click an empty area of the Stage to deselect the text block. See Figure 3-21.

Figure 3-21 ▶ **Sign with text**

rectangle and text for the sign

▶ 11. On the menu bar, click **View**, point to **Guides**, and then click **Clear Guides**. The guides are cleared from the Stage.

Be sure to select both the rectangle and the text block so they are skewed together.

▶ 12. In the Tools panel, click the **Free Transform Tool** button $\boxed{\text{\k:}}$, and then draw a selection marquee around the rectangle. Both the rectangle and the text block are selected. You will skew the selected rectangle.

Trouble? If the fish is selected, the selection marquee you drew probably encompassed the fish. Click an empty area of the Stage, and then redraw the selection marquee, being sure to include only the rectangle and the text block.

TIP

You can also press the Q key to select the Free Transform tool.

13. In the Tools panel, click the **Rotate and Skew** modifier button, move the pointer over the bottom side of the rectangle until it changes to, and then drag the bottom side of the rectangle slightly to the left to skew the rectangle.
14. In the Tools panel, click the **Line Tool** button, and then, if necessary, click the **Snap to Objects** button to select it.
15. In the Property inspector, set the stroke color to **black** (#000000), set the stroke height to **1,** and set the stroke style to **Solid**, if necessary.
16. On the Stage, draw a line from the fish's lower-left fin to the top of the rectangle, and then draw a line from the fish's lower-right fin to the top of the rectangle. The two lines should be drawn at a slight angle and connect the sign to the fish. See Figure 3-22.

Figure 3-22 Sign attached to the fish

The graphic of the fish pulling the sign is complete. You are ready to animate the graphic using the fly-in-left motion preset. The animation of the fish and sign will start on the Stage to the left of the aquarium tank, move across the tank, and end near the right side of the tank. Before you can apply the motion preset, you must convert the sign, lines, and fish to a symbol.

To add the fly-in-left motion preset to the Katie's Pet Shop banner:

1. In the Tools panel, click the **Selection Tool** button, and then draw a selection marquee around the sign, lines, and fish graphic to select all the objects.
2. Convert the selected objects to a movie clip symbol with the name **fish sign**.
3. Change the zoom magnification to **Fit in Window**. The magnification level of the Stage is reduced.
4. Using the Selection pointer, move the **fish sign** instance to the left of the aquarium tank. The fish sign animation will start to the left of the tank and then will move in to the right side of the tank.
5. In the docked panel group, click the **Motion Presets** button. The Motion Presets panel opens.

   Trouble? If the preset folders are not visible, drag the bottom edge of the preview pane up to reduce the size of the pane and display the preset folders.

6. To the left of the Default Presets folder, click the **Expand arrow** ▶,
if necessary, to expand the list of motion presets, scroll down, and then
click **fly-in-left**. The fly-in-left motion preset is selected, and a preview of
the animation is displayed in the preview pane of the Motion Presets panel.
See Figure 3-23.

Figure 3-23   **Motion Presets panel**

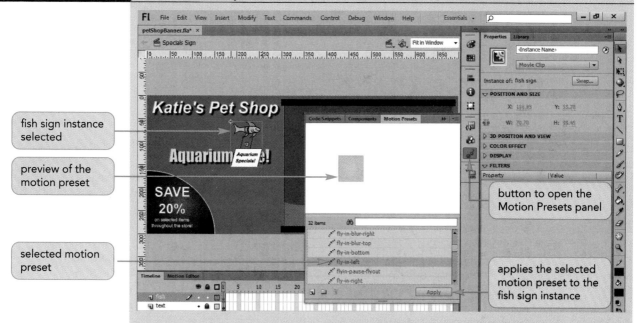

fish sign instance
selected

preview of the
motion preset

selected motion
preset

button to open the
Motion Presets panel

applies the selected
motion preset to the
fish sign instance

7. In the Motion Presets panel, click the **Apply** button. In the Timeline, select
the **fish** layer. The Motion Presets panel closes, and the motion preset is
applied to the selected fish sign instance on the Stage. The fish layer's icon
in the Timeline changes to indicate that a motion tween has been created,
new frames are added to the layer, and the fish sign instance becomes
transparent. See Figure 3-24.

Figure 3-24   **Motion tween created from a motion preset**

motion preset
applied to the
fish sign instance

tween span for
the motion preset

▶ **8.** In the Timeline, drag the end of the tween span to the right to extend the tween span to Frame 40.

▶ **9.** In the Timeline, drag down **Frame 60** of all the layers to select them at the same time.

▶ **10.** On the menu bar, click **Insert**, point to **Timeline**, and then click **Frame** to insert a regular frame. The graphics in all of the layers are displayed through Frame 60. All of the layers exist for 60 frames, and the contents of all the layers will display 20 frames after the end of the tween span.

▶ **11.** In the Timeline, click the **Play** button ▶. The fish and sign move across the Stage from the left to the right, starting quickly and slowing down slightly when they reach the end of the animation.

▶ **12.** Save the banner.

Testing an Animation

After you create a document with animation, you need to test it to make sure it works correctly. To test the document's animation, you have several options. You can play the full animation on the Stage. You can test some or all of the animation by scrubbing the playhead back and forth through the frames, which is useful for testing a short animation sequence. Another way to test a document's animation is to create a SWF file from the document, and then play the file using Flash Player. Finally, you can test an animation in a Web page. Flash publishes the document as a SWF file and also creates a Web page. The Web page with the SWF file is displayed in your computer's default browser. The SWF files created when testing the animation are saved in the same folder as the FLA file.

PROSKILLS

Problem Solving: Testing Your Animations

When you complete an animation, be sure to take that final step of testing the animation. You can use this final step to check for any problems with the animation. First make sure that the animation effectively conveys the intended message. Check that you haven't overused or underused animation effects, as too much action in one animation can turn off the viewer just as much as not enough action. Then confirm that the animation runs smoothly from the first frame through the final frame. You might also ask peers or an intended viewer to review the finished animation so you can get feedback on the content and presentation. During this testing process, you might need to modify the animation to correct problems you or others notice. Each time you make a correction, be sure to test the entire animation again. Thorough testing helps to ensure that the animation provides viewers with the experience you intended.

When you test a document's animation on the Stage, Flash plays only the current scene. To see how all of the scenes work together, you need to test the movie in Flash Player. Each scene then plays in sequence with the animation repeating until you close the Flash Player window.

Testing a Document's Animation

- To test an animation on the Stage, on the menu bar, click Control, and then click Play; or press the Enter key; or click the Play button in the Timeline.
- To test a few frames of animation, scrub the playhead along the Timeline header.
- To test the animation in Flash Player, on the menu bar, click Control, point to Test Movie, and then click in Flash Professional.
- To test the animation in a Web page, on the menu bar, click File, point to Publish Preview, and click Default - (HTML).

You will test the banner document in Flash Player so you can see the animations in both scenes.

To test the document's animation in Flash Player:

1. On the menu bar, click **Control**, point to **Test Movie**, and then click **in Flash Professional**. The movie plays in Flash Player, starting with the Specials Sign scene. You can control how the animation plays.

2. On the Flash Player menu bar, click **Control**, and then click **Loop** to turn off the loop feature and stop the animation from repeating. The animation stops at the current scene.

   Trouble? If the Loop command is not active, continue with Step 3.

3. On the Flash Player menu bar, click **File**, and then click **Close**. Flash Player closes.

The fish animations for both scenes of the banner are complete. In the next session, you will add animations to text blocks using a motion tween, you will modify a motion path, and you will animate plant leaves using a frame-by-frame animation.

Session 3.2 Quick Check

1. Briefly describe the difference between a frame-by-frame animation and a motion tween.
2. What type of animation would you create to have an object move from one side of the Stage to the other?
3. How many objects can you have in a layer with a motion tween?
4. After you create a motion tween in your document, how can you change its properties?
5. How can you make an object in a motion tween move in a more natural way?
6. What is a motion preset?
7. True or False. Each motion preset is created in its own layer.
8. Why is it important to test an animation after you create it?

SESSION 3.3 VISUAL OVERVIEW

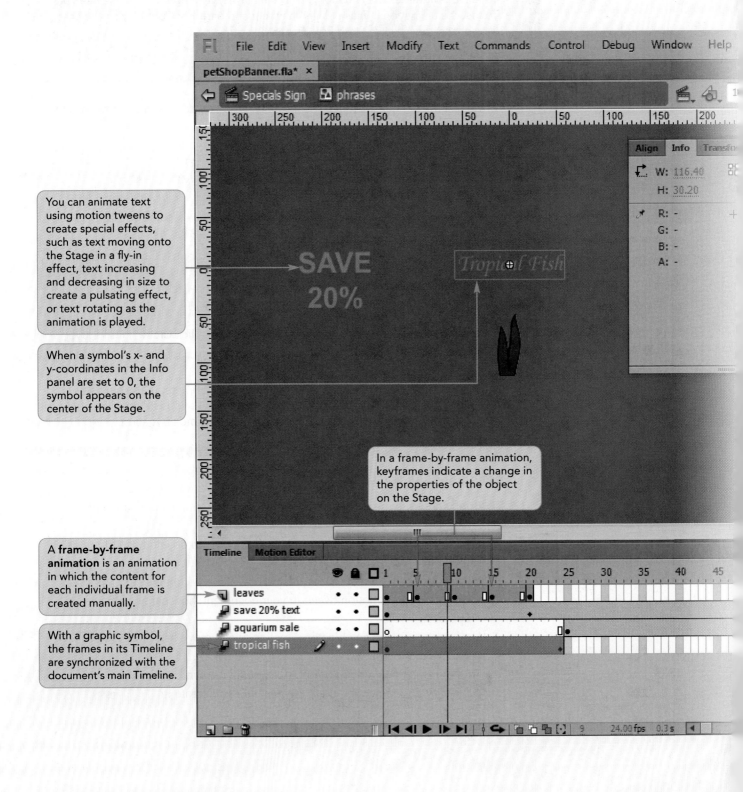

You can animate text using motion tweens to create special effects, such as text moving onto the Stage in a fly-in effect, text increasing and decreasing in size to create a pulsating effect, or text rotating as the animation is played.

When a symbol's x- and y-coordinates in the Info panel are set to 0, the symbol appears on the center of the Stage.

In a frame-by-frame animation, keyframes indicate a change in the properties of the object on the Stage.

A **frame-by-frame animation** is an animation in which the content for each individual frame is created manually.

With a graphic symbol, the frames in its Timeline are synchronized with the document's main Timeline.

TEXT AND SYMBOLS ANIMATION

Click the Registration/Transformation point in the Info panel to display a circle in the lower-right corner. This will display the registration coordinates in the X and Y boxes.

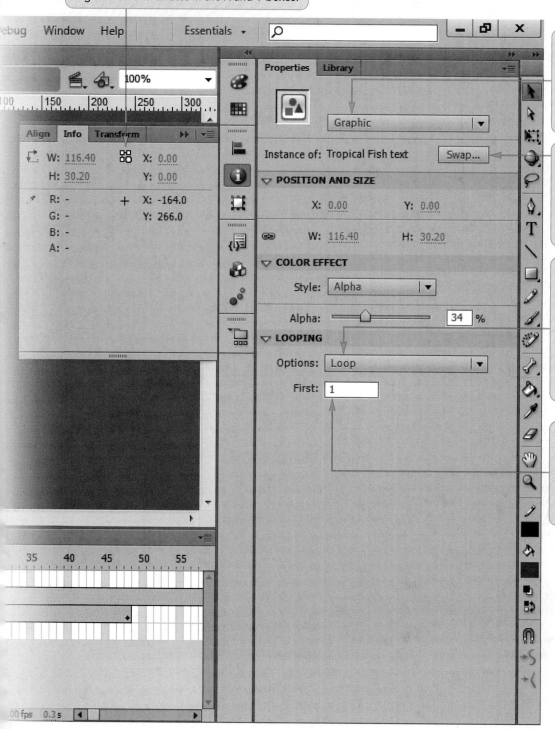

The behavior of a movie clip instance can be changed to Graphic. The graphic instance can be animated so that its Timeline operates in sync with the document's Timeline.

In a motion tween, you can swap the symbol instance with an instance of another symbol. This is helpful when you want to create a similar animation for a different symbol.

Options specify how a graphic instance's animation will play. The **Loop** option plays the animation continuously. The Play Once option plays the animation only one time. The Single Frame option plays only the frame specified in the First frame box.

The Timeline for a graphic instance is synchronized with the main Timeline. The First box specifies which frame within the graphic symbol instance is to be played first.

Animating Text Blocks

You can animate text using motion tweens to create special effects. For example, you can have text move onto the Stage in a fly-in effect, animate text so that it increases and decreases in size to create a pulsating effect, or animate a text block so that it rotates or changes in size as the animation is played. To animate text, you do not need to convert the text block to a symbol. However, if you convert the text block to a symbol and then apply a motion tween, you can have the text block exhibit other changes throughout an animation such as fading in or changing color.

Creating Text Animations

- Select the text block in the first frame of the animation, and then, optionally, convert the text block into a symbol.
- Right-click the text block, and then click Create Motion Tween on the context menu.
- In the last frame of the animation, change the text block's position, size, or orientation or change the symbol instance's tint or transparency.

Adding Animated Text

Based on Aly's notes for completing the banner, shown in Figure 3-25, you need to modify and animate the "SAVE 20% on selected items throughout the store!" text block so that it drops down along a curved path from the pasteboard above the Stage to below the Aquarium Sale! text block on the Stage. The text block will also fade in throughout the animation.

Figure 3-25	Animation plan for the text block

- have text move from the pasteboard above the Stage to the bottom of the Stage following a curved path
- have text fade in

© 2013 Cengage Learning

You will start by adding a new layer and editing the existing text block.

To add a new layer and modify a text block for the text animation:

1. If you took a break after the previous session, make sure the petShopBanner.fla file is open and Flash is reset to the Essentials workspace.

2. In the Timeline, select the **text** layer of the Specials Sign scene, if necessary, and then insert a new layer and rename it **save 20% text**. The new layer appears above the text layer.

   Next, you will cut the text block in the lower-left corner of the Stage, paste it in the new layer, modify the text block, and then reposition it on the pasteboard.

3. In the Timeline, click the **lock** icon 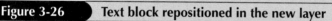 to unlock the text layer.

4. In the Tools panel, click the **Selection Tool** button, click the **pasteboard** to deselect all of the text blocks, and then click the text block in the lower-left corner of the Stage to select it.

5. On the menu bar, click **Edit** and then click **Cut**. The text block is removed and a copy is placed on the Windows Clipboard.

6. In the Timeline, select the **save 20% text** layer, and then, on the menu bar, click **Edit**, and click **Paste in Center**. The text block is placed in the center of the Stage.

7. Double-click the text block so you can edit its contents, and then delete the last two lines of the text block.

8. In the Tools panel, click the **Selection Tool** button, and then reposition the text block on the pasteboard above the Katie's Pet Shop text block, as shown in Figure 3-26.

Figure 3-26	Text block repositioned in the new layer

edited text block positioned on the pasteboard

new layer for the text block

9. In the Tools panel, click the **Text Tool** button T, and then, in the Property inspector, set the font rendering method to **Anti-alias for animation**.

10. In the Timeline, click the oval graphic layer to select it, and then, in the Timeline, click the **Delete** button 🗑 to delete the oval graphic layer. You deleted the oval graphic layer because it will not be part of the text animation.

Next, you will create a motion tween in the save 20% text layer so that the text moves in from above the Stage following a curved path and stops below the Aquarium Sale! text block.

To animate a text block:

1. In the Tools panel, click the **Selection Tool** button ▶.

2. On the pasteboard, right-click the **SAVE 20%** text block, and then click **Create Motion Tween** on the context menu. A tween span is created from Frame 1 through Frame 60.

3. In the Timeline, click **Frame 20** of the save 20% text layer, and then, on the Stage, drag the **SAVE 20%** text block to reposition it below the Aquarium Sale! text block, as shown in Figure 3-27.

Figure 3-27	Ending position for the SAVE 20% text block

text block on the Stage

tween span created from Frame 1 through Frame 60

4. On the Stage, use the Selection pointer ▶, to curve the motion path to the right, as shown in Figure 3-28.

Figure 3-28   **Motion path being modified**

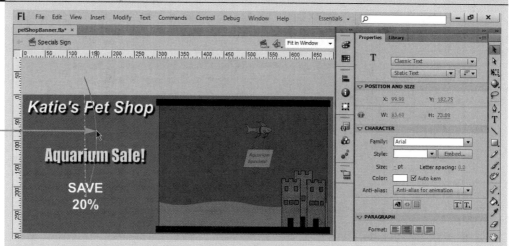

motion path curved slightly to the right

5. Scrub the playhead from Frame 1 through Frame 20. The text block moves from the top of the Stage to below the Aquarium Sale! text block, following a curved path.

6. In the Timeline, select **Frame 20** of the save 20% text layer.

7. In the Tools panel, click the **Subselection Tool** button, and then click the top endpoint of the motion path. The tangent handles on the motion path are displayed. See Figure 3-29.

Figure 3-29   **Motion path tangent handles**

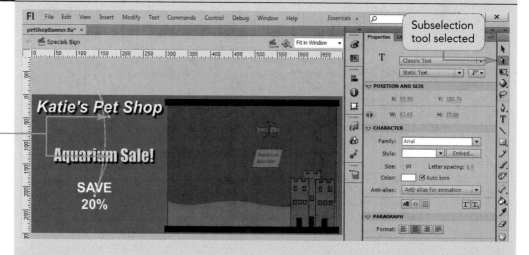

Subselection tool selected

tangent handles

8. On the Stage, drag the top tangent handle to the left of the motion path and drag the bottom tangent handle slightly to the right. The motion path forms an S shape. See Figure 3-30.

Figure 3-30   **Reshaped motion path**

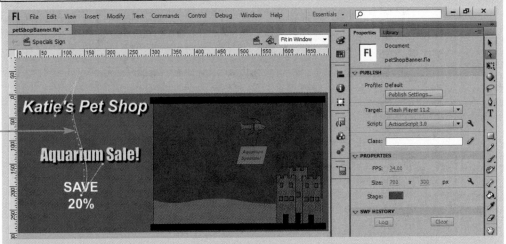

final motion
path shape

9. In the Timeline, move the playhead to Frame 1, and then click the **Play** button ▶. The SAVE 20% text flies in from the pasteboard above the Stage, follows a curved path and stops below the Aquarium Sale! text block.

In addition to flying in from above the Stage, the text block will fade in throughout the animation. To change a text block's transparency or color, it must first be converted to a symbol. To create the fade-in effect, you need to convert the SAVE 20% text block to a movie clip symbol. The text block will not be visible at the start of the motion tween and will become completely opaque by Frame 20 of the motion tween. You will adjust the movie clip's alpha property to create the fade-in effect.

To add a fade-in effect to the SAVE 20% text block:

1. In the Timeline, select **Frame 1** of the save 20% text layer.

2. In the Tools panel, click the **Selection Tool** button ▶, and then click the **SAVE 20%** text block to select it.

3. Convert the SAVE 20% text block into a movie clip symbol named **save 20% text**. The text block is now an instance of a movie clip symbol.

4. In the Color Effect section of the Property inspector, click the **Color styles** button, and then click **Alpha**. The Alpha amount slider and box appear.

5. Drag the **Alpha** slider to the left to set the alpha amount to **0**. The text block becomes transparent. See Figure 3-31.

| Figure 3-31 | Transparent movie clip instance |

6. In the Timeline, click **Frame 20** of the save 20% text layer, and then, on the Stage, select the **SAVE 20%!** text block, indicated by the blue outline.

7. In the Property inspector, drag the **Alpha** slider to the right to set the alpha amount to **100**. The text block becomes opaque at Frame 20.

8. Scrub the playhead between Frame 1 and Frame 20 to see the SAVE 20% text block fade in throughout the animation.

Using Graphic Symbols in Animations

Movie clip instances always start playing from their first frame. With a graphic instance, however, you can specify which of its frames to play first. As a result, if you create an animation with a graphic symbol and then create several instances of the symbol, each instance can have a different starting frame. For example, one instance can start playing at Frame 1 of its Timeline, while another instance can start playing at Frame 20. Using this technique, you can create multiple instances of one graphic symbol in the same scene and have each instance exhibit a different behavior.

Both movie clip and graphic symbols have their own Timelines. With a movie clip symbol, the frames in its Timeline play independently of the document's main Timeline. However, with a graphic symbol, the frames in its Timeline are synchronized with the document's main Timeline. Suppose, for instance, you insert a movie clip instance that contains an animation with 10 frames into a document whose main Timeline has only one frame. Even though the main Timeline contains only one frame, the movie clip's 10 frames still play in their entirety. However, if you insert a graphic instance that contains an animation with 10 frames into a document whose main Timeline has only one frame, then only one frame of the graphic instance will play. If you want all 10 frames of the graphic instance to play, you must extend the length of the document's main Timeline to at least 10 frames. Graphic symbols are useful when you want to synchronize the animations in the symbol to that of the main Timeline.

The Katie's Pet Shop banner should contain an animation that displays the phrases *Tropical Fish* and *Aquarium Supplies* on the Stage. These phrases will appear one at a time and continuously change from one phrase to another. The animation will be placed in several places in the document. You will create the animation only once, as a graphic symbol, and then create several instances of this symbol in the Specials Sign scene.

Using Registration Points

The registration point of a symbol is usually at the center of the symbol, and it can be used to control how the symbol is animated. To align several symbols in an animation, make each symbol's registration point the same. You can set the registration point when you create the symbol in symbol-editing mode by setting the symbol's x- and y-coordinates. You can set the symbol's coordinates in the Info panel, which displays the registration point coordinates when the Registration/Transformation button displays a small circle in its lower-right corner. When the x- and y-coordinates are set to 0, the symbol appears on the center of the Stage.

You will create the animation with the phrases.

To create the phrases graphic symbol:

1. On the menu bar, click **Insert**, and then click **New Symbol**. The Create New Symbol dialog box opens.

2. Type **phrases** in the Name box, click the **Type** button, and then click **Graphic**.

3. Click the **OK** button to create the phrases graphic symbol and display it in symbol-editing mode.

4. In the Tools panel, click the **Text Tool** button ⊤ , and then, in the Property inspector, set the font family to **Monotype Corsiva**, the point size to **24**, the text (fill) color to **white** (#FFFFFF), the font rendering method to **Anti-alias for animation**, and the format to **Align center**.

5. On the center of the Stage, create a single-line text block, and then type **Tropical Fish**.

6. In the Tools panel, click the **Selection Tool** button ▶ to select the text block.

7. In the docked panel group, click the **Info** button 🛈 to open the Info panel.

8. In the Info panel, click the **Registration/Transformation point** button ▦ so that it displays a small circle in its lower-right corner ▦ , if necessary. You can now set the x- and y-coordinates for the symbol.

9. In the Info panel, type **0** in the X box, type **0** in the Y box, and then press the **Enter** key. The text block is centered on the Stage. See Figure 3-32.

Figure 3-32   Settings in the Info panel

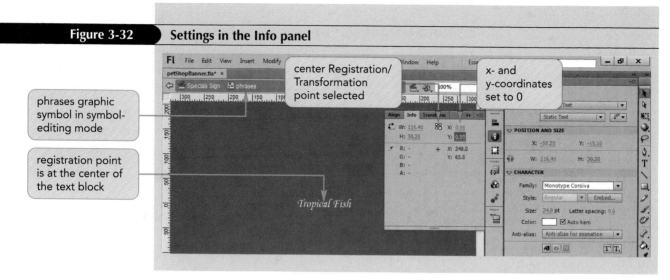

Next, you will convert the text block to a movie clip and duplicate it. To apply a fade-in animation effect, the text block must be a symbol.

To convert the text block to a symbol and duplicate it:

1. With the text block still selected, convert the text block to a movie clip symbol named **Tropical Fish text**, clicking the center registration point in the Convert to Symbol dialog box. The movie clip symbol is created inside the phrases symbol.

2. Open the Library panel, right-click the **Tropical Fish text** symbol, and then click **Duplicate**. The Duplicate Symbol dialog box opens.

3. Type **Aquarium Supplies text** as the name of the duplicate symbol, and then click the **OK** button.

4. On the Edit bar, click the **Edit Symbols** button ⬚, and then click **Aquarium Supplies text**. The symbol opens in symbol-editing mode so you can change the text in this duplicate symbol.

5. In the Tools panel, if necessary, click the **Selection Tool** button ▶ to select it.

6. On the Stage, double-click the text block, and then change the text to **Aquarium Supplies**.

7. In the Tools panel, click the **Selection Tool** button ▶ again.

8. Expand the Info panel, and then set the X and Y values to **0**, if necessary.

You will create the Tropical Fish text animation in the phrases symbol.

To create the Tropical Fish text animation:

1. On the Edit bar, click the **Edit Symbols** button [icon], and then click **phrases**. The phrases symbol opens in symbol-editing mode.

2. In the Timeline, rename Layer 1 to **tropical fish**.

3. On the Stage, right-click the **Tropical Fish text** instance, and then click **Create Motion Tween**. A motion tween is created in Frames 1 through 24.

4. In the Timeline, click **Frame 1**, and then, in the Tools panel, click the **Selection Tool** button [icon], if necessary.

5. On the Stage, select the **Tropical Fish text** instance.

6. In the Property inspector, in the Color Effect section, click the **Style** button, click **Alpha**, type **0** in the Alpha amount box if necessary, and then press the **Enter** key. The Tropical Fish text disappears.

7. In the Timeline, click **Frame 24**, and then, on the Stage, select the instance and set its alpha value to **100**. The Tropical Fish text becomes completely opaque.

8. Press the **Enter** key to play the animation. The Tropical Fish text instance fades in throughout the animation.

   Trouble? If the animation doesn't play, click the Play button in the Property inspector.

You need to create a similar animation for the next phrase. Instead of repeating all of these steps in a new layer, you can duplicate the tropical fish layer. Then, in the motion tween, you can swap the Tropical Fish text symbol with an instance of the Aquarium Supplies text symbol. Finally, you will reposition the frames that contain the Aquarium Supplies motion tween so that the animation for the second phrase starts later than the animation for the first phrase.

To create the tween animation for the Aquarium Supplies text symbol:

1. In the Timeline, right-click the **tropical fish** layer name, and then click **Duplicate Layers**. A copy of the tropical fish layer is created.

2. In the Timeline, rename of the tropical fish copy layer to **aquarium supplies**.

3. In the Timeline, click **Frame 1** of the aquarium supplies layer, and then click the instance of the **Tropical Fish text** symbol at the center of the Stage. You can tell the instance is selected because the Property inspector shows "Instance of: Tropical Fish text."

4. In the Property inspector, click the **Swap** button to open the Swap Symbol dialog box, and then click **Aquarium Supplies text**. See Figure 3-33.

Figure 3-33   Swap Symbol dialog box

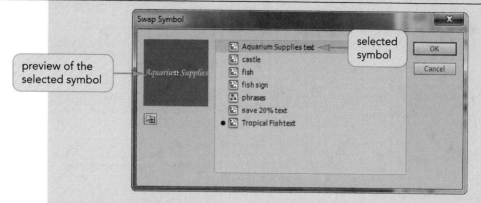

5. Click the **OK** button. The Tropical Fish instance is replaced with the Aquarium Supplies text instance. The text blocks for the two layers overlap on the Stage. You will fix this in the next set of steps.

The animation in the aquarium supplies layer works the same as the one in the tropical fish layer, except that the symbol being animated is the Aquarium Supplies text symbol and not the Tropical Fish text symbol.

Now that both animations are complete, you need to reposition the Aquarium Supplies text animation so that the two animations do not occur at the same time. You want the Tropical Fish text animation to start first, followed by the Aquarium Supplies text animation. This means that the Aquarium Supplies text animation will begin at Frame 25 after the Tropical Fish text animation ends. The Aquarium Supplies text animation's 24 frames will end at Frame 48. You can easily change the location of frames within a layer.

To reposition the frames within the aquarium supplies layer:

1. In the Timeline, select the **aquarium supplies** layer. All of the frames that make up the Aquarium Supplies text animation are selected.

2. Drag the selected frames to the right so that the beginning keyframe starts on Frame 25 of the aquarium supplies layer, as shown in Figure 3-34. The selected frames start on Frame 25 and end on Frame 48.

Figure 3-34   Frames repositioned within the layer

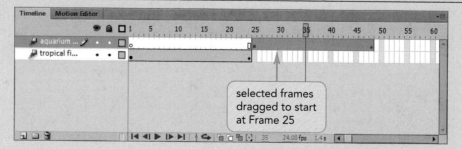

3. In the Timeline, move the playhead to **Frame 1**, and then click the **Play** button 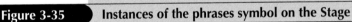. The phrases appear and fade in one after the other as the animation plays.

4. On the Edit bar, click the **Specials Sign** scene to exit symbol-editing mode and return to the Specials Sign scene.

The phrases symbol is complete. You will insert two instances of the phrases symbol onto the Stage for the Specials Sign scene.

To insert the phrases symbol instances and test the scene:

1. In the Timeline of the Specials Sign scene, insert a new layer above the save 20% text layer, rename the layer **phrases**.

2. Drag two instances of the **phrases** symbol from the Library panel to the bottom part of the Stage, as shown in Figure 3-35.

Figure 3-35　Instances of the phrases symbol on the Stage

instances of the phrases symbol

instances added to the selected phrases layer

3. In the Timeline, move the playhead to **Frame 1**, and then click the **Play** button 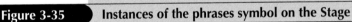. The phrases instances display their animations on the Stage. You will also test the scene's animation in Flash Player.

> **4.** On the menu bar, click **Control**, and then click **Test Scene**. The scene opens in Flash Player, the SAVE 20% text block drops in from above the Stage, and the fish moves across the tank as the phrases instances display the two text blocks in turn.

> **5.** On the Flash Player menu bar, click **File**, and then click **Close**. Flash Player closes.

The two instances of the Phrases symbol display their respective text blocks at the same time. Aly wants you to change one of the instances so that its animation starts at a different frame and is not in sync with the other instance. Because the phrases symbol is a graphic symbol, you can have each instance start at a different frame within its Timeline.

To change the starting frame of the phrases symbol instance:

> **1.** On the right side of the Stage, select the **phrases** symbol instance.

> **2.** In the Property inspector, expand the Looping section, if necessary, type **30** in the First box, and then press the **Enter** key. This instance will start at Frame 30 of the phrases Timeline.

> **3.** In the Property inspector, make sure **Loop** is selected in the Options list. The animation will play continuously.

> **4.** On the menu bar, click **Control**, and then click **Test Scene**. The scene opens in Flash Player, and the phrases instances each start at a different frame as they fade in.

> **5.** On the Flash Player menu bar, click **File**, and then click **Close**. Flash Player closes.

> **6.** Save the banner.

Creating Frame-by-Frame Animations

A frame-by-frame animation requires that the graphic elements of the animation be created for each of its individual frames. If, for example, the animation will have 15 frames, you need to create the content for each of the 15 frames. Some of the content can be the same from one frame to the next, and other content can be slightly modified. As the frames are displayed one after another, the perception of movement is achieved.

To create a frame-by-frame animation, you start with a graphic object in the initial frame. Then, for each place in the animation where the object changes, you add a keyframe. As you add keyframes, you change the position or properties of the graphic object. Depending on the animation, every frame can have a keyframe, or only some frames can have keyframes while the graphic object does not change in the intervening frames. After you have created all of the keyframes, you test the animation.

Decision Making: Choosing an Animation Type

As you create animations, keep in mind that the file size affects the viewer's experience with the animation. You want to use the smallest possible file size to create an animation that effectively conveys your message. In animations, each keyframe indicates a change in action. Because Flash stores the contents of every keyframe, the number of keyframes in an animation affects the document's file size. As you decide which type of animation to create, consider the following information.

- Frame-by-frame animations produce larger file sizes because they tend to have many keyframes.
- Motion tweens have smaller file sizes because Flash stores only the contents of the target object and the property keyframes.

So, to keep file sizes small, choose frame-by-frame animations only when you cannot achieve the same results with motion tweens.

The Fish and Plant scene contains a graphic element that looks like the leaves of a plant. You will convert this graphic into a symbol with a movie clip behavior, and then create a frame-by-frame animation so that the plant's leaves appear to be moving in the tank. The leaves will be animated within the Timeline of the plant symbol and not in the main Timeline of the document. Recall that a movie clip symbol has its own Timeline that is independent of the document's Timeline. By adding the animation in the symbol's Timeline, every instance of the symbol automatically includes the animation. This means that each plant instance you create on the Stage will have the same animation built in as part of the instance.

Before you can create the frame-by-frame animation of the leaves, you need to convert the plant object to a symbol.

To convert the leaves graphic in the Fish and Plant scene to a symbol:

1. On the Edit bar, click the **Edit Scene** button 🎬, and then click the **Fish and Plant** scene to make it the current scene. You will create a symbol of the leaves graphic.

2. In the Timeline, select the **leaves** layer. The leaves graphic on the Stage is selected.

3. Convert the leaves graphic to a movie clip symbol named **leaves**.

You are ready to animate the leaves symbol. You first need to select the symbol from the Library panel so you can edit it to create an animation within its Timeline.

To create a frame-by-frame animation of the leaves symbol:

1. On the Edit bar, click the **Edit Symbols** button 🔷 and then click **leaves**. The symbol opens in symbol-editing mode.

2. In the symbol's Timeline, click **Frame 5**. This is the frame where you want to change the animation. See Figure 3-36.

Figure 3-36   **Leaves symbol in symbol-editing mode**

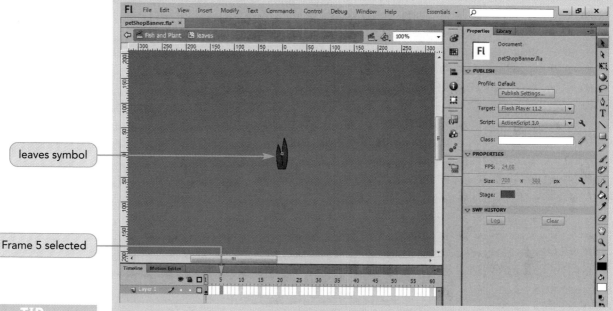

leaves symbol

Frame 5 selected

TIP

You can also press the F6 key to insert a keyframe at the selected location.

3. On the menu bar, click **Insert**, point to **Timeline**, and then click **Keyframe**. A keyframe is inserted in Frame 5 and regular frames are added to Frames 2, 3, and 4 to fill the empty intervening frames. The leaves graphic is automatically copied to all the new frames. See Figure 3-37.

Figure 3-37   **Keyframe added in the Timeline of the leaves symbol**

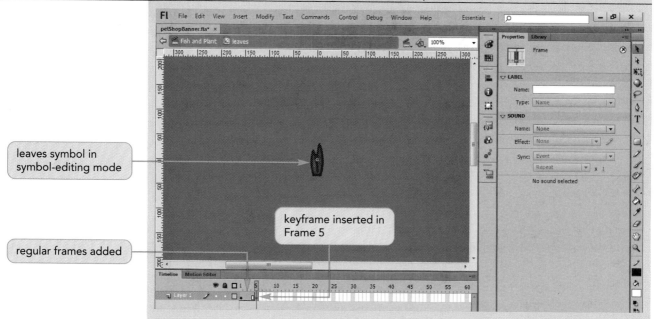

leaves symbol in symbol-editing mode

keyframe inserted in Frame 5

regular frames added

In Frame 5, you will move the tips of the leaves slightly to the right.

4. Change the zoom magnification to **400%**. The magnification level of the Stage increases to make it easier to edit the leaves graphic.

5. In the Tools panel, click the **Selection Tool** button ▶ if necessary, and then click the **Snap to Objects** button 🔲, if necessary, to deselect it.

6. Click another area of the Stage to deselect the leaves, move the pointer over the tip of the right leaf until it changes to ◥⌐, click and drag the tip of the leaf slightly to the right, and then click and drag each of the leaf's sides slightly to the right to reshape them.

7. Repeat Step 6 to reposition the other leaf's tip and sides slightly to the right. See Figure 3-38.

Figure 3-38 **Tips and sides of the plant leaves modified**

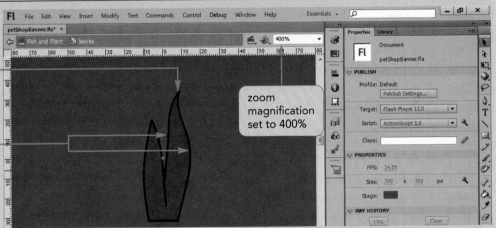

leaf tip moved to the right

leaf sides moved to right

zoom magnification set to 400%

You will repeat this process to add a keyframe every fifth frame and reposition the leaves' tips and sides farther right, then back left, and finally back to their starting positions.

8. Click **Frame 10**, insert a keyframe, and then repeat Steps 6 and 7 to reposition both of the leaves' tips and sides slightly more to the right.

9. Click **Frame 15**, insert a keyframe, and then repeat Steps 6 and 7 to reposition the leaves' tips and sides back slightly to the left.

10. Click **Frame 20**, insert a keyframe, and then repeat Steps 6 and 7 to move the leaves' tips and sides slightly more to the left to almost the same positions where they started in Frame 1.

11. Scrub the playhead through these frames to get a sense of what the animation looks like. This frame-by-frame animation is complete.

12. On the Edit bar, click the **Fish and Plant** scene to exit symbol-editing mode.

13. Change the zoom magnification to **Fit in Window**.

You have created a frame-by-frame animation within the leaves symbol. Because the animation was created within the symbol's Timeline, each instance of the symbol has the same animation. You can, therefore, place several instances of the leaves symbol in the document, and all of the instances will be animated.

The banner should have three animated plants in the lower-left corner of the tank. Because one instance of the animated plant leaves is already on the Stage, you need to add two more instances. The second instance needs to be modified to make it larger than the first, and the third instance needs to be modified so its leaves point to the right.

To create and modify two instances of the animated leaves symbol:

1. In the Timeline, select the **leaves** layer, if necessary.

2. Drag an instance of the **leaves** symbol from the Library panel to the Stage and place it to the right of and slightly overlapping the existing instance.

3. In the Tools panel, click the **Free Transform Tool** button 🔲, and then click the **Scale** button 🔲.

4. On the Stage, drag one corner of the bounding box around the plant outward to make this leaves instance slightly larger than the other instance. See Figure 3-39.

Figure 3-39	Enlarged leaves instance

corner dragged outward to enlarge the selected instance

5. In the Tools panel, click the **Selection Tool** button � to select it, and then reposition this instance as needed to align it with the bottom edge of the other leaves instance.

6. Drag another instance of the **leaves** symbol from the Library panel to the Stage and place it to the right of and slightly overlapping the larger leaves instance.

7. With the third leaves instance still selected on the Stage, on the menu bar, click **Modify**, point to **Transform**, and then click **Flip Horizontal**. The leaves of the instance now face to the right.

8. If necessary, line up the bottoms of the leaves with the bottom part of the Stage. See Figure 3-40.

Figure 3-40   **Three leaves instances arranged on the Stage**

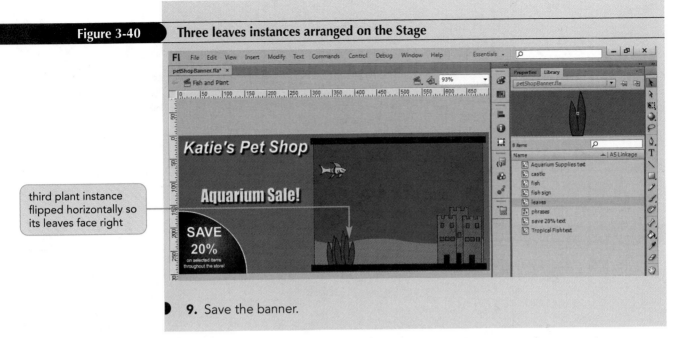

third plant instance flipped horizontally so its leaves face right

9. Save the banner.

Because the leaves symbol's animation is within its own Timeline, you need to test the animation as a SWF file. The movie will appear in a Flash Player window. If you test the animation on the Stage, the leaves symbol's animation will not play. You can also test the animation in a Web page.

To test the animation in a Flash Player window and a Web page:

1. On the menu bar, click **Control**, point to **Test Movie**, and then click **in Flash Professional**. The movie plays in Flash Player, starting with the Specials Sign scene. The leaves display their animation, as shown in Figure 3-41.

Figure 3-41   **Flash Player window with the leaves animation**

leaves animation

TIP

You can also press the F12 key to preview the animation in a Web page in your computer's default browser.

2. On the Flash Player menu bar, click **File**, and then click **Close**. Flash Player closes.

3. On the menu bar, click **File**, point to **Publish Preview**, and then click **Default - (HTML)**. Your computer's default browser opens, and the animation plays in a Web page.

   Trouble? If Internet Explorer restricted this Web page from running scripts or the ActiveX controls warning displays, allow blocked content.

4. Close the browser when you are finished viewing the animation.

5. Save and close the banner.

The animation for the Katie's Pet Shop Web site banner is complete.

INSIGHT

Creating a Shape Tween

Shape tweens are created similarly to motion tween animations. A **shape tween** is an animation that takes one shape and transforms it into another shape. To create a shape tween, you create the graphic content in the beginning and ending frames of the animation, and Flash creates the tweened frames to complete the animation. The object in a shape tween must *not* be a symbol or a grouped object. This is different from a motion tween where the object must be a symbol. A shape tween is indicated in the Timeline by a black arrow and a light green color for the frames. You can also control the shape tween's acceleration and deceleration by changing the Ease value in the Property inspector. The Katie's Pet Shop banner does not require a shape tween.

In this session, you created animations using motion tweens and frame-by-frame animations, and you learned how to create shape tweens. You also learned how to create animations using graphic symbols. Aly is pleased with the completed banner for Katie's Pet Shop Web site and is looking forward to showing it to Katie.

REVIEW

Session 3.3 Quick Check

1. How can you animate a movie clip symbol so that each of its instances automatically contains the animation?

2. List two differences between a movie clip symbol and a graphic symbol.

3. Why do animations within graphic symbols play in a document's main Timeline without the document having to be tested in Flash Player?

4. In a frame-by-frame animation, what kind of frame do you need to have in the Timeline when the content changes on the Stage?

5. True or False. To create a frame-by-frame animation, the object being animated does not need to be converted to a symbol.

6. Can you include regular frames in a frame-by-frame animation? Why or why not?

7. True or False. To create a shape tween, the object being animated must first be converted to a symbol.

Practice the skills you learned in the tutorial using the same case scenario.

PRACTICE

Review Assignments

Data File needed for the Review Assignments: adDraft.fla

Aly wants you to modify the animated ad banner so that a text animation in the first scene includes the words *Tropical*, *Fish*, and *Aquariums!* displayed one after the other. She also wants you to animate the fish and sign so that they move across the Stage. Finally, she wants you to add two instances of an animated fish that swim in opposite directions in a second scene.

1. Open the **adDraft.fla** file located in the Flash3\Review folder included with your Data Files, save the file as **katiesAd.fla** in the same folder, and then reset Flash to the Essentials workspace.

2. Select the entire fish and sign graphics on the Stage, and then convert them to a movie clip symbol named **fish and sign**.

3. Move the fish and sign instance to the pasteboard in the lower-left side of the Stage. Apply the motion preset fly-in-blur-left to the fish and sign instance. Modify the endpoint of the motion path so that the instance will stop on the upper-right side of the Stage just below the title. The fish and sign instance will fly in from the pasteboard on the lower-left side of the Stage onto the upper-right side of the tank. Insert regular frames in Frame 50 of all of the layers to extend them.

4. In the Library panel, make two duplicates of the tropical text symbol, and name one duplicate **fish text** and the other **aquariums text**. Edit the fish text symbol by changing the Tropical text to **Fish**. Edit the aquariums text symbol by changing the Tropical text to **Aquariums!**.

5. Create a new graphic symbol named **text animation**. In symbol-editing mode, change the Layer 1 name to **tropical**. Drag an instance of the tropical text symbol from the Library panel to the center of the Stage. In the Info panel, change its x- and y-coordinates to 0.

6. Using the Selection tool, right-click the tropical text instance and create a motion tween. With the playhead on Frame 24 and the tropical text instance selected on the Stage, set the alpha amount to 0% in the Color Effect section of the Property inspector to make the instance transparent. Hide the contents of the tropical layer.

7. In the Timeline, insert a new layer and name it **fish**, and then drag an instance of the fish text symbol from the Library panel to the center of the Stage. In the Info panel, change its x- and y-coordinates to 0.

8. Right-click the fish text instance and create a motion tween. Move the playhead to Frame 24, if necessary, and then select the fish text instance on the Stage. Set its alpha amount to 0% to make it transparent. Hide the contents of the fish layer.

9. In the Timeline, insert a new layer and name it **aquariums**, and then drag an instance of the aquariums text symbol from the Library panel to the center of the Stage. In the Info panel, change its x- and y-coordinates to 0.

10. Right-click the aquariums text instance and create a motion tween. Move the playhead to Frame 24, if necessary, and then select the aquariums text instance on the Stage. Set its alpha amount to 0% to make it transparent.

11. Select the fish layer and then drag its tween span so that it starts in Frame 24 of the same layer. Drag the tween span in the aquariums layer so that it starts in Frame 47 of the same layer. Unhide the tropical and fish layers and test the text animation. The words appear and fade out in turn. Exit symbol-editing mode.

12. Insert a new layer above the text layer and rename it **animated text**, and then add two instances of the text animation symbol to the Stage. Place one on the lower-left side of the Stage. Place the other on the lower-right side of the Stage and set its First frame to 35 so that its animation starts in Frame 35.

13. In the Library panel, make a duplicate of the small fish symbol and name it **second small fish**, and then edit the second small fish symbol by changing the color of each of its fins to teal (#339966) and the color of its body to light yellow (#FFFF99). Change the color of the yellow bands on the fish body to dark red (#993300). Exit symbol-editing mode.

14. Create a duplicate of Scene 1. Name the duplicate scene **Swimming fish** and rename Scene 1 **Specials sign**.

15. In the Swimming fish scene, delete the fish layer and then insert a new layer and rename it **swimming fish1**.

16. Drag an instance of the small fish symbol to the pasteboard next to the lower-left side of the Stage. Create a motion tween so that the small fish instance moves from the pasteboard on the left side of the Stage to the pasteboard on the right side of the Stage in Frames 1 through 30. The motion tween should end at Frame 30. The small fish will move across the Stage from left to right.

17. Insert a new layer and rename it **swimming fish2**. In this layer, drag an instance of the second small fish symbol to the pasteboard next to the upper-right side of the Stage. Flip the second small fish instance so that it faces to the left.

18. Create a motion tween for this second fish instance so that the fish swims from right to left across the Stage in Frames 1 through 30. You want the second small fish instance to start from the pasteboard on the right side of the Stage, and then swim left across the Stage to the pasteboard.

19. Curve each motion path up slightly and orient the fish to the curved motion paths.

20. Test the animation. The fish and sign move across the banner while the text animation plays, and then the small fish swim across the banner.

21. Submit the finished file to your instructor.

Add motion tweens, a motion preset, and a frame-by-frame animation to a Web site banner.

APPLY

Case Problem 1

Data File needed for this Case Problem: jsBanner.fla

Jackson's Sports Store   Planning is well under way at Jackson's Sports Store for the grand opening celebration. Dan asks Chris to make the banner for the Web site more festive by adding animation to it. Chris started developing the revised banner shown in Figure 3-42 and wants you to add animations for the text and the balloon graphics. The balloons will float up as the text blocks fly in from the sides. You will also add a fly-in animation to the Grand Opening Celebration! text.

| Figure 3-42 | Starting banner for Jackson's Sports Store |

create different colored copies of the balloon and animate them to float up

add a drop in animation to the text block

animate the square graphic to rotate

© 2013 Cengage Learning; iStockphoto.com/Bill Grove

1. Open the **jsBanner.fla** file located in the Flash3\Case1 folder included with your Data Files, and then save the banner as **sportsBanner.fla** in the same folder.

2. Convert the balloon into a movie clip symbol named **balloon1**. Be sure to include both the balloon and the string.

3. Create a duplicate of the balloon1 symbol and name it **balloon2**. Edit the balloon2 symbol to change the color of the balloon to blue (#0000FF). Create another duplicate of the balloon1 symbol and name it **balloon3**. Edit the balloon3 symbol to change its color to green (#00FF00).

4. Create a motion tween with the balloon1 instance on the Stage. Extend the tween span to Frame 50. At Frame 1, move the balloon1 instance to the pasteboard below the Stage and at Frame 50, move the balloon1 instance to the pasteboard above the Stage. The balloon1 instance will move from the below the Stage to the pasteboard right above the Stage. Modify the motion path to curve it slightly to the right.

5. Rename the balloon layer to **balloon1**. Insert a new layer above the balloon1 layer and rename it **balloon2**. In this layer, select Frame 1, and then drag an instance of the balloon2 symbol to the pasteboard below the middle part of the Stage. Create a motion tween so that the balloon moves up to the pasteboard above the Stage. Modify the motion path to curve it slightly to the left.

6. Insert a new layer above the balloon2 layer and rename it **balloon3**. In this layer, select Frame 1, and then drag an instance of the balloon3 symbol to the pasteboard below the left corner of the Stage. Create a motion tween so that the balloon moves up to the pasteboard above the Stage. Modify the motion path to curve it slightly to the left.

7. Insert a layer folder above the balloon3 layer and rename it **balloons**. Move the balloon1, balloon2, and balloon3 layers into the balloon layer folder and then collapse the folder.

8. Add a regular frame to Frame 50 of each of the other layers.

9. Select Frame 1 of the grand opening text layer, convert the Grand Opening Celebration! text on the Stage to a movie clip symbol named **grand opening**, and then move the instance to the pasteboard above the Stage.

10. From the Motion Presets panel, apply the fly-in-top motion preset found in the Default Presets folder to the grand opening instance so that the Grand Opening Celebration! text drops in from above the Stage to its original position below the Sports Store text block. Extend the tween span to Frame 40 of the grand opening text layer. Add a regular frame to Frame 50 of the same layer.

11. Select the grouped object in the lower-left corner of the Stage with the blue square and the word *Sports*. Convert the object to a graphic symbol named **square**.

12. Double-click the square symbol in the Library panel to open it in symbol-editing mode. In the square's Timeline, insert a keyframe in Frame 5. Use the Transform tool with the Rotate and Skew modifier to rotate the square and text graphic to the right so that the *Sports* text is horizontal.

13. Insert a keyframe at Frame 10 and rotate the square and text graphic to the left to its original position. Insert a keyframe at Frame 15 and rotate the square and text graphic to the right so that the text is horizontal. Insert a keyframe at Frame 20 and rotate the square and text graphic to the left to its original position. Insert a regular frame at Frame 25. Return to Scene 1.

14. In the squares layer, insert another instance of the square symbol and place it in the lower-right corner of the Stage. Have the second instance start its animation in Frame 5 of its Timeline.

15. Test the animation. The Grand Opening Celebration! text drops in as the balloons float up and out of sight and the squares at the bottom shift back and forth.

16. Submit the finished files to your instructor.

Add text animations, motion tweens, and a motion preset to a banner.

APPLY

Case Problem 2

Data File needed for this Case Problem: aczDraft.fla

Alamo City Zoo   Janet wants to add animation to the banner that Alex developed promoting the new bear exhibit. The banner should include new animations that highlight the Alamo City Zoo name and display a text message on the banner that promote the zoo's new bear exhibit. You will add two text blocks that will be animated and animate the bear and bear paw graphics. The document Alex provides contains some of the graphic elements that will be used to create the animated banner, as shown in Figure 3-43.

Figure 3-43   Animated banner for Alamo City Zoo

add a text block and animate it to increase in size

duplicate paw print and animate to appear one at a time

animate bear to bounce in and out from the side of the banner

add a text block here and animate it to fade in

© 2013 Cengage Learning

1. Open the **aczDraft.fla** file located in the Flash3\Case2 folder included with your Data Files, and then save the banner as **aczBanner.fla** in the same folder.

2. Delete the bear and bear paw instances from the Stage, and rename Layer 1 as **tracks**.

3. Create a new movie clip symbol named **bear tracks**. In symbol-editing mode, add a horizontal guide at the center of the Stage that aligns with the 0 mark on the left vertical ruler. Add another horizontal guide approximately 40 pixels above the first guide.

4. Drag an instance of the bear paw symbol from the Library panel to the center of the Stage. If necessary, select the instance and set both the X and Y values in the Position and Size section of the Property inspector to 0 so that the center of the instance is exactly centered on the Stage.

5. Insert a keyframe at Frame 5, and then drag another instance of the bear paw symbol so that its center is on the top guide and approximately 30 pixels to the right of the first instance. Insert a keyframe at Frame 10, and then drag an instance of the bear paw symbol so that its center is on the bottom guide and approximately 30 pixels to the right of the second bear paw instance.

6. Insert a keyframe at Frame 15, and then drag an instance of the bear paw symbol so that its center is on the top guide and approximately 30 pixels to the right of the third instance. Insert a keyframe at Frame 20, and then drag an instance of the bear paw symbol so that its center is on the bottom guide and approximately 30 pixels to the right of the fourth bear paw instance. Insert a keyframe at Frame 25, and then drag an instance of the bear paw symbol so that it is positioned on the top guide approximately 30 pixels from the fifth bear paw.

7. Insert a regular frame at Frame 40 of Layer 1 in the Timeline to extend the end of the animation, and then test the animation. The bear paws should be displayed one at a time.

8. In the main Timeline, in the tracks layer, drag an instance of the bear tracks symbol from the Library panel to the Stage. Position the instance so that it is on the left side of the Stage in the bear paw instance's original position. Drag another instance of the bear tracks symbol and place it in the lower-right corner of the Stage. Flip this instance horizontally so that it faces to the left. Reduce each bear track instance to 75% of its original size using the Transform panel.

9. Insert regular frames at Frame 70 of the tracks layer and background layer.

10. Insert a new layer above the tracks layer and name it **bear**. Drag an instance of the bear symbol to the center of the Stage. In the Motions Preset panel, select the wave preset from the Default Presets, and then apply the preset to the bear instance.

11. Insert a new layer above the bear layer and name it **title**. In Frame 1 of this layer, create a classic text block with the text **Alamo City Zoo**. Use a fancy font such as Monotype Corsiva and use a point size such as 24. Select maroon (#660000) for the font color and select Align center for the paragraph format. Center the text block on the banner above the bear tracks and bear.

12. Select the text block and convert it to a movie clip symbol named **title text**. Reduce the size of the text block instance to 50% of its original size. Right-click the title text instance and create a motion tween. Select Frame 20 of the title layer, and then select the title text instance on the Stage. In the Transform panel, change the width of the instance to 150%. Make sure the height value changes proportionally.

13. Insert a new layer and name it **exhibit**. Create a classic text block in Frame 1 of the exhibit layer with the text **Visit the Bear Exhibit!** using the same font family as the title text, and select 30 for the font size. Use a red-orange (#FF3300) for the font color. Center the text block at the bottom of the Stage.

14. Select this text block and convert it to a movie clip symbol named **exhibit text**. Right-click the text instance and create a motion tween. Select Frame 1 of the exhibit layer, and then select the exhibit text instance on the Stage. In the Color Effect section of the Property inspector, select the Alpha style and change the alpha amount to 0%.

15. Select Frame 30 of the exhibit layer, and then select the exhibit text instance. In the Color Effect section of the Property inspector, change the alpha amount to 100%.

16. Test the animation. The title text expands, the bear tracks are displayed one after the other, the bear bounces out and in from the side of the banner, and the exhibit text fades in.

17. Submit the finished files to your instructor.

Create a logo with shape tweens, motion tweens, and a frame-by-frame animation using a graphic symbol.

CHALLENGE

Case Problem 3

Data File needed for this Case Problem: glLogo.fla

G&L Nursery   Amanda and Alice agree that the logo for the G&L Nursery Web site could be enhanced by adding some animation. Amanda wants you to revise the logo by adding a shape tween to the G&L Nursery company name, applying a motion tween to the word *FLOWERS*, and animating the wheel graphics. The banner will look similar to the one shown in Figure 3-44.

Figure 3-44	Animated banner for G&L Nursery

© 2013 Cengage Learning

1. Open the **glLogo.fla** file located in the Flash3\Case3 folder included with your Data Files, and then save the file as **nurseryLogo.fla** in the same folder.

2. Rename Layer 1 to **graphics**, and then insert regular frames so that the layer extends to Frame 60.

3. Insert three layers and name them **g&l**, **nursery**, and **flowers**, respectively.

4. Select the G&L text block. Use the Cut command on the Edit menu to cut the text block. Then, on Frame 1 of the g&l layer, use the Paste in Place command on the Edit menu to place the text in the same relative position as it was in the graphics layer.

5. Select the Nursery text block. Use the Cut command to cut the text. Insert a keyframe on Frame 30 of the nursery layer. In this frame, use the Paste in Place command to place the text in the same relative position as it was in the graphics layer.

6. In Frame 1 of the graphics layer, select the FLOWERS text block in the center of the Stage. Make sure you do not select any other graphics besides the text. Use the Cut command to cut the text block. Then, on Frame 1 of the flowers layer, use the Paste in Place command to place the text in the same relative position as it was in the graphics layer.

7. Use the Scene panel to create a duplicate of Scene 1. Rename Scene 1 copy **wheel animation** and rename Scene 1 **flowers animation**.

⊕ EXPLORE
8. In the flowers animation scene, select the G&L text and use the Break Apart command to break the text apart into individual letters. Use the command a second time to break the letters into filled shapes.

⊕ EXPLORE
9. Insert a keyframe in Frame 30 of the g&l layer. In Frame 1, draw a rectangle over the G&L text block. Use green (#009900) for the rectangle's fill and do not include a stroke. If necessary, turn off Snap to Objects to make it easier to draw the rectangle. The size of the rectangle should be just slightly larger than the text block itself.

⊕ EXPLORE
10. Insert a shape tween between Frames 1 and 30 of the g&l layer. Test the animation. The rectangle should transform into the text *G&L*.

11. In Frame 30 of the nursery layer, select the *Nursery* text and apply the Break Apart command twice to break the text into filled shapes. Insert a keyframe in Frame 50 of the nursery layer.

12. In Frame 30 of the nursery layer, draw a rectangle with a green (#009900) fill and no stroke over the Nursery text block. The rectangle should be slightly larger than the text block. Insert a shape tween between Frames 30 and 50. Test the animation. The rectangle should transform into the text *Nursery*.

13. In the same scene, select the *FLOWERS* text in Frame 1 of the flowers layer and convert the text block into a movie clip symbol named **flowers text**. Right-click the symbol instance and create a motion tween. Select Frame 1 of the flowers layer, and then, if necessary, select the flowers text instance on the Stage. In the Property inspector, select Alpha for the style and change the alpha amount to 0%.

14. Select Frame 30 of the flowers layer, and then, if necessary, select the flowers text instance. Change the alpha amount to 100%.

EXPLORE

15. Select Frame 45 of the flowers layer, and then, if necessary, select the flowers text instance. Press the Left arrow key four times to move the instance four pixels to the left.

16. Preview the motion tween to see the text block fade in gradually and then move slightly to the left.

17. Switch to the wheel animation scene. Select the left oval representing a wheel below the FLOWERS text and convert it to a graphic symbol named **wheel**. Open the wheel symbol in symbol-editing mode.

18. Zoom in on the wheel graphic, and then draw a short horizontal line across the middle of the empty area of the wheel graphic to represent a wheel spoke. Use black as the color and 2 for the stroke height. Draw a short vertical line across the middle of the empty area of the wheel graphic to represent another wheel spoke.

EXPLORE

19. Create a frame-by-frame animation to rotate the wheel, as follows:

   a. Insert a keyframe in Frame 2.

   b. Select the wheel graphic, if necessary, and in the Transform panel enter a value of 30 for the number of degrees to rotate the wheel. (Be sure to press the Enter key to apply the Rotate value.)

   c. Insert another keyframe at Frame 3 and enter 30 for the rotate value in the Transform panel to rotate the wheel again.

   d. Repeat inserting keyframes and entering 30 for the rotate value in the Transform panel for Frames 4, 5, and 6.

   e. Exit symbol-editing mode and return to the wheel animation scene.

20. Delete the original wheel under the *R* of *FLOWERS* on the Stage and add an instance of the wheel graphic symbol in the same position. In the Looping section of the Property inspector, change the First frame of the instance to 3.

21. Switch to the flowers animation scene and replace the two wheel graphics with instances of the wheel symbol. In the Looping section of the Property inspector, set the Looping for each instance to Single Frame and make sure the First frame of each instance is set to 1.

22. Test the animation. Two rectangles transform into the G&L Nursery company name, the FLOWERS text shifts left, and then the wheels rotate.

23. Submit the finished files to your instructor.

Create tween shape and frame-by-frame animations.

CREATE

Case Problem 4

Data File needed for this Case Problem: rcBanner.fla

River City Conservation Society   Brittany and Anissa decide that adding animation to the new banner for the River City Conservation Society's Web site will enhance its appearance. Anissa started to develop the banner shown in Figure 3-45, and you will complete it by adding animation using the shapes she created. You will also create an animation of the key phrases Preserve History, Volunteer Opportunities, Special Tours, and Join Now! on the banner.

| Figure 3-45 | Animated banner for River City Conservation Society |

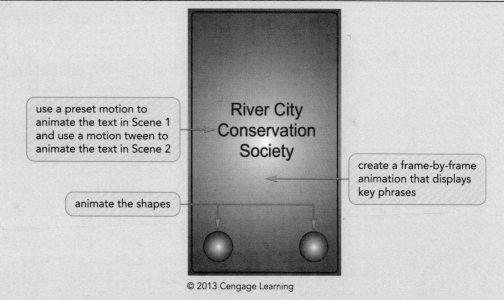

© 2013 Cengage Learning

1. Open the **rcBanner.fla** file located in the Flash3\Case4 folder included with your Data Files, and then save the file as **societyBanner.fla** in the same folder. The document contains some of the graphic elements that will be used to create the animated banner.

2. Use a preset motion to animate the River City Conservation Society text.

3. Animate the circle shapes on the Stage using motion or shape tweens to provide interest. For example, the shapes could move from corner to corner or they can change into triangles. The Timeline should extend to at least 70 frames. (*Hint*: You will need to create each animation in its own layer.)

4. Create a duplicate of Scene 1 in which to create animation for the key phrases. Delete the circle tween layers from Scene 2, and then rename both scenes appropriately.

5. In the second scene, remove the title text motion tween and create a new motion tween to animate the River City Conservation Society text block in the first 20 frames so that it fades in and is positioned in the middle of the Stage.

6. Insert a new layer in which to create a frame-by-frame animation that changes a text block to a different phrase periodically, and then rename the layer with a descriptive name.

7. In Frame 6 of the new layer, create a text block with the words **Preserve History** below the River City Conservation Society text block, using the font family, color, and size of your choice. Convert the text block to a graphic symbol.

8. Edit the graphic symbol to create a frame-by-frame animation that changes the text block to a different phrase periodically between Frame 1 and Frame 30 and extend the Timeline to Frame 60. If necessary, use the Info panel to set x- and y-coordinates to 0. Add the following phrases: **Volunteer**, **Special Tours**, and **Join Now!** (For example, in symbol-editing mode, you can insert a keyframe every tenth frame, edit the text block at each keyframe to change the key phrase, and then insert a regular frame at Frame 60 to extend the symbol's Timeline.) Exit symbol-editing mode.

9. Test the animation.

10. Submit the finished files to your instructor.

ENDING DATA FILES

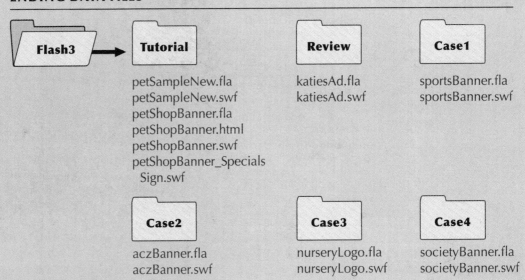

Flash3 → **Tutorial**

petSampleNew.fla
petSampleNew.swf
petShopBanner.fla
petShopBanner.html
petShopBanner.swf
petShopBanner_Specials
 Sign.swf

Review

katiesAd.fla
katiesAd.swf

Case1

sportsBanner.fla
sportsBanner.swf

Case2

aczBanner.fla
aczBanner.swf

Case3

nurseryLogo.fla
nurseryLogo.swf

Case4

societyBanner.fla
societyBanner.swf

Creating Complex Animations

OBJECTIVES

Session 4.1
- Modify motion tweens using the Motion Editor
- Create a mask
- Create an animation using a mask layer
- Create a bitmap animation

Session 4.2
- Animate individual letters within a text block
- Apply 3D rotation effects to movie clips

Session 4.3
- Create nested movie clips
- Test animations using onion skinning
- Create an inverse kinematic animation
- Use the Movie Explorer

Animating with Masks, Onion Skinning, 3D Rotations, and Inverse Kinematics

Case | *Katie's Pet Shop*

Aly wants to develop a second banner for the Katie's Pet Shop Web site to provide Katie a choice of banners. The second banner will consist of two scenes. Aly started the first scene, which will have two fish swimming across the banner. You need to create an animated fish that exhibits more natural movements of its fins and tail, and you will create an animation showing a spotlight effect on the Katie's Pet Shop title text block. The second scene will include a complex animation of the individual letters of Katie's name so that the letters rotate in three-dimensional (3D) space one after another on the screen. The scene will also contain several bitmaps fading in one after the other within a mask.

In this tutorial, you will create an animation using a mask layer and you will modify motion paths using the Motion Editor. You will create complex animations using individual letters and nested movie clips. You will apply a 3D animation to text, and you will create an animation using inverse kinematics with the Bone tool. You will also test an animation using onion skinning. Finally, you will use the Movie Explorer to review the document's elements.

STARTING DATA FILES

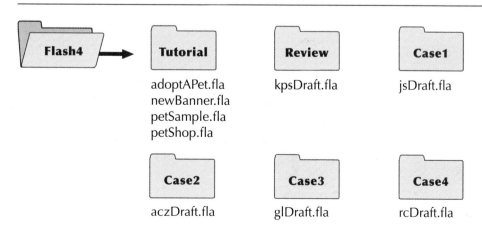

Flash4 → **Tutorial**

adoptAPet.fla
newBanner.fla
petSample.fla
petShop.fla

Review

kpsDraft.fla

Case1

jsDraft.fla

Case2

aczDraft.fla

Case3

glDraft.fla

Case4

rcDraft.fla

Adobe product screenshot(s) reprinted with permission from Adobe Systems Incorporated.

FL 181

SESSION 4.1 VISUAL OVERVIEW

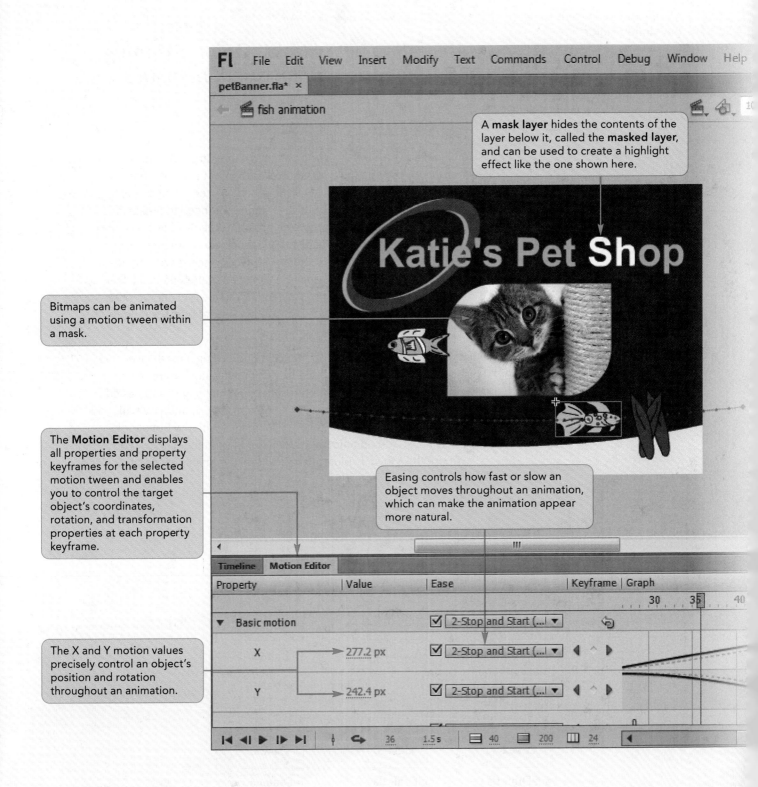

A **mask layer** hides the contents of the layer below it, called the **masked layer**, and can be used to create a highlight effect like the one shown here.

Bitmaps can be animated using a motion tween within a mask.

The **Motion Editor** displays all properties and property keyframes for the selected motion tween and enables you to control the target object's coordinates, rotation, and transformation properties at each property keyframe.

Easing controls how fast or slow an object moves throughout an animation, which can make the animation appear more natural.

The X and Y motion values precisely control an object's position and rotation throughout an animation.

MOTION TWEENS AND MASK LAYERS

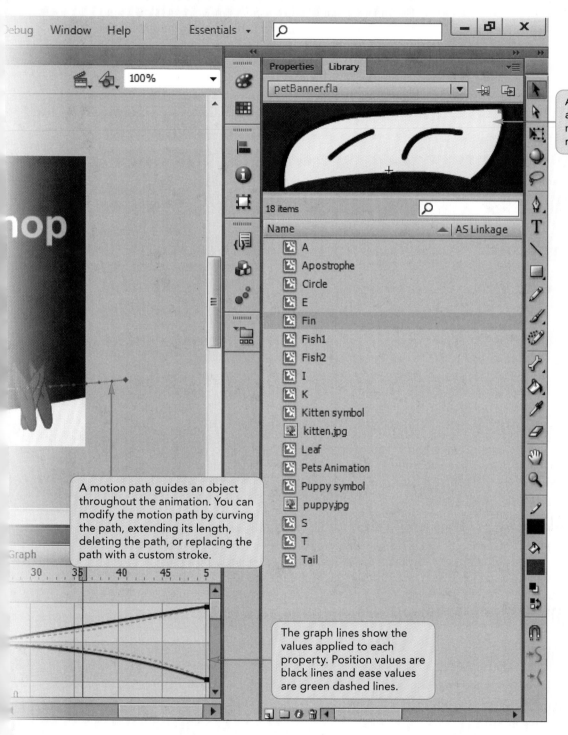

A movie clip containing a motion tween can be nested within another movie clip.

A motion path guides an object throughout the animation. You can modify the motion path by curving the path, extending its length, deleting the path, or replacing the path with a custom stroke.

The graph lines show the values applied to each property. Position values are black lines and ease values are green dashed lines.

Modifying Motion Tweens

As discussed in Tutorial 3, there are several ways to modify a motion path to control how an object is animated and to have it exhibit a more natural movement. To refine a motion tween, you can use the Motion Editor to control an object's position, rotation, and speed throughout the animation.

The alternate banner for Katie's Pet Shop includes a fish swimming across the banner. Aly's notes, shown in Figure 4-1, indicate that the fish needs to move more slowly during the middle part of the animation. You will change the fish's speed by modifying the motion tween's properties using the Motion Editor. Also, a second fish needs to have its fins and tail animated, and the title text needs to have an animated spotlight effect.

| Figure 4-1 | Animation plan for the alternate banner |

- Add an animated spotlight effect so that the spotlight moves back and forth across the title text

- Animate the fish to swim along a curved path
- Orient the fish to the path
- Make the fish swim more slowly in the middle of the animation

- Animate two pet picture bitmaps to create a fade in/fade out effect
- Make this animation independent of the main Timeline
- Use a mask to frame the photos

- Add a second fish
- Animate its fins and tail
- Animate it to swim in the opposite direction of the first fish

© 2013 Cengage Learning

Changing Tween Properties in the Motion Editor

The Motion Editor is based on a feature of the Adobe After Effects program, an industry-standard tool used to create motion graphics and visual effects for video. Using the Motion Editor in Flash, you can control individual tween properties within their own Timeline and modify a motion tween more precisely by setting the values of individual property keyframes, adding or removing property keyframes, and adding or removing filters or color effects. The Motion Editor displays the values of a motion tween's properties both numerically and graphically to make it simpler to change the properties and create complex animations. In addition to controlling an object's position and rotation throughout a motion tween, you can use the Motion Editor to change the object's ease value, which makes the object move faster or slower throughout the animation. You can also add preset eases to a motion tween to modify its properties.

PROSKILLS

Decision Making: Deciding When to Use the Motion Editor

Decision making is the process of choosing between alternative courses of action. When creating a tween, you need to decide the best way to create and modify the animation. This requires determining the level of complexity you want to use for the animation, and then determining the best method for creating it. For most standard or simple tweens such as animating a fish to move across the Stage, you can create and modify the animation using the Timeline and tools from the Tools panel. For more complex animations in which you modify various properties of the animated object at different points in the tween span, consider using the Motion Editor.

With the Motion Editor, you can change the position, scale, color, or ease attributes of the animated object at multiple frames within the tween span. For example, you should use the Motion Editor if you need to animate a fish to increase in size throughout part of the tween span as its transparency changes and exhibit a filter effect during certain frames. You can also use the Motion Editor to precisely control how an animated object starts and stops by selecting a preset ease and then modifying the ease effect before you apply it to the tweened object. After you test the animation, you can make additional adjustments to the ease effect in the Motion Editor to obtain the desired animation effect. As you modify a tweened object's properties in the Motion Editor, you can test the effect of the changes by playing the animation in both the Timeline and the Motion Editor.

Careful review of end results you want to achieve with an animation will help you decide on the best way to accomplish those goals.

You will use the Motion Editor to explore and modify a sample animation that Aly created for another project.

To view a motion tween's properties in the Motion Editor:

1. Open the **petSample.fla** file located in the Flash4\Tutorial folder included with your Data Files, save it as **petRevised.fla** in the same folder, and then reset Flash to the Essentials workspace.

2. Press the **Enter** key to play the animation. The Katie's text block moves into the Stage and the Annual Sale text fades in.

3. In the Timeline, move the playhead to **Frame 1**, and then select the **katies** layer.

4. In the Timeline and Motion Editor panel group, click the **Motion Editor** tab to open the panel. You want to resize the Motion Editor to see more of the panel.

5. Point to the top edge of the Timeline and Motion Editor panel group until the pointer changes to ↕, and then drag up to increase the size of the panel group, as shown in Figure 4-2.

Figure 4-2   **Timeline and Motion Editor panel group being resized**

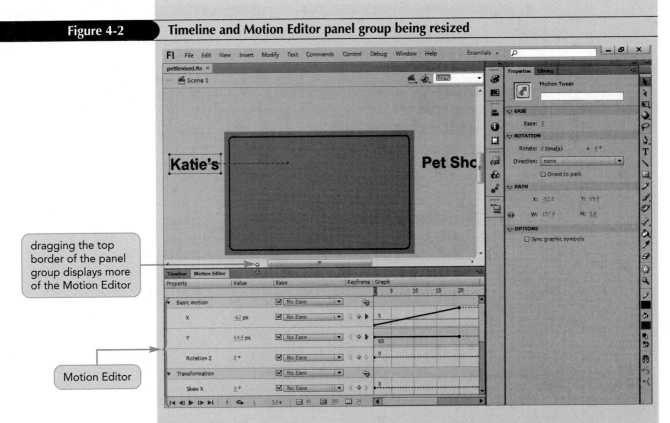

dragging the top border of the panel group displays more of the Motion Editor

Motion Editor

▶ **6.** In the Motion Editor, scroll up to the Basic motion category, if necessary, and then in the Property column, click the **expand arrow** ▶ next to the Basic motion category to expand the category, if necessary. The Motion Editor displays the X, Y, and Rotation Z properties for the motion tween, along with their associated values in the Value column. At Frame 1, the X property value is -62 px, which places the Katie's text block to the left of the Stage.

▶ **7.** In the Motion Editor, in the Graph column, scroll to the right and move the playhead to **Frame 20**. The Katie's text block moves to the center of the Stage, and the X property value in the Motion Editor changes to 135 px. See Figure 4-3.

Figure 4-3	Basic motion values in the Motion Editor

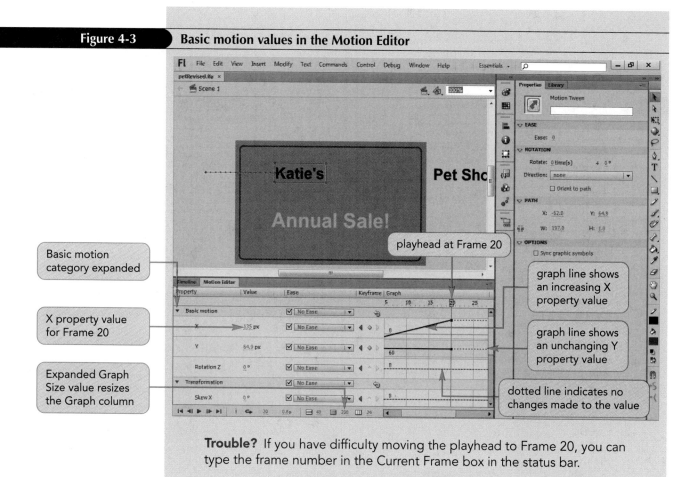

Basic motion
category expanded

X property value
for Frame 20

Expanded Graph
Size value resizes
the Graph column

playhead at Frame 20

graph line shows
an increasing X
property value

graph line shows
an unchanging Y
property value

dotted line indicates no
changes made to the value

Trouble? If you have difficulty moving the playhead to Frame 20, you can type the frame number in the Current Frame box in the status bar.

As you can see in Figure 4-3, in the Graph column of the Motion Editor, the X property curve is a straight line with an upward slope because the X property value increases from -62 pixels in Frame 1 to 135 pixels in Frame 20. The Y property curve is a flat line because the text block does not change vertical position. The Rotation Z property contains a dashed line because no changes have been made to the rotation value.

You will create a new motion tween and modify it using the Motion Editor.

To create and modify a motion tween:

1. On the Stage, right-click the **Pet Shop** text block, and then click **Create Motion Tween** on the context menu. The Graph column of the Motion Editor displays dashed lines because no motion paths have been created yet.

2. Make sure the playhead is on **Frame 20**, and then, if necessary, in the Graph column, scroll to the left until Frame 20 is at the right side of the column.

3. In the Motion Editor, in the Keyframe column of the X property, click the **Add or Remove keyframe** icon ⌃ to add a property keyframe. Flat lines appear in the Graph column for the X and Y property curves. See Figure 4-4.

| Figure 4-4 | Property curves added in the Graph column |

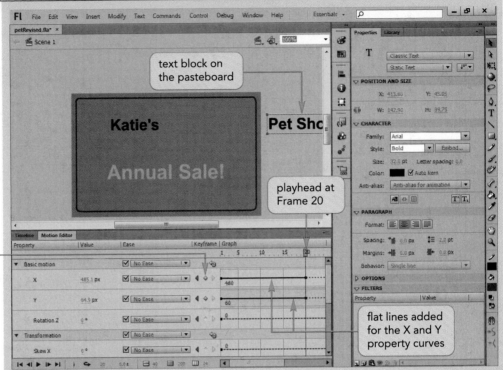

adds a property keyframe at the current frame

text block on the pasteboard

playhead at Frame 20

flat lines added for the X and Y property curves

4. In the Value column, drag the X position value to the left to change the value to **265**. A downward slope is added to the property curve in the Graph column, reflecting the new X property value. The Pet Shop text block moves to the center of the Stage. See Figure 4-5.

| Figure 4-5 | X position changed |

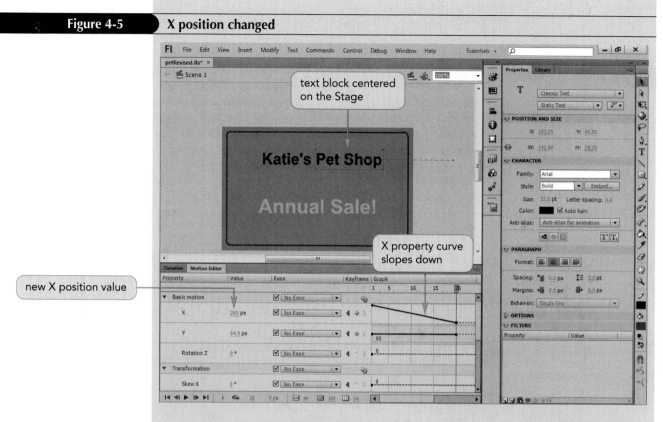

Trouble? If you reach the left side of the screen before reaching 265, release the mouse button, and then repeat Step 4 to continue to reduce the X position value.

▶ 5. Click the **Timeline** tab, move the playhead to **Frame 1**, and then press the **Enter** key to play the animation. The Pet Shop text block moves from the right of the Stage as the Katie's text block moves in from the left of the Stage.

▶ 6. Save and close the petRevised.fla file.

Next, you will use the Motion Editor to modify the motion tweens for the fish in the banner for Katie's Pet Shop. Based on Aly's notes, you need to add easing to the motion tweens to make the fish slow down in the middle of the animation. You will add a preset ease to the motion tweens for both fish instances.

To add an easing effect to a motion tween:

▶ 1. Open the **newBanner.fla** file located in the Flash4\Tutorial folder included with your Data Files, save the document as **petBanner.fla**, and then reset Flash to the **Essentials** workspace.

▶ 2. In the petBanner.fla document, click **Frame 1** of the fish1 layer to select its motion tween.

▶ 3. Click the **Motion Editor** tab to display the Motion Editor, and then scroll to the last row to view the Eases category.

▶ 4. In the Eases category, click the **Add Color, Filter or Ease** button 🔁, and then click **Stop and Start (Slow)** in the menu that opens. The preset ease is available and can be added to the motion tween.

5. In the Motion Editor, scroll down to see the preset ease property, value, and graph in the Eases category. See Figure 4-6.

Figure 4-6   **Stop and Start (Slow) ease added to the Eases category**

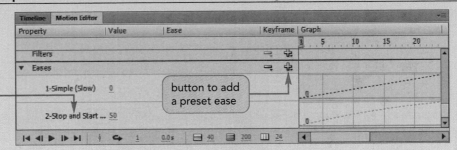

preset ease added to the motion tween

button to add a preset ease

6. In the Motion Editor, scroll up as needed to display the Basic motion category.

7. In the Basic motion category, click the first **Selected Ease** button, and then click **2-Stop and Start (Slow)** to add the preset ease to the motion tween's X and Y properties. The ease appears as green dashed lines next to the X and Y property curves in the Graph column. See Figure 4-7.

Figure 4-7   **Ease curves in the Graph column**

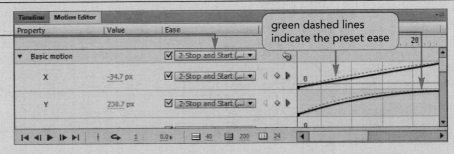

preset ease added to the motion tween's X and Y properties

green dashed lines indicate the preset ease

8. Click the **Timeline** tab to display the Timeline, and then click **Frame 50** of the fish2 layer to select its motion tween.

9. Click the **Motion Editor** tab to display the Motion Editor, and then scroll down to view the Eases category.

10. In the Eases category, click the **Add Color, Filter or Ease** button ⊞, and then click **Stop and Start (Slow)**. The preset ease is now available.

11. In the Motion Editor, scroll up to view the Basic motion category.

12. In the Basic motion category, click the first **Selected Ease** button, and then click **2-Stop and Start (Slow)** to add the ease preset to the motion tween's X and Y properties. The Stop and Start (Slow) ease has been added to both motion tweens.

13. Click the **Timeline** tab to display the Timeline, move the playhead to **Frame 1**, and then press the **Enter** key to play the animation. The fish swims across the Stage as before, but now it slows down in the middle of the motion tweens.

14. Save the banner.

Using a Mask Layer in an Animation

You can create animations that incorporate a mask layer to create special effects. A mask layer can also be used with motion tweens and frame-by-frame animations. For example, you can create an animation in a mask layer to show different areas of a masked layer throughout the animation.

INSIGHT

Creating an Animated Picture Masked with Text

You can create an interesting effect with mask layers by using text for the mask object and having another object such as a picture show through the text. With this technique, the text acts like a window for the content behind it. For example, if you animate a picture on the masked layer, as the picture moves, only the parts of the picture that are behind the text will be visible.

To create an animation using a mask layer, you create the object to be masked in one layer and add a new layer above it that will contain the mask. When you change the top layer to a mask layer, the bottom layer becomes the masked layer. The masked layer is indented below the mask layer in the Timeline.

The object in the mask layer can be a filled shape, such as an oval or a rectangle. It can also be text or an instance of a symbol. The fill of the shape in the mask layer will reveal the content in the underlying masked layer. This shape determines what part of the masked layer's content is visible. The color of the shape is irrelevant because its color is not displayed. You can animate either the object in the mask layer or the object in the masked layer. For example, you can animate an oval shape in the mask layer so that it moves over some stationary text in the masked layer. This technique creates a spotlight effect, as shown in Figure 4-8.

Figure 4-8   **Masked layer example**

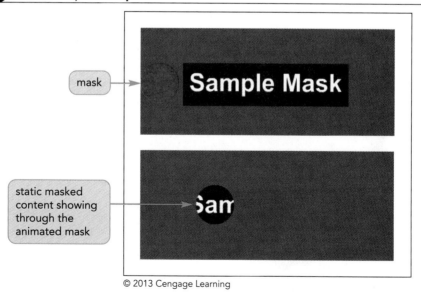

mask

static masked content showing through the animated mask

© 2013 Cengage Learning

If you animate the object in the masked layer while the object in the mask layer remains stationary, you can create a different type of effect. For example, you can create a scrolling text effect by drawing a rectangle in the mask layer and then animating a block of text in the masked layer. As the text block moves across the mask, only the portion of the text behind the rectangle is visible, as shown in Figure 4-9.

Figure 4-9   **Masked layer with scrolling text effect**

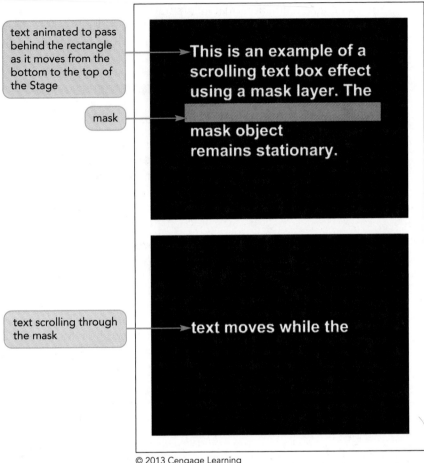

text animated to pass behind the rectangle as it moves from the bottom to the top of the Stage

mask

This is an example of a scrolling text box effect using a mask layer. The

mask object
remains stationary.

text scrolling through the mask

text moves while the

© 2013 Cengage Learning

When you first create a mask layer, Flash locks both the mask and the masked layers. These layers must be locked to preview the effects of the mask on the Stage. When the layers are locked, the mask layer object is not visible, and only the content in the masked layer that is behind the mask layer object becomes visible. You need to unlock the layers to work with the objects on both layers, and then lock the layers again to test the animation.

REFERENCE

Creating a Mask Layer Animation

- Select the layer whose content will be masked.
- In the Timeline, click the New Layer button.
- Add content to the new layer that will be used as the mask.
- Right-click the new layer's name, and then click Mask.
- Unlock the layers and create an animation in either the mask layer or the masked layer.
- Lock the layers, and then test the animation.

You will explore a sample mask layer animation Aly has created for an upcoming pet adoption event.

To explore the mask layer animation in the Adopt a Pet banner:

▶ 1. Open the **adoptAPet.fla** file located in the Flash4\Tutorial folder included with your Data Files, and then reset the Essentials workspace. The adoptAPet.fla document opens, but the mask layer content is not visible because the layer is locked.

▶ 2. In the Timeline, unlock the mask layer and hide the white text layer. The mask layer is unlocked, and you can see its contents. See Figure 4-10. The content of the mask layer is just a motion tween animation of a circle shape. As the circle moves across the Stage, different parts of the underlying white Adopt a Pet text become visible.

Figure 4-10 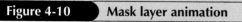 **Mask layer animation**

mask object

mask layer

masked layer

iStockphoto.com/Sarah Salmela

▶ 3. In the Timeline, show the white text layer.

▶ 4. In the Timeline, lock the mask layer. When a mask layer is locked, the masking effect is visible on the Stage.

▶ 5. Press the **Enter** key to play the animation. The part of the white text layer under the circle becomes visible as the circle moves across the Stage.

▶ 6. Close the adoptAPet.fla document without saving any changes.

Creating an Animation Using a Mask Layer

Aly's notes for the Katie's Pet Shop banner shown in Figure 4-1 indicate that the Katie's Pet Shop text block should have a spotlight effect. You will create a spotlight effect where the spotlight moves across the Katie's Pet Shop text block. To do this, you need to create a mask layer animation. You will start by creating a duplicate of the title text block.

To add layers for the mask layer animation:

▶ **1.** On the Stage, click the **Katie's Pet Shop** text block to select it. You will create a duplicate of this text block.

▶ **2.** On the menu bar, click **Edit**, and then click **Copy**. The text is copied to the Windows Clipboard.

▶ **3.** In the Timeline, insert a new layer above the ovals layer, and then rename the new layer **gray text**.

▶ **4.** On the menu bar, click **Edit**, and then click **Paste in Place** to paste the text block in the new gray text layer in the same relative position as it is in the title layer.

▶ **5.** In the Timeline, hide the title layer. The layer's content is no longer visible, although you cannot tell because the pasted text block is still visible.

▶ **6.** On the Stage, make sure the text block is selected, and then, in the Property inspector, change its text fill color to **gray** (#999999).

▶ **7.** In the Timeline, lock the gray text layer, and then show the title layer. The text in the title layer will provide the white text in the spotlight effect.

▶ **8.** In the Timeline, insert a new layer above the title layer, and then rename the new layer **title mask**. The title mask layer will be the mask layer and will contain a motion tween of a circle.

▶ **9.** In the Timeline, right-click the **title mask** layer name, and then click **Mask** on the context menu. The layer changes to a mask layer and the title layer changes to a masked layer indented below the title mask layer. Both layers are locked. See Figure 4-11.

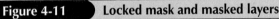

Figure 4-11   **Locked mask and masked layers**

mask and masked layers are locked

Now you need to create a motion tween of a circle and have it move across the text. You will draw the circle shape, convert it to a symbol, and then create a motion tween.

To create the mask layer animation:

1. In the Timeline, unlock the title mask layer, and then click **Frame 1** of the title mask layer. You will draw a circle in the title mask layer to represent the spotlight.

2. In the Tools panel, click the **Oval Tool** button to select the Oval tool, and then set the fill color to **white** (#FFFFFF) and the stroke color to **no color**.

3. On the Stage, draw a circle to the left of the letter K in the Katie's Pet Shop text block. See Figure 4-12.

Figure 4-12   Circle drawn in the title mask layer

4. In the Tools panel, click the **Selection Tool** button, and then, on the Stage, select the circle.

5. Convert the circle to a movie clip symbol named **Circle**. You will create a motion tween for the circle instance.

6. On the Stage, right-click the **Circle** instance, and then click **Create Motion Tween** on the context menu. A motion tween is created in the title mask layer.

   You will create a highlight effect by moving the circle to the right of the title text block and then back to its starting point.

7. Click **Frame 50** of the title mask layer, and then drag the **Circle** instance to the right of the last letter of the text block.

8. Select **Frame 100** of the title mask layer, and then drag the **Circle** instance back to the left of the first letter in the text block. Frame 100 represents the end of the motion tween where the circle moves back to its starting point. See Figure 4-13.

Figure 4-13 **Circle instance at the end of the motion tween**

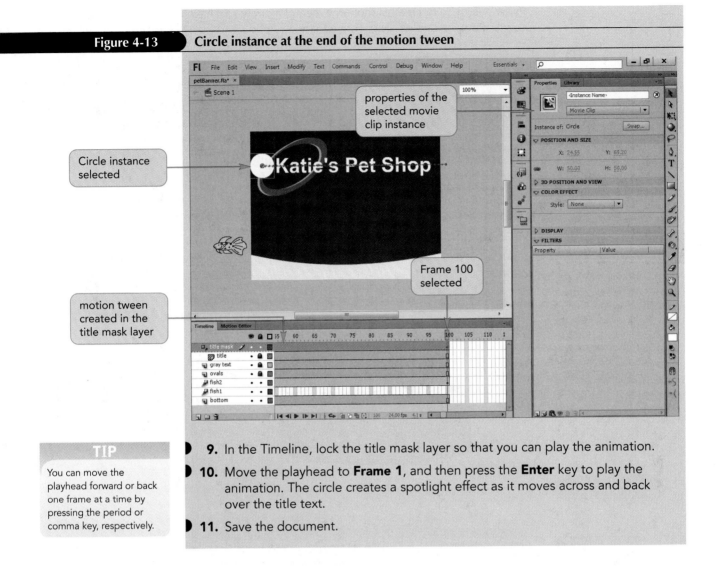

TIP

You can move the playhead forward or back one frame at a time by pressing the period or comma key, respectively.

9. In the Timeline, lock the title mask layer so that you can play the animation.

10. Move the playhead to **Frame 1**, and then press the **Enter** key to play the animation. The circle creates a spotlight effect as it moves across and back over the title text.

11. Save the document.

Animating Bitmaps

You animate an imported bitmap the same way you animate any other object. For instance, you can create a motion tween that causes the bitmap to move, rotate, change in size (scale), or fade in or out. To animate a bitmap in a motion tween, you first need to convert the bitmap instance on the Stage to a symbol.

Aly's instructions for the banner shown in Figure 4-1 indicate that the kitten.jpg and puppy.jpg bitmaps are part of an animation where one bitmap appears and then fades away, while the second bitmap fades in over the first. To accomplish the fade effect, you change the alpha amount for each instance. The **alpha amount** controls the transparency of an image. The alpha amount is a percentage from 0 to 100. An alpha amount of 0% makes the object completely transparent; an alpha amount of 100% makes the object completely opaque, which means it has no transparency. A motion tween that starts the object at an alpha amount of 100% and changes it at the end of the tween to 0% makes the object appear to fade out of view. You reverse the amounts to make the object appear to fade into view.

Because this animation should be independent of any other animation that might be added to the banner, you will create a movie clip symbol that contains the pet pictures animation within its own Timeline, independent of the main document's Timeline. To create a separate Timeline for the bitmap animation, you will make a duplicate of the current scene, and then rename the scenes.

To create a duplicate scene:

1. On the menu bar, click **Window**, point to **Other Panels**, and then click **Scene**. The Scene panel opens, showing one scene named Scene 1. You will create a duplicate scene.

2. In the Scene panel, click the **Duplicate Scene** button . A duplicate scene is created named Scene 1 copy.

3. In the Scene panel, double-click **Scene 1** and type **fish animation** to rename the scene. Rename Scene 1 copy as **bitmaps animation**. The scenes are renamed with more meaningful names.

4. In the Timeline, in the bitmap animations scene, delete the fish1, fish2, gray text, and title mask layers. These layers will not be used in this scene. See Figure 4-14.

Figure 4-14	The bitmaps animation scene

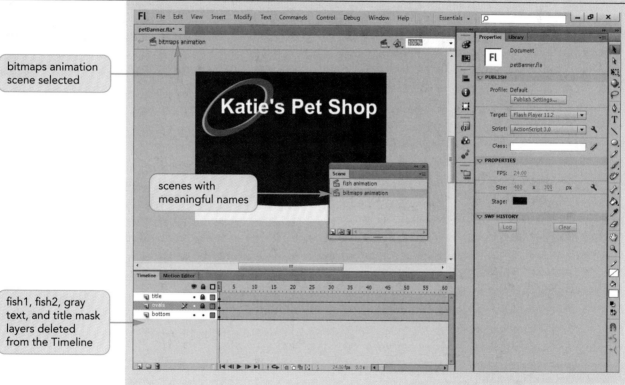

bitmaps animation scene selected

scenes with meaningful names

fish1, fish2, gray text, and title mask layers deleted from the Timeline

5. Close the Scene panel.

You will create the pet pictures animation in the bitmaps animation scene.

To create the pet pictures animation:

1. Make sure the bitmaps animation scene is the current scene, and then create a new movie clip symbol named **Pets Animation**. The new movie clip symbol opens in symbol-editing mode.

2. Drag an instance of the **kitten.jpg** bitmap from the Library panel to the Stage.

TIP

You can press the Ctrl+T keys to open or close the Transform panel; you can press the Ctrl+I keys to open or close the Info panel.

3. On the docked panel group, click the **Transform** button 🔲 to open the Transform panel.

4. In the Transform panel, click the **Constrain** button 🔗, if necessary, to change it to 🔗.

5. In the Transform panel, click the **Scale Width** value, type **50** in the Scale Width box, and then press the **Enter** key. The width and height of the bitmap is reduced to 50%.

6. Click the **Info** tab to open the Info panel, click the **Registration/Transformation point** button 🔳, if necessary, to change it to 🔳 and then change the X and Y values to **0**. The selected bitmap instance is centered within the editing window. See Figure 4-15.

Figure 4-15	The kitten.jpg bitmap instance centered

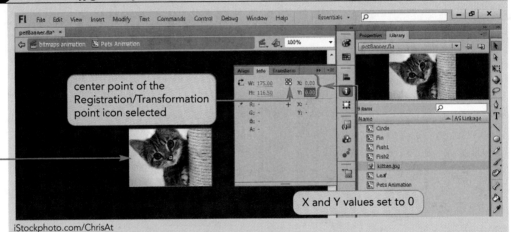

center point of the Registration/Transformation point icon selected

centered bitmap

X and Y values set to 0

iStockphoto.com/ChrisAt

7. Convert the **kitten.jpg** bitmap instance on the Stage to a movie clip symbol named **Kitten symbol**, and then click the center registration point in the Registration icon 🔳, if necessary, as shown in Figure 4-16. The registration point specifies what part of the symbol is used for alignment. Because the kitten.jpg and the puppy.jpg images need to be in the same position on the Stage, you specify a point in the kitten image to use for alignment when you position the puppy image. See Figure 4-16.

Figure 4-16	Convert to Symbol dialog box

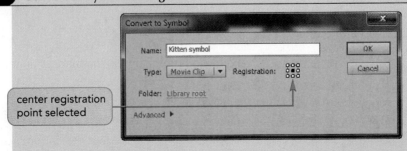

center registration point selected

8. Click the **OK** button. The Kitten symbol is created, and you can use it in a motion tween animation.

9. Close the Info panel, if necessary.

In the animation, the kitten.jpg bitmap fades out of view after a period of time, and then the puppy.jpg bitmap fades in. Aly provides the sketch, shown in Figure 4-17 that outlines how the animation should occur. Based on the sketch, the animation of the pictures takes place over six seconds. During the first two seconds, the kitten.jpg picture is displayed. During the third second, the kitten.jpg picture fades out as the puppy.jpg picture fades in. Then, during the next two seconds, the puppy.jpg picture is displayed. Finally, during the last second, the puppy.jpg picture fades out and the kitten.jpg picture fades back in. Because the frame rate is 24 frames per second, each second requires 24 frames. Converting these time specifications to frame numbers means that you need keyframes at Frames 1, 48, 72, 120, and 144. These are the frames where a change occurs from the previous frames.

| Figure 4-17 | Fade animation plan |

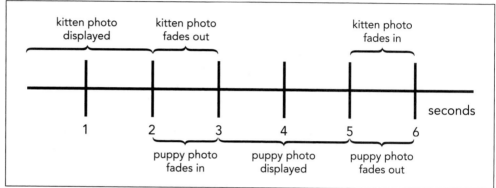

© 2013 Cengage Learning

You will insert keyframes for the kitten animation, create a motion tween, and then set the alpha amounts for the kitten instance to control the transparency, which creates the fade-in and fade-out effects.

To create the kitten animation:

1. In the Timeline, rename Layer 1 as **kitten**, and then select the **Kitten symbol** instance on the Stage.

2. In the Color Effect section of the Property inspector, click the **Style** button, and then click **Alpha**. The Alpha setting appears in the Property inspector.

3. If necessary, drag the **Alpha** slider to the right until **100** appears in the % box. The Kitten symbol instance is fully opaque with the alpha amount set to 100%.

4. In the Timeline, right-click **Frame 1** and then click **Create Motion Tween**. The motion tween span ends at Frame 24.

5. In the Timeline, drag the right border of Frame 24 to the right to extend the motion tween span to Frame 144. The Timeline will scroll to the right as you drag. You extended the span so that the animation will last six seconds.

6. In the kitten layer, right-click **Frame 48**, point to **Insert Keyframe** on the context menu, and then click **Color**. A property keyframe is added to the motion tween, so you can set the starting alpha amount for the motion tween.

7. Select the **Kitten symbol** instance on the Stage, and then, in the Color Effect section of the Property inspector, make sure the alpha amount remains set to 100%.

8. In the Timeline, click **Frame 72**, select the **Kitten symbol** instance on the Stage, and then, in the Property inspector, set the alpha amount to **0%**. The kitten instance is transparent. See Figure 4-18.

Figure 4-18 | **Transparent Kitten symbol instance**

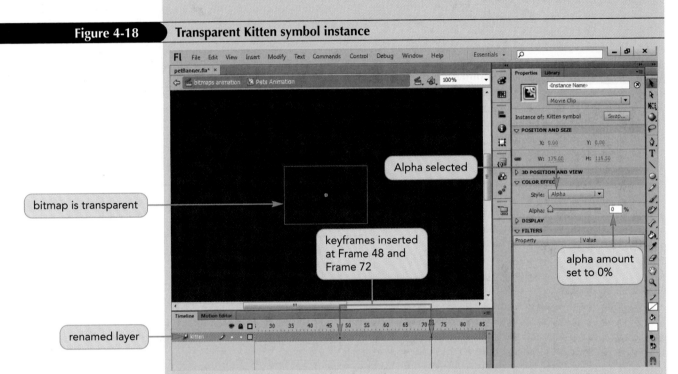

bitmap is transparent

Alpha selected

keyframes inserted at Frame 48 and Frame 72

alpha amount set to 0%

renamed layer

9. Move the playhead to **Frame 1**, and then play the animation. As the motion tween plays, the Kitten symbol instance is displayed and then fades out. See Figure 4-19.

Figure 4-19   **Kitten bitmap animation**

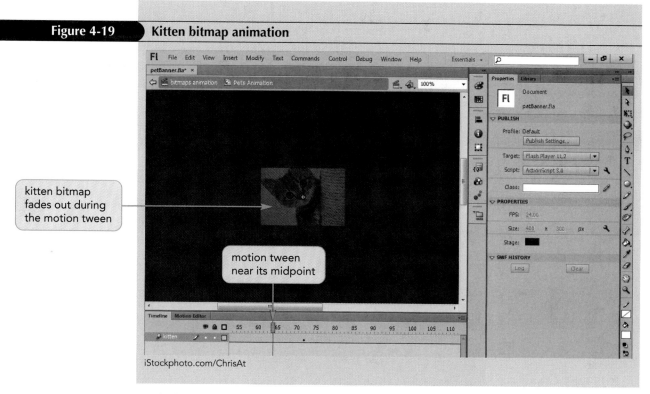

kitten bitmap fades out during the motion tween

motion tween near its midpoint

iStockphoto.com/ChrisAt

The kitten photo is supposed to fade out and then fade back into view at the end of the animation. You will modify the motion tween to fade in the kitten.

To modify the motion tween to fade in the Kitten symbol instance:

1. In the Timeline, right-click **Frame 120**, point to **Insert Keyframe** on the context menu, and then click **Color**. A property keyframe is added to the motion tween, so you can set the starting alpha amount for the motion tween.

2. In the Timeline, click **Frame 144**, select the **Kitten symbol** instance on the Stage, and then, in the Property inspector, set the alpha amount to **100%**. The motion tween is modified to fade in the Kitten symbol instance.

3. Move the playhead to **Frame 1**, and then play the animation. The Kitten symbol instance is displayed, fades out, and then fades back in at the end of the animation.

You will follow a similar process to make the puppy.jpg bitmap fade in as the kitten.jpg bitmap fades out. The puppy.jpg bitmap will then fade out as the kitten.jpg bitmap fades back in. You will place the puppy animation in a separate layer.

To add the puppy.jpg bitmap to the animation:

1. In the Timeline, insert a new layer, name the layer **puppy**, and then insert a keyframe at **Frame 48**. The puppy instance will start at this frame.

2. Drag an instance of the **puppy.jpg** bitmap from the Library panel to the center of the Stage.

3. Open the **Transform** panel, and then reduce the width and height of the bitmap to **50%**.

4. Open the **Info** panel, set the X and Y values to **0**, and then close the Info panel. The puppy.jpg bitmap instance is centered within the editing window at the same relative position as the kitten instance. See Figure 4-20.

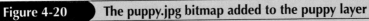

Figure 4-20 | **The puppy.jpg bitmap added to the puppy layer**

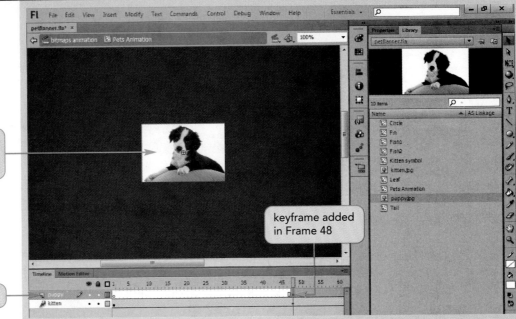

puppy bitmap centered on the Stage

keyframe added in Frame 48

puppy layer inserted

iStockphoto.com/Sarah Salmela

5. Convert the **puppy.jpg** bitmap instance to a movie clip symbol named **Puppy symbol** with the center registration point selected in the Registration icon. The Puppy symbol is created, and you can use it in a motion tween animation.

6. Right-click the **Puppy symbol** instance on the Stage and create a motion tween.

7. Make sure the Puppy symbol instance is still selected, and then in the Property inspector, select **Alpha** in the Style list of the Color Effect section, and set the alpha amount to **0%**. The Puppy symbol instance is transparent, allowing the Kitten symbol instance to show through.

8. In the Timeline, right-click **Frame 72** of the puppy layer, point to **Insert Keyframe** on the context menu, and then click **Color**. A property keyframe is added to the motion tween, so you can set the ending alpha amount for the motion tween.

9. Select the **Puppy symbol** instance on the Stage, and then, in the Property inspector, set the alpha amount to **100%**. The motion tween is created to fade in the Puppy symbol instance.

10. In the Timeline, scrub the playhead between Frame 48 and Frame 72 to preview how the puppy picture fades in while the kitten picture fades out. See Figure 4-21.

Figure 4-21 **Motion tweens fade the pictures**

one bitmap fades out while the other fades in

property keyframe added at Frame 72

motion tween created between Frame 48 and Frame 72

iStockphoto.com/ChrisAt; iStockphoto.com/Sarah Salmela

You will create the motion tween for the Puppy symbol instance to fade out of view and the Kitten symbol instance to fade back into view.

To create the motion tween to fade out the Puppy symbol instance:

1. In the Timeline, right-click **Frame 120** of the puppy layer, point to **Insert Keyframe** on the context menu, and then click **Color**. A property keyframe is added to the motion tween, so you can set the starting alpha amount for the motion tween.

2. In the Timeline, at **Frame 120** of the puppy layer, click the **Puppy symbol** instance on the Stage to select it, and then, in the Property inspector, set the alpha amount to **100%**, if necessary.

3. In the Timeline, click **Frame 144** of the puppy layer, click the **Puppy symbol** instance on the Stage, and then, in the Property inspector, set the alpha amount to **0%**. The motion tween fades out the Puppy symbol instance.

4. In the Timeline, move the playhead to **Frame 1**, and then play the animation. The kitten picture appears and then fades out when the puppy picture fades in. Then the kitten picture fades back in while the puppy picture fades out. The Pets Animation is complete.

Based on Aly's instructions, you need to add a mask. Recall that a mask is created in a separate mask layer. The layer below the mask layer becomes the masked layer. The contents of the masked layer that are covered by the filled shape in the mask layer appear when the movie is played. In this case, you need to create a mask layer, draw a filled shape that covers the Pets Animation, and then make both the kitten layer and the puppy layer masked layers. The filled shape determines how much of the Pets Animation shows through.

To create the mask layer for the Pets Animation:

1. In the Timeline, select the **puppy** layer, if necessary, and then insert a new layer and name it **mask**. This new layer will be the mask layer.

2. Right-click the **mask** layer, and then click **Mask** on the context menu. The mask layer's icon changes to represent the layer's Mask property. The puppy layer is indented, and its icon changes to indicate it is a masked layer.

3. Right-click the **kitten** layer, and then click **Properties** on the context menu. The Layer Properties dialog box opens so you can change the kitten layer's properties to Masked. See Figure 4-22.

Figure 4-22 Layer Properties dialog box

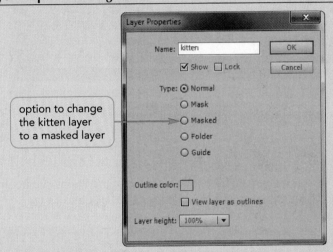

option to change the kitten layer to a masked layer

4. Click the **Masked** option button, and then click the **OK** button. The dialog box closes. The kitten layer in the Timeline is indented, and its icon changes to indicate that it is a masked layer. The mask layer starts out locked to display its effect. See Figure 4-23.

Figure 4-23 Layers converted to masked layers

mask layer

masked layers are indented

5. In the Timeline, click the **mask** layer, and then click the **lock** icon 🔒 to unlock the layer. With the layer unlocked, you can draw the shape for the mask, which can be any shape that contains a fill. The area covered by the shape's fill determines which part of the masked layer's contents is displayed.

6. In the Tools panel, click and hold the **Oval Tool** button, click the **Rectangle Primitive Tool** button to select it, and then set the fill color to **yellow** (#FFFF00). Although you set the fill to yellow, the shape's fill can be any color because it is not displayed.

7. On the Stage, drag the crosshair pointer ✛ from the upper-left corner of the Kitten symbol instance to its lower-right corner. The yellow rectangle covers the entire picture.

8. Open the **Info** panel, set the rectangle's width to **175**, set its height to **116**, set its X and Y values to **0**, select the center registration point in the Registration icon, if necessary, and then close the Info panel. The rectangle frames the Pets Animation.

   Trouble? If the rectangle is not selected, click the Selection Tool button in the Tools panel, click the rectangle on the Stage to select it, and then repeat Step 8.

9. In the Property inspector, click the **lock** icon for the corner radius boxes to unlock the values, enter **50** in the upper-left corner radius value box, and then enter **50** in the lower-right corner radius value box. The rectangle shape has two rounded corners. See Figure 4-24.

Figure 4-24	Mask covers the bitmaps

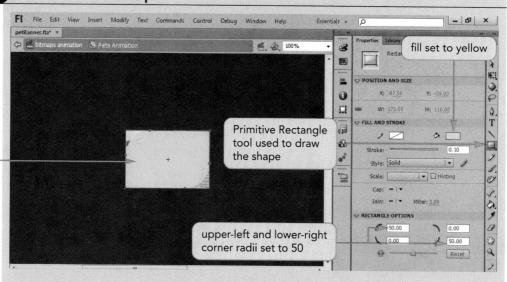

10. In the Timeline, click the **Lock or Unlock All Layers** icon to lock all of the layers and display the result of the mask. The kitten picture shows through the mask. The mask for the Pets Animation is complete. See Figure 4-25.

Figure 4-25   **Bitmaps show through the mask**

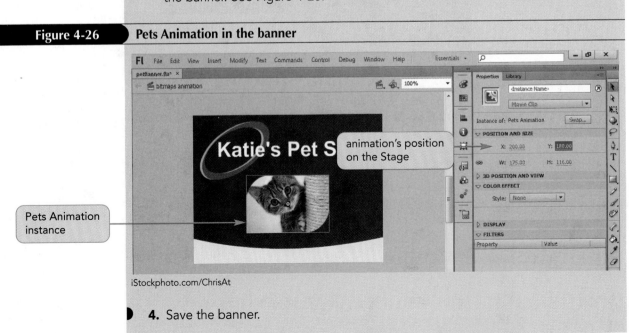

bitmap visible
through the mask

iStockphoto.com/ChrisAt

▶ **11.** Click the **bitmaps animation** link on the Edit bar to exit symbol-editing
mode and return to the document's main Timeline.

▶ **12.** In the Tools panel, click the **Selection Tool** button ▶ to select the
Selection tool.

You need to add the completed Pets Animation movie clip to the center of the
banner based on the specifications that Aly provided.

To add the Pets Animation to the banner:

▶ **1.** In the Timeline, insert a new layer above the title layer and name it **bitmaps**.
You will add the Pets Animation to the banner in this layer.

▶ **2.** Drag the **Pets Animation** symbol from the Library panel to the center of the
Stage below the title text block. The animation is added to the banner.

▶ **3.** In the Position and Size section of the Property inspector, enter **200** for the
X value and **180** for the Y value. The animation is positioned on the center of
the banner. See Figure 4-26.

Figure 4-26   **Pets Animation in the banner**

animation's position
on the Stage

Pets Animation
instance

iStockphoto.com/ChrisAt

▶ **4.** Save the banner.

Because the animation was created inside the movie clip's Timeline, you cannot preview it within the main document's Timeline. To preview the Pets Animation with the banner, you need to create a SWF file and play it in a separate window or in a Web page.

To preview the animation in the banner:

▶ **1.** On the menu bar, click **Control**, and then click **Test Scene**. A Flash Player window opens with the banner and the Pets Animation.

▶ **2.** View the animation in the banner, and then close the Flash Player window.

In this session, you modified a motion path by changing the tween's properties in the Motion Editor. You also created a mask layer animation to create a spotlight effect. Finally, you created a bitmap animation with a fade in and fade out effect. In the next session, you will create text animations on the Katie's Pet Shop banner.

REVIEW

Session 4.1 Quick Check

1. Name three motion tween properties you can modify in the Motion Editor.
2. What is the difference between a mask layer and a masked layer?
3. How can you see the effect that a mask layer has on a masked layer when testing an animation within the Flash workspace?
4. True or False. Text can be used as a mask in a mask layer.
5. True or False. In a mask layer animation, the contents of the mask layer are revealed when the object in the masked layer moves over it.
6. What alpha amount makes an object transparent?
7. What is the first thing you need to do to animate a bitmap in a motion tween?

SESSION 4.2 VISUAL OVERVIEW

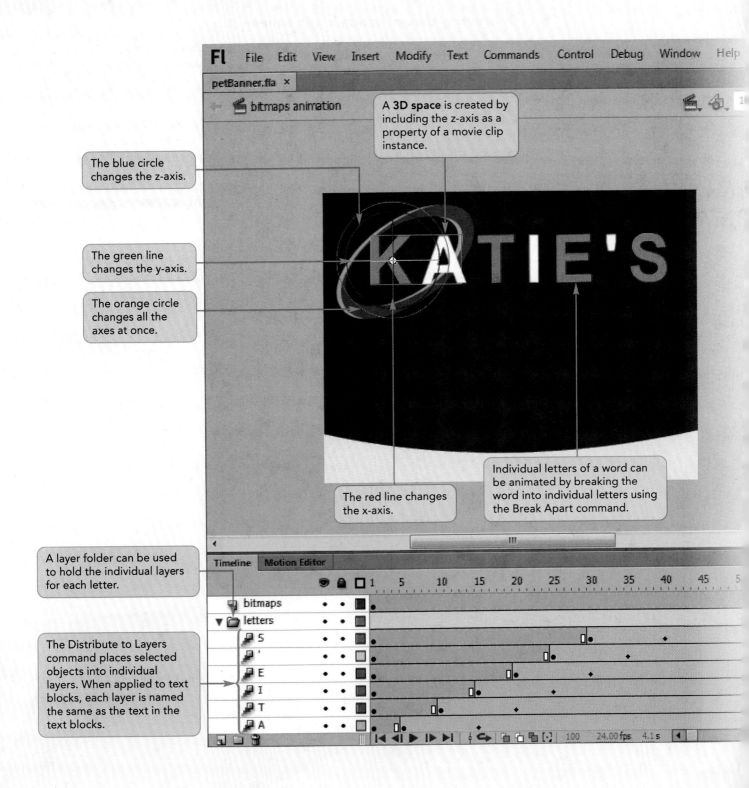

The blue circle changes the z-axis.

The green line changes the y-axis.

The orange circle changes all the axes at once.

A **3D space** is created by including the z-axis as a property of a movie clip instance.

Individual letters of a word can be animated by breaking the word into individual letters using the Break Apart command.

The red line changes the x-axis.

A layer folder can be used to hold the individual layers for each letter.

The Distribute to Layers command places selected objects into individual layers. When applied to text blocks, each layer is named the same as the text in the text blocks.

TEXT ANIMATIONS AND 3D GRAPHICS

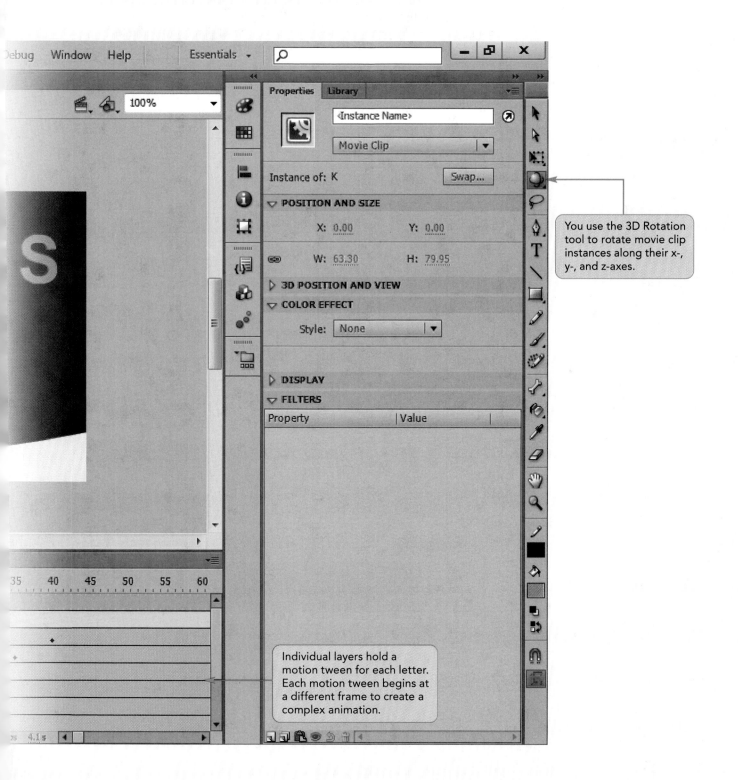

You use the 3D Rotation tool to rotate movie clip instances along their x-, y-, and z-axes.

Individual layers hold a motion tween for each letter. Each motion tween begins at a different frame to create a complex animation.

Creating Complex Text Animations

In addition to animating text blocks to move from one part of the Stage to another or to fade in and increase in size, you can also create complex text animations. For example, you can make the individual letters of a text block rotate and fade in as they appear one at a time on the Stage to form a word or phrase or even have the individual letters exhibit a 3D effect as they rotate into place.

You can also apply a shape tween to text. However, you must first convert the text to fills by using the Break Apart command. When you apply the Break Apart command to a text block, each character in the text block becomes an individual text block. You apply the command again to the individual letters to convert them to fills. After the text blocks are converted to fills, you can apply a shape tween to them. For example, you can make the letters change into a rectangle shape, as shown in Figure 4-27.

Figure 4-27   **Sample shape tween**

various stages of FLASH text block changing to a rectangular shape

© 2013 Cengage Learning

Be aware that after you convert the text to fills, you can no longer edit the fills as text.

REFERENCE

Creating Text Shape Tweens

- Select the text block in the first frame of the animation.
- On the menu bar, click Modify, and then click Break Apart to break the text into individual letters.
- On the menu bar, click Modify, and then click Break Apart a second time to convert the text to fills.
- Create a keyframe in the last frame of the animation and change the shape of the text fills or create a new shape.
- Right-click between the first and last keyframe, and then click Create Shape Tween on the context menu.

Animating Individual Letters

You can animate individual letters in a word or phrase to create interesting text effects. For example, you can animate the letters of a word to fall into place on the Stage one at a time. Or you can have a word explode with the individual letters flying off the Stage in different directions. Another example is to have the individual letters of a word increase and decrease in size to create a pulsating effect. To create most of these text effects, you first need to break a word into its individual letters and then animate each letter separately. The simplest way to animate each letter is to create motion tweens. This means that each letter must reside in its own layer.

INSIGHT

Creating Symbols when Animating Text Blocks

When animating text blocks, it is a good idea to create a symbol for each text block even though converting text to symbols is not required in certain types of animations. Converting text blocks to symbols enables you to use the text block instances more than once in a document without increasing the file size. You can also add color or transparency changes as part of an existing animation without having to create new duplicate text blocks. And, with text blocks as symbols, advanced users of Flash can manipulate the text block instances through programming code to create more complex animations.

Aly has been working on a sample banner that includes individual letter text animation. In this banner, each letter has the same motion tween applied to it to create a pulsating effect. The text blocks in this animation did not have to be converted to symbols because the motion tweens only include changes to the dimensions of the text blocks.

To explore the sample banner with individual letters text effect:

1. Open the **petShop.fla** file located in the Flash4\Tutorial folder included with your Data Files.

2. Press the **Enter** key to play the animation. Each letter increases and decreases in size one after the other. Notice that each letter resides in its own layer.

3. In the Timeline, click **Frame 1** of the P layer, and then look at the size of the letter *P* on the Stage.

4. In the Timeline, click **Frame 5** of the P layer, and then look at how the letter *P* increases in size on the Stage. The property keyframe in this frame represents the change in the text block's dimensions.

5. In the Timeline, click **Frame 10** of the P layer, and then look at the letters *P* and *E* on the Stage. In this frame, the letter *P* returns to its original size. At the same time, the next letter, *E*, increases in size. A property keyframe in this frame represents the change in dimensions for the *P* text block. See Figure 4-28.

Figure 4-28   **Sample letters animation**

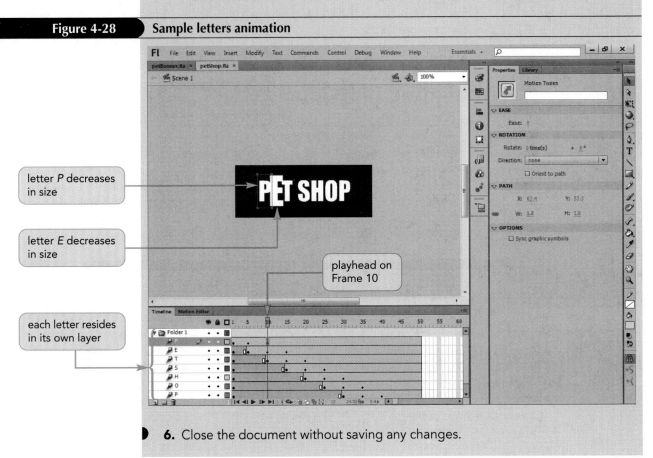

letter *P* decreases in size

letter *E* decreases in size

playhead on Frame 10

each letter resides in its own layer

6. Close the document without saving any changes.

Creating a Complex Text Animation

The next animation you will create for the Katie's Pet Shop banner consists of individual letters rotating one after the other, as described in Aly's notes shown in Figure 4-29. Each letter will rotate around an imaginary axis in three-dimensional space. Three-dimensional graphics are discussed later in this session. Each letter will also increase and decrease in size as it rotates. This effect involves animating the individual letters of the word in a similar way to the animated text in the sample banner Aly created.

Figure 4-29   Animation plan for the title text

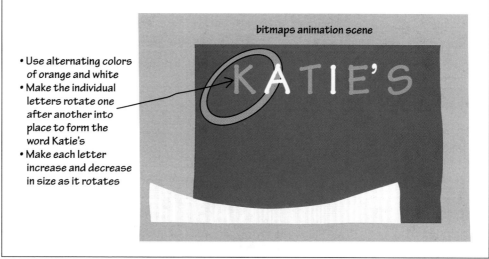

© 2013 Cengage Learning

To create the animations for the individual letters, you will first create the Katie's text block, convert each letter in that text block into its own individual text block, and then distribute these individual letter text blocks onto their own layers.

Animating Individual Letters

- On the Stage, select the text block containing the letters to be animated.
- On the menu bar, click Modify, and then click Break Apart.
- On the menu bar, click Modify, point to Timeline, and then click Distribute to Layers.
- Delete the original layer, which is now empty.
- If necessary, convert each letter that will be animated to a symbol with an appropriate name.
- Create a motion tween for each letter.

Before animating the letters, you will change the colors of the letters in the KATIE's text block to alternate between yellow and orange to enhance the special effect. You will initially create the Katie's text block in a new layer folder. Then, when you distribute the letters to individual layers, all of the new layers will be inside the folder. This new animation will reside in the bitmaps animation scene, which will play after the fish animation scene in the document. You will create a new layer folder for the new text block.

To create the KATIE'S text block in the bitmaps animation scene:

1. In the Timeline, unlock the title layer and delete the Katie's Pet Shop text block.

2. In the Tools panel, click the **Text Tool** button $\boxed{\text{T}}$ to select the Text tool.

3. In the Property inspector, set the font family to **Arial**, set the font style to **Bold**, set the point size to **68**, set the text fill color to **white** (#FFFFFF), set the font rendering method to **Anti-alias for animation**, and then set the paragraph format to **Align center**.

4. On the Stage, create a text block, and then type **KATIE'S**.

5. In the Tools panel, click the **Selection Tool** button  to select it.

6. In the Property inspector, set the letter spacing to **10**, set the text block's X value to **44**, and then set its Y value to **30**. See Figure 4-30.

Figure 4-30	KATIE'S text block

text block centered 30 pixels from the top of the Stage

properties for the text block

title layer unlocked

iStockphoto.com/ChrisAt

7. In the Timeline, click the **New Folder** button to create a new layer folder, and then rename the new layer folder as **letters**. The letters layer folder is created above the title layer.

8. In the Timeline, drag the **title** layer into the letters folder, and then click **Frame 1** of the title layer.

9. On the Stage, double-click the **KATIE's** text block, click and drag in the text block to select the letter **K**, and then change the letter's text fill color to **light orange** (#FF9900).

10. Repeat Step 9 to change the color of the letter **T**, the letter **E**, and the letter **S** to the same light orange color. The letters in the word *KATIE'S* alternate between light orange and white.

11. In the Tools panel, click the **Selection Tool** button. The KATIE'S text block remains selected.

Distributing Objects to Individual Layers

Animating a word's individual letters as in the sample Pet Shop banner requires each letter to be placed in its own layer. A quick way to place each letter into its own layer is to use the Distribute to Layers command. This command takes a group of selected objects and places each individual object into its own layer. Each new layer is named based on its content. For example, if the objects distributed are text blocks, the names of the new layers are the same as the text in the text blocks. If the objects are symbols, the names of the new layers are the same as the names of the symbols. Other layers are named "Layer" followed by a number. This helps you to identify to which layers the selected objects have been distributed. The layer that originally contained the grouped objects will be empty after you apply the Distribute to Layers command and can be deleted. Before you apply the Distribute to Layers command, be sure to select all of the objects you want distributed.

PROSKILLS

Written Communication: Organizing Layers in a Layer Folder

File organization is critical to keeping track of and working effectively with the documents you create. The same is true for layer organization within a Flash document. As a Flash document becomes more intricate and includes complex animations, the number of layers and objects expands and can quickly become unmanageable. To help keep layers organized and logical, use layer folders to combine layers into logical groups. Although you can create layer folders at any time and move existing layers into them, it can be easier to create the layer folder first. A clear naming convention makes it simpler and faster to locate layers and objects.

For example, when you animate individual letters in a text block, each letter needs to be in a separate layer. Before distributing a group of objects to layers, you can create a new layer folder and move the layer containing the objects into the layer folder. After the objects are distributed to layers, all of the new layers will reside within the layer folder. You can then collapse the layer folder to hide the individual layers when you are not working with them. This makes it easier to work with the document's Timeline and other layers in the document.

A well-planned organization and clear, descriptive naming convention makes it easier to work with a Flash document. It also ensures that someone else can quickly determine how you structured the objects and layers in the document if you need to collaborate on an animation.

To convert the KATIE'S text block into individual letters so they can be distributed to individual layers, you need to break the text block into separate text blocks, one for each letter, using the Break Apart command. When you apply the Distribute to Layers command to the selected text blocks, each letter is placed in its own layer. You then can create the necessary motion tween animations for each of the letters.

You will start by separating the letters into individual text blocks and distributing the text blocks into individual layers.

To create the individual letters from the word *KATIE'S*:

1. On the menu bar, click **Modify**, and then click **Break Apart**. Each letter is placed in its own text block, and all the text blocks are selected. See Figure 4-31.

Figure 4-31   **Individual letter text blocks**

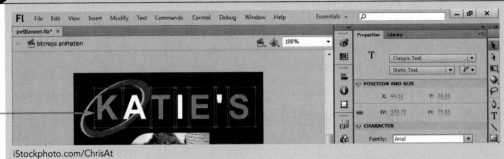

each letter in the title layer is a text block

iStockphoto.com/ChrisAt

2. With all of the letters still selected, on the menu bar, click **Modify**, point to **Timeline**, and then click **Distribute to Layers**. Each letter is placed in its own layer that is named with the letter it contains. The title layer is empty and is no longer needed.

3. In the Timeline, delete the **title** layer. The empty title layer is removed from the Timeline.

Now that the letters in the *KATIE'S* text have been split into individual text blocks and on separate layers, you can animate each letter to create the animation. You will convert each letter into a movie clip symbol and then create a motion tween for each letter instance. The motion tween for letter *K*, the first letter, will start in Frame 1. The other motion tweens will start every fifth frame.

To convert each letter to a symbol and create motion tweens:

1. On the Stage, select the letter **K**, and then convert the letter to a movie clip symbol named **K**. The symbol is added to the document's library.

2. Repeat Step 1 for each of the remaining letters, naming each symbol for the letter it represents, using **Apostrophe** as the symbol name for the apostrophe. All of the letters are converted to symbols.

3. In the Timeline, insert a keyframe at **Frame 5** of the A layer. The animation for the letter A will start in the fifth frame of the layer. You did not insert a keyframe for the letter K because it will start in the first frame of the layer.

4. Repeat Step 3 to insert a keyframe in layer T at **Frame 10**, in layer I at **Frame 15**, in layer E at **Frame 20**, in layer ' (apostrophe) at **Frame 25**, and in layer S at **Frame 30**. See Figure 4-32. The order of your layers might be different.

Figure 4-32   **Keyframes inserted in each layer**

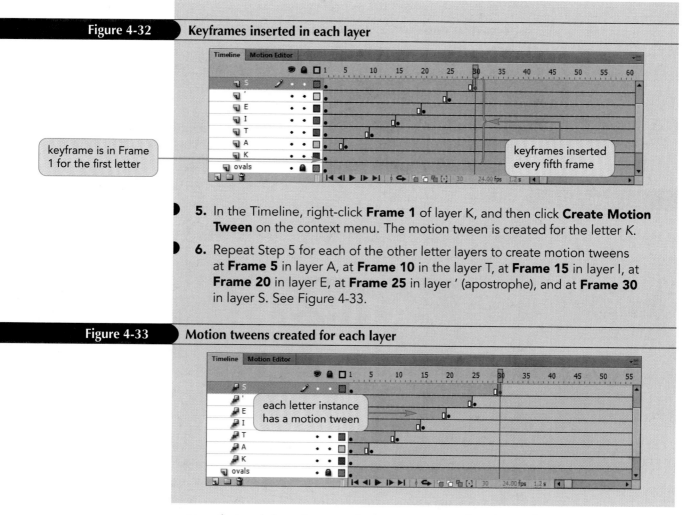

keyframe is in Frame 1 for the first letter

keyframes inserted every fifth frame

5. In the Timeline, right-click **Frame 1** of layer K, and then click **Create Motion Tween** on the context menu. The motion tween is created for the letter *K*.

6. Repeat Step 5 for each of the other letter layers to create motion tweens at **Frame 5** in layer A, at **Frame 10** in the layer T, at **Frame 15** in layer I, at **Frame 20** in layer E, at **Frame 25** in layer ' (apostrophe), and at **Frame 30** in layer S. See Figure 4-33.

Figure 4-33   **Motion tweens created for each layer**

each letter instance has a motion tween

Now that each layer has a motion tween, you need to change the properties of each instance at the starting frame for its tween span.

Creating 3D Graphic Effects

Every object in Flash has x and y properties, which represent the object's horizontal and vertical coordinates relative to the Stage. By adding a third property, the z property, you can create an illusion of depth, where an object appears to be closer or farther away than other objects. You can also manipulate an object in three dimensions along its x-, y-, or z-axis. To create this illusion in Flash, you create three-dimensional (3D) effects by moving and rotating movie clips in 3D space. You can only apply 3D properties to movie clip instances. These instances can be moved along their z-axis using the 3D Translation tool or rotated along their x- or y-axis with the 3D Rotation tool.

You will use the 3D Rotation tool to rotate each letter along its y-axis.

To rotate each letter instance in 3D space:

1. In the Timeline, click **Frame 1** of the K layer.

2. In the Tools panel, click the **3D Rotation Tool** button 🔵 to select it. The K instance is overlaid with 3D axes. You change the 3D properties of an instance by dragging one of its axes.

3. On the Stage, drag the green line on the right of the K movie clip instance to its left to rotate the letter so that it faces to its left. The K movie clip instance rotates along its y-axis in 3D space. See Figure 4-34.

Figure 4-34	K instance being rotated

drag the green line left to rotate the letter along its y-axis

iStockphoto.com/ChrisAt

4. In the Timeline, click **Frame 10** of the K layer.

5. On the Stage, drag the green line on the left of the K movie clip instance to its right to rotate the letter so that it faces to its right. The K instance rotates back to its original orientation in Frame 10.

6. Scrub the playhead from Frame 1 through Frame 10 to see the 3D rotation effect on the letter K. Because the letter instance was rotated with the 3D Rotation tool, Flash converts the movie clip into a 3D movie clip.

7. Repeat Steps 1 through 5 for each letter instance to rotate each letter left in the starting keyframe of its tween span and rotate the letter back to its original orientation 10 frames later. Make sure you select the starting frame for each letter and that you select only one letter at a time.

8. Drag the playhead to **Frame 1**, and then press the **Enter** key to play the animation. Each letter in *KATIE'S* rotates in 3D space one after the other. See Figure 4-35.

TIP

To prevent selecting more than one letter at one time, lock layers you are not working with and then unlock the layers as needed to modify them.

Figure 4-35   Completed KATIE'S text animation

letters rotating in 3D space one after the other

iStockphoto.com/ChrisAt

You will test the movie to see how the animations play in each scene one after the other.

▶ **9.** On the menu bar, click **Control**, point to **Test Movie**, and then click **in Flash Professional**. A Flash Player window opens, showing the SWF file as it plays the animation of the fish animation scene followed by the animation of the bitmaps animation scene.

▶ **10.** Close the Flash Player window.

▶ **11.** Save the document.

In this session, you created an animation of the individual letters of the *KATIE'S* name and applied a 3D rotation effect to each letter. In the next session, you will complete the banner by adding a complex animation to the first scene.

Session 4.2 Quick Check

REVIEW

1. List two examples of how text can be animated.
2. To apply a shape tween to a text block, what must you do first to the text?
3. If you apply the Distribute to Layers command to a group of selected text blocks, how will the new layers be named in the Timeline?
4. Why must each letter to be animated be in its own layer?
5. Why is it a good idea to place all of the individual letter layers in a layer folder?
6. True or False. A layer whose contents are distributed to separate layers with the Distribute to Layers command retains a copy of its original contents.
7. True or False. A 3D space is created by including the z-axis as a property of a movie clip instance.

SESSION 4.3 VISUAL OVERVIEW

Inverse kinematics is an animation method used to create bone structures. When one bone moves, the other bones move in relation to it.

You can show or hide elements in the movie, including text, movie clips, buttons and graphics, and frames and layers.

A **bone** is a link from one symbol instance to another or from one interior part of a shape to another.

A chain of bones is called an **armature**.

With onion skinning toggled on, the Start Onion Skin and End Onion Skin markers appear on either side of the playhead.

When you add bones to a symbol instance or to a shape, the instance or shape and its armature are moved to a new layer called a **pose layer**.

Onion skinning displays more than one frame at a time on the Stage. The Onion Skin button toggles the feature on and off.

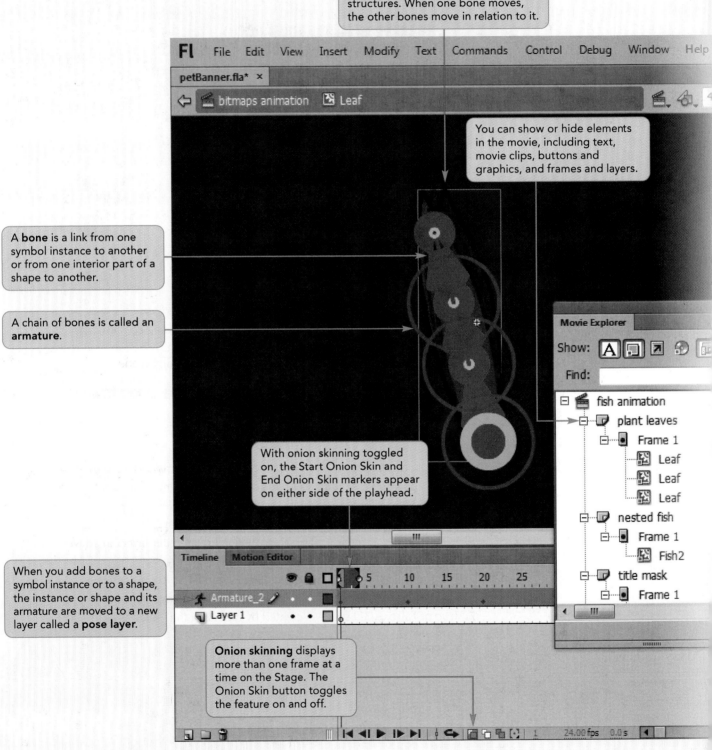

NESTED SYMBOLS AND INVERSE KINEMATICS

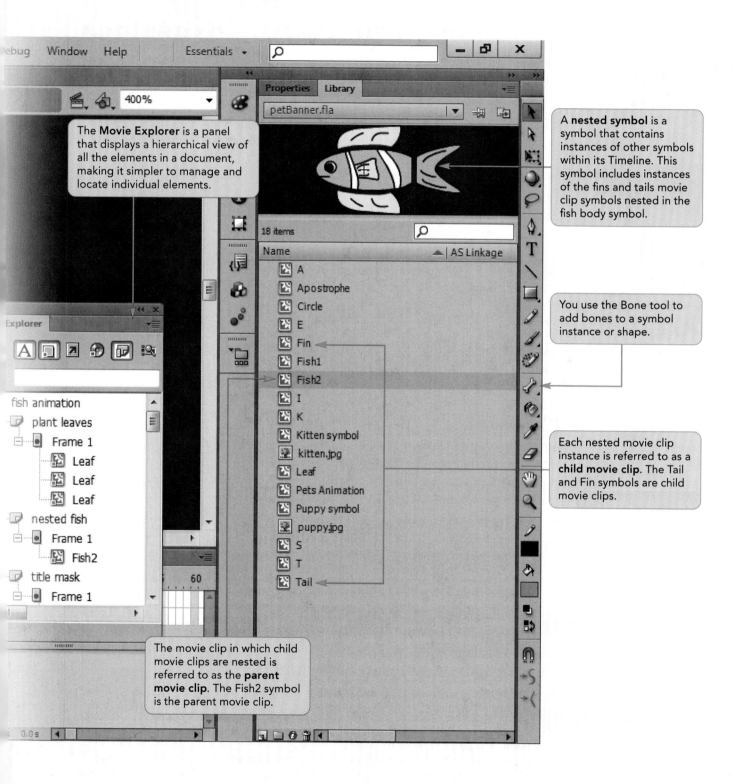

The **Movie Explorer** is a panel that displays a hierarchical view of all the elements in a document, making it simpler to manage and locate individual elements.

A **nested symbol** is a symbol that contains instances of other symbols within its Timeline. This symbol includes instances of the fins and tails movie clip symbols nested in the fish body symbol.

You use the Bone tool to add bones to a symbol instance or shape.

Each nested movie clip instance is referred to as a **child movie clip**. The Tail and Fin symbols are child movie clips.

The movie clip in which child movie clips are nested is referred to as the **parent movie clip**. The Fish2 symbol is the parent movie clip.

Animating Nested Symbols

As you have seen, complex animations can be created by animating objects in separate layers. For example, you can animate one object to move across the Stage in one layer while at the same time another object in another layer rotates and increases in size. So, by adding more layers to the document's main Timeline, you can create complex animation effects.

You cannot always achieve a desired special effect by just adding layers with more animations. For example, the Katie's Pet Shop banner has a fish swimming across the Stage, but the fish's fins and tail remain stationary in relation to the fish. A better design creates animations for the fins and the tail so that the fish moves more realistically. You could separate the fins and the tail from the body of the fish, convert them to movie clip symbols, and then create animations for each one in separate layers. Then you could animate the fish body, fins, and tail to move across the Stage at the same time as one object, which creates a more natural look. This is difficult to do, however, because all the animations must be synchronized to work together. A simpler way to achieve this same result is to create a nested symbol.

Creating Complex Animations with Nested Symbols

A nested symbol contains instances of other symbols within its Timeline. So, the Timeline of a movie clip symbol can include instances of other symbols that in turn can contain their own animations within their own Timelines. Instances of the parent movie clip can then be inserted into the document's main Timeline, and modified and animated just like any other symbol instance. When you modify or animate the parent movie clip, the child movie clips are also affected.

In the case of the fish, the parent movie clip can consist of the fish body plus nested instances of the fins and the tail, as shown in Figure 4-36. The fins and tail movie clip instances can contain their own animations to make them change slightly to simulate the movement of a real fish. These animations are independent of the fish body. The whole fish, which is the parent movie clip, can then be inserted in the document's main Timeline and animated to move across the Stage. When you apply a motion tween to the whole fish to make it move across the Stage, the motion tween is also applied to its nested instances. As a result, the fish body, fins, and tail all move across the Stage as one object while the fins and tail exhibit their own animations.

| Figure 4-36 | Example of a nested movie clip symbol |

© 2013 Cengage Learning

Creating a Nested Movie Clip Symbol

The first scene of the banner requires a fish that has its fins and tail animated to appear more natural. To do this, you will create a fish using separate fin and tail symbols that contain their own animations. Aly already created movie clip symbols for the fish body, fin, and tail. You will use these to create frame-by-frame animations for the fin and the tail. Then you will add two instances of the fin movie clip and one instance of the tail movie clip to the fish body. You will then insert the resulting nested movie clip symbol into the fish animation scene of the banner and animate it to move across the Stage.

You will start by creating a frame-by-frame animation for the fin. To create the animation for the fin, you will add keyframes at every other frame of the fin Timeline starting at Frame 3. You will then change the shape of the fin slightly at each keyframe for a total of nine frames.

To insert frames for the fin frame-by-frame animation:

▶ **1.** If you took a break after the previous session, make sure the petBanner.fla file is open and Flash is reset to the Essentials workspace.

▶ **2.** On the Edit bar, click the **Edit Symbols** button 🔄, and then click **Fin**. The Fin symbol opens in symbol-editing mode.

▶ **3.** Change the zoom magnification to **400%**. The magnification of the Stage increases, making it easier to see the Fin symbol on the Stage.

▶ **4.** In the Timeline, insert keyframes in the Layer 1 layer at **Frame 3**, **Frame 5**, **Frame 7**, and **Frame 9**. The fin is copied to each of the new frames.

Using Onion Skinning with Complex Animations

When working with complex animations, it is often helpful to use onion skinning. Onion skinning shows the current frame plus two or more frames on the Stage at once. The contents of the frames within the onion skin markers are displayed on the Stage. The content of the current frame, indicated by the position of the playhead, appears in full color as usual. The contents of the frames before and after the current frame appear dimmed. Onion skinning can be especially helpful when creating a frame-by-frame animation where you need to compare the current frame's contents to the previous frame's contents.

You can also click the Onion Skin Outlines button to display only the outlines of the content on the Stage, which can be helpful when working with complex animations. The Edit Multiple Frames button makes the content of all the frames in a frame-by-frame animation that are within the onion skin markers available for editing.

INSIGHT

Locking Layers While Onion Skinning

When using onion skinning with a complex document, a confusing array of images might be displayed on the Stage. Because the content of locked layers is not affected when onion skinning is turned on, lock any layers you are not editing. You can then focus on the contents of the layers you are editing. Remember to toggle off onion skinning when you are finished so that you again see only one frame at one time.

You will toggle on onion skinning to help you as you create the fin frame-by-frame animation.

To create the fin frame-by-frame animation:

▶ **1.** In the Timeline, click the **Onion Skin** button 🔲. The onion skin markers appear in the Timeline header.

▶ **2.** In the Timeline, click the **Modify Markers** button 🔲, and then click **Marker Range 2**. The two frames before and after the current frame appear on the Stage.

▶ **3.** In the Timeline, click **Frame 3** of the Layer 1 layer. This is the frame where you will first modify the fin.

▶ **4.** In the Tools panel, click the **Selection Tool** button ▶.

▶ **5.** Click an empty area of the Stage to deselect the fin, and then drag the right side of the fin slightly to the left. The onion skinned frames provide a reference of the changed fin. See Figure 4-37.

Figure 4-37 **Fin movie clip modified in Frame 3**

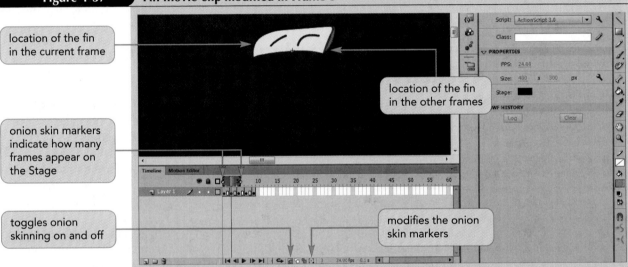

location of the fin in the current frame

location of the fin in the other frames

onion skin markers indicate how many frames appear on the Stage

toggles onion skinning on and off

modifies the onion skin markers

In Frame 5 and Frame 7, you will repeat this process to modify other parts of the fin. In Frame 9, the fin returns to its original state, so you won't make any changes in this frame.

▶ **6.** In the Timeline, click **Frame 5**, deselect the fin on the Stage, and then drag the top edge of the fin slightly up. See Figure 4-38.

Figure 4-38 **Fin movie clip modified in Frame 5**

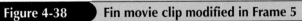
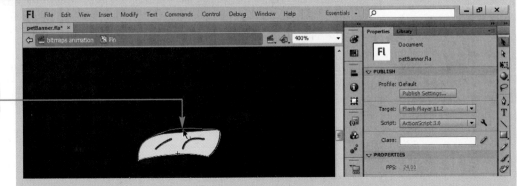

top edge of the fin moved up

7. In the Timeline, click **Frame 7**, deselect the fin on the Stage, and then drag the upper-right tip of the fin slightly to the right. The fin animation is complete.

8. Drag the playhead to **Frame 1**, and then press the **Enter** key to play the frame-by-frame animation. The fin changes slightly at each keyframe throughout the animation.

The frame-by-frame animation for the fin is complete. You will create a similar frame-by-frame animation for the Tail symbol. You will use the same number of key-frames for the Tail symbol as you did for the Fin symbol and change the shape of the tail slightly at each keyframe.

To create the tail frame-by-frame animation:

1. On the Edit bar, click the **Edit Symbols** button, and then click **Tail**. The Tail symbol opens in symbol-editing mode.

2. In the Timeline, insert keyframes in the Layer 1 layer at **Frame 3**, **Frame 5**, **Frame 7**, and **Frame 9**. The tail is copied to each of the new frames. Onion skinning is still on and will remain that way until you click the Onion Skin button.

3. In the Timeline, click **Frame 3** of the Layer 1 layer, and then click an empty area of the Stage to deselect the tail.

4. On the Stage, drag the two tips on the right side of the tail slightly inward. The dimmed tail from the previous frame provides a reference as you change the shape of the tail. See Figure 4-39.

Figure 4-39	Tail movie clip modified in Frame 3

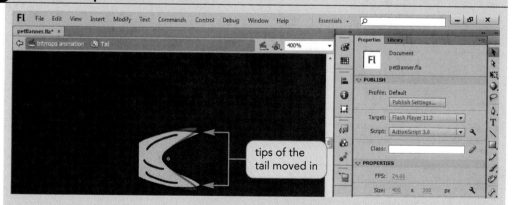

tips of the tail moved in

5. In the Timeline, click **Frame 5**, deselect the tail on the Stage, and then drag the tail's top edge near the left side of the tail slightly down. See Figure 4-40.

Figure 4-40   Tail movie clip symbol modified in Frame 5

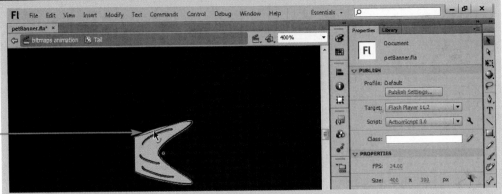

top edge of the
tail moved down

6. In Frame 5, drag the tail's bottom edge near the left side of the tail slightly up.
   The midsection of the tail is narrower.

7. In the Timeline, click **Frame 7**, deselect the tail on the Stage, and then drag
   the two tips on the right side of the tail slightly inward as you did in Step 4.
   In Frame 9, the tail returns to its original state, so no changes are needed
   in this frame.

8. In the Timeline, click the **Onion Skin** button. Onion skinning toggles off.

9. In the Timeline, click **Frame 1**, and then press the **Enter** key to play the
   frame-by-frame animation. The tail changes slightly at each keyframe
   throughout the animation.

Now that you have created the animations for the Fin movie clip symbol and the Tail
movie clip symbol, you are ready to insert instances of these symbols in the Fish2 symbol,
which contains the fish body. The instances will be nested inside the Fish2 symbol.

To create the Fish2 nested movie clip symbol:

1. On the Edit bar, click the **Edit Symbols** button, and then click **Fish2**. The
   Fish2 symbol opens in symbol-editing mode.

2. Click the **Library** tab, if necessary, and then drag an instance of the **Fin
   symbol** from the Library panel and place it directly above the fish body on
   the Stage. See Figure 4-41.

Figure 4-41   **Fin instance placed on top of the fish**

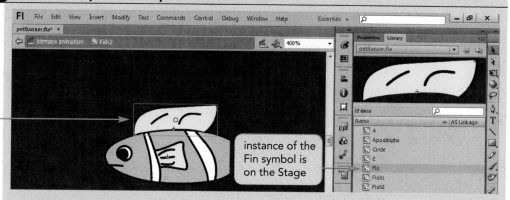

fin positioned directly above the fish body

instance of the Fin symbol is on the Stage

 3. If necessary, press the arrow keys to nudge the fin into place.

 4. Drag another instance of the **Fin symbol** from the Library panel and place it below the fish body.

 5. On the menu bar, click **Modify**, point to **Transform**, and then click **Flip Vertical**. The fin will now fit below the fish body.

 6. Position the **Fin** instance right below the fish body, pressing the arrow keys as needed to nudge the fin into place.

 7. Drag an instance of the **Tail symbol** from the Library panel and place it to the right side of the fish, positioning the tail precisely against the fish body.

 8. Click an empty area of the Stage to deselect the fish. The fish is now complete. See Figure 4-42.

Figure 4-42   **Completed nested symbol**

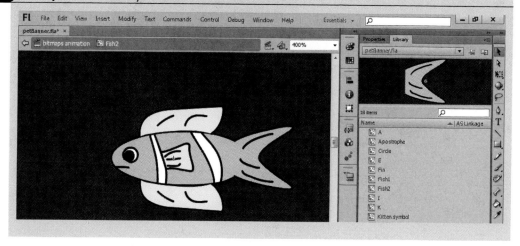

The Fish2 symbol is complete with its nested movie clip symbols. You will place the complete fish in the fish animation scene and apply a motion tween to make the fish swim across the Stage. The fins and tail will move together with the fish.

To insert and animate the Fish2 symbol in the fish animation scene:

▶ 1. On the Edit bar, click the **Edit Scene** button, and then click **fish animation**. The fish animation scene appears.

▶ 2. Change the zoom magnification to **100%**.

▶ 3. In the Timeline, insert a new layer above the title mask layer and name it **nested fish**. The nested fish layer is selected in the Timeline.

▶ 4. Drag an instance of the **Fish2** symbol from the Library panel and place it on the pasteboard to the right of the Stage about 150 pixels from the top of the Stage.

▶ 5. In the Tools panel, click the **Free Transform Tool** button, and then click the **Scale** button.

▶ 6. On the pasteboard, drag a corner handle of the Fish2 symbol to reduce the size of the instance so that it is about the same size as the Fish1 instance. See Figure 4-43.

| Figure 4-43 | Nested movie clip instance in the fish animation scene |

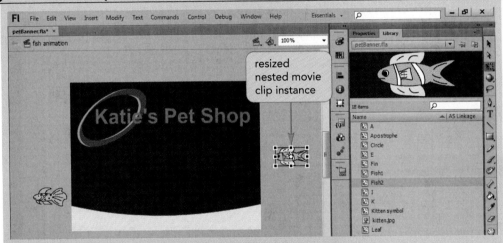

▶ 7. In the Tools panel, click the **Selection Tool** button.

▶ 8. On the pasteboard, right-click the **Fish2** instance, and then click **Create Motion Tween** on the context menu. A tween span is added to the nested fish layer.

▶ 9. In the Timeline, click **Frame 50** of the nested fish layer, and then move the **Fish2** instance to the pasteboard on the left side of the Stage. The fish will move across the Stage as the frames play.

The motion tween animation is complete for the Fish2 instance. You will test the animation next. Because the Fin and Tail symbols are movie clip symbols and their Timelines are independent of the main document's Timeline, their animations will not play when you test the animation of the fish within the Document window. To see their animations, you will play the current scene as a SWF file in Flash Player.

To test the nested movie clip animation:

▶ **1.** In the Timeline, click **Frame 1** of the nested fish layer, and then press the **Enter** key to play the motion tween animation. The Fish2 instance moves across the Stage, but the nested fin and tail animations do not play.

▶ **2.** On the menu bar, click **Control**, and then click **Test Scene**. The fish animation scene plays in Flash Player. As the Fish2 instance moves across the Stage, its fins and tail exhibit their animations.

You will stop the main document's Timeline from playing to see only the animations for the Fin and Tail instances.

▶ **3.** When the Fish2 instance moves across the Stage, press the **Enter** key. The fish stops swimming. The fins and tail of the Fish2 instance continue their animations because they are on independent Timelines.

▶ **4.** Press the **Enter** key. The fish starts swimming again.

▶ **5.** Close the Flash Player window, and then save the banner.

TIP

You can also press the Ctrl+Enter keys to test the current scene in Flash Player.

Using Inverse Kinematics

In Flash, you use inverse kinematics to animate one or more objects in relation to each other. With inverse kinematics, you can easily create complex animations and natural movement. For example, you can create character animation in which the arms and legs of a body are connected to each other with bones. When a bone in one part of the character moves, the other bones move accordingly without you defining every single movement. You specify only the start and end positions of an object by positioning its bones, and the other bones shift into a different pose.

Bones can be added to connect one symbol instance to another, or they can be added to the interior of a shape object so that you can move or animate parts of the shape without having to draw the shape multiple times. When you add bones to a symbol instance or shape, the instance or shape and its armature are moved to a pose layer named Armature.

The Katie's Pet Shop banner requires a plant leaf animation. You will use the Bone tool to add bones to a leaf shape that Aly created. You will then move the bones slightly at different frames in the pose layer to create the animation.

To create a plant leaf animation using inverse kinematics:

▶ **1.** On the Edit bar, click the **Edit Symbols** button, and then click **Leaf**. The Leaf symbol opens in symbol-editing mode.

▶ **2.** Increase the zoom magnification to **400%**.

▶ **3.** In the Tools panel, click the **Bone Tool** button to select it. You use the Bone tool to add bones to an instance or to a shape. Each time you click and drag with the Bone tool, a new bone is created.

▶ **4.** On the Stage, click the base of the plant leaf, and then drag the pointer up to about one-third of the length of the leaf shape. A bone is added to the shape, and a new layer named "Armature" is created. See Figure 4-44.

Figure 4-44   Bone added to the plant leaf shape

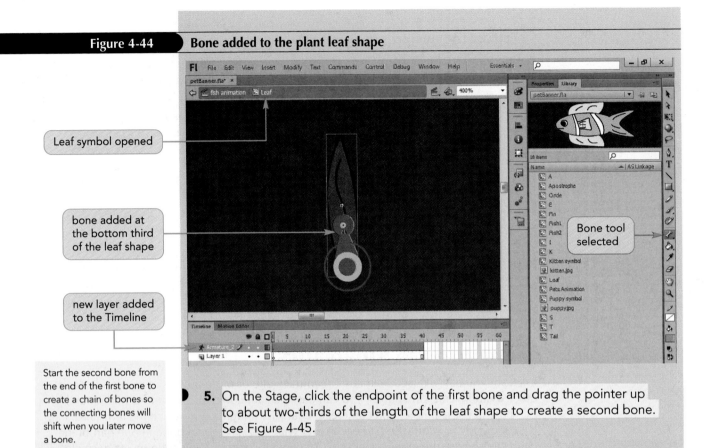

Leaf symbol opened

bone added at the bottom third of the leaf shape

Bone tool selected

new layer added to the Timeline

Start the second bone from the end of the first bone to create a chain of bones so the connecting bones will shift when you later move a bone.

▶ **5.** On the Stage, click the endpoint of the first bone and drag the pointer up to about two-thirds of the length of the leaf shape to create a second bone. See Figure 4-45.

Figure 4-45   Second bone added to the plant leaf shape

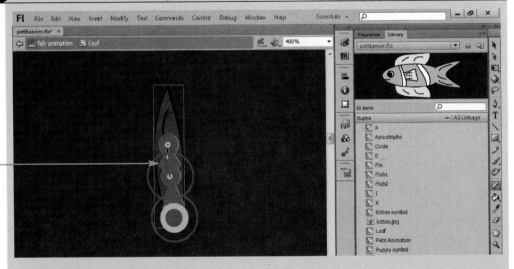

bone added at the middle third of the leaf shape

Trouble? If an additional Armature layer is created, you did not start the new bone from the end of the previous bone. On the menu bar, click Edit, click Undo, and then repeat Step 5, being sure to start the second bone from the end of the first bone.

▶ **6.** On the Stage, click the end point of the second bone and drag the pointer up to right below the tip of the leaf shape to create a third bone. You will move the bones to create an inverse kinematic animation.

▶ **7.** In the Tools panel, click the **Selection Tool** button ▶ to select it, and then, in the Timeline, click **Frame 1** of the Armature layer, if necessary.

8. On the Stage, drag the endpoint of the top bone slightly to the left. Moving the bones creates an inverse kinematic animation. See Figure 4-46.

Figure 4-46 **Leaf starting position**

bone pointer over the bone endpoint

top bone moved to the left

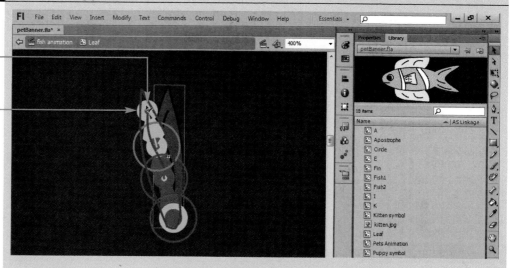

9. In the Timeline, click **Frame 10** of the Armature layer, and then, on the Stage, drag the endpoint of the top bone slightly to the right of the leaf's original position. A new pose is created at Frame 10. See Figure 4-47.

Figure 4-47 **New pose created in the Leaf symbol**

top bone moved to the right

middle and bottom bones move in response to the top bone's new position

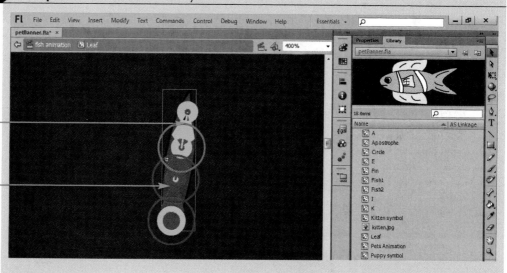

10. In the Timeline, click **Frame 20** of the Armature layer, and then, on the Stage, drag the top bone slightly further to the right of the leaf's original position. A new pose is created at Frame 20.

11. In the Timeline, click **Frame 30** of the Armature layer, and then, on the Stage, drag the top bone slightly to the left to approximately the leaf's original position. A new pose is created at Frame 30.

12. In the Timeline, click **Frame 40** of the Armature layer, and then, on the Stage, drag the top bone slightly to the left to approximately the leaf's position in Frame 1. A new pose is created at Frame 40.

▶ **13.** Scrub the playhead between Frame 1 and Frame 40 to see the inverse kinematic animation.

The plant leaf animation is complete. Several instances of the plant leaf symbol will be added to the fish animation scene. One instance will be flipped horizontally so that its animation moves in the opposite direction of the other two instances.

To add the plant leaf animation to the fish animation scene:

▶ **1.** On the Edit bar, click the **fish animation** link. The fish animation scene is the current scene.

▶ **2.** In the Timeline, move the playhead to **Frame 1**, insert a new layer above the nested fish layer, and then name the new layer **plant leaves**.

▶ **3.** Drag an instance of the **Leaf** symbol from the Library panel and place it in the lower-right corner of the Stage, and then drag two more instances of the **Leaf** symbol and place them next to the first instance. See Figure 4-48.

Figure 4-48   Leaf instances arranged on the Stage

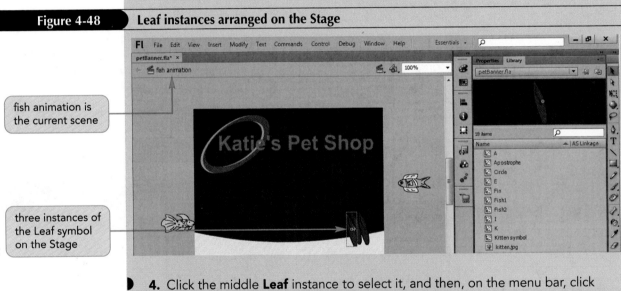

fish animation is the current scene

three instances of the Leaf symbol on the Stage

▶ **4.** Click the middle **Leaf** instance to select it, and then, on the menu bar, click **Modify**, point to **Transform**, and click **Flip Horizontal**. The middle leaf instance faces the other direction.

▶ **5.** On the menu bar, click **Control**, point to **Test Movie**, and then click **in Flash Professional**. The movie plays in Flash Player. The Leaf instances exhibit their animation.

▶ **6.** Close the Flash Player window, and then save the banner.

Using the Movie Explorer

As a Flash document gets more complex with many symbols, text blocks, layers, and scenes, it can become difficult to manage all the elements or to find a specific element. The Movie Explorer can help you view each of the document's elements, to search for a specific element, to find all instances of a particular symbol, or even to print a list of the document's elements as listed in the Movie Explorer.

You can choose which elements to display in the Movie Explorer. For example, you can display only the text blocks used in the document, and then each text block appears in the Movie Explorer with information about the font and point size used in the text block. Likewise, you can choose to display each instance of the symbols used in the document. When you select an instance in the Movie Explorer, information about where the instance is located in the document appears at the bottom of the panel. The Movie Explorer's panel menu button provides access to additional options, including the following:

- Go to Symbol Definition, which selects the symbol definition for the symbol selected in the Movie Explorer
- Show in Library, which displays the selected symbol in the Library panel
- Show Movie Elements, which displays the document's elements such as its layers, frames, and symbol instances
- Show Symbol Definitions, which displays all elements associated with a symbol
- Show All Scenes, which displays the elements and symbols for all scenes in the document, not just the current scene

PROSKILLS

Teamwork: Using the Movie Explorer to Troubleshoot Problems

Creating a Flash document is often a collaborative process that could involve clients, designers, artists, and others. If you are working with a team of people to create a new Flash document, then you will already be familiar with how the document is organized. If you are working with a Flash document developed by someone else, the organization might not be as clear. In that case, you can use the Movie Explorer to become familiar with the way the scenes, symbols, and other elements are organized. You can explore how and where each of the document's symbols is used as well as how the symbol is constructed. You can then more easily modify the document.

You can also use the Movie Explorer to troubleshoot problems that arise, which might occur when you are working with complex animations. For example, if an animation is not working correctly, you can check the symbol instances that are part of the animation and determine whether they are in the correct scene, layer, and frame.

Teams commonly work together to create Flash documents. The Movie Explorer provides a good tool to help you evaluate the document if you didn't create it, saving you time and energy when you try to locate specific elements or determine specifics about the element.

Because the banner you created for the Katie's Pet Shop Web site has multiple scenes, layers, and symbols, you can use the Movie Explorer to review all of its elements and view how all the various symbol instances throughout the document are organized.

TIP

If a text block does not reside in a locked layer, you can double-click the text block in the Movie Explorer to change its contents.

To use the Movie Explorer to examine the banner's elements:

1. On the menu bar, click **Window**, and then click **Movie Explorer**. The Movie Explorer opens.

2. If necessary, click the **Show text** button $\boxed{A}$ to select it and click the other Show buttons to deselect them.

3. Click the **Movie Explorer panel menu** button, and then click **Show Movie Elements** to select it, if necessary.

4. Repeat Step 3 to select **Show Symbol Definitions** and **Show All Scenes**. The panel displays the scenes that contain text blocks as well as the symbols that contain text. This will make it easier to locate text blocks within the document.

5. Drag the bottom edge of the Movie Explorer window down to increase its size so you can see more of the elements in the window.

6. If necessary, click the **plus sign** next to the fish animation scene name to expand its contents. The Movie Explorer displays all of the text blocks for the scene, including the text properties. You can compare the text properties of all the text blocks in the scene. This information can be useful if you need to maintain consistency across all of the text blocks within a scene. See Figure 4-49.

| Figure 4-49 | Movie Explorer displaying text blocks |

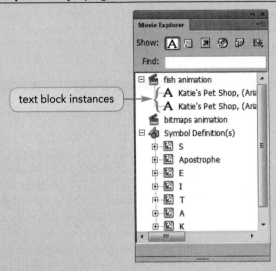

text block instances

7. In the Movie Explorer, click the **Show frames and layers** button to select it, and then click the **plus sign** next to the fish animation scene to expand its display, if necessary. Each layer of the fish animation scene is displayed in the panel. Selecting a layer name in the panel also selects the layer in the document, enabling you to find specific layers in a complex document.

8. In the Movie Explorer, scroll down the panel, click the **fish2** layer name under the fish animation scene, and then, if necessary, click the **plus sign** next to it. Each keyframe within the fish2 layer is displayed. See Figure 4-50.

| Figure 4-50 | Movie Explorer displaying the fish2 layer and its keyframes |

fish2 layer

keyframes

9. In the Movie Explorer, click the **Show movie clips, buttons, and graphics** button to select it, scroll down in the Movie Explorer panel, and then click the **Fish1** instance in Frame 50 of the fish2 layer. The path of the instance at the bottom of the panel indicates where the instance is located within the document. See Figure 4-51.

| Figure 4-51 | Fish1 instance in Frame 50 of the fish2 layer |

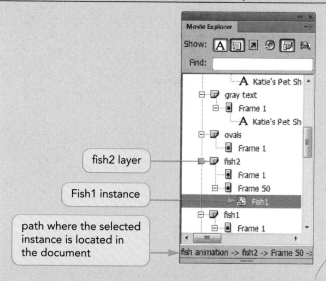

fish2 layer

Fish1 instance

path where the selected instance is located in the document

TIP

You can also press the Alt+F3 keys to open and close the Movie Explorer.

10. In the Movie Explorer, click the **Movie Explorer panel menu** button , and then click **Go to Symbol Definition**. The Movie Explorer shows the Fish1 symbol under the Symbol Definitions area. The Symbol Definitions area shows all the elements associated with the selected symbol.

11. Close the Movie Explorer, and then close the petBanner.fla file.

Aly is pleased with the document elements and is ready to show the banner to Katie. In this session, you used onion skinning to display the contents of multiple frames on the Stage. You created nested movie clips, which contain instances of other movie clips within their Timelines. You also created an inverse kinematic animation using bones. Finally, you used the Movie Explorer to review the elements of a complex document.

Session 4.3 Quick Check

1. What is a nested movie clip symbol?
2. What is a movie clip that has other movie clips nested within it called?
3. How can onion skinning help you when working with a complex animation?
4. How can you change the position of the onion skin markers in the Timeline header?
5. Why will the animations of movie clips embedded in a nested movie clip not play when you test them within the Document window?
6. Explain how inverse kinematics works.
7. When you add bones to a symbol instance or shape, the instance or shape and its armature are moved to a pose layer named _____.
8. What is the purpose of the Movie Explorer?

Review Assignments

Data File needed for the Review Assignments: kpsDraft.fla

Based on Katie's feedback, Aly wants you to create a third banner for the Katie's Pet Shop Web site. This banner will have two fish swimming back and forth on the Stage, one following a curved path, and both slowing down in the middle of the banner. The banner will include a mask effect on the Katie's Pet Shop title that makes the text block appear gradually from left to right. This banner also requires a new animation of a small circular sign that contains rotating text inside. An instance of the sign will be animated to move in the scene.

1. Open the **kpsDraft.fla** document located in the Flash4\Review folder included with your Data Files, and then save the file as **kpsBanner.fla** in the same folder.

2. In Frame 1 of the fish1 layer, add an instance of the Fish1 symbol to the pasteboard on the left side of the Stage so its center is about 170 pixels from the top of the Stage.

3. Insert a keyframe in Frame 36 of the fish1 layer, and then create a motion tween at Frame 1 of the fish1 layer.

4. At Frame 35, move the Fish1 instance to the pasteboard on the right side of the Stage. Curve the center of the motion path slightly up. Orient the fish to the path.

5. At Frame 36 of the fish1 layer, move the Fish1 instance to the right side of the pasteboard, and then flip the Fish1 instance to face to the left. Create a motion tween at Frame 36 of the fish1 layer.

6. At Frame 70, move the Fish1 instance to the pasteboard on the left side of the Stage. Curve the center of the motion path slightly down. Orient the fish to the path.

7. Insert a new layer above the fish1 layer and name it **fish2**. In the fish2 layer, add an instance of the Fish2 symbol on the pasteboard on the right side of the Stage so its center is about 250 pixels from the top of the Stage.

8. Insert a keyframe in Frame 36 of the fish2 layer, and then create a motion tween at Frame 1 of the fish2 layer. At Frame 35, move the Fish2 instance to the pasteboard on the left side of the Stage.

9. At Frame 36 of the fish2 layer, move the Fish2 instance to the left side of the pasteboard, and then flip the Fish2 instance to face to the right. Create a motion tween at Frame 36 of the fish2 layer. At Frame 70, move the Fish2 instance to the pasteboard on the right side of the Stage.

10. Use the Motion Editor to apply the Stop and Start (Medium) ease to the basic motion properties of both motion tweens in the fish1 layer. Apply the Stop and Start (Fastest) ease to the basic motion properties of both motion tweens in the fish2 layer.

11. Insert a new layer above the title layer, name it **text mask**, and then change its type to Mask. Make sure the title layer's type is changed to Masked and that it is indented below the text mask layer.

12. Unlock the text mask layer. In the text mask layer, draw a rectangle with no stroke and a fill color of your choice that covers the entire Katie's Pet Shop text block. The rectangle's width should be the same width as the text block and its height should be only as high as the text block. Convert this rectangle to a movie clip symbol named **Rectangle**.

13. Insert a keyframe at Frame 35 of the text mask layer. At Frame 1, move the rectangle to the left of the text block to reveal the entire text block. Create a motion tween from Frame 1 to Frame 34 so that the rectangle moves from left to right to gradually cover the text block. Lock the text mask layer and test the mask animation effect. The text block should appear gradually from left to right.

14. Create a new movie clip symbol named **Rotating text**. In symbol-editing mode, add a text block to the center of the symbol's Stage. Use Arial for the font family, Bold for the font style, 12 for the point size, 0 for the letter spacing, white for the text (fill) color, and Align center for the paragraph format. Type **Puppies** in the text block. In the Property inspector, set the text block's X and Y values to 0.

15. Create a motion tween in Frame 1, and then, in the Property inspector, set the text to rotate clockwise one time.

16. Rename Layer 1 to **puppies**, hide the puppies layer, and then insert a new layer named **kittens** above the puppies layer. In the kittens layer, create a text block with the word **Kittens** using the same properties as the Puppies text block. Create a motion tween so that the Kittens text block will rotate counterclockwise one time.

17. Hide the kittens layer, and then insert a new layer named **fish** above the kittens layer. In the fish layer, create a text block with the word **Fish** using the same properties as the Puppies text block. Create a motion tween so that the Fish text block will rotate clockwise one time.

18. Select the kittens layer, and then move its motion tween span so that it starts in Frame 26. Select the fish layer, and then move its motion tween span so that it starts in Frame 49. In the fish layer, insert a regular frame at Frame 95. Unhide the puppies and kittens layers. Test the animation. Exit symbol-editing mode.

19. Create a new movie clip symbol named **Rotating sign**. In symbol-editing mode, add a small circle with a dark blue (#003366) fill color and no stroke to the center of the symbol's Stage. Use the Property inspector to make the circle 60 pixels wide and 60 pixels high, and to set its X and Y values to 0. Drag an instance of the Rotating text symbol to the center of the circle. Exit symbol-editing mode.

20. Insert a new layer above the text mask layer and name it **rotating sign**. In this layer, drag an instance of the Rotating sign symbol to the pasteboard at the lower left of the Stage, and then create a motion tween. Insert a keyframe at Frame 35, and then move the Rotating sign instance to the bottom center of the Stage so that the instance moves from the pasteboard in Frame 1 to the bottom center of the Stage in Frame 35.

21. Test the new animations for the document using the Test Movie command.

22. Submit the finished files to your instructor.

Case Problem 1

Animate letters, add motion tweens, and create a mask animation.

APPLY

Data File needed for this Case Problem: jsDraft.fla

Jackson's Sports Store Dan asks Chris about creating a new Flash document to use on the Jackson's Sports Store Web site to promote the store's softball extravaganza sale. You will create the advertisement based on a document Dan has developed. You will add new text messages promoting the sale and the supplies provided by the store. The store's name will be animated to display one letter at a time. After the store's name appears, the next text message will fade in. Another text message will appear and will increase in size and change in color. You will add a softball picture animation and you will also add several instances of the balloon symbol. The finished advertisement is shown in Figure 4-52.

Figure 4-52   **Finished advertisement for Jackson's Sports Store**

iStockphoto.com/Bill Grove

1. Open the **jsDraft.fla** file located in the Flash4\Case1 folder included with your Data Files, and then save the document as **jsSoftball.fla** in the same folder.

2. Create a new layer folder named **letters** above the jackson's layer, and then move the layer inside the folder. Convert the text block in the jackson's layer to individual text blocks, one for each character. Distribute the characters to individual layers inside the letters layer folder, and then delete the empty jackson's layer.

3. Move the keyframes in Frame 1 of each letter layer so that each starts one frame after the previous character. The first letter, *J*, starts in Frame 1. The second letter, *a*, starts in Frame 2. The third letter, *c*, starts in Frame 3. The fourth letter, *k*, starts in Frame 4, and so on. The characters will appear one at a time to form the store's complete name. Collapse the letters layer folder.

4. Insert regular frames at Frame 100 of each layer to extend the movie.

5. Insert a new layer above the background layer and name it **sale**. At Frame 25 of the sale layer, insert a keyframe, and then drag an instance of the Sale symbol from the Library panel to the center of the Stage. Animate the text block instance to fade in over the next 15 frames. (*Hint*: Insert a keyframe at Frame 40 of the sale layer. At Frame 25, create a motion tween and change the alpha amount of the Sale instance to 0%. At Frame 39, change the alpha amount to 100%.)

6. Do the following to animate the text of the Sale text block instance to change from red to blue. At Frame 55, insert a keyframe. At Frame 40, create a motion tween. At Frame 54, change the tint of the Sale text instance to 100% blue (#0000FF). At Frame 55, change the tint to 100% blue (#0000FF) to match the text block's tint at the end of the motion tween.

7. Do the following to change the tint of the Sale text block back to red. At Frame 55, create a motion tween. At Frame 70, change the text block's tint to 100% red (#FF0000). Lock the sale layer.

8. Insert a new layer above the sale layer and name it **equipment**. At Frame 40, insert a keyframe, drag an instance of the Equipment symbol to the lower part of the Stage, and then create a motion tween.

9. At Frame 40, use the Transform panel to reduce the size of the Equipment instance to 50% of its original size and change the alpha amount to 0%. At Frame 55, change the size of the instance back to 100% and change its alpha amount to 100%. The text block will fade in as it increases in size from Frame 40 to Frame 55.

10. At Frame 60 of the equipment layer, reduce the size of the Equipment instance to 80% of its original size. At Frame 65, increase the size of the text block to 100%. The text block will decrease in size slightly and increase back to its original size. Lock the equipment layer.

11. Insert a new layer above the background layer and name it **balloon1**. Drag an instance of the Balloon symbol to the lower-left side of the Stage. At Frame 1 of the balloon1 layer, create a motion tween. At Frame 50, move the Balloon instance to

the upper-right corner of the Stage. Use the Selection tool to curve the motion path down slightly.

12. Insert a new layer above the balloon1 layer and name it **balloon2**. At Frame 20, insert a keyframe, drag an instance of the Balloon symbol to the lower-right side of the Stage, and then create a motion tween. At Frame 70, move the Balloon instance to the upper-left corner of the Stage. Use the Selection tool to curve the motion path down slightly.

13. Create a new movie clip symbol named **Bitmap animation**. In symbol-editing mode, drag the softball1.jpg bitmap to the center of the Stage, and in the Info panel, select the center Registration/Transformation point, and change the X and Y values to 0.

14. Convert the bitmap to a movie clip symbol named **Softball pic1**, and select its center registration point in the Registration icon, if necessary.

15. Rename Layer 1 as **softball1**, and set the alpha amount of the Softball pic1 instance to 100%. Create a motion tween, extend the motion tween span to Frame 144, and add a Color property keyframe at Frame 48. Select the Softball pic1 instance on the Stage, and make sure the alpha amount remains set at 100%.

16. At Frame 72, set the alpha amount of the Softball pic1 instance to 0%. At Frame 120, add a Color property keyframe, and at Frame 144, set the alpha amount to 100%.

17. Insert a new layer and name it **softball2**, and then insert a keyframe at Frame 48. Drag an instance of the softball2.jpg bitmap to the center of the Stage, and in the Info panel, select the center Registration/Transformation point, and change the X and Y values to 0.

18. Convert the bitmap to a movie clip symbol names **Softball pic2**, and select its center registration point in the Registration icon, if necessary. At Frame 48, create a motion tween, set the alpha amount of the Softball pic2 instance to 0%, and then add a Color property keyframe at Frame 72. At Frame 72, set the alpha amount of the Softball pic2 instance to 100%.

19. At Frame 120, add a Color property keyframe, and at Frame 145, set the alpha amount to 0%.

20. Insert a new layer above the softball2 layer, name it **bitmap mask**, and then convert the new layer to a Mask layer. Convert the softball1 layer to a masked layer.

21. In the bitmap mask layer, draw a filled circle shape that is 150 pixels high by 150 pixels wide, and center it on the Stage. Lock all of the layers and test the animation. Each bitmap will display one after the other inside the masked area. Exit symbol-editing mode.

22. Insert a new layer above the background layer and name it **bitmaps**. In the bitmaps layer, drag an instance of the Bitmap animation symbol and place at the center of the Stage.

23. Test the animation in both Flash and Flash Player.

24. Submit the finished files to your instructor.

Add a mask layer effect, animate letters and text blocks, and apply an ease effect.

APPLY

Case Problem 2

Data File needed for this Case Problem: aczDraft.fla

Alamo City Zoo   Janet asks Alex to develop a new advertising banner for the Alamo City Zoo Web site. The banner should include new animations that highlight the Alamo City Zoo name. It should also display several text messages that promote the zoo's attractions, including the new bear exhibit. You will create the new advertisement based on a banner that Alex started. You will add a mask effect where the spotlight starts small at the center of the banner and increases to reveal the banner. You will develop a special text effect for the zoo's name where the letters increase in size one after the other to give it a pulsating effect. Finally, you will add the text messages promoting the zoo and you will add graphics that drop down from the top of the banner. The finished banner is shown in Figure 4-53.

| Figure 4-53 | Finished advertising banner for Alamo City Zoo |

© Luis A Lopez

1. Open the **aczDraft.fla** file located in the Flash4\Case2 folder included with your Data Files, and then save the document as **aczAd.fla** in the same folder.

2. Create a new movie clip symbol named **Circle**. In symbol-editing mode, draw a circle with a brown (#663300) fill and no stroke at the center of the Stage. Select the circle and in the Info panel, set its dimensions to 40 pixels wide and 40 pixels high, select the center Registration/Transformation point, and set the X and Y values to 0. Exit symbol-editing mode.

3. Insert a regular frame at Frame 20 in all layers. Insert a new layer above the title layer and name it **mask**. At Frame 1 of the mask layer, drag an instance of the Circle symbol from the Library panel to the center of the Stage. In the Property inspector, set the instance's X and Y values to 175 each to center it on the Stage.

4. Select the Circle instance and create a motion tween. At Frame 20 of the mask layer, change the size of the Circle instance to 350 pixels wide by 350 pixels high.

5. Show the mask layer, right-click the layer, and then change its type to Mask. Make sure the title layer is masked, and then change the bear background layer's type to masked. Test the animation. The mask gradually reveals the company name and bear picture.

6. Hide the mask layer temporarily, unlock the title layer if needed, and then copy the text block on the Stage. Insert a new layer above the mask layer and name it **name**. Use the Paste in Place command to paste the text block in the name layer in the same relative position as in the title layer.

7. Insert a layer folder above the name layer, name it **letters**, and then move the name layer inside the letters folder.

8. Select the text block in the name layer, convert the text to individual letters, and then distribute the letters to individual layers. Delete the empty name layer. Move all of the letter keyframes to Frame 20 by selecting all the Frame 1s of the individual letter layers and dragging them all to start in Frame 20. This is where the individual letters' animation will begin.

9. Extend all of the layers except the mask and title layers by inserting regular frames at Frame 130 of each layer.

10. To make each letter change in size for a moment, insert two keyframes in each layer where the size of the letter is increased slightly in the first of the two new keyframes and where the second keyframe is inserted three frames after the first. So for the

A layer, add keyframes at Frames 22 and 25, and then use the Transform panel to change the size of the instance in Frame 22 to 130% larger. For the next letter in layer l, insert keyframes at Frames 26 and 29, and then increase the size of the instance in Frame 26 to 130%. For the letter *a* in layer a, insert keyframes at Frame 30 and Frame 33, and then increase the size of the letter in Frame 30 to 130%.

11. Repeat Step 10 for each letter, starting one frame after the last keyframe of the previous letter. The last layer (for the second *o* in Zoo) will have keyframes at Frame 66 and Frame 69. Show the mask layer, lock the title layer, and then test the animation. The individual letters should increase in size one at a time after the mask effect. Collapse the letters folder.

12. Place horizontal guides about 150 pixels and 250 pixels from the top of the Stage.

13. Insert two new layers above the mask layer, and rename them **text1** and **text2**. At Frame 60 of the text1 layer, insert a keyframe, and then create a Classic text block centered just below the guide 150 pixels from the top of the Stage. Use the Monotype Corsiva font family, a 22 point size, centered alignment, and light yellow (#FFFFCC) text fill color. Type **Monkeys, Gorillas, and Elephants!** in the text block.

14. Create a motion tween in Frame 60 of the text1 layer. At Frame 60, use the Transform panel to reduce the size of the text block to 50% of its original size. At Frame 65, increase the size of the text back to 100%. The text will increase in size throughout the motion tween.

15. Create another text motion tween in the text2 layer between Frame 65 and Frame 70. Create a text block with the words **New Bear Exhibit!** on the pasteboard to the right of the Stage just below the guide 250 pixels from the top of the Stage. This text block should fly in from the right of the Stage to the center of the banner about 250 pixels from the top. Clear the guides.

16. Insert a new layer above the text2 layer and name it **paw1**. Insert a keyframe at Frame 80. Drag an instance of the bear paw symbol to the upper-left corner of the banner, staying within the rectangle. Insert a keyframe at Frame 90 and move the bear paw instance toward the bottom so that it is below the letters *Ne* in the New Bear Exhibit! text. Create a motion tween at Frame 80 of the paw1 layer and have the bear paw instance rotate clockwise twice. At Frame 89, move the bear paw instance to the same position as it is in Frame 90.

⊕ EXPLORE   17. Use the Motion Editor to apply the Spring ease to the motion tween in the paw1 layer. The paw instance will exhibit a spring effect at the end of its motion tween.

18. Insert a new layer above the paw1 layer and rename it **paw2**. Insert a keyframe at Frame 100. Drag an instance of the bear paw symbol to the upper-right side of the banner, staying within the rectangle. Insert another keyframe at Frame 110 and move the bear paw instance toward the bottom so that it is below the letters *it!* in the New Bear Exhibit! text. Create a motion tween at Frame 100 and have the bear paw instance rotate counterclockwise twice. At Frame 109, move the bear paw instance to the same position as it is in Frame 110.

⊕ EXPLORE   19. Use the Motion Editor to apply the Spring ease to the motion tween in the paw2 layer. The paw instance will exhibit a spring effect at the end of its motion tween.

20. Test the banner's animation in Flash and Flash Player to view all the animations.

21. Submit the finished files to your instructor.

Create 3D
animations of
letters, text block
animations, a
nested movie
clip, and a curved
motion path.

CHALLENGE

Case Problem 3

Data File needed for this Case Problem: glDraft.fla

G&L Nursery   G&L Nursery is expanding and opening a store at a new location. To
advertise the new location and promote her business, Alice started a new marketing
campaign. As part of this campaign, she asks Amanda to develop an ad to place on
the local newspaper's Web site. To help Amanda, you will create several animations,
including one where the letters *G&L* drop in and the letters in the word *Nursery* fall
into place to create the title for the ad. Then several animated text blocks will move into
place on the ad, followed by a graphic of the word *Flowers* that will move across the ad
banner simulating a truck. The graphic will have animated tires. Figure 4-54 shows the
completed advertisement.

| Figure 4-54 | Completed advertisement for G&L Nursery |

1. Open the **glDraft.fla** file located in the Flash4\Case3 folder included with your
   Data Files, and then save the document as **nurseryAd.fla** in the same folder.
2. Create horizontal guides at 50 pixels, at 150 pixels, and at 200 pixels from the
   top of the Stage.
3. Insert a new layer and name it **title1**, and then create a text block with the word
   Nursery. Use white for the text (fill) color, Arial for the font family, Bold Italic for
   the font style, and 40 for the point size. Center the word on the guide 200 pixels
   from the top of the Stage.
4. Insert a layer folder above the title1 layer and name it **nursery text**. Move the title1
   layer to the new layer folder. Then select the title1 text block, break it apart, and
   distribute the individual letters to separate layers. The new layers for the letters
   should be inside the layer folder. Delete the title1 layer.

⊕ **EXPLORE**   5. Convert each of the letters into symbols with movie clip behavior. Use the following names for the symbols to match the letters they represent: **N, U, R1, S, E, R2,**
   and **Y**. Create a new folder in the Library, name it **Nursery Letters**, and then move
   all the letter symbols inside the folder.

   Each letter will be animated to drop in from the top part of the Stage to its current
   location 200 pixels from the top. The letters will move one at a time, rotating in
   3D space, and fading in as they move to form the word *Nursery*. The first letter will
   start in Frame 1 and the next letters will start every 10 frames.

6. Move each of the letters' keyframes that are in Frame 1 of their respective layers to start every 10 frames. The keyframes should be moved to the following frames: N—Frame 1; u—Frame 10; r—Frame 20; s—Frame 30; e—Frame 40; r—Frame 50; y—Frame 60. Be sure to keep each letter in its own layer.

7. Create a motion tween for each letter in its own layer.

8. Select Frame 10 of the N layer, open the Motion Editor, and insert a property keyframe for the X property under the Basic motion category. A property keyframe is automatically added for the Y property. Select Frame 1 and use the 3D Translation tool to move the N instance up so that its center is on the guide 50 pixels from the top of the Stage. Move the instance slightly to its left. In the Motion Editor, at Frame 1, set the Rotation X and the Rotation Y properties to 90 degrees. At Frame 10, insert a property keyframe for the Rotation X and the Rotation Y properties, and then set their values to 0 degrees. At Frame 10, select the Alpha property under the Color Effect category and add a property keyframe. Set the alpha amount in Frame 1 to 0% and in Frame 10 to 100%. The N instance will rotate, fade in, and move into place from Frame 1 to Frame 10.

9. Repeat Step 8 for each letter instance so that it rotates, fades in, and falls into place using the following starting and ending frames: u layer—Frames 10–20; first r layer—Frames 20–30; s layer—Frames 30–40; e layer—Frames 40–50; second r layer—Frames 50–60; y layer—Frames 60–70. Test the letter animations. The letters for the word *Nursery* drop into place one at a time. They fade in and rotate as they fall. Collapse the nursery text folder and lock it to make it easier to work with the other layers in the Timeline.

10. Insert a layer above the frame layer and name it **title2**. Insert a keyframe at Frame 91. Create a text block using the same type settings as in Step 3. Type **G&L** in the text block. Center this text block on the guide 50 pixels from the top of the Stage.

11. Convert the G&L text block to a movie clip symbol named **G&L text**. Create a motion tween for the G&L text instance. At Frame 91, change the alpha amount of the instance to 0%. At Frame 100, move the instance so that it is centered above the Nursery text and change its alpha amount to 100%. The G&L text should move from its initial position to above the Nursery text and should fade in as it moves into position.

12. Insert a new layer and name it **text1**. Insert a keyframe at Frame 100 of this layer, and then create a text block in this frame. The text should be white, Arial for the font, 26 for the point size, and Bold for the font style. Place the text block on the pasteboard to the left of the Stage about 50 pixels from the top. Type **Always Fresh!** in this text block. Create a motion tween on this text block, and at Frame 105, move the text block to the center of the Stage, keeping it about 50 pixels from the top. The text block moves in from the left of the Stage.

13. Insert a new layer and rename it **text2**. Insert a keyframe at Frame 105 and create a text block using the same settings used in Step 12, but change the font size to 20 and use Bold Italic for the font style. Place the text block in the pasteboard to the right of the Stage about 350 pixels from the top. Type **Delivered on Time!** in this text block. Create a motion tween on this text block, and at Frame 110, move the text block to the center of the Stage, keeping it about 350 pixels from the top. The text block moves in from the right of the Stage.

14. Create a graphic that will simulate a truck moving across the Stage. Start by creating a rotating wheel symbol that will be embedded in the truck graphic. Create a new movie clip symbol named **Rotating wheel**. In symbol-editing mode, insert an instance of the Wheel symbol from the library to the center of the Stage. In the Property inspector, if necessary, set the X and Y values to 0. Create a motion tween on the Wheel instance, select Frame 1, and then in the Property inspector, set the Wheel instance to rotate clockwise one time. The Rotating wheel symbol is complete. Exit symbol-editing mode.

15. Create a new movie clip symbol named **Truck**. In symbol-editing mode, create a text block at the center of the Stage using Arial for the font, Bold Italic for the style, 36 for the point size, and green (#66FF99) for the font color. Type the word **FLOWERs** in all uppercase, except for the letter *s*. Reduce the font size of the

letter *s* to 30. Use the Info panel to set the X and Y registration point coordinates to 0 to center the text on the Stage.

16. Use the Line tool to draw a short horizontal line about 30 pixels wide using a stroke color of yellow (#FFFF00), a stroke height of 1, and Solid for the stroke style. Draw the line about 5 pixels to the left of the letter *F*. Create two copies of this line and place the lines to the left of the letter *F*. Each line should be a little farther distance from the letter *F* and equally spaced from each other. The lines will add to the effect of the FLOWERs text moving.

17. Drag an instance of the Rotating wheel symbol to the Stage and place it right below the letter *L* in FLOWERs. Drag another instance and place it below the letter *R*. These instances will be the wheels for the truck. The Truck symbol is complete. Exit symbol-editing mode.

18. Insert a new layer above the text2 layer and name it **truck**. Insert a keyframe at Frame 70 and drag an instance of the Truck symbol in the pasteboard to the upper-left side of the Stage. Create a motion tween at Frame 70 for the Truck instance. At Frame 100, move the Truck instance to the center of the Stage below the Nursery text block.

⊕ **EXPLORE** 19. Use the Selection tool to drag the center of the motion path for the Truck instance down slightly to curve it.

⊕ **EXPLORE** 20. Use the Subselection tool to click an endpoint on the motion path to reveal the curve's Bezier handles, which are used to modify the curve of the motion path. Drag the top endpoint Bezier handle to the left to further curve the top part of the motion path. Drag the bottom endpoint Bezier handle up and to the right to create an upward curve on the bottom part of the motion path.

21. Test the animation in Flash and Flash Player.

22. Submit the finished files to your instructor.

Create an ad banner with a mask animation, motion tween animations, and individual letters.

CREATE

Case Problem 4

Data File needed for this Case Problem: rcDraft.fla

River City Conservation Society Brittany meets with Anissa to discuss the development of a new advertisement banner that the River City Conservation Society can use to promote the organization in various Web sites. The ad will contain the society's name, an animation of a star moving across the banner, and several graphics containing text messages. You will create the new ad, which will be similar to the one shown in Figure 4-55.

Figure 4-55   **Sample advertisement banner for River City Conservation Society**

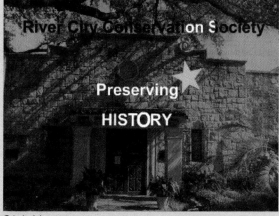

© Luis A Lopez

1. Open the **rcDraft.fla** file located in the Flash4\Case4 folder included with your Data Files, and then save the document as **rcAd.fla** in the same folder.

2. In a new layer, create a text block with the text **River City Conservation Society** at an appropriate location on the Stage, using the text properties of your choice.

3. Create a spotlight effect for the text using a mask animation.

4. In a new layer, create an animation of an instance of the star symbol that rotates as it moves. For example, the Star instance could move from the lower-left corner of the Stage in a curved path up toward the center of the Stage, move back down to the lower-right corner of the Stage, and then move in a curved path back toward the lower-left corner.

5. At the frame(s) of your choice, in separate layers, create a text block for each word of the text **Preserving HISTORY**. The words should appear on the Stage in an appropriate location. Use the text properties of your choice.

6. Create a pulsating effect on the individual letters of the word *HISTORY*.

7. Make any other changes you feel enhance the advertisement.

8. Test the document's animation in Flash and Flash Player.

9. Submit the finished files to your instructor.

ENDING DATA FILES

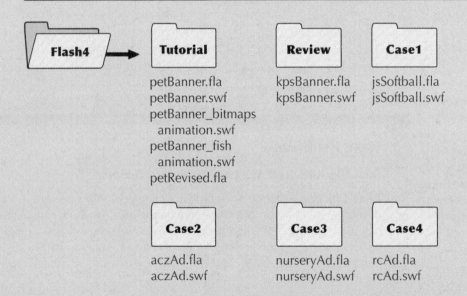

Flash4 → Tutorial

Tutorial
petBanner.fla
petBanner.swf
petBanner_bitmaps
 animation.swf
petBanner_fish
 animation.swf
petRevised.fla

Review
kpsBanner.fla
kpsBanner.swf

Case1
jsSoftball.fla
jsSoftball.swf

Case2
aczAd.fla
aczAd.swf

Case3
nurseryAd.fla
nurseryAd.swf

Case4
rcAd.fla
rcAd.swf

TUTORIAL 5

Making a Document Interactive with ActionScript 3.0

Adding Buttons, Actions, and Sounds

OBJECTIVES

Session 5.1
- Explore the different button states
- Add a button from the Buttons library
- Edit a button instance
- Create a custom button
- Align objects on the Stage

Session 5.2
- Review the basics of ActionScript programming
- Compare ActionScript 2.0 and ActionScript 3.0
- Learn ActionScript 3.0 syntax
- Create ActionScript 3.0 code using the Code Snippets panel
- Modify ActionScript code to create functions and handle events
- Create links to external Web sites

Session 5.3
- Compare different types of sound effects
- Import sounds from a file or the Sounds library
- Add sound to buttons and as a background sound
- Change sound settings and add sound effects

Case | *Katie's Pet Shop*

Aly is designing a pet adoption banner for the Katie's Pet Shop Web site. Katie wants the new banner design to be similar to the site's other banners and to include a background sound as well as the option to view pictures of pets available for adoption. Aly suggests providing the option to turn off the background sound, which some users might find distracting while they view the banner. She suggests adding several buttons to the banner to control which picture is displayed and to mute the sound. She also suggests that the buttons include their own sound effects to help the user know when the button has been clicked.

In this tutorial, you will create and add buttons to a document, and use ActionScript 3.0 to make the buttons interactive. You will use the Code Snippets panel to write ActionScript code to control the buttons and to create a link to a Web site. Finally, you will add sound to the banner.

STARTING DATA FILES

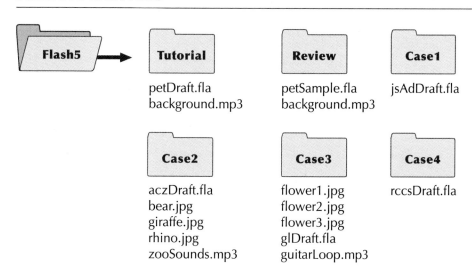

Flash5 → Tutorial
petDraft.fla
background.mp3

Review
petSample.fla
background.mp3

Case1
jsAdDraft.fla

Case2
aczDraft.fla
bear.jpg
giraffe.jpg
rhino.jpg
zooSounds.mp3

Case3
flower1.jpg
flower2.jpg
flower3.jpg
glDraft.fla
guitarLoop.mp3

Case4
rccsDraft.fla

SESSION 5.1 VISUAL OVERVIEW

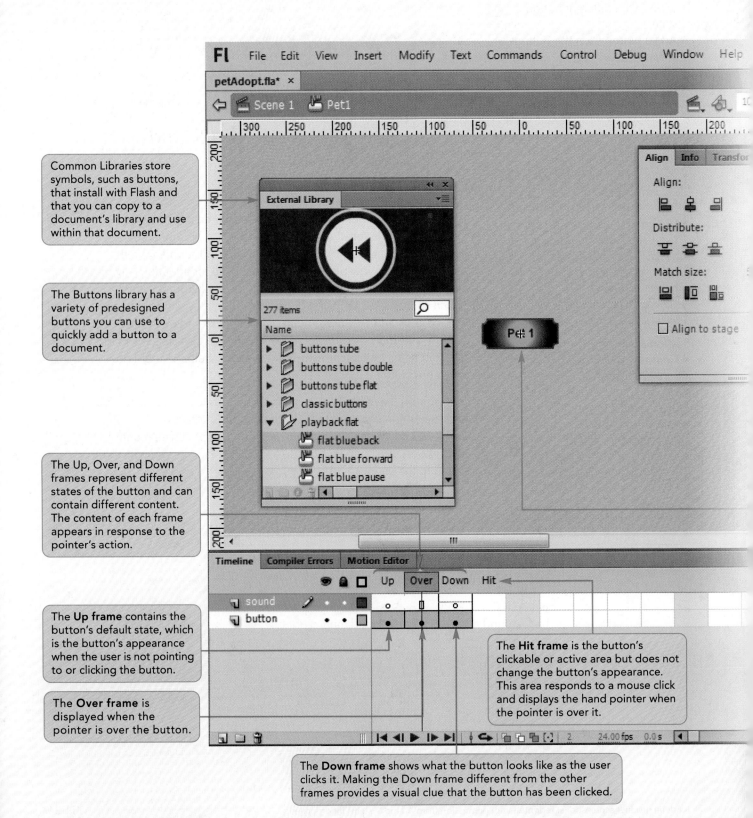

Common Libraries store symbols, such as buttons, that install with Flash and that you can copy to a document's library and use within that document.

The Buttons library has a variety of predesigned buttons you can use to quickly add a button to a document.

The Up, Over, and Down frames represent different states of the button and can contain different content. The content of each frame appears in response to the pointer's action.

The **Up frame** contains the button's default state, which is the button's appearance when the user is not pointing to or clicking the button.

The **Over frame** is displayed when the pointer is over the button.

The **Hit frame** is the button's clickable or active area but does not change the button's appearance. This area responds to a mouse click and displays the hand pointer when the pointer is over it.

The **Down frame** shows what the button looks like as the user clicks it. Making the Down frame different from the other frames provides a visual clue that the button has been clicked.

BUTTONS AND BUTTON STATES

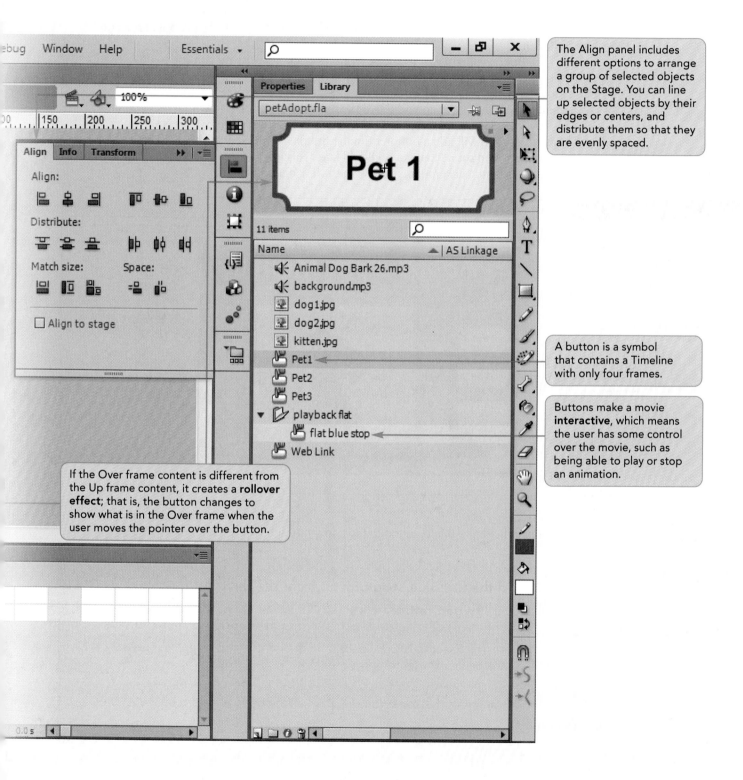

The Align panel includes different options to arrange a group of selected objects on the Stage. You can line up selected objects by their edges or centers, and distribute them so that they are evenly spaced.

A button is a symbol that contains a Timeline with only four frames.

Buttons make a movie **interactive**, which means the user has some control over the movie, such as being able to play or stop an animation.

If the Over frame content is different from the Up frame content, it creates a **rollover effect**; that is, the button changes to show what is in the Over frame when the user moves the pointer over the button.

Adding a Button from the Buttons Library

Published Flash SWF files, also called movies, can include interactive elements. Adding interaction to a movie draws the viewer in because the viewer is able to do more than passively watch the animation. One of the simplest ways to include interactivity is to add buttons that perform an action, such as stopping and starting an animation or muting sound. A button can take many forms, can include sound effects, and can even change appearance or behavior when the user positions the pointer over it or clicks it.

The Buttons library has a variety of predesigned buttons you can use to quickly add a button to a document. The Buttons library is one of the Common Libraries, which store symbols that install with Flash and can be copied to your documents. The library's button symbols can be copied to a document's library and used within that document.

Aly included a background sound in the new banner design, which is shown in Figure 5-1. You will add a button from the Buttons library that allows the user to mute the background sound that you will add later. This way, users can decide whether they want to listen to background sounds when viewing the banner.

| Figure 5-1 | Initial banner design |

© 2013 Cengage Learning

You will add the Mute button to the banner design that Aly started.

To add the flat blue stop button from the Buttons library:

1. Open the **petDraft.fla** file located in the Flash5\Tutorial folder included with your Data Files, and then save the file as **petAdopt.fla** in the same folder.

2. Reset the **Essentials** workspace, and then display the rulers, if necessary. All of the banner contents are visible.

3. In the Timeline, add a new layer above the text layer, and then rename the new layer **buttons**. You will place all the buttons for the banner in the buttons layer.

4. On the menu bar, click **Window**, point to **Common Libraries**, and then click **Buttons**. The Buttons External Library panel opens in the middle of the program window. The library contains 277 items organized into folders by categories such as "buttons oval" and "classic buttons."

5. In the Buttons Library panel, scroll down, and then double-click the **playback flat** folder icon. The folder expands, displaying a list of buttons.

6. In the playback flat folder, click the **flat blue stop** button to select it. A preview of the button appears at the top of the panel. See Figure 5-2. You want to copy the flat blue stop button into the buttons layer of the document.

Figure 5-2	Buttons Library panel

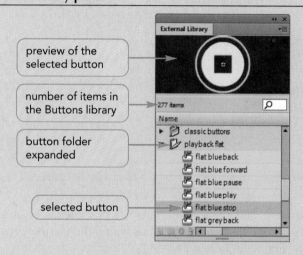

preview of the selected button

number of items in the Buttons library

button folder expanded

selected button

7. In the Timeline, make sure that the buttons layer is still selected, and then drag the **flat blue stop** button from the Buttons External Library panel to the lower-left corner of the Stage to create an instance of the button. The flat blue stop button is added to the document's library as a symbol with a button behavior.

8. On the Stage, drag the **flat blue stop** button instance approximately 10 pixels from the left edge of the Stage and approximately 270 pixels from the top of the Stage.

9. On the Buttons External Library panel tab, click the **Close** button [x]. The Buttons library closes.

10. Click the **Library** tab to open the Library panel, expand the **playback flat** folder, and then click the **flat blue stop** symbol. The library contains the flat blue stop button you just added. See Figure 5-3.

Figure 5-3   **Button symbol added to the banner**

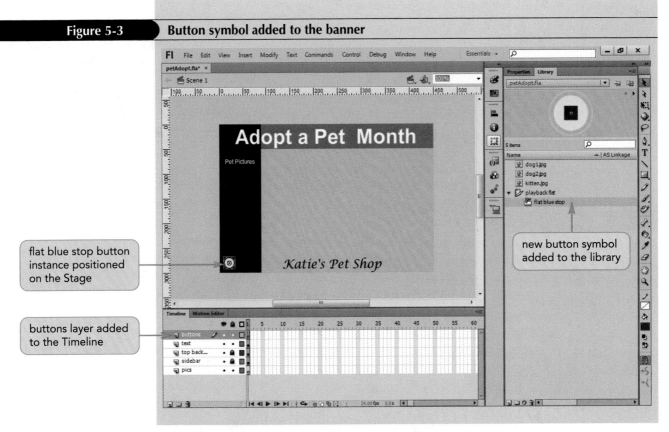

flat blue stop button instance positioned on the Stage

buttons layer added to the Timeline

new button symbol added to the library

After you add a button instance to a document, you should test it to be sure that it works as expected. You can do this within the Flash program window by turning on the Enable Simple Buttons command. When you turn on this command, the button exhibits its behavior on the Stage. When you move the pointer over the button, the pointer changes to a hand pointer and the button displays any rollover effects that are part of the button. After you review the button's behavior, you must turn off the Enable Simple Buttons command to select the button instance on the Stage and continue to modify it. You cannot select a button with the hand pointer.

You will use the Enable Simple Buttons command to test the new button instance.

To view the flat blue stop button's behaviors:

1. On the menu bar, click **Control**, and then click **Enable Simple Buttons**. The command is toggled on so you can test the button.

2. On the Stage, click an empty area away from the button to deselect the button.

3. On the Stage, point to the **flat blue stop** button instance. The pointer changes to 🖑, indicating that an action will occur after the button is clicked.

4. Click the **flat blue stop** button. The button changes color when clicked.

Editing a Button Instance

Every button has four frames—Up, Over, Down, and Hit, as described in the Session 5.1 Visual Overview. The Up, Over, and Down frames represent different states of the button and can contain different content that appears in response to the pointer's action. You can edit any button you add from the Buttons library. For example, you can change the contents of the Over frame to change the button's rollover effect, or you can change the contents of the Down frame to change the effect that occurs when the button is clicked. You can also change the colors or graphics in a predesigned button to match the design of the document and to make it look less like a predesigned button. You can even delete the contents in one of the button's frames if you don't want the button to exhibit a certain behavior such as a rollover effect.

PROSKILLS

Decision Making: Including a Button's Hit Frame

Creating a button requires a certain amount of decision making. You first need to evaluate how the button should look and function in all states. The button's appearance in the Up, Over, and Down frames should fit with the design of the movie and be placed in an accessible area of the movie.

Each button you create should also be simple to use. You need to decide whether to add a shape to the Hit frame, which is the area of the button the user can roll over or click to perform an action. When a button is a solid shape, such as a rectangle or oval, the button area is easy to click and you can leave the Hit frame empty. When a button consists of text, the user must click the letters in the text to activate the button. This can be difficult, especially if the text is small. To make it easier to click the button, you can draw a filled shape such as a rectangle to cover the text in the Hit frame. The shape is not visible in the published movie, but it represents the area the user can click to activate the button. This will enhance the user's experience and help avoid the frustration that can occur when the button does not work as expected.

You will modify the flat blue stop button so that it uses a different color for its Down frame. This frame is displayed when the button is clicked, giving the user visual feedback that the button has been clicked. Because the button is a symbol, you must be in symbol-editing mode to modify it.

To edit the Down frame of the flat blue stop button:

1. In the Library panel, double-click the **flat blue stop** button icon [icon]. The button opens in symbol-editing mode, and its four-frame Timeline appears.

   Trouble? If the button does not open in symbol-editing mode, you might be clicking the button instance on the Stage and not the button icon in the library. Try double-clicking the button icon in the library. If the button still does not open in symbol-editing mode, click Control on the menu bar, and then click Enable Simple Buttons to toggle off the command, complete Steps 1 through 6, toggle on the Enable Simple Buttons command, and then continue with Step 7.

2. Change the zoom magnification to **400%** to get a better view of the button. See Figure 5-4.

Figure 5-4   Flat blue stop button in symbol-editing mode

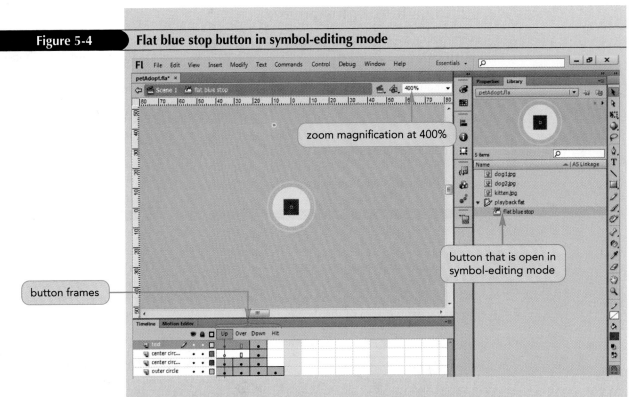

zoom magnification at 400%

button that is open in symbol-editing mode

button frames

3. In the Timeline, drag the playhead back and forth between the Up frame and the Down frame to see how the button changes.

4. In the Timeline, click the **Down** frame of the text layer. The small white square in the center of the button is selected, which is indicated by the dot pattern.

5. In the Tools panel, change the fill color of the square to **yellow** (#FFFF00). See Figure 5-5.

Figure 5-5   Fill color changed in the button's Down frame

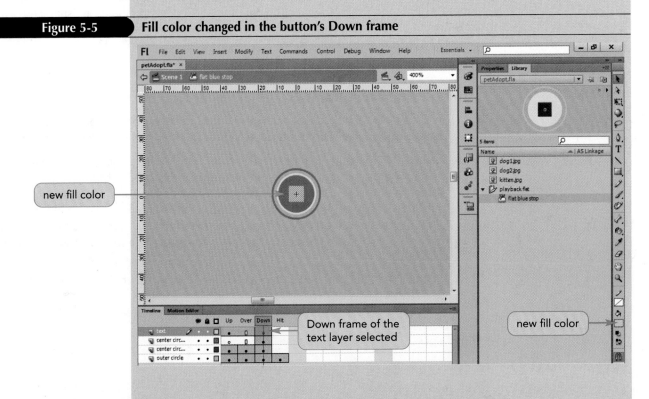

new fill color

Down frame of the text layer selected

new fill color

6. On the Edit bar, click the **Scene 1** link to exit symbol-editing mode and return to the document.

7. On the Stage, click the **flat blue stop** button instance. The small gray square in the center of the button turns yellow when you click the button instance.

8. On the menu bar, click **Control**, and then click **Enable Simple Buttons**. The Enable Simple Buttons command is toggled off, so you can select the button instance on the Stage.

INSIGHT

Anti-Aliasing Text

To improve readability, Flash uses a rendering engine that provides high-quality, clear text in Flash documents. Anti-aliasing, which is part of the rendering process, smoothes the edges of text displayed on the computer screen. Anti-aliasing is especially effective when using small font sizes. When text is selected on the Stage, you can choose a font-rendering method in the Property inspector. Two of the methods available are Anti-alias for animation and Anti-alias for readability. You should select Anti-alias for animation when the text will be animated, such as when you apply a motion tween to a text object. This results in a smoother animation. If the text will not be animated, you should select Anti-alias for readability. This improves the legibility of the text.

Labels often identify the purpose of each button so that it is clear to the user what will happen when a button is clicked. You should add a label either within the button's frames or to an instance of a button on the Stage. You will add text next to the flat blue stop button instance on the Stage to label it as the Mute button. This tells the user what happens when the button is clicked. Otherwise, the user might not know what purpose the button serves.

To add text to identify the Mute button instance:

1. Change the zoom magnification to **200%**.

2. In the Tools panel, click the **Hand Tool** button 👋, and then drag the document to center the button instance in the Document window.

3. In the Tools panel, click the **Text Tool** button ⊤. You will set the text properties and add a text block next to the button.

4. In the Property inspector, set the font family to **Arial**, set the font style to **Bold**, set the point size to **10**, the letter spacing to **0**, and then set the text fill color to **white** (#FFFFFF).

5. In the Property inspector, if necessary, click the **Anti-alias** button, and then click **Anti-alias for readability**. This anti-aliasing option improves the legibility of the text.

6. On the Stage, add a text block to the right of the button, and then type **Mute** in the text block.

7. In the Tools panel, click the **Selection Tool** button ▶.

8. On the Stage, reposition the text block as shown in Figure 5-6, and then deselect the text block.

TIP

You can also hold down the Spacebar to change the pointer to a hand pointer, drag the document on the Stage, and then release the Spacebar to return to the previous pointer.

Figure 5-6   Mute label added to the button

9. Save the document.

Creating a Custom Button

The buttons in the Buttons library provide many choices to use in documents. For a more professional look, you will often want to create unique buttons that match your project's design. Flash has the tools to create almost any kind of button you need. Buttons can be any shape, such as rectangles and ovals, or even text.

You can convert an existing object on the Stage, such as a rectangle, into a button symbol and then edit the button in symbol-editing mode, creating or modifying the contents for each of the button's four frames as needed. The object on the Stage becomes an instance of the button symbol, and the symbol is added to the library. You can also create a new symbol with a button behavior and then draw the button shape in symbol-editing mode as well as create or modify the contents for each of the button's four frames. The button you created is stored in the document's library, available for you to create instances of the button on the Stage.

REFERENCE

Creating a Custom Button

- On the Stage, create the button's shape, and then select the shape.
- On the menu bar, click Modify, and then click Convert to Symbol.
- Type a name in the Name box, click the Type button, click Button, and then click the OK button.
- Switch to symbol-editing mode, and then modify the contents for each of the button's four frames as needed.

or

- On the menu bar, click Insert, and then click New Symbol.
- Type a name in the Name box, click the Type button, click Button, and then click the OK button.
- Create the button's shape on the Stage.
- Switch to symbol-editing mode, and then modify the contents for each of the button's four frames as needed.

Based on Aly's instructions, you need to create three buttons for the banner. The buttons are modified rectangles. Each button, when clicked, will display a different picture of a pet. Because the buttons have a similar appearance, you can create one button, and then modify a copy of the button to create the other buttons.

To create the first button:

1. On the menu bar, click **Insert**, and then click **New Symbol** to open the Create New Symbol dialog box.

2. Name the symbol **Pet1**, set the symbol type to **Button**, and then click the **OK** button. The symbol opens in symbol-editing mode.

3. In the Tools panel, click and hold the **Rectangle Tool** button to display submenu of tools, and then click the **Rectangle Primitive Tool** button to select it.

4. In the Property inspector, lock the corner radius controls and enter **–5** as the Rectangle corner radius. Each corner radius is set to -5.

5. In the Property inspector, set the stroke color to **brown** (#996600), set the fill color to **light yellow** (#FFFFCC), set the stroke height to **2**, and then set the stroke style to **Solid**.

6. In the center of the Stage, draw a rectangle that is approximately **80** pixels wide and **30** pixels high.

7. In the Info panel, set the width to **80** and the height to **30**, if necessary, verify that the center registration point is selected, and then set the rectangle's X and Y values to **0**. See Figure 5-7.

Figure 5-7	Rectangle button shape

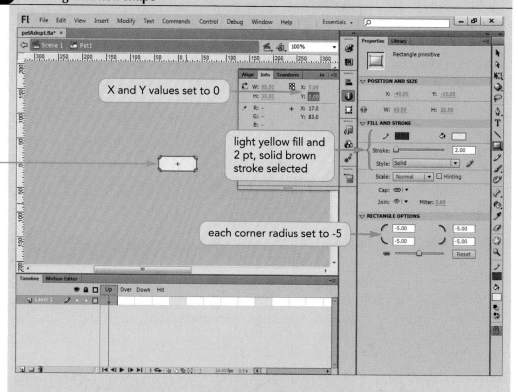

8. In the Tools panel, click the **Selection Tool** button to select it. The rectangle remains selected.

You will add a text label to the button and create the different states of the button. The button will have a rollover effect so that when the pointer moves over the button, the button's fill color changes from yellow to a green radial gradient. This provides a visual clue to the user that something will happen if the button is clicked. The button will also move when it is clicked, providing visual feedback that reinforces the user's action. You will make these changes in the four frames of the button's Timeline. The Up frame has a keyframe and contains the rectangle you created for the default state of the button. You will add text to the Up frame, and then add keyframes to the Over and Down frames to create the different states of the button. You don't need to add anything to the Hit frame because the rectangle shape provides the clickable, or active, area for the button. You will add the text in a new layer.

To add text to the button and create the different button states:

1. In the Timeline, rename Layer 1 to **button**, and then change the zoom magnification to **200%**.

2. In the Tools panel, click the **Text Tool** button T to select it, and in the Property inspector, if necessary, set the font family to **Arial**, set the font style to **Bold**, set the point size to **12**, and set the text fill color to **dark green** (#003300). See Figure 5-8.

Figure 5-8	Text settings for the button

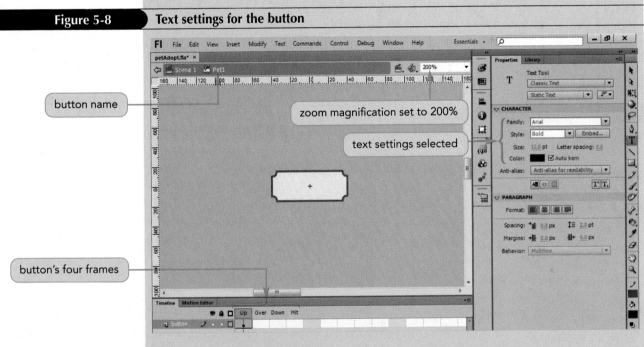

3. Inside the rectangle, create a text block, and then type **Pet 1**. You want the text block to be centered inside the rectangle.

4. In the Tools panel, click the **Selection Tool** button ➤ to select it, and then click the **Snap to Objects** button 🔟 to deselect it.

5. On the Stage, drag the text block so that it is centered inside the rectangle, as shown in Figure 5-9.

Figure 5-9   **Label added to the button**

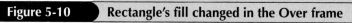

text block centered
within the rectangle

6. In the Timeline, click the **Over** frame to select it, and then insert a keyframe. The contents of the Up frame are automatically copied to the Over frame. You will change the button's fill color in the Over frame so that the button's color changes when the user moves the pointer over the button.

7. Deselect the rectangle and the text block, and then select the rectangle but not the text block.

8. In the Tools panel, change the fill color to the **green radial gradient**, which is the fourth swatch in the bottom row of the color palette. The green radial gradient replaces the rectangle's yellow fill. See Figure 5-10.

Figure 5-10   **Rectangle's fill changed in the Over frame**

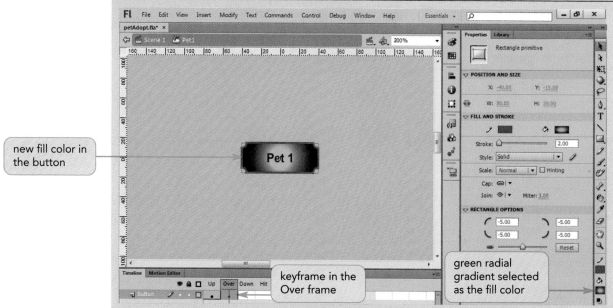

new fill color in
the button

keyframe in the
Over frame

green radial
gradient selected
as the fill color

9. In the Timeline, click the **Down** frame, and then insert a keyframe. The contents of the Over frame are copied to the Down frame. You need to change the button's position in the Down frame so that when the user clicks the button, the button appears as if it has been pressed and released.

▶ **10.** With the rectangle and text block still selected, press the **Down arrow** key three times, and then press the **Right arrow** key three times. The rectangle moves three pixels down and three pixels to the right, which makes the button appear to shift when the user clicks it.

▶ **11.** On the Edit bar, click the **Scene 1** link to exit symbol-editing mode and return to the document.

The first button and its different states are complete. You will preview the behavior of the button instance on the Stage to make sure the different effects you created appear correctly. You will use the Enable Simple Buttons command to preview the effects.

To insert a Pet1 instance and test its rollover effects:

▶ **1.** Change the zoom magnification to **100%**, center the banner in the Document window, and then add an instance of the **Pet1** button to the Stage.

▶ **2.** Position the Pet1 button instance on the left side of the banner below the Pet Pictures text block and approximately **100** pixels from the top of the Stage. See Figure 5-11.

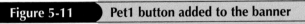

| Figure 5-11 | Pet1 button added to the banner |

button instance positioned in the banner

Pet1 button

▶ **3.** On the menu bar, click **Control**, and then click **Enable Simple Buttons**. The command is toggled on and you can test the button.

▶ **4.** On the Stage, click a blank area to deselect the button, and then move the pointer over the **Pet 1** button. Because of the rollover effect, the button changes color. See Figure 5-12.

Figure 5-12	Pet 1 button's rollover effect

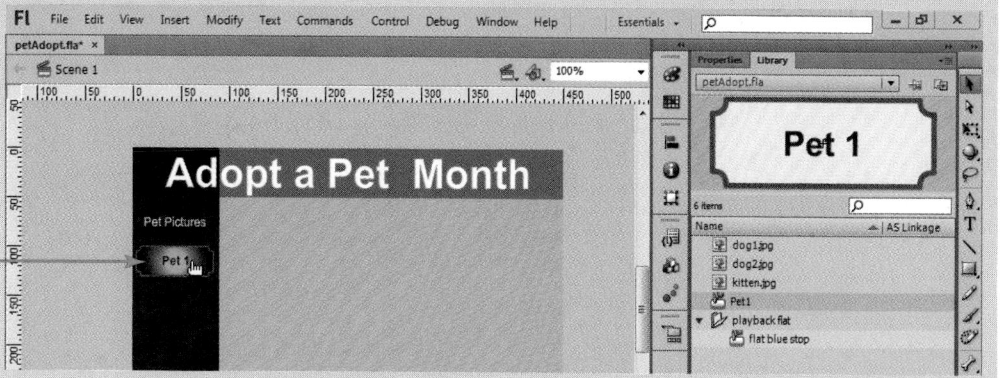

rollover effect changes the button's color

> **5.** Click the **Pet 1** button. The button shifts down and right when clicked, providing a visual cue that the button was clicked. You are done testing the visual effects of the Pet 1 button.

> **6.** On the menu bar, click **Control**, and then click **Enable Simple Buttons**. The command is toggled off, and you can again select button instances on the Stage.

Copying and Editing a Custom Button

Many times, a Flash document requires two or more buttons that are similar. Rather than creating each button individually, you can create the first button and then copy and modify the button for each remaining button. This method is faster and helps to ensure consistency in the design of the buttons.

The banner requires two more buttons, which look the same as the first button. Instead of creating new buttons, you will make copies of the first button, and then modify them to create the two additional buttons.

To create two copies of the Pet 1 button:

> **1.** In the Library panel, right-click the **Pet1** symbol, and then click **Duplicate** on the context menu. The Duplicate Symbol dialog box opens with the duplicate button's name, "Pet1 copy," selected. You will rename the button.

> **2.** In the Name box, type **Pet2**. The symbol type remains set to Button and the folder in which the Pet2 button symbol is stored remains the root folder of the library.

> **3.** Click the **OK** button. The Duplicate Symbol dialog box closes, and the Pet2 symbol is added to the document's library. See Figure 5-13.

Figure 5-13   **Pet2 button symbol in the library**

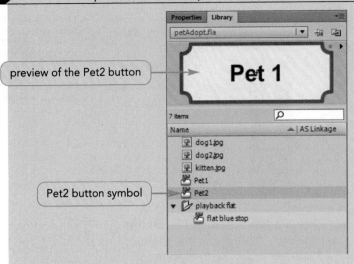

preview of the Pet2 button

Pet2 button symbol

▶ **4.** Repeat Steps 1 through 3 to create another duplicate of the Pet1 symbol named **Pet3**.

You need to modify the text in the duplicate button symbols. The button's colors will remain the same. After you modify the Pet2 and Pet3 symbols in the document's library, you need to create an instance of each button symbol in the document.

To edit the duplicate button symbols and add instances to the Stage:

▶ **1.** In the Library panel, double-click the **Pet2** button symbol icon 🖰. The button opens in symbol-editing mode.

▶ **2.** Change the zoom magnification to **200%**. The close-up view of the button makes the button easier to edit.

▶ **3.** In the Timeline, select the **Up** frame, if necessary. You need to change the text in the text block.

▶ **4.** On the Stage, double-click the **Pet 1** text block, and then edit the text in the text block to **Pet 2**. You also need to change the text blocks in the Over and Down frames.

▶ **5.** In the Timeline, select the **Over** frame, and then, on the Stage, edit the Pet 1 text in the text block to **Pet 2**.

▶ **6.** In the Timeline, select the **Down** frame, and then edit the Pet 1 text in the text block to **Pet 2**. The text blocks in all three frames are changed to reflect the button's purpose.

▶ **7.** On the Edit bar, click the **Edit Symbols** button 🖰, and then click **Pet3** to open the symbol in symbol-editing mode.

▶ **8.** Repeat Steps 3 through 6 to change the Pet 1 text blocks to **Pet 3**.

▶ **9.** Exit symbol-editing mode.

10. Drag the **Pet2** symbol from the Library panel to the Stage, placing the instance below the Pet1 button instance.

11. Drag the **Pet3** symbol from the Library panel to the Stage, placing the instance below the Pet2 button instance. See Figure 5-14.

| Figure 5-14 | Pet button instances added to the document |

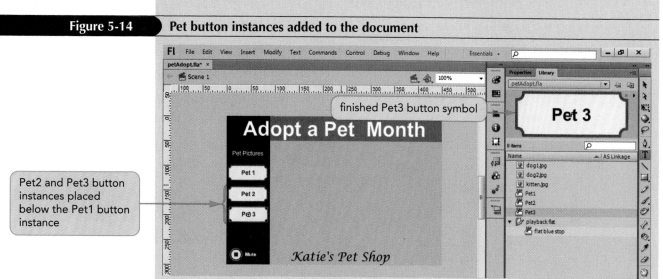

Pet2 and Pet3 button instances placed below the Pet1 button instance

finished Pet3 button symbol

Aligning Objects on the Stage

When a document includes multiple objects similar in design, you should align them with each other. If several objects are placed vertically, you should align them by their left or right edges. If the objects are placed horizontally, you should align them by their top or bottom edges. Also, be sure to make the space between the objects the same. Taking the time to align and space objects evenly gives a document a more polished and professional appearance.

The Align panel includes different options to arrange a group of selected objects on the Stage. You can line up selected objects by their edges or centers, and you can also distribute them so that they are evenly spaced. Objects will align with the far left or far right selected object when aligned by their left edges or right edges, respectively. They will align with the highest or lowest selected object when aligned by their top edges or bottom edges, respectively.

The Pet1, Pet2, and Pet3 button instances should be aligned by their left edges. You also need to make sure that they are positioned with an equal amount of space between them. You will use the Align panel to make these changes.

To align the instances of the Pet buttons:

1. In the Tools panel, click the **Selection Tool** button to select it.

2. On the Stage, click the **Pet1** button instance, press and hold the **Shift** key, click the **Pet2** button instance, click the **Pet3** button instance, and then release the **Shift** key. All three button instances are selected on the Stage.

3. In the docked panel group, click the **Align** button. The Align panel opens. See Figure 5-15.

TIP

You can also press the Ctrl+K keys to open and close the Align panel.

Figure 5-15   **Align panel**

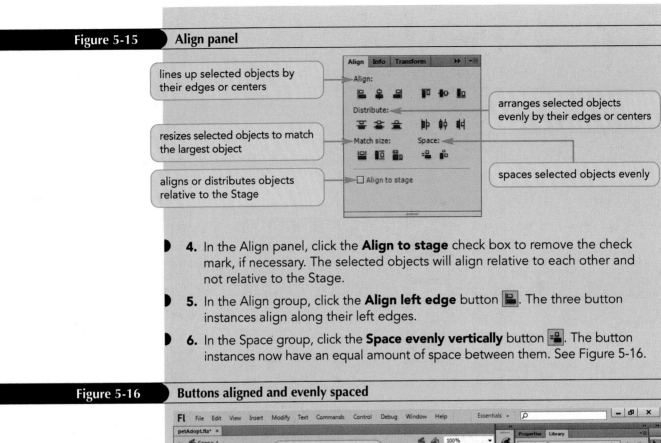

lines up selected objects by their edges or centers

resizes selected objects to match the largest object

aligns or distributes objects relative to the Stage

arranges selected objects evenly by their edges or centers

spaces selected objects evenly

4. In the Align panel, click the **Align to stage** check box to remove the check mark, if necessary. The selected objects will align relative to each other and not relative to the Stage.

5. In the Align group, click the **Align left edge** button 🔲. The three button instances align along their left edges.

6. In the Space group, click the **Space evenly vertically** button 🔲. The button instances now have an equal amount of space between them. See Figure 5-16.

Figure 5-16   **Buttons aligned and evenly spaced**

aligns the buttons' left edges

buttons aligned and evenly spaced

buttons align relative to each other

evenly spaces the buttons vertically

7. Close the Align panel, click a blank area of the Stage to deselect the buttons, and then save the document.

In this session, you created buttons to mute the background sound and to select different pictures to display. You added a button from the Buttons library to the banner, and then modified it to create a Mute button. You also created custom buttons for the picture buttons. You then aligned the buttons along their left edges and spaced the buttons evenly. The buttons, though attractive and professional looking, do not control anything yet. You will modify them in the next session to control the banner's interactivity.

REVIEW

Session 5.1 Quick Check

1. What is a button?
2. Why would you add buttons to a document?
3. How can you add a button from the Buttons library to your document's library?
4. What are the four frames in a button's Timeline?
5. How do you create a rollover effect for a button?
6. How can you test a button in Flash?
7. How can you align several objects on the Stage?

SESSION 5.2 VISUAL OVERVIEW

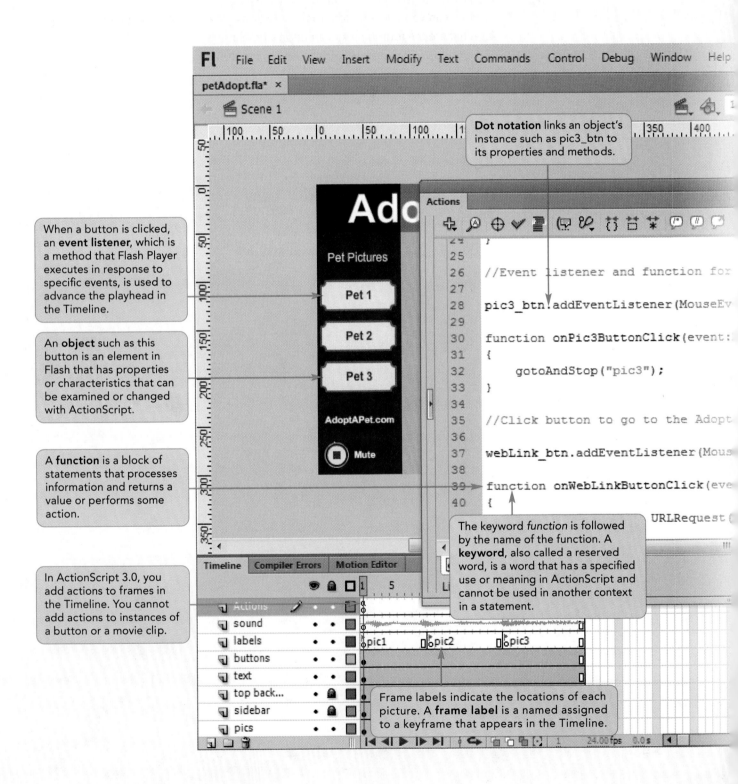

When a button is clicked, an **event listener**, which is a method that Flash Player executes in response to specific events, is used to advance the playhead in the Timeline.

An **object** such as this button is an element in Flash that has properties or characteristics that can be examined or changed with ActionScript.

A **function** is a block of statements that processes information and returns a value or performs some action.

In ActionScript 3.0, you add actions to frames in the Timeline. You cannot add actions to instances of a button or a movie clip.

Dot notation links an object's instance such as pic3_btn to its properties and methods.

```
24      }
25
26      //Event listener and function for
27
28      pic3_btn.addEventListener(MouseEv
29
30      function onPic3ButtonClick(event:
31      {
32          gotoAndStop("pic3");
33      }
34
35      //Click button to go to the Adopt
36
37      webLink_btn.addEventListener(Mous
38
39      function onWebLinkButtonClick(eve
40      {
                              URLRequest (
```

The keyword *function* is followed by the name of the function. A **keyword**, also called a reserved word, is a word that has a specified use or meaning in ActionScript and cannot be used in another context in a statement.

Frame labels indicate the locations of each picture. A **frame label** is a named assigned to a keyframe that appears in the Timeline.

ACTIONSCRIPT 3.0 AND CODE SNIPPETS

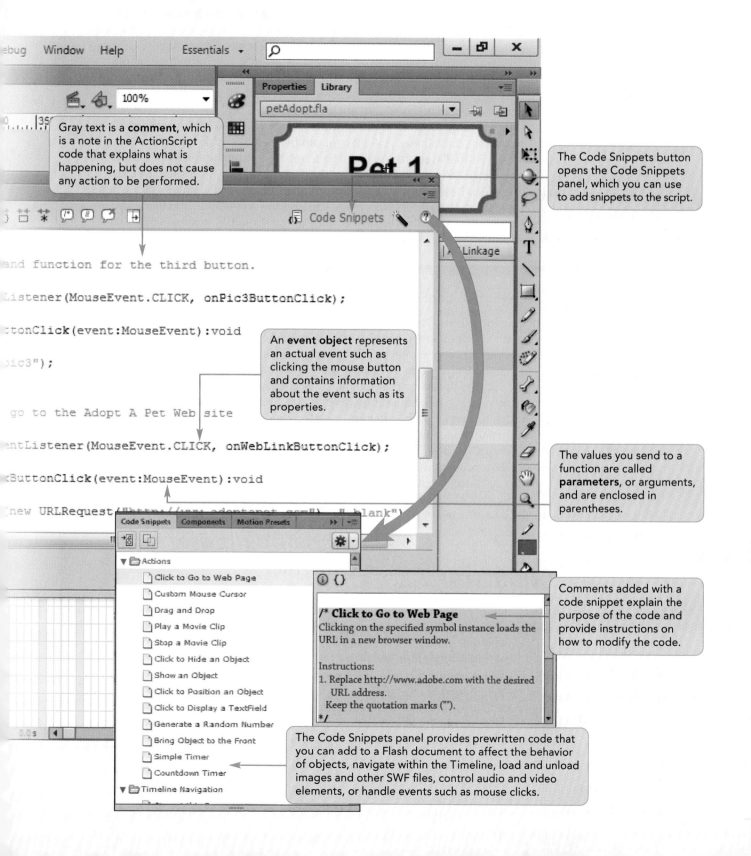

Gray text is a **comment**, which is a note in the ActionScript code that explains what is happening, but does not cause any action to be performed.

The Code Snippets button opens the Code Snippets panel, which you can use to add snippets to the script.

An **event object** represents an actual event such as clicking the mouse button and contains information about the event such as its properties.

The values you send to a function are called **parameters**, or arguments, and are enclosed in parentheses.

Comments added with a code snippet explain the purpose of the code and provide instructions on how to modify the code.

The Code Snippets panel provides prewritten code that you can add to a Flash document to affect the behavior of objects, navigate within the Timeline, load and unload images and other SWF files, control audio and video elements, or handle events such as mouse clicks.

Programming with ActionScript 3.0

The buttons you added to the banner do not yet allow the user to control the document's interactivity. When the button is clicked, the pictures do not display. According to Aly's instructions, clicking the buttons should display different pet pictures. To make a button fully functional and interactive, you need to add actions. Actions are part of **ActionScript**, the programming language used in Flash.

ActionScript is a robust programming language that gives Flash developers a virtually unlimited number of ways to make a Flash document interactive. ActionScript can be used to create actions that control multimedia elements, such as buttons, and to control the way the different parts of a movie are played. ActionScript programming requires writing scripts that consist of actions, event handlers, and other programming statements to control how the actions are executed.

In addition to controlling the order in which frames play in a document's Timeline or making buttons operational, ActionScript can be used to enable the viewer to input data and have Flash Player process that data to return a result. ActionScript can also be used to change the properties of movie clips while they play in Flash Player. For example, you can have a movie clip with a graphic of a car that changes color when a button is clicked. With ActionScript, you can also test a condition and then execute different actions based on the test results. For example, you can create a script that compares an input value with a set value to determine what actions to execute.

INSIGHT

Comparing ActionScript 3.0 and ActionScript 2.0

ActionScript 3.0, introduced in 2006, is the latest version of the ActionScript programming language. ActionScript 3.0, unlike ActionScript 2.0, is based on object-oriented programming (OOP) principles. These principles make the programming language more flexible and powerful, but also increase the learning curve for someone new to programming. OOP-based programming languages enable developers to create programs based on objects that work together, allowing for more flexibility in program development. ActionScript 3.0 is a robust programming language designed to enable Flash developers to create highly complex applications. The Flash Player plug-in has built-in code that plays Flash movies. You can run SWF files that contain ActionScript 2.0 or earlier in current versions of Flash Player. As newer versions of the Flash Player code are developed, Flash movies can include newer features and can run faster and more efficiently than in previous versions. You will use only ActionScript 3.0 in this textbook.

Working with Objects and Properties

ActionScript is used to control and modify objects which are instances of classes. A **class** is a blueprint for an object that describes the properties, methods, and events for the object. All objects in ActionScript are defined by classes. The multimedia elements you work with in Flash, such as buttons, movie clips, and text blocks, are considered objects. For example, a button has properties such as width, height, and location on the Stage. An instance of a movie clip symbol has similar properties. ActionScript code can be written to read or change these properties in response to certain events, such as a mouse click, a key press, or a certain frame in the Timeline being played. The properties for an object include alpha (which controls the movie clip's transparency), rotation (which controls the movie clip's orientation), and visible (which controls the movie clip's visibility). These properties can be examined and modified using ActionScript.

Any object you want to reference in ActionScript requires a name. Recall that you can have multiple instances of one movie clip symbol, which means that multiple objects are based on the same symbol. When using ActionScript to refer to a specific instance, you must refer to its instance name.

After you assign a name to an instance, you can refer to it in the action using dot notation. For example, if a movie clip instance is named circle_mc, the following code changes the alpha property of the instance to 30%:

```
circle_mc.alpha = .30
```

The values for an object's alpha property range from 0 to 1, where 1 represents 100%. The dot (.) links the property to the particular instance or object.

Before adding ActionScript code to the banner, you will assign names to the objects representing the buttons for the banner's interactivity, and then extend the Timeline of the document to add the pictures.

To name the button objects and extend the Timeline:

1. If you took a break after the previous session, make sure the petAdopt.fla file is open and the Essentials workspace is reset.

2. In the Timeline, insert a new layer above the buttons layer and rename it **labels**.

3. In the Tools panel, click the **Selection Tool** button ![selection tool icon], and then, on the Stage, click the **Pet1** button instance to select it.

4. In the Property inspector, type **pic1_btn** in the Instance name box to assign a name to the Pet1 button instance. See Figure 5-17.

| Figure 5-17 | Pet1 button instance name |

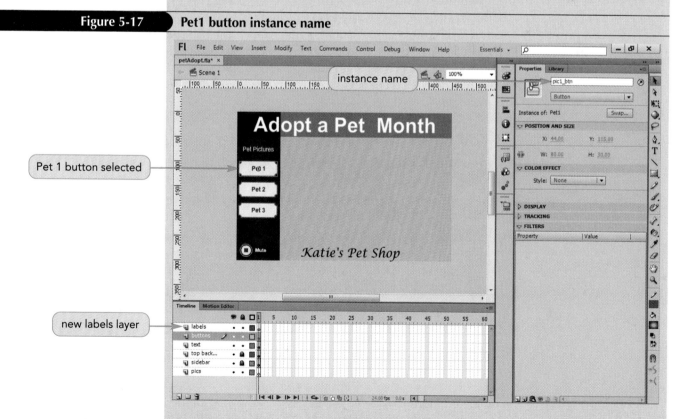

5. On the Stage, click the **Pet2** button instance to select it, and then, in the Property inspector, type **pic2_btn** in the Instance name box and press the **Enter** key. The name pic2_btn is assigned to the button instance.

6. Repeat Step 5 to assign the instance name **pic3_btn** to the Pet3 button instance and the instance name **mute_btn** to the flat blue stop button instance.

7. In the Timeline, insert regular frames at **Frame 30** of all the layers, and then, in the labels layer, insert keyframes at **Frame 10** and **Frame 20**.

8. In the labels layer, select **Frame 1**, and then, in the Label section of the Property inspector, type **pic1** in the Name box and press the **Enter** key. The pic1 frame label appears in the Timeline next to Frame 1 in the labels layer.

9. Repeat Step 8 to select **Frame 10** and enter the frame label **pic2**. The pic2 frame label appears in the Timeline next to Frame 10 in the labels layer.

10. Repeat Step 8 to select **Frame 20** and enter the frame label **pic3**. The pic3 frame label appears in the Timeline next to Frame 20 in the labels layer. See Figure 5-18.

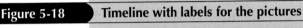

Figure 5-18   **Timeline with labels for the pictures**

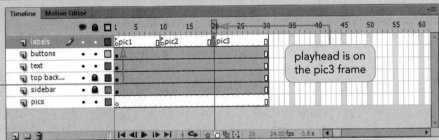

frame labels added for each picture

Next, you will add the pet pictures to the banner. The pictures will be added in the pics layer. Each frame that will contain a picture is labeled. In the pics layer, you will insert keyframes in the frames that are labeled. Then, for each, you will drag an instance of a different bitmap to the Stage and reduce its size by 60%.

To add the pet pictures to the banner:

1. In the Timeline, in the pics layer, insert keyframes in **Frame 10** and **Frame 20**, and then select **Frame 1**.

2. Open the document's Library panel, and drag an instance of the **dog1.jpg** bitmap to the center of the Stage.

3. Use the Transform panel to reduce the size of the bitmap to **60%** of its original size, and then reposition the bitmap as needed so that it is centered on the Stage.

4. In the Timeline, select **Frame 10** in the pics layer, and then drag an instance of the **dog2.jpg** bitmap from the library to the center of the Stage.

5. Use the Transform panel to reduce the size of the bitmap to **60%** of its original size, and then reposition the bitmap as needed so that it is centered on the Stage.

6. In the Timeline, select **Frame 20** in the pics layer, drag an instance of the **kitten.jpg** bitmap from the library to the center of the Stage, reduce its size to **60%** of its original size, and then reposition the bitmap as needed so that it is centered on the Stage. See Figure 5-19.

Figure 5-19   **Pictures added to the Stage**

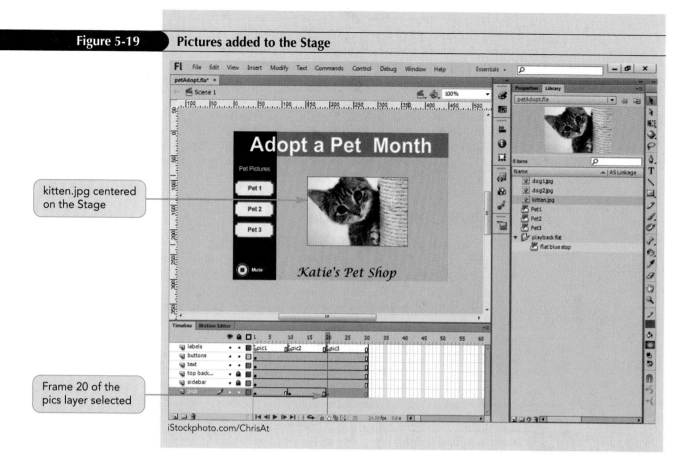

kitten.jpg centered on the Stage

Frame 20 of the pics layer selected

iStockphoto.com/ChrisAt

Using Actions, Methods, and Functions

An **action** is a statement, such as `gotoAndStop()`, that instructs the SWF file to do something. The terms *action* and *statement* are often interchangeable.

Flash includes a number of prebuilt functions, or sets of instructions, such as the `trace()` function, which displays values in the Output panel, and the `math.Random()` function, which returns a random number. You can also create your own functions. For example, you can create a function that accepts the temperature value in Fahrenheit degrees and returns the value in Celsius degrees. Then you can **call**, or execute, the function from different parts of the script in which it is defined. To use a function, you need to know what value or values to send to it and what value or values to expect in return. For example, the text "You are here" in the function `trace ("You are here")` is a parameter of the function. Not all functions require parameters. For example, the `math.Random()` function requires no parameters, so nothing is enclosed in the parentheses.

A **method** is a function specific to a particular object. It is a built-in capability of the object that performs a certain action or responds to a certain event. Methods are similar to other functions and actions, but they are part of an object and can be used to control the object. For example, if you have a movie clip instance named circle_mc in the document's main Timeline that has 20 frames in its own Timeline, you can control which of the 20 frames will play. You do this with the `gotoAndPlay()` method for the movie clip. Using dot notation, you code the object name followed by a dot followed by the method's name. The following code sets the movie clip instance to start playing at Frame 10 of its Timeline:

```
circle_mc.gotoAndPlay(10);
```

The parameter value of 10 in the parentheses specifies to which frame the playhead will go. Because `gotoAndPlay()` is a method of the movie clip object, the movie clip knows how to respond when the method is executed. The `gotoAndPlay()` method is also considered an action in the main Timeline because the main document is considered an object. When using the `gotoAndPlay()` method for the document's main Timeline, it is not necessary to specify an object name.

The Adopt a Pet banner will use functions to move the playhead to specific frames in the Timeline by referring to frame labels. For example, the `gotoAndStop("pic1")` action will move the playhead to the frame labeled pic1, Frame 1 of the labels layer, which contains the first picture for the banner. The pictures in the banner will be in separate frames that will be referred to by their labels.

Writing ActionScript Code

When writing ActionScript code, you must follow certain rules, which are known as the **syntax** of the language. As shown in previous examples, actions and functions are often written in mixed uppercase and lowercase letters. For example, the `gotoAndPlay()` function uses the uppercase letters A and P, but lowercase for the remainder of the letters. Because ActionScript is case sensitive, writing this function as `gotoandplay()`, with all lowercase letters, will generate an error message. Also, even though most statements work without an ending semicolon, it is good programming practice to include it. Ending the statements with a semicolon follows the format of other programming languages. Other required syntactical elements are parentheses, which are used to group arguments in methods and functions, and curly braces, which group a block of related statements. Figure 5-20 shows a sample ActionScript syntax.

Figure 5-20	Sample ActionScript syntax

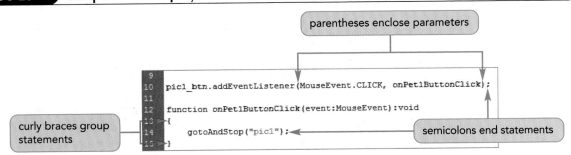

```
 9
10   pic1_btn.addEventListener(MouseEvent.CLICK, onPet1ButtonClick);
11
12   function onPet1ButtonClick(event:MouseEvent):void
13   {
14       gotoAndStop("pic1");
15   }
```

parentheses enclose parameters

curly braces group statements

semicolons end statements

Line 12 of code in Figure 5-20 contains `function onPet1ButtonClick (event:MouseEvent):void`, which defines the `onPet1ButtonClick` function. To define a function, you use the function keyword followed by the function name. The function name is a user-defined name and should be unique. The name should not start with a number, but it can include letters, numbers, the underscore character, and the dollar sign character. Within the parentheses following the function name, you specify the parameter of the function, which in this case is an event object with the user-defined name of the event. The event object must be assigned an event type—in this case, `MouseEvent`. Object types are coded with a colon followed by the type identifier. The event type, `MouseEvent`, distinguishes the event parameter from other types of events.

Written Communication: Using a Standard Naming Convention

Programming requires writing code correctly. Within that standard coding language are names that you assign to objects, such as functions, variables, movie clips, and buttons. The names you assign can mean the difference between easily understood code and difficult-to-interpret code. To ensure that you can later quickly recall what object you are referencing, you should use a standard naming convention.

When assigning names to objects, use a mixed-case format where the first letter of the name is lowercase and the first letter of each word that is part of the name is capitalized such as onHomeButtonClick. This naming convention makes it easier to read names within the ActionScript code and is consistent with other programming languages such as Java. This naming convention is sometimes called camel case because the uppercase letters form humps in the name.

One benefit of using a consistent naming convention is that the programs are easier to understand by other programmers. Also, it makes previously written code simpler to read when it needs to be reused at a later time. This naming convention also makes it possible to write more meaningful names because you can use multiple words that are joined together without spaces that are still easy to read. Multiword names can be more descriptive than single-word names.

A function can return a value, such as the result of a calculation, based on the actions in the function. The results of the function, such as a return value, must also be assigned a data type. If the function does not return a value, you include the void keyword after the colon to indicate no value is returned. The statements in a function must be enclosed in curly braces. In this case, the curly braces enclose the statement `gotoAndStop("pic1");`, which is the action to be performed when the function is called. Although this function requires only one statement, functions can include multiple statements. When the `onPet1ButtonClick` function is called, the playhead will move to the frame labeled pic1 and the movie will stop playing. The function structure is shown in Figure 5-21.

| Figure 5-21 | Structure of the onPet1ButtonClick function |

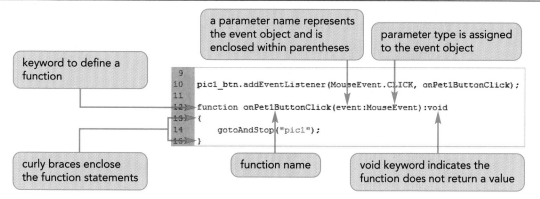

keyword to define a function

a parameter name represents the event object and is enclosed within parentheses

parameter type is assigned to the event object

curly braces enclose the function statements

function name

void keyword indicates the function does not return a value

```
9
10    pic1_btn.addEventListener(MouseEvent.CLICK, onPet1ButtonClick);
11
12    function onPet1ButtonClick(event:MouseEvent):void
13    {
14        gotoAndStop("pic1");
15    }
```

Using the Code Snippets Panel

Writing ActionScript code from scratch can be a challenging task for a beginning programmer, especially if easy-to-follow examples of code are not available. Fortunately, the Code Snippets panel makes it simple for beginning programmers to use ActionScript 3.0 by providing snippets of prewritten code that can be added to a Flash document. The panel includes code snippets you can add to affect the behavior of objects on the Stage, to enable navigation within the Timeline, to load and unload images and other SWF files, to control audio and video elements, or to handle events such as mouse clicks. (Events are covered later in this session.) You can display a description of any code snippet and you can display the code for the code snippet.

When code snippets are applied to a Flash document, the ActionScript code is added to the current frame in the Timeline and in an Actions layer if one exists. If no Actions layer exists, one is added above all other layers. The code snippets also contain instructions on how to customize the code to achieve the desired results. After you insert the code, you can modify it using the Actions panel.

INSIGHT

Learning to Write ActionScript

Adding prebuilt code using the Code Snippets panel is a good way to learn ActionScript 3.0 because the panel does not require knowledge of the ActionScript language. The code snippets contain the lines of code needed to add interactivity to a Flash document, they are error free, and they contain instructions about the purpose of the code and which lines can be customized. By reviewing the code snippets, you can begin to understand the structure of ActionScript code and how the various elements of the language are used to control objects in Flash. This makes it easier to write similar lines of code from scratch.

You will use the Code Snippets panel to add functions to move the playhead to each frame containing a pet picture.

To add a new function for the banner:

1. In the Timeline, select **Frame 1** of the labels layer.

2. On the Stage, click the **Pet1** button instance to select it. You will add ActionScript code to control what happens when the button is clicked.

3. In the docked panel group, click the **Code Snippets** button ⧉. The Code Snippets panel opens.

4. In the Code Snippets panel, click the **expand arrow** ▶ to the left of the Timeline Navigation folder, if necessary, to display the list of snippets.

5. Click the **Click to Go to Frame and Stop** snippet to display the Show description ⓘ and Show code {} buttons. See Figure 5-22. Clicking the Show description button displays a window with a brief description of the code snippet. Clicking the Show code button displays the actual code in the snippet.

Figure 5-22   Code Snippets panel

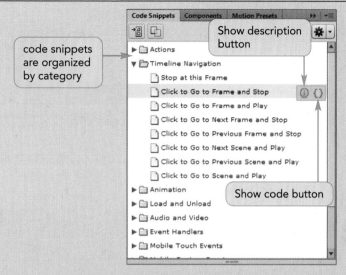

6. In the Code Snippets panel, click the **Show description** button 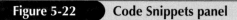. The description for the Click to Go to Frame and Stop code snippet is displayed. See Figure 5-23.

Figure 5-23   Description of the Click to Go to Frame and Stop code snippet

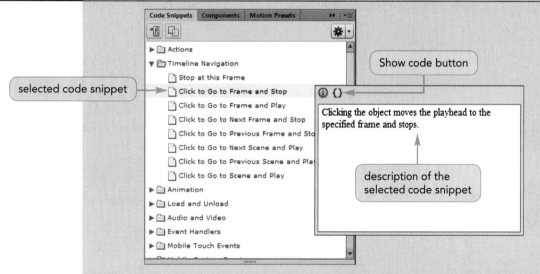

7. In the Code Snippets panel, click the **Show code** button {}, and then scroll down to see the code for the snippet below the instructions. See Figure 5-24. Notice that the name of the Pet1 instance, pic1_btn, is already embedded in the code as part of the addEventListener line. Because you selected the button instance before selecting the code, Flash automatically added the name assigned to the button instance.

Figure 5-24   Click to Go to Frame and Stop code snippet

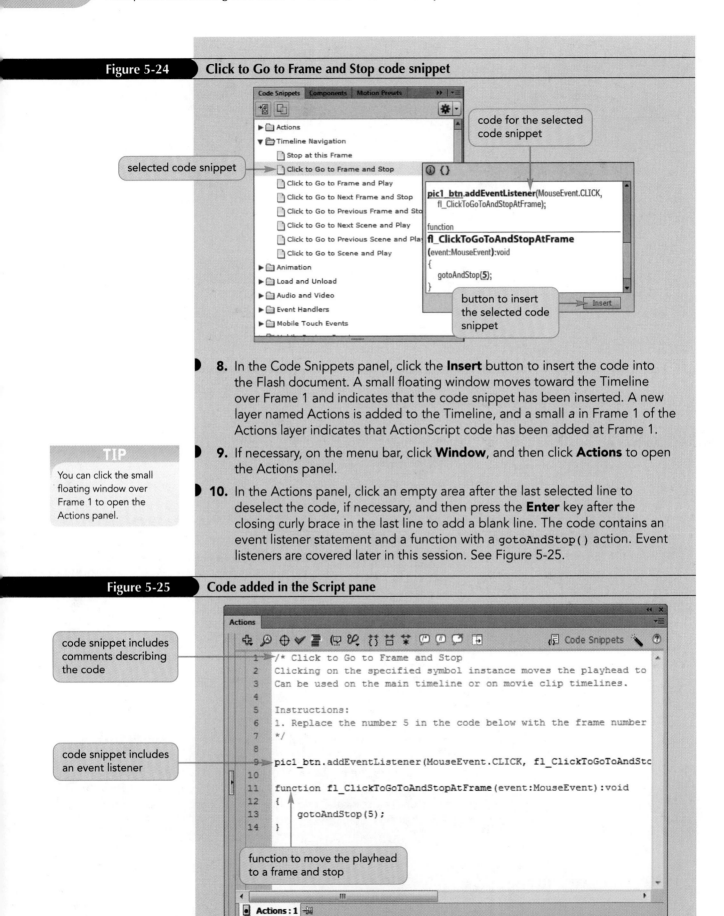

8. In the Code Snippets panel, click the **Insert** button to insert the code into the Flash document. A small floating window moves toward the Timeline over Frame 1 and indicates that the code snippet has been inserted. A new layer named Actions is added to the Timeline, and a small a in Frame 1 of the Actions layer indicates that ActionScript code has been added at Frame 1.

TIP

You can click the small floating window over Frame 1 to open the Actions panel.

9. If necessary, on the menu bar, click **Window**, and then click **Actions** to open the Actions panel.

10. In the Actions panel, click an empty area after the last selected line to deselect the code, if necessary, and then press the **Enter** key after the closing curly brace in the last line to add a blank line. The code contains an event listener statement and a function with a gotoAndStop() action. Event listeners are covered later in this session. See Figure 5-25.

Figure 5-25   Code added in the Script pane

Using Events and Event Listeners

An **event** is something that happens when a movie is playing, such as when the user clicks a button or presses a key. ActionScript can respond to or handle an event by carrying out instructions based on the event. The code to respond to or handle events consists of three elements: the event source, the event, and the response. The **event source**, also known as the event target, is the object to which the event will happen, such as a button instance. The event is the thing that will happen to the object, such as a button click or a key press. The **response** is the steps that are performed when the event occurs. The ActionScript code to handle events must include these three elements. The code snippets added in the previous steps contain all three elements.

Creating an Event Listener

In the Katie's Pet Shop banner, clicking a button with the mouse is the event that will control which function is called. If the Pet 1 button is clicked, for example, then the `fl_ClickToGoToAndStopAtFrame` function should be called to move the playhead to the pic1 frame. To call a function when a button is clicked, you need an event listener. An event listener is a method that Flash Player executes in response to specific events. Every object that has an event has an event listener.

The event listener method, `addEventListener()`, establishes a connection between the function, such as `fl_ClickToGoToAndStopAtFrame`, and the event source, such as the pic1_btn instance. The `addEventListener()` method registers the function to be called with the event source to listen for a specified event. When the event occurs, Flash Player can respond by calling the associated function. The `addEventListener()` method has two parameters: the event to listen for and the function to call when the event happens. The code for the event listener for the pic1_btn is:

```
pic1_btn.addEventListener(MouseEvent.CLICK,
  fl_ClickToGoToAndStopAtFrame);
```

This code contains the three elements required to respond to an event. The event source is the `pic1_btn`, which is the instance name of the Pet 1 button. The event is `CLICK`, which is a property of the MouseEvent object and represents the clicking of the mouse. The response is the call to the `fl_ClickToGoToAndStopAtFrame` function. The `addEventListener()` method is called to register the fl_ClickToGoToAndStopAtFrame function with the button instance. The code structure is shown in Figure 5-26.

Figure 5-26	Format of an event listener

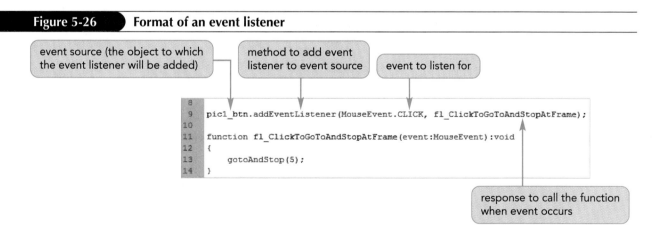

Next, you will add code snippets for the Pet2 and Pet3 button instances.

To add functions for the other buttons:

1. On the Stage, click the **Pet 2** button to select it. You will add ActionScript code to control what happens when the Pet 2 button is clicked.

2. In the Actions panel, click the **Code Snippets** button, if necessary, to open the Code Snippets panel.

3. Expand the **Timeline Navigation** group if necessary, click the **Click to Go to Frame and Stop** code snippet to select it, click the **Show code** button {}, and then click the **Insert** button. The code for the snippet is added to the Actions panel after the existing code.

4. In the Actions panel, scroll down in the Script pane to see the newly added code. The name of the function is similar to the function name added for the Pet 1 button. Each time you add the same code snippet, the function name is changed by adding a number at the end of its name.

5. Press the **Enter** key after the last line to add a blank line, and then repeat Steps 1 through 3 to add the same code snippet for the Pet 3 button.

The code snippets added in the previous steps use predefined names for the functions such as `fl_ClickToGoToAndStopAtFrame()`. When you add the same code snippet more than once, Flash adds a number at the end of the function name to distinguish it from the existing function with the same name. Also, the action within the function references Frame 5 and in the comments you are instructed to change the frame number. You will modify the function names to be more descriptive and you will change the frame reference to move the playhead to the frame label associated with the button.

To modify the function names and actions:

1. In the Script pane of the Actions panel, scroll up to see the `pic1_btn.addEventListener()` line, and then select the function reference within the parentheses, `fl_ClickToGoToAndStopAtFrame`.

2. Type `onPic1ButtonClick` to change the name of the function that is called when the Pet 1 button is clicked.

3. In the Script pane, below the `pic1_btn.addEventListener()` line, select the function name `fl_ClickToGoToAndStopAtFrame`, and then type `onPic1ButtonClick` to change the name of the function to match the function referenced in the `pic1_btn.addEventListener()` line.

4. In the next line located within the curly braces, select the number **5** in the `gotoAndStop(5);` function and type `"pic1"` to change the frame referenced in the `gotoAndStop()` function. The function will now cause the playhead to move to the frame labeled pic1. See Figure 5-27.

| Figure 5-27 | Updated function names and frame reference |

function names changed to be more descriptive

frame reference changed from 5 to "pic1"

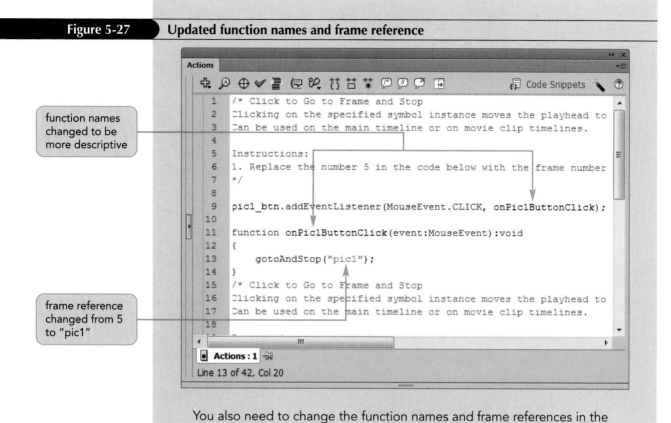

```
1   /* Click to Go to Frame and Stop
2   Clicking on the specified symbol instance moves the playhead to
3   Can be used on the main timeline or on movie clip timelines.
4
5   Instructions:
6   1. Replace the number 5 in the code below with the frame number
7   */
8
9   pic1_btn.addEventListener(MouseEvent.CLICK, onPic1ButtonClick);
10
11  function onPic1ButtonClick(event:MouseEvent):void
12  {
13      gotoAndStop("pic1");
14  }
15  /* Click to Go to Frame and Stop
16  Clicking on the specified symbol instance moves the playhead to
17  Can be used on the main timeline or on movie clip timelines.
18
```

Actions : 1

Line 13 of 42, Col 20

You also need to change the function names and frame references in the code snippets inserted for the Pet 2 button and the Pet 3 button.

5. In the Script pane, scroll down to the `pic2_btn.addEventListener()` line, select **fl_ClickToGoToAndStopAtFrame_2** (the function name within the parentheses), and then type **onPic2ButtonClick** to change the name of the function that is called when the Pet 2 button is clicked.

6. In the Script pane, below the `pic2_btn.addEventListener()` line, select the function name **fl_ClickToGoToAndStopAtFrame_2**, and then type **onPic2ButtonClick** to change the name of the function.

7. In the next line located within the curly braces, select the number **5** in the `gotoAndStop(5);` function, and then type **"pic2"** to change the frame referenced within the function. The function will now cause the playhead to move to the frame labeled pic2.

8. Repeat Steps 5 through 7 to change the function name and frame reference for the Pet 3 button, using **onPic3ButtonClick** as the name of the function that is called when the Pet 3 button is clicked and **"pic3"** as the reference in the `gotoAndStop()` statement. The code for the Pet 3 button is updated.

You have modified the code snippets to use more descriptive names for the functions and to reference the frame labels in the `gotoAndStop()` statements. Because you have made multiple changes to the code, you should check the code to make sure you have not introduced any syntax errors. If your code contains syntax errors, the errors will be listed in the Compiler Errors panel. You should make the necessary corrections, and then retest the syntax until the code is error free. Once you are certain the code syntax is correct, you should test the movie to make sure that when the navigational buttons are clicked, the playhead moves to the associated frame.

To check for errors and test the movie:

1. In the Actions panel, click the **Check syntax** button ✔ to check for syntax errors in the code. If no errors are displayed in the Compiler Errors panel, the script is correct.

   Trouble? If your code contains errors, the errors will be listed in the Compiler Errors panel at the bottom of the screen. Review your script to compare it with the code you modified in the previous steps, make any necessary corrections, and then repeat Step 1 until no errors are found.

2. Save the document. You will test the Katie's Pet Shop banner.

3. On the menu bar, click **Control**, point to **Test Movie**, and then click **in Flash Professional**. The movie opens in Flash Player. The banner displays and each picture is displayed in turn.

   The frames in the banner's Timeline play one after the other because there is nothing instructing the playhead to stop. To have the playhead stop at Frame 1, the stop(); statement needs to be added to the code. The stop(); statement will stop the playhead from advancing and will prevent the movie from playing continuously. You will add the stop(); statement to the beginning of the existing code in the Actions panel.

4. Close the Flash Player window and return to the document.

5. In the Script pane, place the insertion point to the left of the first line, type **stop();**, and then press the **Enter** key to move the existing statement to the next line. See Figure 5-28.

| Figure 5-28 | The stop(); statement added to the code |

stop(); code added to the first line

6. On the menu bar, click **Control**, point to **Test Movie**, and then click **in Flash Professional**. The movie opens in Flash Player. The banner displays and only the first picture is displayed.

> **7.** Click the **Pet 2** button to display the second pet picture, click the **Pet 3** button to display the third pet picture, and then click the **Pet 1** button to display the first picture.

> **8.** Close the Flash Player window and return to the document.

> **Trouble?** If the Output panel displays a message about embedding fonts, ignore the message and click the Timeline tab to display the Timeline. You will not need to embed fonts in the SWF file.

Adding Comments

The gray lines at the beginning of a code snippet are comments that explain what is happening, but do not cause any action to be performed. The comments added with the code snippet explain the purpose of the code and provide instructions on how to modify the code. After you modify the code snippets, you can delete these comments. However, as scripts get longer and more complex, comments become increasingly helpful. Even though comments are not necessary for the actions to work, they can be very useful to the programmer writing the code and to other programmers who might later modify the code. Single-line comments are indicated by two forward slashes (//). Any text after the slashes in the same line is not interpreted by Flash Player. Comments that span multiple lines are enclosed with the /* and */ characters.

You will delete existing comments and add new comments to the code in the Katie's Pet Shop banner.

To delete and add comments to the Katie's Pet Shop banner script:

> **1.** In the Actions panel, click to the left of `stop();` on the first line, and then type the following code, pressing the **Enter** key after each line to create a multiple-line comment:

```
/* ActionScript code to make the buttons in
the Katie's Pet Shop banner functional.
The first action will stop the playhead to
keep it from advancing automatically. */
```

> **2.** Press the **Enter** key to add a blank line between the last line of the comments and the `stop()` code.

> **3.** In the Actions panel, select the multiple-line comment above the event listener for the pic1_btn, and then delete the selected comment.

> **4.** Type the following code, and then press the **Enter** key to create a single-line comment, as shown in Figure 5-29:

```
// Event listener and function for the first button.
```

Figure 5-29   **Multiline comment replaced**

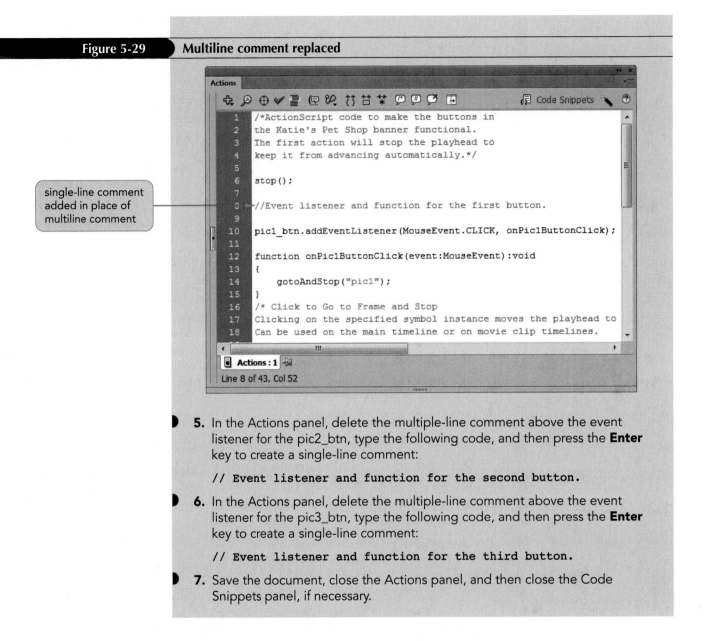

single-line comment added in place of multiline comment

```
1   /*ActionScript code to make the buttons in
2   the Katie's Pet Shop banner functional.
3   The first action will stop the playhead to
4   keep it from advancing automatically.*/
5
6   stop();
7
8   //Event listener and function for the first button.
9
10  pic1_btn.addEventListener(MouseEvent.CLICK, onPic1ButtonClick);
11
12  function onPic1ButtonClick(event:MouseEvent):void
13  {
14      gotoAndStop("pic1");
15  }
16  /* Click to Go to Frame and Stop
17  Clicking on the specified symbol instance moves the playhead to
18  Can be used on the main timeline or on movie clip timelines.
```

Actions : 1

Line 8 of 43, Col 52

▶ **5.** In the Actions panel, delete the multiple-line comment above the event listener for the pic2_btn, type the following code, and then press the **Enter** key to create a single-line comment:

   `// Event listener and function for the second button.`

▶ **6.** In the Actions panel, delete the multiple-line comment above the event listener for the pic3_btn, type the following code, and then press the **Enter** key to create a single-line comment:

   `// Event listener and function for the third button.`

▶ **7.** Save the document, close the Actions panel, and then close the Code Snippets panel, if necessary.

Creating Links to Web Sites

A Flash document can include links in the form of buttons or movie clips that use ActionScript to direct Flash Player to open a specified Web site. Aly's instructions are to include a link to a Web site that might be of interest to customers who are considering adopting a pet. You will complete the banner by creating a button that represents a link to the external Web site and add the corresponding ActionScript code. When the viewer clicks a button, a browser window will open, displaying an external Web site.

You will start by creating the button and assigning a name to the button instance on the Stage so that the button instance can be referenced by ActionScript code.

To add a button to link to an external Web site:

1. In the Tools panel, click the **Text Tool** button $\boxed{T}$ to select the Text tool, and then set the font family to **Arial**, set the font style to **Bold**, set the point size to **10**, set the text color to **white**, set the paragraph format to **Align center**, and set the font rendering method to **Anti-alias for readability**.

2. In the Timeline, select the **buttons** layer.

3. On the Stage, add a text block above the Mute button instance, type **AdoptAPet.com** in the text block, and then deselect the text. See Figure 5-30.

Figure 5-30	Text block added to the banner

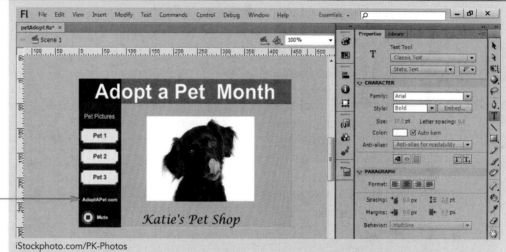

text block to convert to a button symbol

iStockphoto.com/PK-Photos

4. In the Tools panel, click the **Selection Tool** button 🖈, and then select the **AdoptAPet.com** text block.

5. Convert the selected text to a button symbol named **Web Link**. The Web Link button instance remains selected on the Stage.

6. In the Property inspector, type **webLink_btn** in the instance name box, and then press the **Enter** key. You have assigned the button instance a name.

Using the URLRequest Class

To create a link to an external Web site, you need to create a function as you did in the previous session. The function will use the `URLRequest()` class to define an object with the value of the Web address of the site to which you want to link. The ActionScript code for the function to link to a Web site is shown in Figure 5-31.

Figure 5-31   **Function to add a link to a Web site**

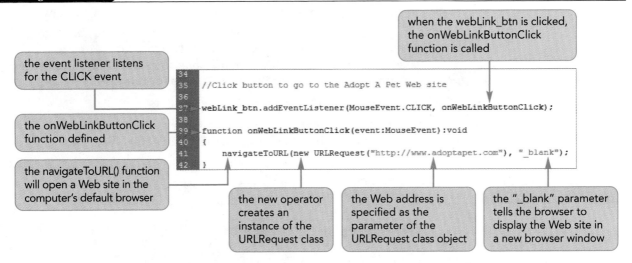

the event listener listens for the CLICK event

when the webLink_btn is clicked, the onWebLinkButtonClick function is called

the onWebLinkButtonClick function defined

the navigateToURL() function will open a Web site in the computer's default browser

the new operator creates an instance of the URLRequest class

the Web address is specified as the parameter of the URLRequest class object

the "_blank" parameter tells the browser to display the Web site in a new browser window

```
34
35    //Click button to go to the Adopt A Pet Web site
36
37    webLink_btn.addEventListener(MouseEvent.CLICK, onWebLinkButtonClick);
38
39    function onWebLinkButtonClick(event:MouseEvent):void
40    {
41        navigateToURL(new URLRequest("http://www.adoptapet.com"), "_blank");
42    }
```

In the `onWebLinkButtonClick` function, the `navigateToURL()` function is used to link to a Web site. The first parameter of the `navigateToURL()` function is an instance of the `URLRequest ()` class that contains the Web address for the Web site. The new operator is a special method used to create instances of objects based on a class.

You will add the code using the Code Snippets panel to create the functions for the Web site link.

To create a script with a function to control the button:

1. Select the **webLink_btn** instance on the Stage, if necessary.

2. In the docked panel group, click the **Code Snippets** button ▦. The Code Snippets panel opens.

3. In the Code Snippets panel, click the **expand arrow** ▶ to the left of the Actions folder to display the list of snippets, and then click the **Click to Go to Web Page** snippet. This is the action you want to insert.

4. In the Code Snippets panel, click the **Show code** button ⟨⟩ to display the code for the selected snippet.

5. Click the **Insert** button to add the code to the Script pane.

6. Open the Actions panel, scroll down in the Script pane to the `webLink_btn.addEventListener()` line, select the function name within the parentheses, **fl_ClickToGoToWebPage**, and then type **onWebLinkButtonClick** to change the name of the function that is called.

7. In the Script pane, below the `webLink_btn.addEventListener()` line, select the function name **fl_ClickToGoToWebPage**, and then type **onWebLinkButtonClick** to change the name of the function.

▶ **8.** In the next line within the curly braces, select **http://www.adobe.com** in the parameter of the URLRequest function and type **http://www.adoptapet.com.** The function will now assign the new URL as the parameter of the navigateToURL function.

Be careful not to delete the closing curly brace from the previous function when deleting the comment to avoid errors in the code.

▶ **9.** Delete the multiple-line comment above the **webLink_btn.addEventListener()** line, and then type the following comment in its place, as shown in Figure 5-32:
// Click button to go to the Adopt A Pet Web site

| **Figure 5-32** | **Function added to link to a Web site** |

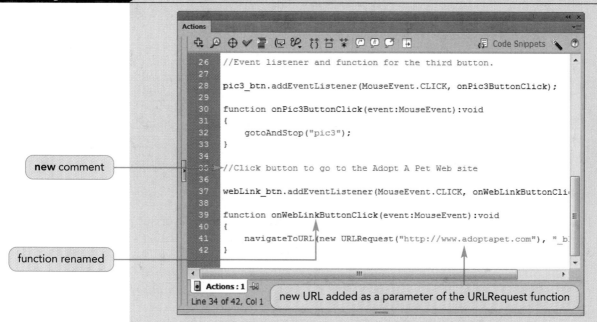

new comment

function renamed

```
26   //Event listener and function for the third button.
27
28   pic3_btn.addEventListener(MouseEvent.CLICK, onPic3ButtonClick);
29
30   function onPic3ButtonClick(event:MouseEvent):void
31   {
32       gotoAndStop("pic3");
33   }
34
35   //Click button to go to the Adopt A Pet Web site
36
37   webLink_btn.addEventListener(MouseEvent.CLICK, onWebLinkButtonCli
38
39   function onWebLinkButtonClick(event:MouseEvent):void
40   {
41       navigateToURL(new URLRequest("http://www.adoptapet.com"), "_b
42   }
```

Actions : 1
Line 34 of 42, Col 1

new URL added as a parameter of the URLRequest function

▶ **10.** In the Actions panel, click the **Check syntax** button ✔ to check for syntax errors in the code. If no errors are displayed in the Compiler Errors panel, the script is correct.

Trouble? If your code contains errors, the errors will be listed in the Compiler Errors panel at the bottom of the screen. If the syntax error, "expecting right-brace before end of program" is listed, add the closing curly brace to the line specified in the Compiler Errors panel. Review your script to compare it with the code you modified in the previous steps, make any necessary corrections, and then repeat Step 10 until no errors are encountered.

▶ **11.** Close the Actions panel, and then save the file.

The code for the event listener and function, necessary to make the Web link button operational, is complete. You will test the link in the banner to ensure that it functions as expected.

To test the Web link button in the banner:

▶ 1. On the menu bar, click **File**, point to **Publish Preview**, and then click **Default – (HTML)**. The Katie's Pet Shop banner opens in the default browser.

   Trouble? If the Web page does not open and a warning indicating that Internet Explorer has restricted this Web page from running scripts appears, you need to allow the blocked content. Click Allow blocked content, and then click the Yes button in the dialog box that opens to confirm that you want to allow the blocked content, if necessary.

▶ 2. In the browser window, click the **AdoptAPet.com** button to open the Web site in a separate window. If necessary, switch to the window displaying the Adopt a Pet Web site.

   Trouble? If an error message appears stating the page cannot be displayed, your computer might not be connected to the Internet. If necessary, connect to the Internet and repeat Step 2. If your computer is connected to the Internet, check the URL in the URLRequest() parameter to make certain it is correct. If you still cannot connect to the Internet, or the Web site does not display in the browser, read the rest of the steps in this section.

   Trouble? If an Adobe Flash Player window opens, stating that an ActionScript error has occurred, click the Continue button.

   Trouble? If an Adobe Flash Player Security dialog box opens, stating that Flash Player stopped a potentially unsafe operation, click the Settings button. A Web page displays the Adobe Flash Player Settings Manager. In the Settings Manager, click the Advanced tab and then scroll down and click the Trusted Location Settings button, click the Add button, click the Add Folder button, navigate to the folder containing the petAdopt.swf file, and then click the OK button. Click Confirm, click Close, close the dialog box, and then repeat Steps 1 and 2.

▶ 3. Close the browser window displaying the Web site, and then switch to the browser window displaying the Katie's Pet Shop banner.

▶ 4. Close the browser to return to the petAdopt.fla document. The banner is complete. You have added the button and ActionScript code to open the external Web site in a browser.

In this session, you learned the basic components and rules for the ActionScript programming language. You learned about actions, functions, methods, and event listeners. You learned how to use the Code Snippets panel to enter code to make the Katie's Pet Shop banner interactive. You also used the URLRequest() function to create a button with a URL link to a Web site on the Internet. In the next session, you will add sound effects to the buttons and a background sound to the banner.

Session 5.2 Quick Check

1. What is ActionScript?
2. A(n) _____ is an element in Flash that has properties or characteristics that can be examined or changed with ActionScript.
3. Why does any object you want to reference in ActionScript require a name?
4. Write the ActionScript expression to change the alpha property of the car_mc instance to 50.
5. What three programming elements are needed to respond to or handle events?
6. What is the purpose of the Code Snippets panel?
7. Why should you add comments to ActionScript code?
8. Write the ActionScript code to create a function named `gotoAdobeSite()` that will use the `navigateToURL()` function and the `URLRequest()` class to open the Web site *http://www.adobe.com*.

SESSION 5.3 VISUAL OVERVIEW

You cannot create sounds in Flash. The sound files you use in documents must first be imported into Flash.

You can add sound effects to instances of buttons to make them more interactive. For example, you can add a sound that plays when a user clicks a button.

You can add an action to the Mute button instance to stop all sounds that are playing when the button is clicked.

You can add a sound to a document that plays continuously and that is independent of the Timeline, such as a background sound.

The External Sounds library includes 185 MP3 sounds from a wide range of categories, such as animal sounds, cartoon sounds, household sounds, sports sounds, technology sounds, transportation sounds, and weather sounds.

A **waveform** is a graphical representation of a sound.

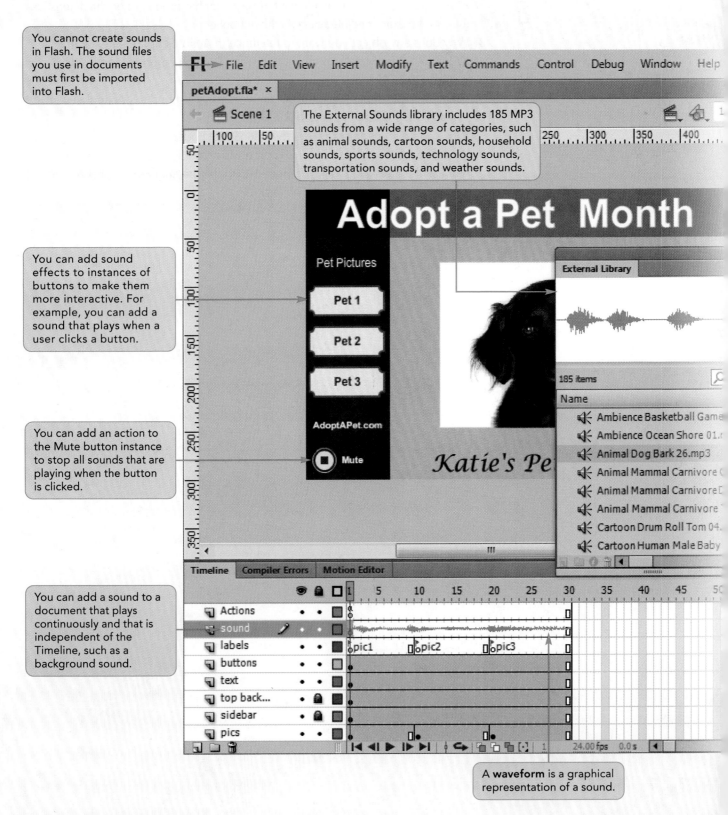

SOUNDS

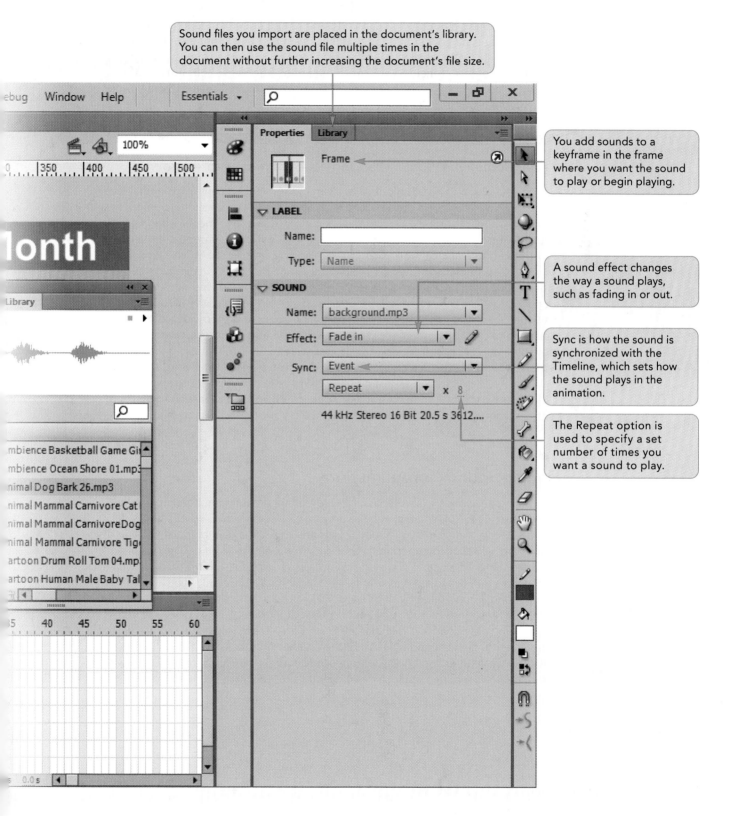

Sound files you import are placed in the document's library. You can then use the sound file multiple times in the document without further increasing the document's file size.

You add sounds to a keyframe in the frame where you want the sound to play or begin playing.

A sound effect changes the way a sound plays, such as fading in or out.

Sync is how the sound is synchronized with the Timeline, which sets how the sound plays in the animation.

The Repeat option is used to specify a set number of times you want a sound to play.

Using Sounds in a Flash Animation

Flash offers a variety of ways to use sounds. You can add sound effects to instances of buttons to make them more interactive. For example, you can add a sound that plays when a user clicks a button. You can add a sound to a document that plays continuously and that is independent of the Timeline, such as a background sound. You can add a sound that is synchronized with the animation, such as a sound simulating a clap of thunder that coincides with an animation of a lightning bolt. You can also add a sound in the form of a voice narration to supplement the information being displayed in the Web page as text or graphics.

PROSKILLS

Verbal Communication: Enhancing an Animation with Audio

Adding sound to an animation can have a very powerful effect, bringing another level of interest to a well-designed document. The sound you use can be subtle or loud. It can be lengthy or short, playing throughout the animation, for a short time, or when the user clicks a button. The sound can use special effects, such as fading in and repeating.

Use sound to enhance the animation, keeping in mind that too much sound can overwhelm an animation. You can use sound to add a mood to an animation, such as adding a bubbling background sound to animation showing fish swimming. You can use sound to highlight an element in an animation. For example, a drumroll sound could play when each sale item appears in an animation about an upcoming sale. You can also use sound to draw attention to or provide an audio cue. For instance, a doorbell ding could play when a user clicks a button. However, keep in mind that using the same sound repeatedly will get tiresome really fast. Also, in certain types of Web sites, such a business Web site, sound might take away from the professional image presented by the Web site.

If you are in doubt whether the sound or effect will enhance what you have to say, consider leaving it out. Your final animations will be more effective and enjoyable to others.

Finding Sounds for Animations

TIP

Sound files you download may be in a compressed format; decompress the file with a utility program such as WinZip before using the sounds.

You can create sounds with a separate sound-editing program and then import the sounds into Flash. Or, you can acquire prerecorded sounds from other sources. Most vendors offer a wide variety of sound effects and music that can be purchased on disk. Sounds are also available for purchase on the Web. You can even download sounds for free from Web sites such as Flash Kit (*www.flashkit.com*). Flash Kit provides a wealth of resources for Flash developers. At its site, shown in Figure 5-33, you can find sounds under Sound FX and under Sound Loops. You can search for sounds using keywords or browse for sounds by category. Sounds listed at the site can also be previewed before being downloaded. Note that the Flash Kit Web site might have been updated or modified since this tutorial was published. Other sites that have free sounds available for download include ccMixter (*dig.ccmixter.org*), The Free Sound Project (*www.freesound.org*), and Incompetech Creative Industries (*www.incompetech.com*).

| Figure 5-33 | Flash Kit Web site |

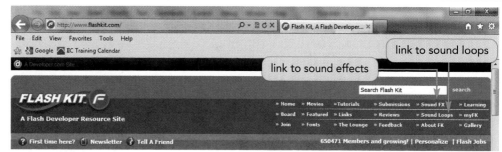

Used with permission from Microsoft Corporation; Copyright 2012 QuinStreet Inc. All Rights Reserved. Reprinted with permission.

Other Web sites offer sounds for purchase. These Web sites have preproduced sounds from which you can select. They will even create customized sounds for a fee. Two examples of such sites are Royalty Free Music (*www.royaltyfreemusic.com*) and SoundShopper (*www.soundshopper.com*). These sites also have a few sounds that you can download for free to use in personal projects such as a family or hobby Web site.

Adding Sounds to a Document

TIP

A good sound format to use in Flash movies is MP3, which produces small sound files, retains very good sound quality, and is compatible with Windows and Macintosh computers.

You cannot create sounds in Flash. As a result, the sound files you use in documents must first be imported into Flash. To be imported, sounds must be in a file format that is compatible with Flash, such as Windows Waveform (WAV), Audio Interchange File Format (AIFF) used with Macintosh computers, MPEG-3 (MP3) used with both Windows and Macintosh operating systems, and Adobe Soundbooth (ASND) used with both Windows and Macintosh operating systems. The WAV and AIFF formats are not compressed and tend to be larger than MP3 files, which are compressed.

Compressed files are smaller because the parts of the sound data that listeners are not likely to notice have been removed. Compressing a sound file basically means that its size has been reduced without sacrificing too much of the sound quality. You need to pay attention to the size of sound files you add to a Flash document because they can significantly increase the overall size of the published file, affecting its download time. You can import a WAV file into a document, and then compress it to MP3 format within Flash.

Sound files you import are placed in the document's library along with any symbols and buttons already in the library. In the library, a sound is preceded by a sound icon. Also, when you select a sound in the library, its waveform appears in the Library panel's preview box. After you have a sound file in the document's library, you can use it as many times as you need in the document. The multiple uses do not further increase the document's file size because only one copy of the sound is stored in the file.

In addition to importing sounds, Flash provides a variety of sound effects in the Sounds library. You can use any of these sounds by dragging them from the library to the Stage. You will use one of the sounds in the Sounds library to add a sound effect to the picture buttons.

Before you add a sound to a document, you should create a separate layer for each and name the layer for the sound it contains. This makes the sound easier to identify in the Timeline. Also, sounds can be added only to keyframes in the main Timeline or a symbol's Timeline. After you add a sound to a keyframe, it plays when the playhead reaches the keyframe.

To add the Animal Dog Bark 26.mp3 sound file to the document's library:

▶ 1. On the menu bar, click **Window**, point to **Common Libraries**, and then click **Sounds**. The Sounds External Library panel opens.

▶ 2. In the Sounds External Library panel, click the **Animal Dog Bark 26.mp3** sound file. The preview box shows the sound's waveform. See Figure 5-34.

Figure 5-34   **The Animal Dog Bark 26.mp3 sound in the Sound External Library panel**

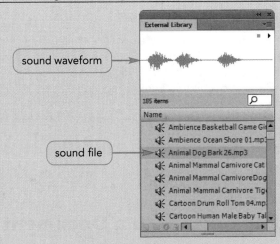

▶ 3. If necessary, click the **Library** tab to open the document's Library panel.

▶ 4. Drag the **Animal Dog Bark 26.mp3** file from the Sounds External Library to the document's Library panel. The Animal Dog Bark 26.mp3 sound is now available in the document's library and can be added to the buttons.

▶ 5. Close the Sounds External Library panel.

Adding Sound to a Button

You can add sounds to buttons to make a button more interactive, such as a sound that plays when the user clicks the button or even when the user moves the pointer over the button. You add a sound to a button's Over frame or to its Down frame. A sound added to the Over frame plays when the pointer is moved over the button. A sound placed in the Down frame plays when the button is clicked.

Adding a Sound to a Button

- Open the button in symbol-editing mode.
- In the button's Timeline, create a new layer for the sound.
- In the frame where the sound will be placed, create a keyframe and then select it.
- In the Sound section of the Property inspector, click the Name button, and then click the sound (or drag the sound from the Library panel to the Stage).

Based on the banner plan, Aly wants you to add a sound effect to the picture buttons. You will add the dog bark sound to the Down frame, so that it plays when the user clicks the button, providing an audio cue that the button was clicked.

To add the Animal Dog Bark 26.mp3 sound to the Pet buttons:

1. On the Stage, double-click the **Pet 1 button** instance. The button opens in symbol-editing mode.

2. In the Timeline, insert a new layer and name the layer **sound**. You will add the Animal Dog Bark 26.mp3 sound to the sound layer.

3. In the sound layer in the Timeline, click the **Down** frame to select it, and then insert a keyframe. You will add the Animal Dog Bark 26.mp3 sound to this keyframe.

4. In the Property inspector in the Sound section, click the **Name** button to display the available sounds, and then click **Animal Dog Bark 26.mp3**. The sound is added to the Down frame. See Figure 5-35.

Figure 5-35	Sound added to the Down frame

Pet1 button instance opened in symbol-editing mode

Animal Dog Bark 26.mp3 sound selected

layer for the sound

Animal Dog Bark 26.mp3 sound waveform appears with the keyframe in the Down frame

iStockphoto.com/PK-Photos

5. On the Edit bar, click the **Scene 1** link to return to the document and exit symbol-editing mode.

You should test sounds you add to make sure they work correctly. You can test sounds within the Flash program window after you toggle on the Enable Simple Buttons command. In this case, when clicked, the Pet1 button should exhibit its rollover effect and play the Animal Dog Bark 26.mp3 sound.

To test the sound effect added to the Pet 1 button:

▶ **1.** On the menu bar, click **Control**, and then click **Enable Simple Buttons**. The command is selected, so clicking the Pet1 button tests the button rather than selects it.

▶ **2.** On the Stage, click the **Pet 1** button. The Animal Dog Bark 26.mp3 sound plays.

   Trouble? If you do not hear a sound when you click the button, your computer's speakers might be off or at a soft volume. Make sure that the speakers are turned on and the volume is turned up.

▶ **3.** On the menu bar, click **Control**, and then click **Enable Simple Buttons**. The command is toggled off.

The Pet 2 and Pet 3 buttons use the same Animal Dog Bark 26.mp3 sound effect. Because the sound file is already part of the document's library, you do not need to add another copy to the library. You will use another method to add the sound to the Pet 2 button.

To add the Animal Dog Bark 26.mp3 sound effect to the Pet2 and Pet3 buttons:

▶ **1.** In the Library panel, double-click the **Pet2 button** icon [icon]. The button opens in symbol-editing mode.

▶ **2.** In the Timeline, insert a new layer and name it **sound**. You will add the sound to this new layer.

▶ **3.** In the sound layer, click the **Down** frame, and then insert a keyframe.

▶ **4.** Drag the **Animal Dog Bark 26.mp3** sound from the Library panel onto the Stage. The sound is added to the Down frame.

▶ **5.** Repeat Steps 1 through 4 to add the Animal Dog Bark 26.mp3 sound to the Pet3 button.

▶ **6.** On the Edit bar, click the **Scene 1** link to return to the document.

▶ **7.** On the menu bar, click **Control**, and then click **Enable Simple Buttons**. You can now test the buttons by clicking them.

▶ **8.** On the Stage, click the **Pet 2** button, and then click the **Pet 3** button to hear the sound.

▶ **9.** On the menu bar, click **Control**, and then click **Enable Simple Buttons**. The command is toggled off, and you can again select the button on the Stage.

Adding a Background Sound

The user's experience with a Flash movie can be enhanced by playing a background sound. You add a background sound in a separate layer and in the keyframe where you want the sound to start playing. Again, you can import into Flash a sound you have purchased or recorded yourself.

Aly wants you to use a sound she obtained as the background sound for the banner. You will import a sound from your Data Files into your document's library, and then add it as a background sound.

To import the background.mp3 sound to the library:

▶ 1. On the menu bar, click **File**, point to **Import**, and then click **Import to Library**. The Import to Library dialog box opens.

▶ 2. Navigate to the **Flash5\Tutorial** folder included with your Data Files, click **All Sound Formats** in the File type list, click the **background.mp3** sound file, and then click the **Open** button. The background.mp3 file is added to the document's library.

▶ 3. In the Library panel, click the **background.mp3** sound, if necessary. The preview box shows the sound's waveform. See Figure 5-36.

Figure 5-36   The background.mp3 sound in the document's library

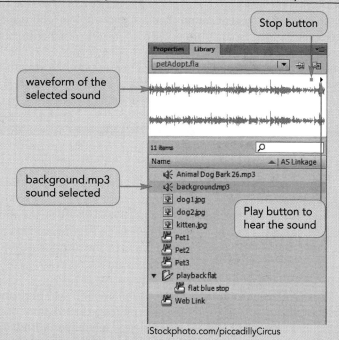

iStockphoto.com/piccadillyCircus

▶ 4. In the preview box, click the **Play** button ▶ to play the sound. The sound starts to play and will continue for 20.5 seconds.

▶ 5. In the preview box, click the **Stop** button ■ to end the sound. You will use this sound as the background sound for the banner.

▶ 6. In the Timeline, insert a new layer above the labels layer, and then name the new layer **sound**. You will add the sound to this layer.

▶ 7. In the Timeline, click **Frame 1** of the sound layer.

8. In the Sound section of the Property inspector, click the **Name** button to view the available sounds, and then click **background.mp3**. The sound is added to the sound layer. See Figure 5-37.

Figure 5-37　　**Background sound waveform in the sound layer**

layer for the sound

waveform for the background.mp3 sound

iStockphoto.com/piccadillyCircus

Changing the Sound Sync Settings

After you have added a sound to a document, you can control the way the sound plays by using the sound settings in the Property inspector. The Sync setting lets you set the sound as an event sound or as a stream sound, which are the two main types of sounds used in Flash. An **event sound** does not play until the entire sound has downloaded completely. Event sounds are not synchronized with the Timeline, which means that after an event sound is started, it continues to play regardless of the Timeline until the entire sound is played or the user takes an action to stop it. A **stream sound** is synchronized with the Timeline and begins playing as soon as enough data has downloaded. Stream sounds are useful when you want the animation in a movie to coincide with the sound.

INSIGHT

Using Stream Sounds

Before adding a stream sound to a Flash document, consider your target audience. When a movie has a stream sound, Flash forces the animation to keep pace with the sound. If a user has a slow computer, Flash Player might skip frames to play the sound. This can result in a less-than-ideal viewing experience for the user. Unless there is a need to synchronize a sound to the Timeline, use the event sound setting.

After an event sound starts, the sound continues to play until it is stopped by the user or finishes. As a result, several instances of the same sound might play at one time. Because event sounds play independently of the Timeline, an event sound starts to play when the playhead reaches the sound's keyframe and continues to play until it is completely finished. If the playhead returns to the keyframe with the sound before the sound has finished playing, another instance of the sound starts playing at the same time. This means that one sound instance overlaps the other.

To prevent sounds from overlapping, you can change the Sync setting of the sound to Start instead of Event. With the Start Sync setting, a new instance of the sound does not start if the first instance of the sound is still playing, preventing the overlap of multiple instances of the same sound. To end a sound that is playing, you can change the Sync setting to Stop. For example, you might want a sound that starts playing in Frame 1 to stop playing in Frame 10. You add the same sound in Frame 1 to Frame 10 but use the Stop Sync setting. Then, when the playhead reaches Frame 10, the sound stops playing.

The Loop and Repeat sound settings let you set how many times a sound replays. If you want a sound to play continuously for a period of time, select Repeat and then specify how many times the sound should play. For example, if you want a sound to play for 2 minutes and the sound is 10 seconds long, enter 12 as the number of times to repeat; the sound will play 12 times for a total of 120 seconds, or 2 minutes. If you want the sound to repeat continuously, select Loop.

The banner's background sound should be an event sound. You will make this change now.

To change the Sync setting for the background sound:

1. In the Property inspector, in the Sound section, click the **Sync** button, and then click **Event**, if necessary. Event is the default setting and is used when you do not need the sound synchronized with the Timeline.

2. Below the Sync button, click the **Sound loop** button, and then click **Repeat**, if necessary. You will set how many times the sound should repeat.

3. Change the Number of times to loop setting to **8**. The information below the Sync settings indicates that the sound is 20.5 seconds long. If the Repeat setting is 0, the sound ends if the user views the animation for more than sound is 20.5 seconds long, looped 8 times will play for 164 seconds or approx. 2 and ¾ minutes. By changing the Repeat setting to 8, the sound continues playing for 164 seconds—approximately 2 and ¾ minutes. See Figure 5-38.

Figure 5-38	Sound settings in the Property inspector

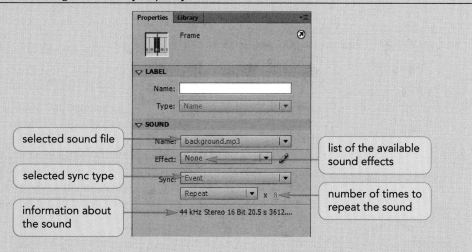

TIP

You can also test a sound by playing the movie in a Web page.

4. On the menu bar, click **Control**, point to **Test Movie**, and then click **in Flash Professional**. The movie opens in Flash Player. The background sound plays.

5. Close the Flash Player window to return to the document.

Adding Sound Effects

The sound effect setting changes the way a sound plays. The Left channel effect plays the sound only in the left speaker, whereas the Right channel effect plays the sound only in the right speaker. The Fade to right effect starts the sound in the left speaker and gradually moves the sound to the right speaker. The Fade to left effect starts the sound in the right speaker and gradually moves the sound to the left speaker. The Fade in effect gradually increases the sound, whereas the Fade out effect gradually decreases the sound. Finally, the Custom setting allows you to create your own sound effects by adjusting the sound's starting point and controlling its volume.

You will explore the sound effect settings to see how they impact the banner's background sound.

To explore the sound effect settings with the background sound:

1. In the Timeline, click **Frame 1** of the sound layer to select it, if necessary. You will try different sound effects for the sound in this layer.

2. In the Property inspector, click the **Effect** button to display the list of effects, and then click **Fade to right**. The effect is applied to the background sound.

3. On the menu bar, click **Control**, point to **Test Movie**, and then click **in Flash Professional** to play the movie and hear the background sound.

4. Close the Flash Player window to return to the document.

5. Repeat Steps 2 through 4 to apply and test at least three other sound effect settings.

6. In the Property inspector, click the **Effect** button, and then click **Fade in**. The effect is applied to the background sound and fits well with the overall design and purpose of the banner. Even though the background sound is set to repeat twice, the fade-in effect will not be repeated. The sound effect is applied only when the sound first starts playing.

Although some users might enjoy the background sound, other users might not want to hear it. You want to give the user the option to turn off the sound. You already added a Mute button for this purpose, but you still need to add an action to the button instance to turn off the sound. Using the Actions panel, you will add an action to the Mute button instance that will stop all sounds that are playing when the button is clicked. Subsequent sounds that are played, such as the sound effects you added to the picture buttons, are not affected because they will not be playing when the Mute button is clicked.

To add an action to mute the background sound:

1. On the Stage, click the **Mute** button to select it. You will add ActionScript code to control what happens when the button is clicked.

2. In the docked panel group, click the **Code Snippets** button. The Code Snippets panel opens.

3. In the Code Snippets panel, click the **expand arrow** ▶ to the left of the Audio and Video folder to expand the list of snippets. See Figure 5-39.

Be sure to select the button and not the Mute text block.

Figure 5-39	Audio and Video folder

selected Mute button

iStockphoto.com/PK-Photos; iStockphoto.com/piccadillyCircus

▶ **4.** Click the **Click to Stop All Sounds** snippet, click the **Show code** button {}, and then click the **Insert** button to insert the code into the Actions panel.

▶ **5.** On the menu bar, click **Control**, point to **Test Movie**, and then click **in Flash Professional**. The banner displays and the background sound plays in Flash Player.

▶ **6.** In the Flash Player window, click the **Mute** button. The sound stops, but you can still click the Pet buttons to display the different pet pictures and play the barking sound.

▶ **7.** Click the **Pet 1**, **Pet 2**, and **Pet 3** buttons to display the different pet pictures.

▶ **8.** Close the Flash Player window, and then save and close the document.

You have completed the banner by adding buttons, actions, and sounds. Katie is pleased with the progress you made on the banner. In this session, you learned how to acquire sounds, the types of sounds Flash uses, and the different sound file formats that can be imported into documents. You imported sounds to the document's library, added the sounds to buttons and as a background sound, and also changed the sound effect settings. Finally, you added a code snippet to a button to stop all sounds from playing.

REVIEW

Session 5.3 Quick Check

1. Where is sound that you import into a document stored?
2. True or False. Sounds can only be added to keyframes.
3. A sound placed in a button's _____ frame plays when the button is clicked.
4. How do you add a background sound to a Flash movie?
5. Describe the two main types of sounds used in a Flash document.
6. To prevent sounds from overlapping, you can change the Sync setting of the sound to _____ instead of Event.
7. True or False. When you select a sound in the document's library, its waveform appears in the Library panel's preview box.

Practice the skills you learned in the tutorial using the same case scenario.

PRACTICE

Review Assignments

Data Files needed for the Review Assignments: petSample.fla, background.mp3

Aly asks you to make some changes to another interactive banner she has started for the adopt a pet month activities. You will modify the Mute button and add an action to stop all sounds when the button is clicked. You will add actions to the Play and Stop buttons to control the animation of the bitmaps. You will import a sound that will play as a background sound. Finally, you will add a sound effect to the Stop and Play buttons and change the text on the Play button to "Start."

1. Open the **petSample.fla** file located in the Flash5\Review folder included with your Data Files, save the document as **petBanner.fla** in the same folder, and then reset the Essentials workspace.
2. Open the mute button symbol in symbol-editing mode, select the Down frame in Layer 2, change the color of the small black square in the middle of the button to green (#00FF00), and then exit symbol-editing mode.
3. Select the mute button instance on the Stage, and then in the Property inspector, type **mute_btn** as the instance name. Select the play button and then enter **play_btn** as the instance name. Select the stop button and then enter **stop_btn** as the instance name.
4. Select the mute button instance on the Stage, and then insert the Click to Stop All Sounds code snippet so that when the button is clicked, all sounds currently playing will stop.
5. Select the play button instance on the Stage, and then insert the Click to Go to Frame and Play code snippet. Change the gotoAndPlay reference from Frame 5 to Frame 1.
6. Select the stop button instance on the Stage, and then insert the Click to Go to Frame and Stop code snippet. Change the gotoAndStop reference from Frame 5 to Frame 1.
7. Import the **background.mp3** file located in the Flash5\Review folder to the document's library.
8. Insert a new layer above the katies layer and name it **music**. With the music layer selected, drag the background.mp3 sound from the library to the Stage. Select Frame 1 of the music layer, and then, in the Property inspector, select Start for the Sync sound option, and enter **4** for the number of times to repeat.
9. Open the stop button symbol in symbol-editing mode, insert a new layer and name it **sound**. Insert a keyframe in the Down frame of the sound layer, and then add the Animal Dog Bark 26.mp3 sound from the Sounds library to the Down frame so that the sound plays when the button is clicked. (*Hint*: You can drag the sound from the library to the Stage to add it to the selected frame.)
10. Open the play button symbol in symbol-editing mode, insert a new layer and name it **sound**, and then add the Animal Dog Bark 26.mp3 sound to the Down frame.
11. Change the text block in the play button from Play to **Start**.
12. Test the banner in Flash Player to make sure the buttons work and the sounds play.
13. Submit the finished files to your instructor.

Add buttons and sounds to an interactive banner for a sports store's Web site.

APPLY

Case Problem 1

Data Files needed for this Case Problem: jsAddDraft.fla

Jackson's Sports   Dan asks Chris about creating a new Flash document to use on the Jackson's Sports Web site to promote the store's softball services. You will create the advertisement based on a document Chris has developed. You will add links to the

Web links section and you will add the ActionScript code to make the navigational buttons and the Web links operational. The finished advertisement is shown in Figure 5-40.

Figure 5-40   **Completed advertisement for Jackson's Sports Store**

1. Open the **jsAdDraft.fla** file located in the Flash5\Review folder included with your Data Files, and then save the file as **jsSoftball.fla** in the same folder.
2. In the labels layer, insert keyframes at Frame 10 and Frame 20, and then add the label **Services** at Frame 10 and the label **Weblinks** at Frame 20.
3. On the Stage, select the Services button instance, and then, in the Property inspector, name the instance **services_btn**, and then name the Links button instance as **weblinks_btn**.
4. In the Timeline, move the playhead to Frame 1.
5. Select the Home button, and then add the Click to Go to Frame and Stop code snippet to make the button operational. Delete the multiline comment, change the function name to **onHomeClick**, and change the frame reference in the **gotoAndStop(5)** action to **gotoAndStop("Home")**.
6. Select the Services button, and then add the Click to Go to Frame and Stop code snippet to make the button operational. Delete the multiline comment, change the function name to **onServicesClick**, and change the frame reference in the **gotoAndStop(5)** action to **gotoAndStop("Services")**.
7. Select the Links button, and then add the Click to Go to Frame and Stop code snippet to make the button operational. Delete the multiline comment, change the function name to **onWeblinksClick**, and change the frame reference in the **gotoAndStop(5)** action to **gotoAndStop("Weblinks")**.
8. In the Actions panel, insert the following comments and statement before the first line:

```
//Keep the playhead from advancing automatically
stop();
//Functions to make buttons operational
```

9. Check the code for syntax errors, make any necessary corrections, and then close the Actions panel.
10. In the Timeline, move the playhead to Frame 20. On the Stage, select the Amateur Softball Association text block, convert the text block to a button symbol, and name the symbol **asaYouth**.
11. Edit the asaYouth symbol by inserting a keyframe in its Over frame. In the Over frame, change the color of the text to white and the font style to italic. Insert a keyframe in the Hit frame, and then draw a rectangle with a black fill and no stroke to cover the text block.

12. In the Library panel, make a duplicate of the asaYouth button symbol named **youthSoftball**, and then edit the youthSoftball button by changing the text in both its Up frame and Over frame to **Youth Softball**.

13. In the Library panel, make a duplicate of the asaYouth button symbol, name the duplicate **USASoftball**, and then edit the USASoftball button by changing the text in both its Up frame and Over frame to **USA Softball**.

14. In Frame 20 of the content layer in the main Timeline, add an instance of the youth-Softball button below the asaYouth button instance, and then add an instance of the USASoftball button below the youthSoftball button instance.

15. Select all three button instances in the center of the Stage, and then, in the Align panel, deselect the Align to stage button, click the Align left edge button, and click the Space evenly vertically button to align the instances and distribute them evenly.

16. On the Stage, select the asaYouth button instance and name the instance **amateurSoftball _btn**, select the youthSoftball button instance and name the instance **youthSoftball _btn**, and then select the USASoftball button instance and name the instance **USASoftball_btn**.

17. On the Stage, select the Amateur Softball Association button and then add the Click to Go to Web Page code snippet. Delete the multiline comment, change the function name to `gotoASAYouthSite`, and change the URL reference in the `URLRequest()` function to `"http://www.softball.org/youth/"`.

18. On the Stage, select the Youth Softball button, and then add the Click to Go to Web Page code snippet. Delete the multiline comment, change the function name to `gotoYouthSoftballSite`, and change the URL reference in the `URLRequest()` function to `"http://www.infosports.com/softball"`.

19. On the Stage, select the USA Softball button, and then add the Click to Go to Web Page code snippet. Delete the multiline comment, change the function name to `gotoUSASoftballSite`, and change the URL reference in the `URLRequest()` function to `"http://www.usasoftball.com"`.

20. In the Actions panel, check the code for syntax errors, make any necessary corrections, and then close the Actions panel.

21. Save the jsSoftball.fla document, and then test it in Flash Player. Click the Services button to go to the Services section, and then click the Links button to go to the Web Links section. In the Weblinks section, click each link button to open its linked Web site in a browser window. (If an error message appears indicating an error opening the Web pages, the URLs for these Web sites might have changed since the printing of this tutorial. See your instructor or technical support person for assistance.)

22. Submit the finished files to your instructor.

Add sound and interactivity to an animated banner for a zoo.

APPLY

Case Problem 2

Data Files needed for this Case Problem: aczDraft.fla, bear.jpg, giraffe.jpg, rhino.jpg, zooSounds.mp3

Alamo City Zoo   Janet meets with Alex to request a new Web site that will display zoo animals. She wants the banner to include sound and Alex suggests using buttons to make the banner interactive. Several frames will display special exhibits and the user will be able to change the display from one exhibit to another. Alex asks you to help him modify a draft page by adding buttons to control the display of each exhibit and by adding each exhibit in a separate frame. Each exhibit will display a picture of a zoo animal and a short message about the exhibit. Alamo City Zoo currently has three special exhibits. You will also add a background sound to the banner and sound effects to the buttons. The finished banner is shown in Figure 5-41.

| Figure 5-41 | Completed banner for Alamo City Zoo |

© Luis A. Lopez

1. Open the **aczDraft.fla** document located in the Flash5\Case2 folder included with your Data Files, and then save the file as **aczExhibits.fla** in the same folder.

2. In the Timeline, insert two new layers above the contents layer, and then name the layers **buttons** and **labels**.

3. In the Timeline, select the buttons layer, open the Buttons Common Library, drag an instance of the flat blue back symbol from the playback flat folder to the Stage, place the instance below the text block and rectangle at the center of the Stage, and then name the instance **prev_btn**.

4. Drag an instance of the flat blue forward symbol from the playback flat folder to the Stage, place the instance just to the right of the flat blue back instance, and then name the instance **next_btn**. Close the Buttons library panel.

5. Select both of the button instances and then top-align the buttons relative to each other.

6. In the Timeline, insert regular frames at Frame 10 of all the layers. Insert a keyframe in Frame 2 of the contents layer, and then delete the bottom and middle text blocks.

7. Import the **bear.jpg, giraffe.jpg**, and **rhino.jpg** files located in the Flash5\Case2 folder included with your Data Files to the document's library.

8. Drag an instance of the rhino.jpg bitmap from the document's Library panel to the center of the rectangle and place it below the title text block.

9. In Frame 2 of the contents layer, add a fixed-width static text block to the left of the rhino picture. Make the text block's width about 140 pixels and place it about 180 pixels from the top of the Stage and about 100 pixels from the left of the Stage. Use Arial for the font family, regular for the font style, 14 for the point size, maroon (#660000) for the text color, and align left for the paragraph format. Type **The rhinoceros stands about 60 inches at the shoulder and weighs between 1 and 1½ tons. Rhinos are vegetarians and live up to 40 years.** in the text block.

10. In the Timeline, insert a keyframe at Frame 3 of the contents layer. On the Stage, swap the instance of the rhino.jpg bitmap with an instance of the giraffe.jpg bitmap. Change the text in the text block to the left of the picture to **The giraffe stands at a height of 14 to 18 feet and weighs up to 2 tons. Giraffes are vegetarians and are able to grasp leaves with their tongues.**

11. In the Timeline, insert a keyframe at Frame 4 of the contents layer. On the Stage, swap the instance of the giraffe.jpg bitmap with an instance of the bear.jpg bitmap. Change the text in the text block to the left of the picture to **Bears, such as the grizzly bear, grow from 5 to 7 feet in length and weigh up to 900 pounds. Bears eat plants, insects, fish, and meat and have a life span of about 25 years.**

12. In the Timeline, select Frame 1 of the labels layer. In the Property inspector, assign the label **Begin** to this frame. Insert a keyframe at Frame 4 of the labels layer, and assign the label **End** to the frame.

⊕ EXPLORE

13. In the Timeline, insert a new layer above the labels layer and name it **actions**. Select Frame 1 of the actions layer, open the Actions panel, and in the Script pane, type the following code (this code stops the playhead at Frame 1; the first function will move the playhead to the previous frame except when the playhead is on Frame 1, in which case the playhead will move to the frame labeled End; the second function will move the playhead to the next frame except when the playhead is on Frame 4, in which case the playhead will move to the frame labeled Begin):

```
//Keep the playhead from advancing
stop();
//Advance the playhead to the previous frame
prev_btn.addEventListener(MouseEvent.CLICK, onPrevClick);
function onPrevClick(event:MouseEvent):void
{
    if (currentFrame == 1)
    {
        gotoAndStop("End");
    }
    else
    {
        prevFrame();
    }
}
//Advance the playhead to the next frame
next_btn.addEventListener(MouseEvent.CLICK, onNextClick);

function onNextClick(event:MouseEvent):void
{
    if (currentFrame == 4)
    {
        gotoAndStop("Begin");
    }
    else
    {
        nextFrame();
    }
}
```

14. Check the code for syntax errors, and make any necessary corrections.

15. Edit the flat blue back button symbol. In symbol-editing mode, insert a new layer above the text layer and name it **sound**. Insert a keyframe in the Down frame of the sound layer. Open the Sounds common library and drag an instance of the Animal Mammal Carnivore Tiger Snarl 01.mp3 sound to the Stage. The sound will play when the button is clicked.

16. Edit the flat blue forward button symbol. In symbol-editing mode, insert a new layer above the text layer and name it **sound**. Insert a keyframe in the Down frame of the sound layer. Drag an instance of the Animal Mammal Carnivore Tiger Snarl 01.mp3 sound from the Sounds common library to the Stage. The sound will play when the button is clicked. Exit symbol-editing mode.

17. Import the **zooSounds.mp3** file located in the Flash5\Case2 folder included with your Data Files to the document's library.

18. In the Timeline, insert a new layer above the actions layer and name it **sound**. With the sound layer selected, drag an instance of the zooSounds.mp3 sound from the document's library to the Stage. The zooSounds.mp3 sound is added to the sound layer.

19. In the Property inspector, select Start for the Sync setting and select Loop to have the sound play continuously.

20. Save the aczExhibits.fla file, and then test it. Click the buttons to hear the sound effect and to display each exhibit in the frames.

21. Submit the finished files to your instructor.

Add ActionScript code to advance the playhead, background sound, and a button to control the sound in a banner for a nursery.

CHALLENGE

Case Problem 3

Data Files needed for this Case Problem: glDraft.fla, guitarLoop.mp3, flower1.jpg, flower2.jpg, flower3.jpg

G&L Nursery Alice requests a photos page to display pictures of flowers and plants for sale. Because the number of pictures varies each week, only one button will be used. Each time the button is clicked, a different picture will appear. This will allow more pictures to be added without adding more buttons. You will modify a photos page developed by Amanda by adding one picture with text per frame and adding a button to advance from one frame to the next. You will also add a background sound and a Mute button to stop the sound from playing. The finished banner is shown in Figure 5-42.

Figure 5-42	Completed banner for G&L Nursery

iStockphoto.com/Carrie Winegarden

1. Open the **glDraft.fla** file located in the Flash5\Case3 folder included with your Data Files, and then save the file as **glBanner.fla** in the same folder.

2. On the Stage, select the G&L Nursery text block and then break the text apart twice so that the letters are converted to filled shapes. In the Timeline, insert a keyframe at Frame 10 of the header layer, and then in Frame 1, draw a rectangle approximately the same size as the text block. Use white for the rectangle's fill and do not include a stroke. The rectangle should cover the entire G&L Nursery text.

◆ EXPLORE

3. In the Timeline, create a shape tween at Frame 1 of the header layer. The rectangle will transform into the G&L Nursery text from Frame 1 to Frame 10.

4. In the Timeline, insert a regular frame at Frame 30 of all layers to extend the movie.

5. In the Timeline, insert two new layers above the header layer and name them **pictures** and **labels**. Insert a keyframe at Frame 10 of the labels layer and at Frame 10 of the pictures layer. Type **Begin** as the label for Frame 10 of the labels layer.

⊕ **EXPLORE**   6. In the Timeline, select Frame 10 of the pictures layer. Use the Import to Stage command to import the **flower1.jpg** file located in the Flash5\Case3 folder included with your Data Files. Click the Yes button to import all of the images in the sequence, which places each of the three pictures in separate frames positioned at the center of the Stage.

7. With Frame 12 selected, select the bitmap on the Stage and in the Property Inspector, enter **60** for the bitmap's Y coordinate. In the Timeline, select Frame 11, select the bitmap on the Stage, and in the Property inspector, enter **60** for the bitmap's Y coordinate. Select Frame 10, select the bitmap on the Stage, and in the Property inspector, enter **60** for the bitmap's Y coordinate.

8. Select Frame 10 of the pictures layer, and then create a static text block in the top center of the picture. Use Arial for the font family, regular for the font style, 24 for the point size, 0 for the letter spacing, align center for the paragraph format, and white for the text color. Type **$19.95–$49.95** in the text block. Add a drop shadow filter effect to the text block.

9. Select Frame 11 of the pictures layer, create a static text block in the top center of the picture using the same properties listed in Step 8, and then type **$24.95–$59.95** in the text block. Add a drop shadow filter effect to the text block.

10. Select Frame 12 of the pictures layer, create a static text block in the top center of the picture using the same properties listed in Step 8, and then type to **$9.95–$29.95** in the text block. Add a drop shadow filter effect to the text block.

11. In the Timeline, insert a new layer above the pictures layer and name it **buttons**. In the buttons layer, insert a keyframe at Frame 10, and then drag an instance of the nextPicture button from the document's library to the Stage and place it to the left of the bitmap at approximately 10 pixels from the left of the Stage and 60 pixels from the top of the Stage.

12. In the Property inspector, name the nextPicture button instance as **next_btn**.

13. Use the Import to Library command to import the **guitarLoop.mp3** sound file located in the Flash5\Case3 folder included with your Data Files.

14. In the Timeline, insert a new layer above the buttons layer and name it **music**. Select Frame 1 of the music layer and then in the Property inspector, select guitarLoop.mp3 from the sound name list.

15. In the Sound section of the Property inspector, select Start for the Sync sound option and Loop for the sound loop option.

16. In the Timeline, select Frame 10 of the buttons layer, and then create a fixed-width static text block in the lower-left side of the Stage. Use Arial for the font family, regular for the font style, 10 for the point size, white for the text color, align center for the paragraph format, and Anti-alias for readability for the font rendering method. Type **Mute**, press the Enter key, and then type **Sound**.

17. Convert the Mute Sound text block to a button symbol and name the symbol **Mute Sound**. In symbol-editing mode, insert a keyframe in the symbol's Over frame.

⊕ **EXPLORE**   18. In the Property inspector, apply a Glow filter to the text block in the Over frame. Change the Glow filter's color to yellow (#FFFF00). Exit symbol-editing mode.

19. On the Stage, select the Mute Sound button, and then in the Property inspector, enter the name **mute_btn** for the instance name.

20. Move the playhead to Frame 10, if necessary, and then select the next_btn instance on the Stage.

⊕ EXPLORE   21. Insert the Mouse Click Event code snippet located in the Event Handlers category. In the Actions panel, change the code snippet function name, `fl_MouseClickHandler`, to **onNextClick** in the event listener and in the function definition.

22. In the Actions panel, replace the multiline comments at the beginning of the script with the following code:

```
//Keep the playhead from advancing
stop();

//Advance the playhead to the begin label or to the next frame
```

⊕ EXPLORE   23. In the Actions panel, within the onNextClick function, replace the comments and the `trace()` statement with the following code. This code will advance the playhead to the next frame each time the button is clicked unless the playhead is on the last frame, in which case the playhead is moved to the frame labeled begin.

```
if (currentFrame == 12) {
    gotoAndStop("Begin");
} else {
    nextFrame();
}
```

24. On the Stage, select the Mute Sound button, and then insert the Click to Stop All Sounds code snippet.

⊕ EXPLORE   25. In the Actions panel, click the Auto format button to apply proper formatting to the code. Check the code for syntax errors and make any necessary corrections.

26. Save the glBanner.fla file, and then test it. After the shape tween is finished, the first picture is displayed. Click the Next picture button to display the next picture. Click the Mute Sound button to stop the music from playing.

27. Submit the finished files to your instructor.

Find sounds, add actions, and create a button to replay an animation.

CREATE

Case Problem 4

Data File needed for this Case Problem: rccsDraft.fla

River City Conservation Society   Brittany wants Anissa to add some interaction with appropriate sounds to enhance the impact of the advertisement banner that River City Conservation Society will use to promote the organization. You will modify the advertisement banner by adding a button that when clicked displays a different message about the organization. You will search the Web to find a background sound for the banner and a sound effect to add to the button. The starting banner is shown in Figure 5-43.

Figure 5-43   **Initial advertisement banner for River City Conservation Society**

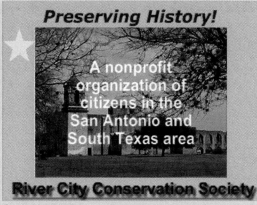

© Luis A. Lopez

1. Open the **rccsDraft.fla** file located in the Flash5\Case4 folder included with your Data Files, and then save the document as **rccsBanner.fla** in the same folder.

 EXPLORE

2. Go to the Flash Kit Web site (*www.flashkit.com*) or another site of your choice that has sound files you can download and use for free. Find two sound files appropriate for the advertisement. One sound should be short to use as a sound effect on a button. The other should be a sound loop to use as a background sound. Download the sounds to the Flash5\Case4 folder.

3. Import the sound loop you downloaded into the document's library, and then add the sound to the first frame of a sound layer that you create above the text layer. Add appropriate sound, sync, and loop settings.

4. In the first frame of a new actions layer, add a stop action that stops the animation and keeps it from repeating.

5. Use the star symbol in the library or create a new symbol using the Button behavior type. Place a button instance in a new layer and position it in the upper left of the Stage aligned with the top of the picture.

6. In the Over frame of the button, change the button in some way to provide a visual clue that the pointer is over the button.

7. In the Down frame, shift the button so that it is offset by a few pixels, and then add the sound effect you imported. Exit symbol-editing mode.

8. In Frame 1 of a new text layer, add a text block with a message about the organization's mission, such as **A nonprofit organization of citizens in the San Antonio and South Texas area**. Place the text block over the picture in the center of the Stage.

9. In Frame 2 of the text layer, add a text block with a message about the organization's mission, such as **Working to preserve historic buildings related to the history of San Antonio and South Texas**. Place the text block over the picture in the center of the Stage.

10. In Frame 3 of the text layer, add a text block with a message about the organization's mission, such as **Bringing awareness to the community and providing a forum to meet and learn about the history of the region**. Place the text block over the picture in the center of the Stage.

11. Insert a new layer above the button layer and name it **label**. Add the label **Start** in Frame 1 of the label layer.

12. Assign a name to the star button instance on the Stage, and then with the button instance selected, insert the Mouse Click Event code snippet located in the Event Handlers category.

13. In the Actions panel, change the statements within the function so that the play-head will advance to the next frame each time the button is clicked unless the playhead is on Frame 3, in which case the playhead is moved to the frame labeled Start. Your code might look like the following:

```
next_btn.addEventListener(MouseEvent.CLICK,
fl_ClickToGoToNextFrame);

function fl_ClickToGoToNextFrame(event:MouseEvent):void
{
if (currentFrame == 3)
{
    gotoAndStop("Start");
}
else {
    nextFrame();
}
}
```

14. Test the banner animation, making sure the sounds play and that the button works properly.
15. Submit the finished files to your instructor.

ENDING DATA FILES

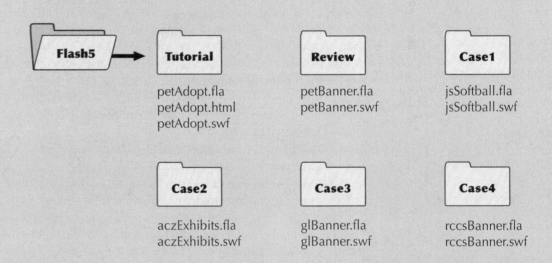

Flash5 → Tutorial
petAdopt.fla
petAdopt.html
petAdopt.swf

Review
petBanner.fla
petBanner.swf

Case1
jsSoftball.fla
jsSoftball.swf

Case2
aczExhibits.fla
aczExhibits.swf

Case3
glBanner.fla
glBanner.swf

Case4
rccsBanner.fla
rccsBanner.swf

Programming with ActionScript 3.0

FLASH

Adding Input and Dynamic Text, Components, and Video

OBJECTIVES

Session 6.1
- Create and test a Flash preloader
- Create input and dynamic text fields
- Create an input form

Session 6.2
- Add Web links using the ComboBox component
- Add pictures using the UILoader and Button components
- Add a ProgressBar component
- Add ActionScript to control components

Session 6.3
- Learn the basics of using digital video
- Format video with Adobe Media Encoder
- Import video
- Modify the FLVPlayback component
- Add button components to control video

Case | *Katie's Pet Shop*

Katie Summers wants changes made to a new banner for the Katie's Pet Shop Web site. Aly asks you to incorporate the changes. You will complete the Pictures, Videos, and Boarding Calculator sections of the banner. You will add a simple animation to provide visual feedback while the site's content loads into Flash Player. The Videos section will include buttons to select each of the two video clips of pets to display as well as controls to play and pause the videos and mute the audio. In the Boarding Calculator section, you will create a section that displays a calculator that visitors can use to estimate the cost of boarding their pets by entering the number of days and the type of activities desired for the pet.

In this tutorial, you will learn how to use components along with ActionScript 3.0 programming to create these interactive elements and to input values and perform calculations in Flash.

STARTING DATA FILES

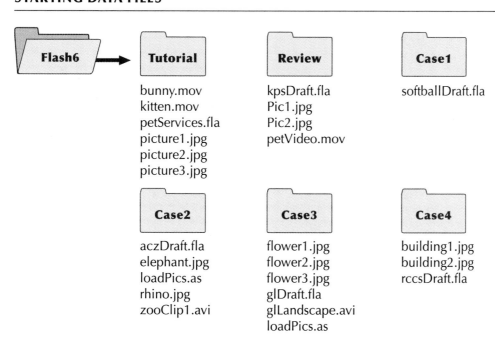

Flash6 → **Tutorial**

bunny.mov
kitten.mov
petServices.fla
picture1.jpg
picture2.jpg
picture3.jpg

Review

kpsDraft.fla
Pic1.jpg
Pic2.jpg
petVideo.mov

Case1

softballDraft.fla

Case2

aczDraft.fla
elephant.jpg
loadPics.as
rhino.jpg
zooClip1.avi

Case3

flower1.jpg
flower2.jpg
flower3.jpg
glDraft.fla
glLandscape.avi
loadPics.as

Case4

building1.jpg
building2.jpg
rccsDraft.fla

Adobe product screenshot(s) reprinted with permission from Adobe Systems Incorporated.

FL 311

SESSION 6.1 VISUAL OVERVIEW

A **preloader** is a short animation or message located in the first few frames of a Flash file that provides visual feedback to assure visitors that the Web site is loading while the frames of the SWF file continue to download.

The green rectangle increases in width as the SWF file is loading.

The event listener calls the preloader function when the file starts loading.

Numeric variables will hold values for the total number of bytes in the SWF file, the number of bytes that have been loaded, and the result of dividing loadedBytes by the totalBytes.

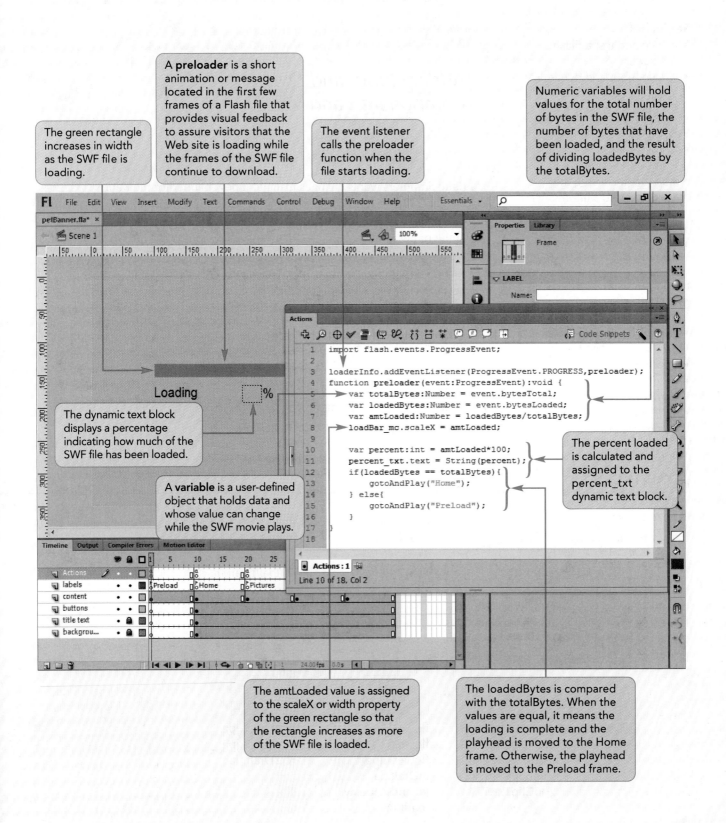

The dynamic text block displays a percentage indicating how much of the SWF file has been loaded.

A **variable** is a user-defined object that holds data and whose value can change while the SWF movie plays.

The percent loaded is calculated and assigned to the percent_txt dynamic text block.

```
1   import flash.events.ProgressEvent;
2
3   loaderInfo.addEventListener(ProgressEvent.PROGRESS,preloader);
4   function preloader(event:ProgressEvent):void {
5       var totalBytes:Number = event.bytesTotal;
6       var loadedBytes:Number = event.bytesLoaded;
7       var amtLoaded:Number = loadedBytes/totalBytes;
8   loadBar_mc.scaleX = amtLoaded;
9
10      var percent:int = amtLoaded*100;
11      percent_txt.text = String(percent);
12      if(loadedBytes == totalBytes){
13          gotoAndPlay("Home");
14      } else{
15          gotoAndPlay("Preload");
16      }
17  }
18
```

The amtLoaded value is assigned to the scaleX or width property of the green rectangle so that the rectangle increases as more of the SWF file is loaded.

The loadedBytes is compared with the totalBytes. When the values are equal, it means the loading is complete and the playhead is moved to the Home frame. Otherwise, the playhead is moved to the Preload frame.

PRELOADERS AND INPUT FORMS

Input text blocks enable the user to enter text that is then stored in a variable and used in an ActionScript script. Input text blocks can be formatted to display with a border around the text.

An input form allows the user to enter data into text blocks.

A function is defined that uses values entered in the input text blocks. In this case, the calculateTotal function will use the values entered in the input text blocks to calculate the total cost of boarding a pet.

Variables are defined to hold numeric data. Numeric data represents numbers rather than characters, which are stored in string variables. These numeric variables hold values for the price per pet and the total cost.

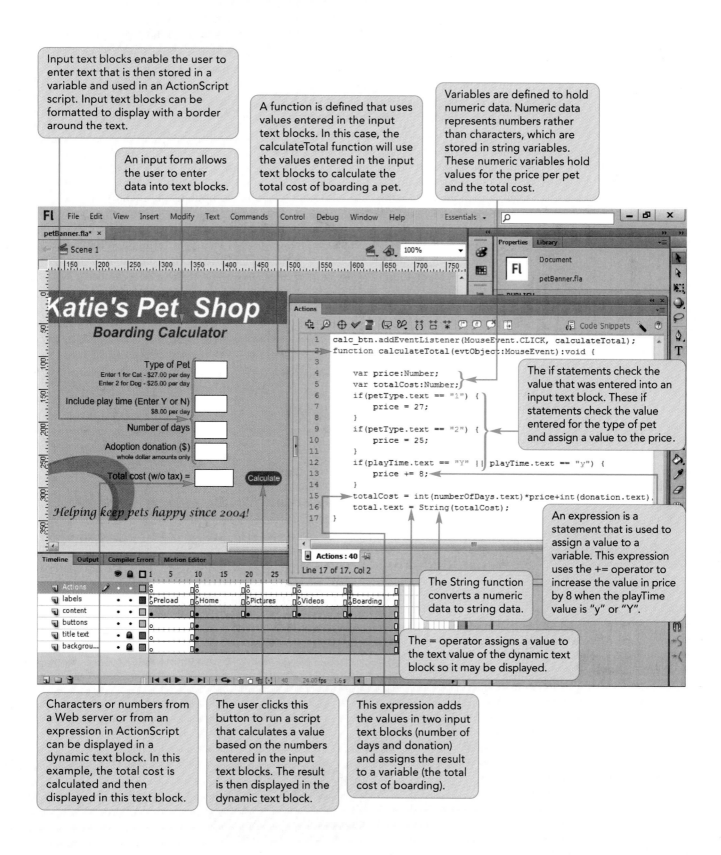

The if statements check the value that was entered into an input text block. These if statements check the value entered for the type of pet and assign a value to the price.

An expression is a statement that is used to assign a value to a variable. This expression uses the += operator to increase the value in price by 8 when the playTime value is "y" or "Y".

The String function converts a numeric data to string data.

The = operator assigns a value to the text value of the dynamic text block so it may be displayed.

Characters or numbers from a Web server or from an expression in ActionScript can be displayed in a dynamic text block. In this example, the total cost is calculated and then displayed in this text block.

The user clicks this button to run a script that calculates a value based on the numbers entered in the input text blocks. The result is then displayed in the dynamic text block.

This expression adds the values in two input text blocks (number of days and donation) and assigns the result to a variable (the total cost of boarding).

Within the Actions panel:

```
1  calc_btn.addEventListener(MouseEvent.CLICK, calculateTotal);
2  function calculateTotal(evtObject:MouseEvent):void {
3
4      var price:Number;
5      var totalCost:Number;
6      if(petType.text == "1") {
7          price = 27;
8      }
9      if(petType.text == "2") {
10         price = 25;
11     }
12     if(playTime.text == "Y" || playTime.text == "y") {
13         price += 8;
14     }
15     totalCost = int(numberOfDays.text)*price+int(donation.text)
16     total.text = String(totalCost);
17 }
```

Katie's Pet Shop
Boarding Calculator

Type of Pet
Enter 1 for Cat - $27.00 per day
Enter 2 for Dog - $25.00 per day

Include play time (Enter Y or N)
$8.00 per day

Number of days

Adoption donation ($)
whole dollar amounts only

Total cost (w/o tax) =   Calculate

Helping keep pets happy since 2004!

Using a Flash Preloader

TIP

Flash can be used to create a complete Web site that consists primarily of Flash SWF files and not HTML documents.

SWF files, like HTML files, are downloaded over the Internet from a Web server to the user's computer, tablet, or other mobile device where the files will reside. A major factor that affects the amount of time a file takes to download is the size of the file, measured in kilobytes. A **kilobyte** is approximately 1000 bytes, and a **byte** is equivalent to one character of information. Flash Web sites typically contain various multimedia elements, such as graphics, animations, pictures, audio, and video. Each element adds to the overall size of the published file. Even though the SWF files are compressed and contain vector graphics that tend to be small, they can still take some time to download.

Another factor that affects download time is the type of Internet connection used by the client computer. The type of Internet connection can be a broadband connection using a cable or DSL modem that provides high-speed download capability, a public wireless connection shared by many users, or a much slower dial-up connection using a telephone modem, as is the case with some personal computers, particularly in rural areas. When the SWF file starts to download from a Web server to a client computer, it is loaded into Flash Player one frame at a time. The first frames start playing in Flash Player as soon as they load, even though other frames of the file are still downloading. This is because of the streaming capability of Flash files. **Streaming** means that as the file is downloading, the initial content can start playing while the rest of the content continues to be downloaded, which reduces the wait time for the user. A problem occurs, however, when the client computer plays all of the loaded frames and then has to wait for additional frames to load. This can happen if a particular frame has a large amount of content such as bitmap images. The wait causes Flash Player to pause the playing of the SWF file while additional frames load. This delay affects the way the SWF file plays and might confuse or frustrate the user. Also, if the wait is more than a few seconds and no visual indication appears that something is still loading, the user may think the Web site is not working and decide to go to another site.

To avoid losing site visitors, Flash developers usually add a preloader, which is a short animation or message located in the first few frames of the Flash file. The preloader typically contains a short animation and the word *Loading* to indicate that the Web site is still loading. This visual feedback helps assure the site visitor that the Web site is loading while the frames of the SWF file continue to download. After all the content has downloaded, the preloader stops and the rest of the SWF file plays. Several examples of preloaders are shown in Figure 6-1.

Figure 6-1 **Examples of preloaders**

Creating the Preloader

Adding a preloader to a Flash file requires ActionScript code along with a loading message and/or an animation placed in the first frame of the Timeline. The preloader message and animation are displayed only while the file is being loaded. A script can be added to a later frame in the Timeline to control the preloader and to check if all of the content has downloaded. The basic logic involves knowing how much of the SWF file has loaded and comparing that with the total size of the file. The amount of content that has loaded and the total size of the file can be measured in either number of frames or number of bytes, both of which can be examined using ActionScript. By checking how much content has been loaded and comparing it with the total size of the file, different actions can be performed. For example, if the number of bytes that have loaded into Flash Player is equal to the total number of bytes for the file, the entire SWF file has loaded. At that point, the SWF file can play as designed. Otherwise, the preloader animation continues to play.

If the SWF file contains a large number of frames, you can create a preloader that checks the number of frames loaded. In the case of the Katie's Pet Shop banner, the number of frames is small, so it is best to check the number of bytes loaded. To create the preloader code, the script will need to get the total number of bytes to be loaded and the number of bytes loaded. The number of bytes loaded will increase as more of the file is loaded into Flash Player. As long as these two values are not the same, the preloader animation will continue to play. When the two values are the same, the SWF has finished loading. At that point, the preloader animation will stop and the rest of the frames in the movie will be played. The steps for the preloader code are as follows:

Get the total number of bytes
Get the number of bytes loaded
Update the preloader animation
If the number of bytes loaded equals the total number of bytes
    play the rest of the SWF file
Otherwise
    continue playing the preloader animation

These steps will be followed to create the code for the preloader for the Katie's Pet Shop banner.

To get the total number of bytes, you will create a function with an instance of the ProgressEvent class as its parameter. The ProgressEvent class has the event type PROGRESS, which includes the properties bytesTotal and bytesLoaded. The bytesTotal property contains the total number of bytes in the SWF file. The bytesLoaded property contains the number of bytes loaded. These numbers will be compared with each other to determine if the SWF file has completed loading into Flash Player. The numbers can also be used to calculate what percentage of the file has loaded.

You will start creating the script for the preloader in the first frame of the Actions layer by creating an event listener and a function, and defining two variables. A variable is a user-defined object that holds data and whose value can change while the SWF movie plays. You define a variable using the **var** keyword followed by the variable's name, which must be one word that includes only alphanumeric, the underscore, and dollar sign characters. A variable must be **typed**, which means you need to specify what type of data it can contain. The data type of the variable is listed after a colon character.

In previous scripts, the event listeners registered button instances with functions to be performed when a button was clicked. In the preloader script, the event listener will call the preloader function when a specific event occurs. In this case, the event is not when a button is clicked. Instead, the event is when a part of the SWF file has loaded into Flash Player. The event.PROGRESS event will indicate when a new part of the SWF file has loaded. Because the event is dispatched or generated by a LoaderInfo object of the main Timeline, you need to register the event listener with the object. You can do this using the `addEventListener()` method of the loaderInfo object. You will add the event listener and function code in the Script pane.

Aly has started the new banner design, which is shown in Figure 6-2. You will add the preloader script and animation.

Figure 6-2   **Initial banner design**

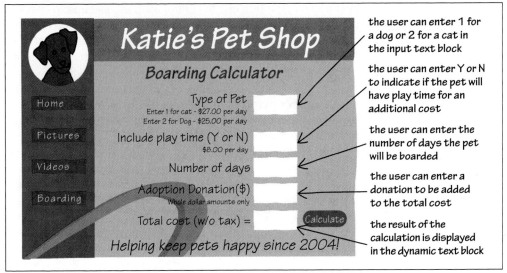

© 2013 Cengage Learning

You will start by adding the ActionScript for the preloader.

To create the first part of the preloader script:

1. Open the **petServices.fla** file located in the Flash6\Tutorial folder included with your Data Files, save the file as **petBanner.fla** in the same folder, reset the workspace to the Essentials layout, and then change the zoom magnification to **Show All**.

2. In the Timeline, click **Frame 1** of the labels layer. You will add the preloader script in this frame.

3. In the Label section of the Property inspector, type **Preload** in the Name box, and then press the **Enter** key. This label will be referred to in the script for the preloader.

4. In the Timeline, click **Frame 1** of the Actions layer, open the Actions panel, click the **collapse arrow** to collapse the Actions Toolbox and expand the Script pane.

5. In the Script pane, type the following lines of code, pressing the **Enter** key after each line:

```
loaderInfo.addEventListener(ProgressEvent.PROGRESS, preloader);
function preloader(event:ProgressEvent):void {
```

The first line defines the event listener. When content is loaded into Flash Player, the PROGRESS event occurs and the `addEventListener()` method calls the preloader function. The second line creates a function named `preloader` with the object event as its parameter. The event object is set as a ProgressEvent data type.

> Flash may add an import statement as the first line of the script and a closing curly brace to indicate the end of the function. Do not delete these statements.

6. In the Script pane of the Actions panel, type the following lines of code after the function preloader() line, pressing the **Enter** key after each line:

```
var totalBytes:Number = event.bytesTotal;
var loadedBytes:Number = event.bytesLoaded;
```

The first var line creates a new variable named totalBytes whose data type is Number. The value of the bytesTotal property of the event object is assigned to the variable. The second var line creates a variable named loadedBytes with a data type of Number. The value of the bytesLoaded property of the event object is assigned to the variable.

Creating the Preloader Animation

The totalBytes and loadedBytes variables can also be used to control the animation used in the preloader. Recall that the properties of a movie clip instance can be modified using ActionScript. You can create a movie clip in the shape of a rectangle and then gradually increase the horizontal size of the rectangle to match how much of the file has been loaded. Because the rectangle instance is an object, you can modify the object's scaleX and scaleY properties, which represent the relative size of the object compared with its original size. The scaleX property can be used to scale the object horizontally. The property uses a fractional value such as 0.5 to represent a percentage of the object's original size. For example, a scaleX value of 0.5 changes the object to display 50% of its original size. So by changing the scaleX property of the rectangle from 0 to 1, the rectangle appears to grow horizontally from 0% to 100% of its original size.

You will create an instance of a movie clip in the shape of a rectangle with a registration point on its upper-left corner. The rectangle will grow horizontally, starting from the left side and growing to the right side. When the rectangle is back to its original size, the SWF file has finished loading.

Calculating the scaleX Property

To determine the value to assign to the scaleX property of the rectangle, divide the loadedBytes value by the totalBytes value, resulting in fractional values ranging from 0 to 1. The result, which represents the percentage of how much of the file has loaded, can be assigned to the scaleX property of the rectangle. It increases gradually until the two values are equal, resulting in a value of 1, which means all of the file's content has loaded and the scaleX property of the rectangle is 100%.

You will add a preloader animation to the content layer.

To add the graphic and code for the preloader animation:

1. Close the Actions panel to see the Stage, and then, in the Timeline, click **Frame 1** of the content layer.

2. In the Tools panel, click the **Text Tool** button T , and then in the Property inspector, set the text type to **Static Text**, if necessary, set the font family to **Arial**, set the font style to **Regular**, set the point size to **20**, set the text fill color to **black**, set the format to **Align left**, if necessary, and set the font rendering method to **Anti-alias for readability** if necessary.

> **3.** On the Stage, display the rulers, if necessary, add a text block approximately 100 pixels from the left of the Stage and 180 pixels from the top of the Stage, and then type **Loading** in the text block.

> **4.** On the Stage, create another text block with the same properties as the first text block, place it to the right of the Loading text block, and then type **%** in the text block. See Figure 6-3.

Figure 6-3	Preload text blocks

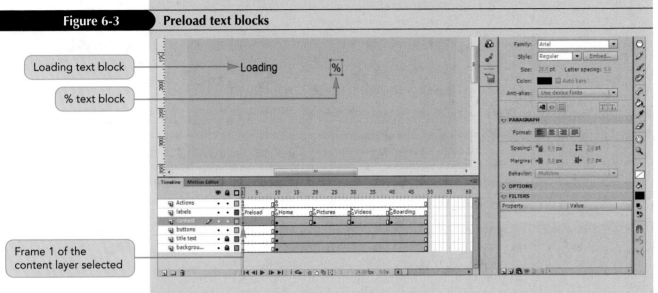

Loading text block

% text block

Frame 1 of the content layer selected

> **5.** Above the Loading text block on the Stage, draw a rectangle with a **dark green** (#009900) fill and no stroke that is **300** pixels wide and **20** pixels high. See Figure 6-4.

Figure 6-4	Rectangle for the preloader animation

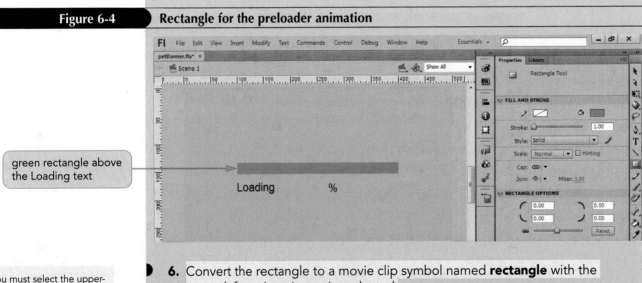

green rectangle above the Loading text

> **6.** Convert the rectangle to a movie clip symbol named **rectangle** with the upper-left registration point selected.

You must select the upper-left registration point of the rectangle movie clip so the rectangle will expand from left to right as the SWF file loads.

> **7.** In the Property inspector, type **loadBar_mc** in the Instance name box, and then press the **Enter** key to name the movie clip instance. The preloader movie clip instance is complete.

> **8.** In the Timeline, click **Frame 1** of the Actions layer, and then open the Actions panel. You will add the code to change the loadBar_mc's scaleX property.

9. In the Script pane after the second var statement, type the following code, pressing the **Enter** key after each line. See Figure 6-5.

```
var amtLoaded:Number = loadedBytes/totalBytes;
loadBar_mc.scaleX = amtLoaded;
```

Figure 6-5   **Partial preloader script**

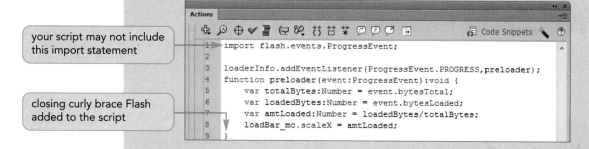

your script may not include this import statement

closing curly brace Flash added to the script

```
import flash.events.ProgressEvent;

loaderInfo.addEventListener(ProgressEvent.PROGRESS,preloader);
function preloader(event:ProgressEvent):void {
    var totalBytes:Number = event.bytesTotal;
    var loadedBytes:Number = event.bytesLoaded;
    var amtLoaded:Number = loadedBytes/totalBytes;
    loadBar_mc.scaleX = amtLoaded;
}
```

Trouble? If Flash did not add the closing brace after the last line of code that you entered, you need to add it yourself. Click in the blank line after the code you entered, and then type } (a closing brace).

The amtLoaded variable will hold the result of dividing loadedBytes by totalBytes. This resulting number is a fractional value that represents the percentage of how much of the SWF file has been loaded. This value is assigned to the scaleX property of the Rectangle movie clip, loadBar_mc, causing it to increase horizontally each time the loadedBytes value changes.

In addition to the loadBar_mc animation, you will add a special type of text block that will display a changing value, from 0% to 100%, indicating how much of the SWF file has loaded. You will add this text block and its associated ActionScript code later in this session.

Completing the Preloader Code

The next part of the function is a comparison using a conditional statement. A **conditional statement** compares one value with another. Based on the result of the comparison, certain actions are performed. Conditional statements use **comparison operators**, such as ==, which is used to test for equality. This is different from the assignment operator =, which is used to assign a value to a variable. Other comparison operators include >, <, and !=, which are used to test for greater than, less than, and not equal to, respectively. You create a conditional statement using the `if` keyword, which tests a condition. If the condition is true, Flash Player performs actions within the curly braces that follow it. You can also include the `else` keyword, which contains the actions to perform when the condition is false.

The `if` statement compares the values of loadedBytes and totalBytes. If the values are not equal, the loading has not finished so the playhead is moved to the Preload frame, which is Frame 1. If the values are equal, the loading has finished and the playhead is moved to the first part of the banner, which is the frame with the Home label. You use the `gotoAndPlay()` function to direct the playhead to a specific frame, referring to a frame by its label. You will add the `if` conditional statement to the script next.

To add code to compare the loadedBytes and totalBytes values:

1. In the Script pane of the Actions panel, click the end of the loadBar_mc statement, and then press the **Enter** key to add a blank line.

▶ **2.** Type the following code, pressing the **Enter** key after each line. Make sure to type the code before the function's closing curly brace. See Figure 6-6.

```
if (loadedBytes == totalBytes) {
    gotoAndPlay("Home");
} else {
    gotoAndPlay("Preload");
}
```

Figure 6-6   **Conditional statement in the preloader script**

If statement code is before the function's ending curly brace

condition compares values in loadedBytes and totalBytes

The condition, enclosed in parentheses, compares the values in the loadedBytes and totalBytes variables. If the values are equal, the gotoAndPlay("Home"); statement is executed, causing the playhead to move to the first page of the Web site. If the values are not equal, the gotoAndPlay("Preload"); statement is executed, causing the playhead to move to the frame labeled Preload. This causes the script to run again.

The function for the preloader script is complete. You will test the script next. Because the SWF file will load from your computer's drive, the file's content will load instantly, and the preloader animation will be visible only for a very short time. This will not be the case when the SWF file is downloaded from the Internet. To better test the preloader, you can use the Simulate Download command. This command simulates the time it takes to download the SWF file based on the type of Internet connection you select.

To test the preloader script:

▶ **1.** In the Actions panel, click the **Check syntax** button ☑ to check for syntax errors in the code. The script is checked. If no errors are displayed in the Compiler Errors panel, the script is correct.

Trouble? If your code contains errors, the errors are listed in the Compiler Errors panel at the bottom of the screen. Review your script to compare it with the code you modified in the previous steps, make any necessary corrections, and then repeat Step 1 until no errors are encountered.

▶ **2.** Save the petBanner.fla document, and then close the Actions panel.

▶ **3.** On the menu bar, click **Control**, point to **Test Movie**, and then click **in Flash Professional**. The SWF file plays in Flash Player; however, the preloader does not appear long enough for you to see it because the SWF file loaded very quickly from your computer's drive.

> **4.** On the Flash Player menu bar, click **View**, point to **Download Settings**, and then click **DSL (32.6 KB/s)** to select it, if necessary, to select the type of Internet connection Aly believes some visitors may use when they load the Katie's Pet Shop Web site.

> **5.** On the Flash Player menu bar, click **View**, and then click **Simulate Download**. After a few seconds, the preloader animation plays, simulating the time it takes to download the SWF file based on the Internet connection you just selected. See Figure 6-7.

Figure 6-7	Simulated download process

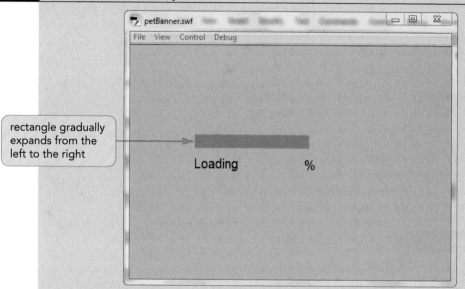

rectangle gradually expands from the left to the right

After the green rectangle is scaled to its original size, the home section of the Katie's Pet Shop banner appears.

> **6.** Close the Flash Player window to return to the petBanner.fla document.

The preloader animation for the Katie's Pet Shop banner is complete. You will add a text field to display a numeric value that represents the amount of content that has been loaded into Flash Player.

Creating Dynamic Text

Text is an important element of a Flash document. All of the text you have created so far has been static text. **Static text** cannot be changed after the document plays in Flash Player. Although static text cannot change, dynamic text can. **Dynamic text** can receive text in the form of characters or numbers from a Web server or from an expression in ActionScript and display the text on a Web page in Flash Player. Dynamic text is defined to display the contents of a variable. The variable can be used in ActionScript to change the value displayed. For example, if a dynamic text block is assigned the variable Amount, you can code an expression in ActionScript that assigns the result of a calculation to the variable. The value stored in the variable Amount will then appear in the text block in the Web page.

In the previous steps, you created an animation for the preloader to provide visual feedback to the user. In the animation, the scaleX property of the rectangle was changed based on how much of the SWF file had loaded into Flash Player. In addition to the visual feedback, Flash developers often include numeric feedback showing what percentage of the file has been loaded. The same value used to change the scaleX property of the rectangle can be displayed as a percentage. To display the number, you need to create a dynamic text block. You will add a dynamic text block for the preloader, and then you will add the code to calculate and display the percentage of the file loaded.

To add a dynamic text block to the preloader:

1. Display the Timeline, if necessary, and then click **Frame 1** of the content layer.

2. On the Stage, deselect the text blocks.

3. In the Tools panel, click the **Text Tool** button T, and then in the Property inspector, set the text type to **Dynamic Text**.

4. On the Stage, create a dynamic text block to the left of the % text block, and then in the Property inspector, set the font family to **Arial**, set the font style to **Regular**, set the point size to **20**, set the font rendering method to **Use device fonts**, set the text color to **black**, set the paragraph format to **Align right**, and deselect the **Show border around text** button, if necessary.

5. In the Property inspector, set the text block's dimensions to **30** pixels wide and **26** pixels high, and then enter **percent_txt** as the instance name of the text block instance.

6. In the Tools panel, click the **Selection Tool** button, and then reposition the text block, as shown in Figure 6-8.

Figure 6-8 **Dynamic text block**

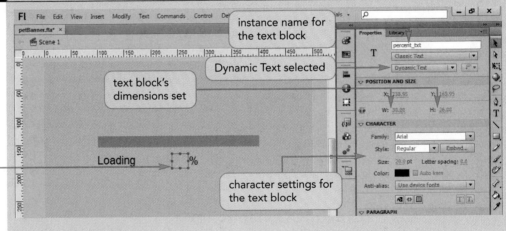

Next, you will add the code to the preloader function to calculate and display the percentage of the file loaded.

To add numeric feedback code, check for errors, and test the script:

1. In the Timeline, click **Frame 1** of the Actions layer, and then open the Actions panel.

2. In the Script pane of the Actions panel, place the insertion point in front of the line with the if conditional statement, press the **Enter** key to add a blank line, and then in the blank line, type the following line of code:

```
var percent:int = amtLoaded*100;
```

This line creates a new variable named percent with integer as its data type. The value in amtLoaded is multiplied by 100 to change the amtLoaded value to a percentage. This percentage is assigned to the percent variable.

3. Press the **Enter** key to add a new line, and then type the following line of code:

```
percent_txt.text = String(percent);
```

The value in the percent variable is converted to a string using the `String()` function and the result is then assigned to the text property of the percent_txt object, which is the dynamic text block instance on the Stage. The result is that the percent value is displayed in the dynamic text block instance.

4. In the Actions panel, click the **Check syntax** button to check for syntax errors in the code. If no errors are displayed in the Compiler Errors panel, the script is correct.

Trouble? If your code contains errors, the errors are listed in the Compiler Errors panel at the bottom of the screen. Review your script to compare it with the code you modified in the previous steps, make any necessary corrections, and then repeat Step 4 until no errors are encountered.

5. Close the Actions panel, and then save the document. You will test the Katie's Pet Shop banner.

6. On the menu bar, click **Control**, point to **Test Movie**, and then click **in Flash Professional**. The movie opens in Flash Player. The Loading text appears briefly, and then the home section of the banner opens.

7. On the Flash Player menu bar, click **View**, and then click **Simulate Download**. After a few seconds, the preloader animation plays and the percent loaded value is displayed. See Figure 6-9. After the percent loaded value reaches 100%, the home section of the Katie's Pet Shop banner appears.

| Figure 6-9 | Simulated download process |

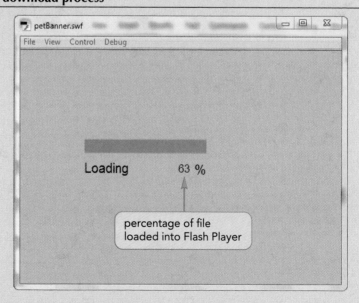

8. Close the Flash Player window.

Creating an Input Form

An input form is a common element found on many Web sites. An **input form** consists of input text blocks and allows the user to enter data into the text blocks. The data entered into the text blocks can be stored in a variable and used in an ActionScript script. The data can then be submitted for storage and processing on a Web server. The server software sends results of the processing back to the user's computer to be displayed on the same form or on another Web page. A banner developed with Flash can also allow the user to enter data, have the data processed, and return a result directly from Flash Player on the user's computer. The developer uses ActionScript to write the underlying functions required to create a form with several input fields coded to accept data from the site visitor, such as the number and type of items to be purchased. Other fields on the form display results based on the site visitor's input, such as a total price. Creating an input form requires the use of dynamic and input text. (Input text is covered later in this tutorial.)

Based on Aly's request, you will create a form for the Calculator section of the Katie's Pet Shop banner. This section will allow a user such as a customer to enter several values for the number of nights of pet boarding desired. The banner will contain a button that when clicked will use the entered values to calculate a total cost and display the result.

You will complete the Calculator section by creating the input and dynamic text blocks. You will also add a Calculate button and write the ActionScript code to make the button operational so that it calculates the total cost. You will start by adding the static text blocks for the section.

To create the static text blocks for the Boarding Calculator:

1. In the Timeline, click **Frame 40** of the content layer. The Boarding Calculator section of the banner appears on the Stage.

2. On the Stage, create a horizontal guide **100** pixels from the top edge of the Stage and a vertical guide **350** pixels from the left edge of the Stage. The guides will be used to place the text blocks.

3. Deselect the title text block, if necessary, click the **Text Tool** button T in the Tools panel, and then, in the Property inspector, set the text type to **Static Text**, set the font family to **Arial**, the font style to **Regular**, the point size to **14**, the text color to **black**, and the paragraph format to **Align right**.

4. On the Stage, click the vertical guide below the horizontal guide to create a text block, type **Type of Pet**, press the **Enter** key to create a new line, type **Enter 1 for Cat - $27.00 per day**, press the **Enter** key to create a new line, and then type **Enter 2 for Dog - $25.00 per day**.

5. Select the last two lines of the text block, and then, in the Property inspector, change the point size to **10**. If necessary, reposition the text block to match that shown in Figure 6-10.

Figure 6-10 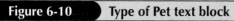 Type of Pet text block

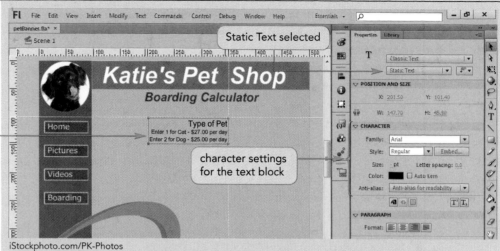

iStockphoto.com/PK-Photos

▶ **6.** Create a second static text block below the Type of Pet text block, use the same text attributes as the first text block with a point size of **14**, type **Include play time (Enter Y or N)**, press the **Enter** key, and then type **$8.00 per day**.

▶ **7.** Select the second line in the text block, and then, in the Property inspector, change the point size to **10**.

▶ **8.** Create a third static text block below the previous text block, use the same text attributes as the previous text block but change the point size to **14**, and then type **Number of days**.

▶ **9.** Create a fourth static text block below the previous text block, use the same text attributes as the previous text block, and then type **Adoption donation ($)**, press the **Enter** key, and then type **whole dollar amounts only**.

▶ **10.** Select the second line in the text block, and then, in the Property inspector, change the point size to **10**.

▶ **11.** Create a fifth static text block below the previous text block, use the same text attributes but change the point size to **14**, and then type **Total cost (w/o tax) =**.

▶ **12.** In the Tools panel, click the **Selection Tool** button ▶, reposition the text blocks on the Stage as needed so that their right edges are aligned, and then deselect the text blocks. See Figure 6-11.

Figure 6-11   **Static text blocks**

iStockphoto.com/PK-Photos

The static text blocks are complete. Each text block provides instructions to the user about the values that can be entered into the input text blocks. You will create the input text blocks next. You will also assign instance names to each input text block so that it can be referenced in the ActionScript code.

To create the input text blocks for the Calculator:

1. In the Tools panel, click the **Text Tool** button **T**, and then, in the Property inspector, click the **Text type** button and click **Input Text**. The next text block you create will be for input text.

2. In the Property inspector, set the font family to **Arial**, set the font style to **Regular**, set the point size to **14**, set the text color to **black**, set the paragraph format to **Align right**, and then set the font rendering method to **Use device fonts**.

3. On the Stage, click to the right of the Type of Pet text block to create an input text block, and then, in the Tools panel, click the **Selection Tool** button. The input text block remains selected on the Stage.

4. In Property inspector, enter **petType** as the instance name, and then, in the Position and Size section, set the dimensions to **50** pixels wide and **26** pixels high.

5. In the Character section of the Property inspector, click the **Show border around text** button to select it.

6. In the Paragraph section of the Property inspector, select **Single line** for the line type.

7. In the Options section of the Property inspector, set the Max chars to **1** to allow only one character in the input box, and then position the text block as shown in Figure 6-12.

Figure 6-12   **Input text block properties**

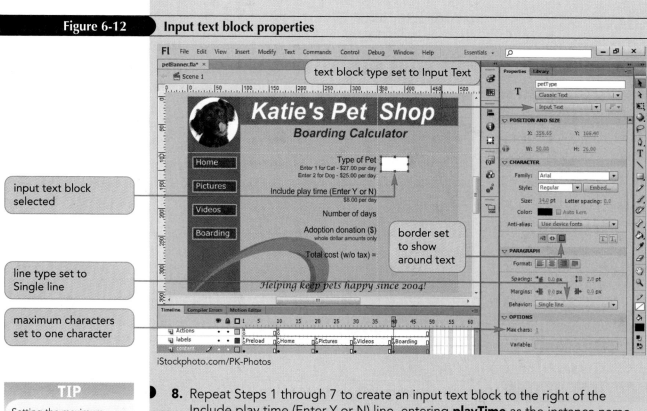

input text block
selected

line type set to
Single line

maximum characters
set to one character

iStockphoto.com/PK-Photos

8. Repeat Steps 1 through 7 to create an input text block to the right of the Include play time (Enter Y or N) line, entering **playTime** as the instance name.

9. Repeat Steps 1 through 7 to create an input text block to the right of the Number of days line, entering **numberOfDays** as the instance name and setting the maximum characters to **0**.

10. Repeat Steps 1 through 7 to create an input text block to the right of the Adoption donation line, entering **donation** as the instance name and setting the maximum characters to **0**.

11. In the Tools panel, click the **Selection Tool** button , reposition the input text blocks as needed so that they are vertically aligned, and then deselect the text blocks. See Figure 6-13.

Figure 6-13   **Completed input text blocks**

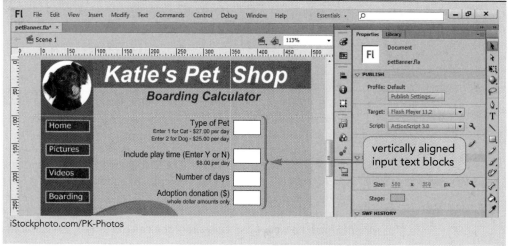

vertically aligned
input text blocks

iStockphoto.com/PK-Photos

The input text blocks the visitor will use to enter data are complete. Next, you will create a dynamic text block. This text block instance must also be assigned a name. You will also create an instance of the Calculate button that Aly created.

> **To add the dynamic text block and button to the Calculator:**
>
> 1. In the Tools panel, click the **Text Tool** button $\boxed{T}$, and then create a text block to the right of the Total cost (w/o tax) = line.
>
> 2. In the Property inspector, set the text type to **Dynamic Text**, set the font family to **Arial**, set the font style to **Regular**, set the point size to **14**, set the text color to **black**, set the paragraph format to **Align right**, and then set the font rendering method to **Use device fonts**.
>
> 3. In the Tools panel, click the **Selection Tool** button $\boxed{\text{▶}}$, and then, in the Property inspector, enter **total** as the instance name, set the text block dimensions to **60** pixels wide and **26** pixels high, and click the **Selectable** button $\boxed{\text{A}}$ to deselect it, if necessary. The properties for the dynamic text block are set.
>
> 4. Drag an instance of the **calcTotal** symbol from the Library panel to the right side of the dynamic text block, and then, in the Property inspector, enter **calc_btn** as the instance name. The button instance is placed on the Stage and assigned a name. See Figure 6-14.

Figure 6-14	Completed dynamic text block and button

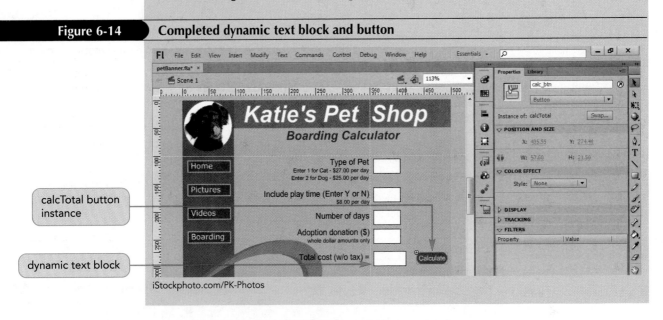

calcTotal button instance

dynamic text block

iStockphoto.com/PK-Photos

Writing ActionScript Code to Do a Calculation

The calcTotal instance requires ActionScript code to make it operational. The user will enter values in the input text blocks you created, and then click the calcTotal instance to compute the total cost for the boarding. As you have done with previous scripts, you need to define a function. The function will process the values entered in the input text blocks and calculate a total cost that will be displayed in the dynamic text block. The first part of the script will create an event listener and a function called `calculateTotal`. After defining the function, you will add several statements to define variables that will be used within the script. These variables do not represent objects on the Stage, but instead hold intermediate values used as part of the calculations. Each variable is defined with the `var` keyword, a name, and the Number data type. The Number data type specifies that the variables will contain numbers.

TIP

You can also right-click the frame, and then click Insert Keyframe to add a keyframe.

To define the function and the initial variables for the script:

▶ **1.** In the Timeline, insert a keyframe at **Frame 40** of the Actions layer. Actions for the Calculator section will be created in Frame 40.

▶ **2.** Open the Actions panel, and then, in the Script pane, type the following lines of code to define the event listener and the function:

```
calc_btn.addEventListener(MouseEvent.CLICK, calculateTotal);
function calculateTotal(evtObject:MouseEvent):void {
```

▶ **3.** Press the **Enter** key twice to insert a blank line, and then type the following lines of code to define the variables, pressing the **Enter** key after each line:

```
var price:Number;
var totalCost:Number;
```

The first input text block will contain either a 1 or a 2 for the type of pet. To determine which price to use for the pet, you must use an if conditional statement. The condition that needs to be checked is whether the petType value the user entered is 1 or 2. You will create two conditional statements: one to check for the value of 1 and one to check for the value of 2. Based on the results of the conditions, the price variable will be assigned a value of 25 or 27, corresponding to the cost of boarding the selected type of pet.

Using Expressions and Operators

An **expression** is a statement that is used to assign a value to a variable. For example, the expression UserName = "Tom" assigns the text "Tom" to the variable UserName. When referring to text in an expression, it is enclosed in quotation marks. The characters within the quotation marks are considered string data, which is handled differently than numeric data. **String data** is a series of characters—such as letters, numbers, and punctuation—and is always enclosed in quotation marks. **Numeric data** is a number or numbers that are not enclosed in quotation marks. So, to assign a numeric value to a variable, you do not enclose the value in quotation marks. For example, the expression Amount = 20 assigns the numeric value 20 to the variable named Amount.

The equal sign in the expression is an example of an operator. Operators are used in expressions to tell Flash how to manipulate the values in the expression. ActionScript uses several types of operators. An **assignment operator**, such as the equal sign, assigns a value to a variable. **Arithmetic operators** such as +, −, *, and / are used to indicate addition, subtraction, multiplication, and division, respectively. A comparison operator is an operator used in conditional statements, as you learned earlier. The script to calculate the results will use expressions and operators.

To code the statements to determine the price per day to charge for boarding:

▶ **1.** In the Script pane of the Actions panel, type the following lines of code after the last var statement, pressing the **Enter** key after each line:

```
if (petType.text == "1") {
     price = 27;
     }
```

In this code, petType is the name assigned to the first input text block and it contains the value entered by the user. The text property of the petType object represents the value contained in the input box. The conditional operator == compares the input box value to the text value of "1". If the values are equal, the next line assigns a value of 27 to the price variable.

2. Type the following lines of code, pressing the **Enter** key after each line to code a second conditional statement to check for a petType value of "2":

```
if (petType.text == "2") {
     price = 25;
     }
```

This code specifies that if the text value of the petType object is "2", a value of 25 is assigned to the price variable.

TIP

You can use shortcuts to combine assignment and arithmetic operators, such as Amount += 5 instead of Amount = Amount + 5 to increment the value in the variable Amount by 5.

After the second if statement is performed, the price variable will contain either a value of 25 or 27 depending on the petType value entered by the user.

The next action to perform is another if statement to determine whether the user entered Y or N. This determines if play time will be included with the boarding. If the user entered Y, you will add 8.00 to the price of the boarding. Because ActionScript is case sensitive, you need to check for both a lowercase y and an uppercase Y. This will ensure that the correct value is calculated, regardless of how the user entered the letter.

There is no need to check for the letter N because if the user entered N, the price will not change. To check for two conditions within the same if statement, you use the logical operator ||, which represents the Or comparison. You will add the ActionScript code for the if statement next.

To code the statement to check if play time will be included:

1. In the Script pane of the Actions panel, type the following lines of code after the lines you typed in the previous steps, pressing the **Enter** key after each line:

```
if (playTime.text =="Y" || playTime.text == "y") {
     price += 8;
}
```

In this code, playTime is the name of the input text block that contains the value the user enters to specify whether play time will be included with the boarding. The text property represents the value entered by the user. The || operator causes the condition to be true if either one of the comparisons is true. If the condition is true, the variable price is increased by 8.

The next input text block contains a value that represents how many days the pet is to be boarded. Another text block contains a value that represents any dollar donation the customer wants to include. These two values will be used in calculating the total cost. Before the values can be used in an arithmetic operation, they need to be converted to numbers. Because the number of days and the dollar donation are whole numbers, you will use the int() function.

INSIGHT

Converting Values to Numeric Data

Values entered into an input text block are considered string data and not numeric data. That is, the values are not treated as numbers, but instead are treated as text characters. Using the + operator to add the two values will not yield the correct result if the values are not first converted to numeric data. The int() function can be applied to the values to convert them to integer numbers, which are whole numbers that do not include decimals.

You can multiply the number of days by the cost per day to get a total cost. You will add the statements to determine the total cost next.

To code the statements to determine the total cost of the boarding and to display the final result:

▶ **1.** In the Script pane of the Actions panel, after the previous lines you added, type the following line of code:

```
totalCost = int(numberOfDays.text) * price + int(donation.text);
```

The numberOfDays variable was defined in the input text block. The text property in numberOfDays.text is used to get the value entered by the user in the text block. The value is converted to an integer and then multiplied by the value in price. The resulting value is then added to the value in donation. text. The end result is then assigned to the variable totalCost.

▶ **2.** In the Script pane of the Actions panel, after the previous line you added, type the following line of code to assign the value in totalCost to the dynamic text block so that it will be displayed for the user:

```
total.text = String(totalCost);
}
```

The dynamic text block can contain only string data. Because the totalCost value is a number, it must first be converted to string data before it can be assigned to the dynamic text block named total. To convert the number to a string, you apply the string() function to the totalCost value. The results of the string() function can then be assigned to the total dynamic text block. The value will then be displayed to the user. See Figure 6-15.

| Figure 6-15 | Complete script for calculation |

```
1  calc_btn.addEventListener(MouseEvent.CLICK, calculateTotal);
2  function calculateTotal(evtObject:MouseEvent):void {
3
4      var price:Number;
5      var totalCost:Number;
6      if(petType.text == "1") {
7          price = 27;
8      }
9      if(petType.text == "2") {
10         price = 25;
11     }
12     if(playTime.text == "Y" || playTime.text == "y") {
13         price += 8;
14     }
15     totalCost = int(numberOfDays.text)*price+int(donation.text);
16     total.text = String(totalCost);
17  }
```

The code is complete. Next you need to check the code for syntax errors and then test it using several input values to make sure you get the correct result. You will test the script next.

TIP

Before testing the script, you should check for syntax errors and make corrections as needed.

To check for errors and test the script:

▶ **1.** In the Actions panel, click the **Check syntax** button ✅ to check for syntax errors in the code. The script is checked. If no errors are displayed in the Compiler Errors panel, the script is correct.

   Trouble? If your code contains errors, the errors are listed in the Compiler Errors panel at the bottom of the screen. Review your script to compare it with the code you modified in the previous steps, make any necessary corrections, and then repeat Step 1 until no errors are encountered.

▶ **2.** Save the document, and then close the Actions panel. You will test the Katie's Pet Shop banner.

▶ **3.** On the menu bar, click **Control**, point to **Test Movie**, and then click **in Flash Professional**. The movie opens in Flash Player. The Loading text appears briefly, and then the Home section of the banner opens.

▶ **4.** Click the **Boarding** button to advance to the Boarding Calculator section, and then enter **1** in the Type of Pet box, **y** in the Include play time box, **3** in the Number of days box, and **4** in the Adoption donation box.

▶ **5.** Click the **Calculate** button. The Total cost field displays 109. See Figure 6-16.

Figure 6-16   **Results of the calculation**

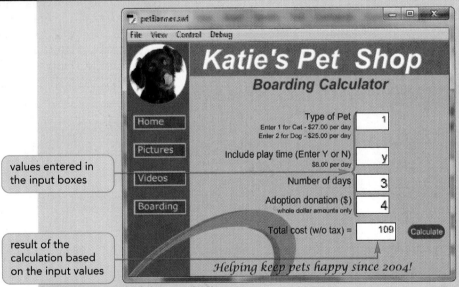

values entered in the input boxes

result of the calculation based on the input values

iStockphoto.com/PK-Photos

   Trouble? If you do not get the correct results, make sure you entered the correct input values and also check the variable names of your input and dynamic text blocks. Remember that ActionScript is case sensitive. If the case of the variable names assigned to the text blocks differs from that used in the code, the result will be incorrect.

▶ **6.** Enter a set of input values of your choice, click the **Calculate** button to see the total cost, and then repeat with another set of input values.

▶ **7.** Close the Flash Player window to return to the petBanner.fla document.

▶ **8.** Clear the guides.

You have completed and tested the input form that allows the user to enter values in input text blocks, calculates the total cost of the boarding based on the values entered, and displays the result in a dynamic text block. You also created a preloader using ActionScript, added a dynamic text block to display the percent loaded value with the preloader animation, and tested the preloader by simulating the download speed of a 56K modem Internet connection.

REVIEW

Session 6.1 Quick Check

1. What is streaming?
2. What is the purpose of a preloader?
3. Explain how you can simulate the downloading of a SWF file within Flash Player.
4. What is an input form?
5. How can you limit the number of characters that can be entered in an input text block?
6. Write a statement to multiply the value in the numeric variable subTotal by 15 and assign the result to the dynamic text block with the instance name of subtotal_txt.
7. Explain the purpose of the || operator in the following conditional statement: `if (Code == "1" || Code == "2")`.
8. What is the purpose of the `int()` function?

SESSION 6.2 VISUAL OVERVIEW

A component is a prebuilt movie clip installed with Flash that includes a set of user interface and video components. Flash components are located in the Components panel.

FL   File   Edit   View   Insert   Modify   Text   Commands   Control   Debug   Window   Help

petBanner.fla* ×

Scene 1

150   200   250   300   350   400   450   500   550   600   650

Katie's Pet Shop

Katie's Pet Shop we value your business and
ll do our best to provide you with exceptional
vice. We have been providing our customers th
t in pet supplies, grooming, boarding, and
ning services for many years.

're also proud supporters of local pet adoption
ncies.

Web Links ○   ▼

Helping keep pets happy since 2004!

The Button component creates a functional button instance. Change the button's text label in its label parameter.

The ComboBox component displays a drop-down list from which the user can make a selection.

When an instance of the ComboBox component is first placed on the Stage, all of its elements are added to the document's library.

The ProgressBar component can display the progress of loading content, such as a photo file, into the UILoader instance.

Code Snippets   Components   Motion Prese

▶ 📁 Flex
▼ 📁 User Interface
   ▢ Button
   ☑ CheckBox
   ▣ ColorPicker
   🗗 ComboBox
   ▦ DataGrid
   T Label
   ▤ List
   10↕ NumericStepper
   ▭ ProgressBar
   ◉ RadioButton
   ▦ ScrollPane
   ⊶ Slider
   ▤ TextArea
   abl TextInput
   ▦ TileList
   🖳 UILoader

Timeline   Output   Compiler Errors   Motion Editor

👁 🔒 ▢   1   5   10   15   20

🔲 Actions   · · ▢
🔲 labels   · · ■   Preload   Home   Pictures   Videos   Boarding
🔲 content   🖉 · · ▢   ·   ·   ·   ·   ·
🔲 buttons   · · ▢
🔲 title text   · 🔒 ■
🔲 backgrou...   · 🔒 ▢

◀◀ ◀▌ ▶ ▌▶ ▶▌   ⬚ ↻   🖫 🖫 🖫 [·]   10   24.00 fps   0.4 s   ◀

The UILoader component can be used to load content such as images and SWF files.

FLASH COMPONENTS

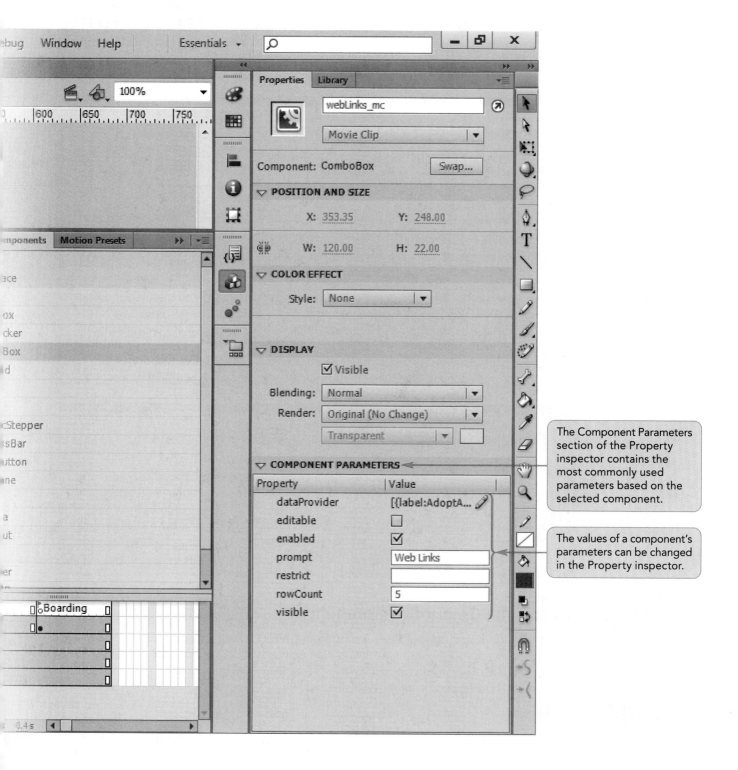

The Component Parameters section of the Property inspector contains the most commonly used parameters based on the selected component.

The values of a component's parameters can be changed in the Property inspector.

Using Flash Components

Components are movie clips that have been exported with the .swc extension. Some components installed with Flash can be used to create user interface elements in documents. For example, you can use the CheckBox component to create check boxes with options that a user can select on a form. When the user clicks a check box, a check mark appears in the check box. This information can then be processed using ActionScript. Using a component such as the CheckBox component means you do not have to create the necessary graphics and functionality because they are already built into the component. Other user interface components include the ComboBox and the ProgressBar, which displays the loading progress of content loading into Flash Player.

The first time you add a component to a document, simply drag an instance of the component from the Components panel to the Stage. The component's movie clip and other elements are added to the document's library. Then, you can add more instances of the same component by dragging them from the Library panel to the Stage and then assigning each instance a different name. A component contains parameters that can be viewed or changed in the Component Parameters section of the Property inspector.

Using the ComboBox Component

The ComboBox component displays a list from which the user can make a selection. In the Home section of the Katie's Pet Shop banner, you will add a drop-down list of Web links based on Aly's instructions, shown in Figure 6-17. The user can then click an item on the list to navigate to another Web site.

Figure 6-17 | **Web links on the banner**

add a list of
Web links to the
home section

© 2013 Cengage Learning

You will create the Web links by adding an instance of the ComboBox component to the Katie's Pet Shop banner, setting its parameters, and adding ActionScript code to make the items in the ComboBox functional.

To add a ComboBox instance to the banner's home section:

1. If you took a break after the previous session, make sure the petBanner.fla file is open, the Essentials workspace is reset, and the zoom magnification is set to Show All.

2. In the Timeline, select **Frame 10** of the content layer. The Home section content appears on the Stage.

3. In the docked panel group, click the **Components** button 🕹️. The Components panel opens.

4. In the Components panel, double-click **User Interface** to expand its list of components, if necessary.

5. Drag an instance of the **ComboBox** component from the Components panel to the Stage.

6. On the Stage, if necessary, reposition the ComboBox instance below the last line of the large text block in the lower-right part of the Stage.

7. In the Property inspector, name the instance **webLinks_mc**, change the width of the instance to **120** pixels, and then make sure the height is **22** pixels. The ComboBox instance is positioned and sized for the banner's home section. See Figure 6-18.

Figure 6-18 **ComboBox added to the banner**

iStockphoto.com/PK-Photos

The ComboBox component instance has **properties**, called parameters, which can be modified in the Component Parameter section of the Property inspector. The data-Provider parameter defines the labels that appear on the drop-down list and the values that are associated with each item. The editable parameter, when set to true, enables the user to edit the items in the list. The contents of the prompt parameter appear on the ComboBox instance on the Stage. The rowCount parameter determines how many rows to allocate to the drop-down list.

You will enter values for the prompt and dataProvider parameters.

To set parameter values for the ComboBox instance:

1. In the Component Parameters section of the Property inspector, type **Web Links** in the prompt box, and then press the **Enter** key. The Web Links text appears in the ComboBox instance on the Stage.

2. In the Component Parameters section of the Property inspector, click the **Value** column next to the dataProvider parameter. The Values dialog box opens.

3. Click the **Add value** button ✚. A label and data without values are inserted.

4. In the label Value column, click **label0**, and then type **AdoptAPet.com**. The label value is added.

5. Press the **Tab** key to move the insertion point to the data Value box, and then type **1** to add the data value. The first value is added to the dataProvider parameter.

6. Repeat Steps 3 through 5 to add two more values to the dataProvider parameter, using **ASPCA Adoption** and **2** for the second label and value, and **PetsAdoption.com** and **3** for the third label and value. See Figure 6-19.

TIP

You can also click the pencil icon in the Value column of the dataProvider parameter to open the Values dialog box.

Figure 6-19   **Values dialog box**

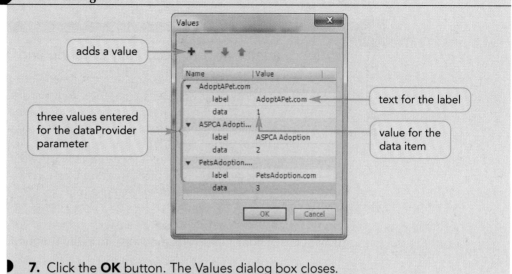

adds a value

three values entered
for the dataProvider
parameter

text for the label

value for the
data item

▶ **7.** Click the **OK** button. The Values dialog box closes.

With the ComboBox component instance added to the Stage and its parameters set, you need to add ActionScript code to make the ComboBox instance operational. When the user clicks an item in the drop-down list, the value associated with the item can be checked using ActionScript code. For example, if a user clicks the AdoptAPet.com item, the value of the ComboBox instance is 1 because that value is associated with AdoptAPet.com.

ActionScript uses the ComboBox value to determine which URL to use to navigate to a Web site. To check which of the three URLs will be used, you can use a switch statement, which is helpful when you need to execute one of several statements or blocks of statements based on the value of the same expression. Each block of statements that might be executed is enclosed between a case statement and a break statement. Each case statement has a value associated with it, as shown in Figure 6-20.

Figure 6-20   **Sample switch statement**

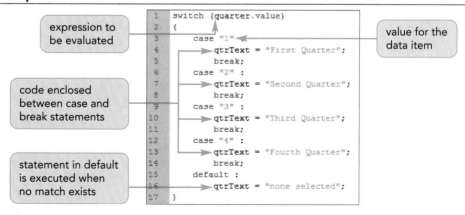

expression to
be evaluated

code enclosed
between case and
break statements

statement in default
is executed when
no match exists

value for the
data item

```
1   switch (quarter.value)
2   {
3       case "1" :
4           qtrText = "First Quarter";
5           break;
6       case "2" :
7           qtrText = "Second Quarter";
8           break;
9       case "3" :
10          qtrText = "Third Quarter";
11          break;
12      case "4" :
13          qtrText = "Fourth Quarter";
14          break;
15      default :
16          qtrText = "none selected";
17  }
```

The expression is evaluated, and its value is compared with the values in each case statement. If a match exists, the statements following the case statement are executed. The break statement is used to exit the switch statement. The default statement executes when there is no match.

You will add a switch statement to check the value of the selected ComboBox item, which can be 1, 2, or 3. When a match is found, the associated code within the case statement assigns a Web site URL to a string variable. No default value is needed because a user can select only three possible values. After the switch statement, the value in the string variable is used to navigate to the corresponding Web site.

Written Communication: Accurately Entering and Testing Code

Programming code can be complex and lengthy. One minor syntax error can yield unexpected or inaccurate results. It is, therefore, very important to be as accurate as possible when you enter the programming code in the Actions panel. This will help reduce the possibility of syntax errors, which can be difficult to find. You should also format the code for readability—not only to help you see how the code is structured, but also to help someone else who might need to work with the code later. It is also very critical to test the code you enter to ensure that it works correctly. Be sure to test the code whenever you make any changes to it.

You will use ActionScript to add functionality to the ComboBox instance.

To add functionality to the ComboBox instance using ActionScript:

1. In the Timeline, select **Frame 10** of the Actions layer, and then open the Actions panel.

2. In the Script pane, place the insertion point at the end of the last line, and then press the **Enter** key to insert a blank line.

3. Starting in the blank line, type the following lines of code, pressing the **Enter** key after each line to create an event listener:

```
// Function to assign URL based on selected option
webLinks_mc.addEventListener(Event.CHANGE, gotoSite);
```

When a change occurs in the ComboBox instance, webLinks_mc, the gotoSite function is called.

4. In the Script pane, type the following lines of code after the last line to create the function that determines which URL will be used:

```
function gotoSite(event:Event):void
{
        // Variable that will hold the URL
        var linkText:String;
        // Switch statement determines which URL to assign
        switch (webLinks_mc.value)
        {
        case "1" :
                linkText = "http://www.adoptapet.com/";
                break;
        case "2" :
                linkText = "http://www.aspca.org/Home/Adoption";
                break;
        case "3" :
                linkText = "http://www.petsadoption.com/home";
                break;
        }
```

5. In the Script pane, type the following lines of code after the closing curly brace for the switch statement to create the URLRequest object that is used in the navigateToURL function. The URLRequest uses the URL assigned to the linkText variable in the switch statement.

> **TIP**
>
> You can click the Auto format button in the Actions panel to align and apply indentation to the code to improve readability.

```
//Open Web site using the selected URL
navigateToURL(new URLRequest(linkText), "_blank");
```

6. In the Script pane, type the following lines of code after the last line to change the value displayed in the ComboBox instance after the Web site is opened:

```
//Set ComboBox to display the prompt, Web Links
webLinks_mc.selectedIndex = -1;
}
```

Without this statement, the ComboBox instance will display the label of the item selected by the user. The last line closes the function.

7. In the Actions panel, click the **Check syntax** button to check for syntax errors in the code. The script is checked. If no errors are displayed in the Compiler Errors panel, the script is correct.

Trouble? If your code contains errors, the errors will be listed in the Compiler Errors panel at the bottom of the screen. Review your script to compare it with the code you modified in the previous steps, make any necessary corrections, and then repeat Step 7 until no errors are encountered.

8. Close the Actions panel, and then save the petBanner.fla document.

You will test the links you added to the ComboBox by opening the movie in Flash Player and clicking each link in the ComboBox.

To test the ComboBox instance:

1. On the menu bar, click **Control**, point to **Test Movie**, and then click **in Flash Professional**. The banner's home section appears in the Flash Player window.

2. On the banner, click the **Web Links** button to display the link selections, and then point to **AdoptAPet.com**. See Figure 6-21.

Figure 6-21   **Web links on the banner**

Web links created by the ComboBox instance

iStockphoto.com/PK-Photos

3. Click **AdoptAPet.com**. The Web site that corresponds to the selected item opens in a browser window.

4. On the banner, click the **Web Links** button, and then click **ASPCA Adoption** to open the Web site that corresponds to the selected item in a browser window.

5. On the banner, click the **Web Links** button, and then click **PetsAdoption.com** to open the Web site that corresponds to the selected item in a browser window.

6. Close the Flash Player window and the browser windows.

Using the UILoader Component to Display Pictures

The UILoader component can be used to load content such as images and SWF files to a Web page. The revised banner created by Aly contains a Pictures section that displays pet pictures, as shown in Figure 6-22. You will add an instance of the UILoader component to the page. The pet pictures can be loaded into an instance of the UILoader component. You will then use the Button component to add buttons that control which pictures are loaded into the UILoader instance.

Figure 6-22	Pictures section

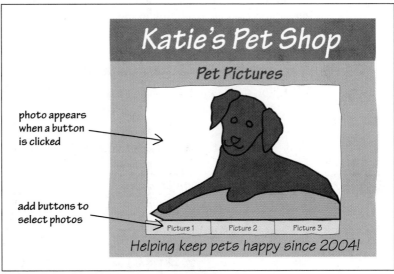

photo appears when a button is clicked

add buttons to select photos

© 2013 Cengage Learning

You will add instances of the UILoader and Button components to complete the Pictures section.

To add the UILoader and Button components to the Pictures section:

1. Display the Timeline, if necessary, and then in the Timeline, select **Frame 20** of the content layer. The Pictures section appears on the Stage.

2. In the docked panel group, click the **Components** button 🔧 to open the Components panel.

3. Drag an instance of the **UILoader** component from the Components panel to the Stage, and then position the UILoader instance about **100** pixels from the top of the Stage and **150** pixels from the left of the Stage.

4. In the Property inspector, name the instance **loader_mc**, change the width of the instance to **300** pixels, and then change the height to **200** pixels.

5. In the docked panel group, click the **Components** button 🔧 to open the Components panel, and then drag an instance of the **Button** component from the Components panel to the Stage, positioning it about **300** pixels from the top of the Stage and **150** pixels from the left of the Stage.

6. Repeat Step 5 to add another instance of the **Button** component to the Stage, positioning it immediately to the right of the first Button instance about **300** pixels from the top of the Stage and **250** pixels from the left of the Stage, right below the instance of the UILoader component.

7. Repeat Step 5 to add a third instance of the **Button** component to the Stage, positioning it immediately to the right of the second Button instance about **300** pixels from the top of the Stage and **350** pixels from the left of the Stage, right below the instance of the UILoader component.

8. Select the first Button instance on the Stage and name the instance **pic1_btn** in the Property inspector, and then repeat to name the second Button instance on the Stage **pic2_btn**, and the third Button instance on the Stage **pic3_btn**.

9. On the Stage, select the **pic1_btn** instance, and then, in the Component Parameters section of the Property inspector, double-click the **label** box, type **Picture 1**, and then press the **Enter** key. The Button instance on the Stage changes to reflect the new label.

10. Repeat Step 9 to select the **pic2_btn** instance and change its label to **Picture 2** and then select the **pic3_btn** instance and change its label to **Picture 3**. The Button instances on the Stage change to reflect their new labels. See Figure 6-23.

Figure 6-23   **UILoader and Button instances**

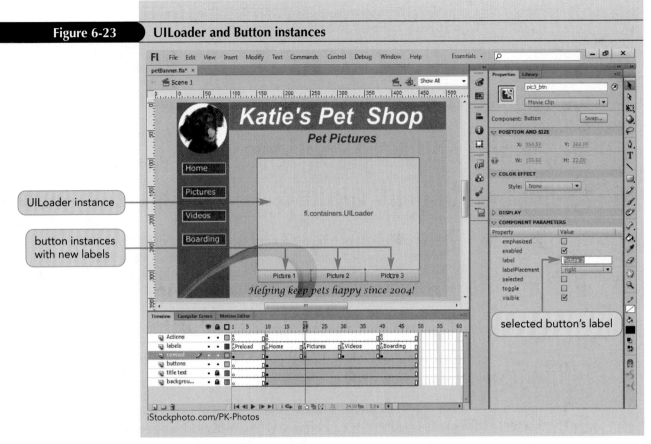

UILoader instance

button instances with new labels

iStockphoto.com/PK-Photos

The UILoader and Button components are added to the document. To make the component instances operational, you need to add ActionScript code similar to the code you used for the Web links in the Home section of the banner. You create a function with the URLRequest object that contains the name of the picture file to be loaded. Then, instead of using the `navigateToURL` function, you use the load function of the UILoader instance. You also add an event listener to each button instance to listen for the CLICK event and to run the respective function that will load the picture.

To make the UILoader and Button instances operational:

1. In the Timeline, select **Frame 20** of the Actions layer, create a keyframe, and then open the Actions panel.

2. In the Script pane, type the following lines of code to create the functions that will create a URLRequest object with the picture's filename. The object will then be used in the load method of the UILoader instance, loader_mc, to load the picture.

```
// Function to load the first picture
pic1_btn.addEventListener(MouseEvent.CLICK, loadPicture1);

function loadPicture1(event:MouseEvent):void
{
    loader_mc.load(new URLRequest("picture1.jpg"));
}
// Function to load the second picture
pic2_btn.addEventListener(MouseEvent.CLICK, loadPicture2);
function loadPicture2(event:MouseEvent):void
```

```
    {
        loader_mc.load(new URLRequest("picture2.jpg"));
    }
    // Function to load the third picture
    pic3_btn.addEventListener(MouseEvent.CLICK, loadPicture3);
    function loadPicture3(event:MouseEvent):void
    {
        loader_mc.load(new URLRequest("picture3.jpg"));
    }
```

3. In the Actions panel, click the **Check syntax** button ✓ to check for syntax errors in the code. The script is checked. If no errors are displayed in the Compiler Errors panel, the script is correct.

   Trouble? If your code contains errors, the errors will be listed in the Compiler Errors panel at the bottom of the screen. Review your script to compare it with the code you modified in the previous steps, make any necessary corrections, and then repeat Step 3 until no errors are encountered.

4. Close the Actions panel, and then save the document.

5. On the menu bar, click **Control**, point to **Test Movie**, and then click **in Flash Professional**. The Home section of the banner appears in Flash Player.

6. On the banner, click the **Pictures** navigation button to display the Pictures section.

7. In the Pictures section, click the **Picture 1** button to load the first picture, click the **Picture 2** button to load the second picture, and then click the **Picture 3** button to load the third picture. Each picture, in turn, is loaded into the UILoader instance and appears on the Stage. See Figure 6-24.

Figure 6-24   UILoader instance operational

photo loaded into the UILoader instance

click a button to load a photo into the UILoader instance

iStockphoto.com/PK-Photos; iStockphoto.com/Sarah Salmela

8. Close the Flash Player window.

Using the ProgressBar Component

The banner now displays pictures in the UILoader instance each time a picture button is clicked. To improve the user experience with the pictures, you will add a preloader that provides visual feedback when the pictures are loading. This is helpful to someone using a slow Internet connection. To create a preloader that requires only a minimal amount of ActionScript and that shows the progress of the pictures loading into Flash Player, you can use the ProgressBar component.

The ProgressBar component can work together with the UILoader component to display the progress of loading the picture file into the UILoader instance. As the picture file loads into the UILoader instance, the ProgressBar instance displays an animation that depicts the loading progress. For the ProgressBar to detect the loading of the content, you enter the name of the UILoader instance into the source parameter of the ProgressBar instance. This establishes a connection between the two component instances.

You will add a ProgressBar component to display a preloader animation for the pictures.

To add an instance of the ProgressBar component to the Stage:

1. Display the Timeline, if necessary, and then, in the Timeline, select **Frame 20** of the content layer.

2. Open the Components panel, and then drag an instance of the **ProgressBar** component from the Components panel to the center of the UILoader instance on the Stage.

> The instance name must be in the source parameter to be associated with the ProgressBar component.

3. In the Property inspector, name the instance **progressBar_mc** and change the height to **10** pixels.

4. In the Component Parameters section of the Property inspector, type **loader_mc** in the source box, and then press the **Enter** key. See Figure 6-25.

| Figure 6-25 | ProgressBar instance added to the Stage |

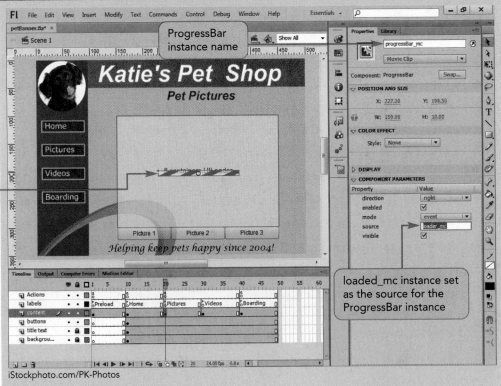

ProgressBar instance added to center of the UILoader instance

ProgressBar instance name

loaded_mc instance set as the source for the ProgressBar instance

iStockphoto.com/PK-Photos

The ProgressBar instance will use the contents of the UILoader instance as the source of the content whose progress will be tracked. As the content loads into the loader_mc movie clip, the progressBar_mc instance will display a preloader animation.

▶ 5. Save the document, and then test the movie.

▶ 6. On the Flash Player menu bar, click **View**, point to **Download Settings**, and then click **DSL (32.6 KB/s)** to select the download speed for the simulation.

▶ 7. On the Flash Player menu bar, click **View**, and then click **Simulate Download**. The initial Home section appears after a few moments.

▶ 8. In the banner, click the **Pictures** button to display the Pictures section. The ProgressBar instance appears in the center of the banner.

▶ 9. In the banner, click the **Picture 1** button to load the first picture. The ProgressBar instance displays an animation indicating the content is being loaded. When the picture appears, the ProgressBar animation stops but remains visible. See Figure 6-26.

| Figure 6-26 | ProgressBar instance on the picture |

ProgressBar instance remains visible after the picture has loaded

iStockphoto.com/PK-Photos; iStockphoto.com/ChrisAt

▶ 10. Close the Flash Player window.

The ProgressBar instance works as expected; however, it appears before and after a picture is loaded. To hide the ProgressBar instance before a picture is being loaded, you need to change its visible property to false. When a picture is about to be loaded into the UILoader instance, you change the visible property of the ProgressBar instance to true so that it appears. After the picture loading is complete, you change the visible property back to false. You also need to add an event listener that will check for the COMPLETE event of the UILoader instance, which indicates that the loading of the content into the UILoader is complete. When the COMPLETE event is detected, the event listener will run a function to set the visible property of the ProgressBar instance to false so the instance disappears from the Stage.

To add ActionScript code to control the ProgressBar instance:

▶ **1.** In the Timeline, select **Frame 20** of the Actions layer, and then open the Actions panel.

▶ **2.** In the Script pane, place the insertion point at the beginning of the first line, press the **Enter** key to add a blank line, and then, starting in the blank line, type the following lines of code to hide the progressBar_mc instance when the Pictures page is displayed:

```
// Hide the ProgressBar instance
progressBar_mc.visible = false;
```

▶ **3.** In the Script pane, place the insertion point after the opening curly brace within the `loadPicture1` function, press the **Enter** key to add a blank line, and then, in this blank line, type the following line of code to display the progressBar_mc instance before the first picture is loaded:

```
progressBar_mc.visible = true;
```

▶ **4.** Repeat Step 3 to type the same line of code after the opening curly brace within the `loadPicture2` function, and then again after the opening curly brace within the `loadPicture3` function. See Figure 6-27.

Figure 6-27   **Visibility set for the ProgressBar instance**

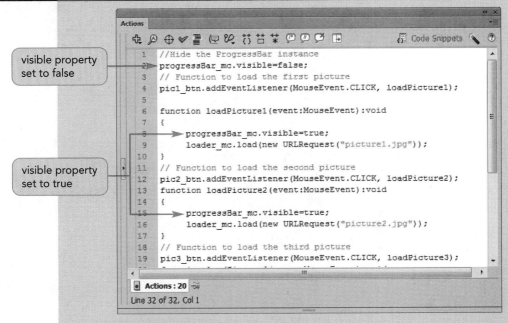

visible property set to false

visible property set to true

▶ **5.** In the Script pane, place the insertion point after the closing curly brace of the `loadPicture3` function, press the **Enter** key to add a blank line, and then, starting in this blank line, type the following lines of code to create a function that will hide the progressBar_mc instance when the loading of a picture is completed. The event listener will run the `hideBar` function when the COMPLETE event occurs for the loader_mc instance.

```
// When the loading is complete, hide the ProgressBar instance
loader_mc.addEventListener(Event.COMPLETE, hideBar);
function hideBar(event:Event)
{
        progressBar_mc.visible = false;
}
```

▶ **6.** In the Actions panel, click the **Check syntax** button ☑ to check for syntax errors in the code. The script is checked. If no errors are displayed in the Compiler Errors panel, the script is correct.

   Trouble? If your code contains errors, the errors will be listed in the Compiler Errors panel at the bottom of the screen. Review your script to compare it with the code you modified in the previous steps, make any necessary corrections, and then repeat Step 6 until no errors are encountered.

▶ **7.** Close the Actions panel, save the document, and then test the movie.

▶ **8.** On the Flash Player menu bar, click **View**, and then click **Simulate Download**. The Home section of the banner appears after a few moments.

▶ **9.** On the banner, click the **Pictures** navigational button to display the Pictures page, and then click the **Picture 1** button to load the first picture. The ProgressBar animation appears, followed by the picture. The ProgressBar instance disappears after the picture is loaded.

▶ **10.** Click the **Picture 2** button to load the second picture. The ProgressBar animation appears, followed by the picture. The ProgressBar instance disappears after the picture is loaded.

▶ **11.** Click the **Picture 3** button to load the third picture. The ProgressBar animation appears, followed by the picture. The ProgressBar instance disappears after the picture is loaded.

▶ **12.** Close the Flash Player window. The Pictures section is complete.

In this session, you learned about components and how to use them in Flash documents. You used the ComboBox, Button, UILoader, and ProgressBar components along with ActionScript to add Web links to the Home section of the banner and buttons to load pictures in the Pictures section.

REVIEW

Session 6.2 Quick Check

1. What is a Flash component?

2. What is the purpose of the dataProvider parameter of the ComboBox component?

3. In the ComboBox component, the contents of the _____ parameter appear on the ComboBox instance on the Stage.

4. Which statement is used to exit a block of code in a switch statement?

5. Write the ActionScript code to hide a ProgressBar component instance named progress_mc.

6. For a ProgressBar instance to detect the loading of content into a UILoader instance, you enter the name of the UILoader instance into the _____ parameter of the ProgressBar instance.

SESSION 6.3 VISUAL OVERVIEW

The Adobe Media Encoder export settings dialog box provides a preview of the source video file and of the video file that will be exported.

Export settings including the preset settings can be changed in this section.

The Video tab includes options such as video frame size and information such as the codec used to encode the video.

You can select how much of the video clip will be exported.

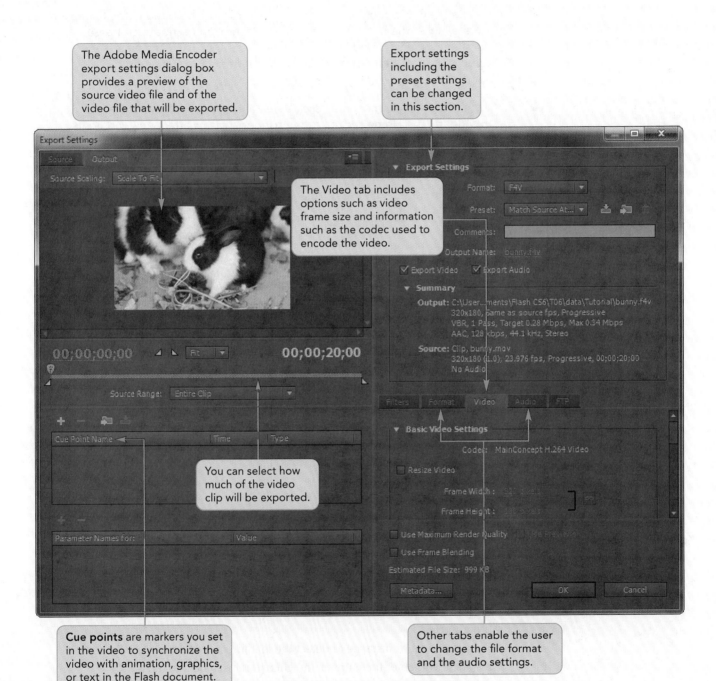

Cue points are markers you set in the video to synchronize the video with animation, graphics, or text in the Flash document.

Other tabs enable the user to change the file format and the audio settings.

DIGITAL VIDEO

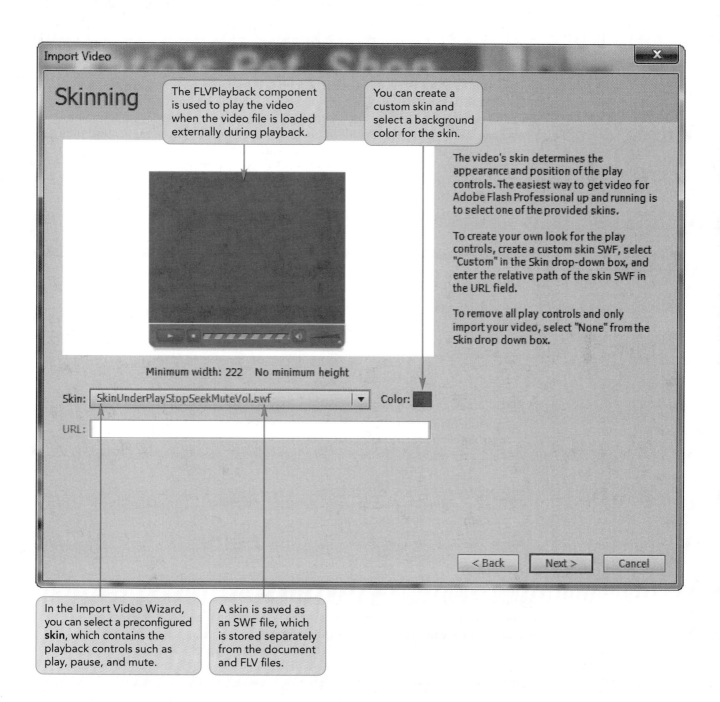

Import Video

Skinning

The FLVPlayback component is used to play the video when the video file is loaded externally during playback.

You can create a custom skin and select a background color for the skin.

The video's skin determines the appearance and position of the play controls. The easiest way to get video for Adobe Flash Professional up and running is to select one of the provided skins.

To create your own look for the play controls, create a custom skin SWF, select "Custom" in the Skin drop-down box, and enter the relative path of the skin SWF in the URL field.

To remove all play controls and only import your video, select "None" from the Skin drop down box.

Minimum width: 222   No minimum height

Skin: SkinUnderPlayStopSeekMuteVol.swf   ▼   Color: ▓

URL:

< Back   Next >   Cancel

In the Import Video Wizard, you can select a preconfigured **skin**, which contains the playback controls such as play, pause, and mute.

A skin is saved as an SWF file, which is stored separately from the document and FLV files.

Adding Video to a Flash Document

So far, the Flash documents you have created include a variety of multimedia elements, such as graphics, bitmaps, and sounds. You can also add video to Flash documents to make them more visually appealing and exciting. Before you work with video in Flash, you should understand some basic terminology and concepts about how video is prepared and in what format video can be imported into Flash. You need to consider the frame size, frame rate, and file size of video files. You also need to understand that using video on your Flash Web site can significantly increase a site's overall download time.

Selecting the Frame Rate and Frame Size

A video's frame rate, which is similar to the frame rate of a document in Flash, represents how many frames play each second. Video frame rates vary, depending on where the video is played. For example, video played on television in many countries plays at 29.97 frames per second, whereas video on film plays at 24 frames per second. Video played on the Web, however, often plays at lower frame rates, such as 12 to 18 frames per second. Frame rate also affects the size of the file. The higher the frame rate, the larger the file size of the video. For example, a 10-second video clip formatted at 30 frames per second contains 300 frames. The same 10-second video clip formatted at 12 frames per second contains 120 frames. Of course, a higher frame rate means better video quality.

PROSKILLS

Decision Making: Deciding on a Video's Frame Rate

Deciding on the frame rate to use is a balance between the quality of the video and the size of the file. Lowering the frame rate lowers the quality of the video but decreases the video's file size. Keep in mind the following factors when deciding the appropriate frame rate to select for a video:

- **Content**. Video with a minimal movement, such as someone talking in front of the camera, can be played on the Web at rates of 10 or fewer frames per second. Video with more movement, such as children playing a sport, is best played at a higher frame rate, such as 15 frames per second.
- **Internet connection of target users.** High frame rates do not play well with a dial-up connection because the connection speed cannot download the frames fast enough to play smoothly on the client computer. A faster broadband connection can better handle higher frame rates.
- **Client computer.** A slow computer with minimal capabilities might not be able to support videos with high frame rates.

Choosing an appropriate frame rate ensures a positive experience for all users.

When editing video clips and preparing them for use in Flash, you should also determine what frame size to use. The **frame size** refers to a video's width and height dimensions. You can decide the frame size by considering the type of Internet access that target users will have and the length of the video. If you are targeting users with dial-up connections, limit the frame size of videos to a smaller size, such as 164 pixels wide by 120 pixels high. If the majority of the target users have faster connections, you can set the video's frame size to higher dimensions, such as 360 pixels wide by 264 pixels high or even 640 pixels wide by 480 pixels high.

Using a High-Quality Video Source File

The quality of the source, or original, file is critical to consider when using video in Flash. The better the quality of the source file, the better the result when the video is imported into Flash. You should start with a high-quality video file before importing the video into Flash.

You can use a digital video camera to record video and then transfer the video from the camera's media to the computer. You can also convert video from an analog format into a digital format that you can store on a computer. However, whenever possible, it is best to use a digital source file. Converting from analog to digital can produce lower-quality video compared with video that is captured in a digital format.

Regardless of the video source, you should edit the video using a video-editing program such as Adobe Premiere after it is transferred to the computer but before it is imported into Flash. Although Flash provides some editing options when video is imported, the options are limited. A video-editing program allows you to trim unwanted parts of the video or select part of the video, depending on how you plan to use it. You can also change other attributes of the video, such as its frame rate and frame size.

Using Compression and Decompression

Another factor affecting the use of video over the Web is the size of the video file. The amount of data required to represent a few seconds of video can make downloading the video over the Internet a slow process. As a result, compression, which removes redundant data, can be used to reduce the size of the video file. You can specify how much to compress a video when you edit it using a video-editing program or by using an encoder program that uses compression, also known as a **compressor**. Before the compressed video can be played, it needs to be decompressed with a decoder program that uses decompression, also known as a **decompressor**.

A video coder/decoder program is called a **codec**. Various codecs are available to work with video. The codecs used by Flash are On2 VP6, Sorenson Spark, and H.264. These codecs compress the video, and Flash Player contains the corresponding decompressor to decompress the video for playback. By default, Flash uses the On2 VP6 codec when you publish video content to Flash Player 8 or higher. The H.264 codec, introduced with Flash Player 9, produces higher-quality video with smaller file sizes but requires that you publish the video to Flash Player 9 or higher. If you publish video content to Flash Player 6 or 7, Flash uses the Sorenson Spark codec. Videos published for older versions of Flash Player will also run on more recent versions of the plug-in, but those published for Flash Player 8 or higher will not work on earlier versions. Because Flash uses codecs that compress video, it is best to avoid compressing the video before bringing it into Flash.

Using Adobe Media Encoder

After video is captured and prepared using a video-editing program, preparing the video for Flash requires two basic steps. First, convert the video to one of the Flash video file formats: FLV or F4V for videos encoded using the H.264 codec. Second, import the video file into a Flash document. To convert the video into a Flash video file format, you can use **Adobe Media Encoder**, an encoder program installed with Flash. Adobe Media Encoder is a separate program that accepts several video file formats, including .mpg, .avi, and .dv. Other formats such as .mov can also be used if your computer has the QuickTime plug-in installed. When you bring a video file into Adobe Media Encoder, you select options for how you want the video to be encoded, and then you encode the video to produce a file in the FLV or F4V format.

Aly prepared two short video clips of pets to add to the Video section of the banner. You will use the Adobe Media Encoder to encode and convert the videos into the FLV format.

To encode the pet video clips using the Adobe Media Encoder:

1. If you took a break after the previous session, make sure the petBanner.fla document is open, the Essentials workspace is reset, and the zoom magnification is set to Show All.

2. Click the **Start** button on the taskbar, click **All Programs**, click the **Adobe** folder, and then click **Adobe Media Encoder CS6**. The Adobe Media Encoder program window opens.

TIP

You can also drag files from the storage location and drop them into the queue.

3. On the menu bar, click **File**, click **Add Source**, navigate to the **Flash6\ Tutorial** folder included with your Data Files, click **bunny.mov**, press and hold the **Ctrl** key, click **kitten.mov** to select both files at the same time, release the **Ctrl** key, and then click the **Open** button to add the selected video files to the queue.

   Trouble? If the encoding process starts automatically, click the Pause button, and then continue with Step 4.

4. Make sure both files are selected in the queue, and then in the Format column, click the **arrow** button ▼ for the bunny.mov file to open a list of formats. See Figure 6-28.

Figure 6-28   Format options in Adobe Media Encoder

format options (yours might differ)

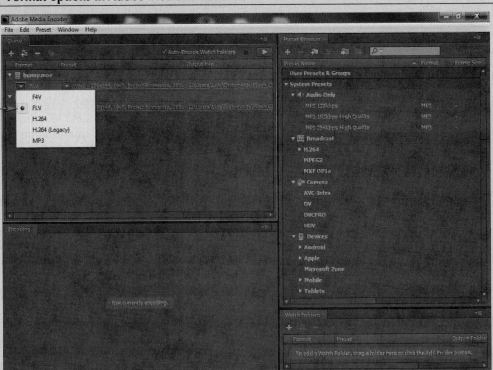

5. Click **FLV**. The selected format is set for both files and listed in the Format column.

6. With both files still selected in the queue, in the Preset column, click the **arrow** button ▼ for the bunny.mov file to open a list of presets. See Figure 6-29.

Figure 6-29 | **Preset formatting options in Adobe Media Encoder**

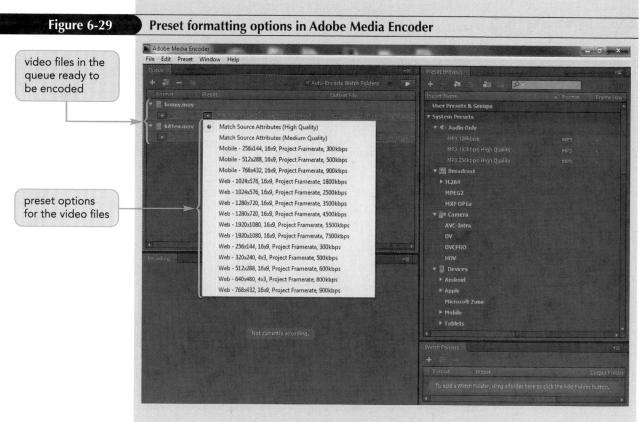

video files in the
queue ready to
be encoded

preset options
for the video files

7. Click **Web - 256×144, 16×9, Project Framerate, 300kbps**. The selected preset is set for both files and listed in the Preset column.

8. Click the **Web - 256×144, 16×9, Project Framerate, 300kbps** link for the bunny.mov file. The Export Settings dialog box opens.

   Trouble? If a dialog box opens to confirm that you are about to edit multiple selected files, click the OK button.

Export settings can be used to modify the way the video will be encoded. You can change the format of the output video to FLV or F4V, change the video's frame rate, change the way the audio is formatted, crop and resize the video clip, as well as add cue points.

To modify export settings in the Adobe Media Encoder:

1. In the Export Settings dialog box, click the **Video** tab, if necessary, scroll down within the Video panel, and then click the **Frame Rate [fps]** button. See Figure 6-30.

Figure 6-30 **Frame rate options**

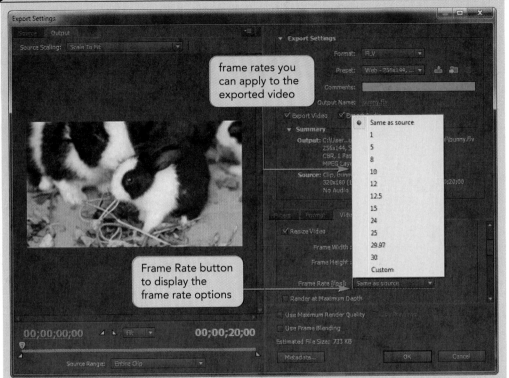

iStockphoto.com/Chanyut Sribua-rawd

▶ **2.** In the Frame Rate list, click **15**. The output video file's frame rate is reduced to 15 frames per second.

▶ **3.** In the Export Settings dialog box, click the **Audio** tab, and then click the **Mono** option button in the Output Channels section, if necessary. Mono creates a smaller output file than Stereo.

Trouble? If no codec is listed in the Audio tab under Basic Audio Settings, ask your instructor or technical support person for help. A codec is needed to ensure proper encoding of the audio.

▶ **4.** Click the **OK** button to close the Export Settings dialog box.

▶ **5.** Click the **Start Queue (Return)** button ▶ to start the encoding process for both video files. The encoding process starts for the first file. The encoding progress is displayed at the bottom of the program window. See Figure 6-31.

Figure 6-31   Video files being encoded

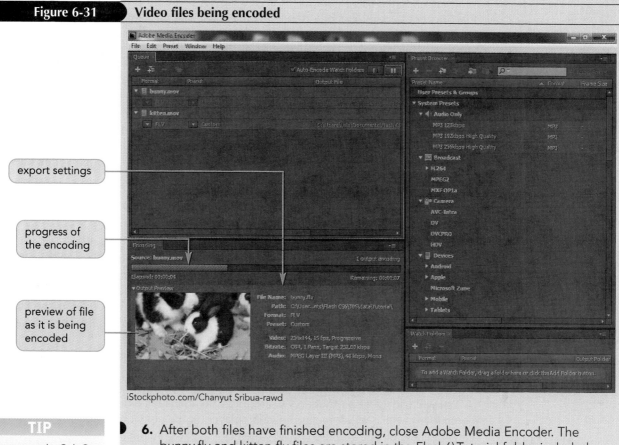

export settings

progress of the encoding

preview of file as it is being encoded

iStockphoto.com/Chanyut Sribua-rawd

TIP

You can press the Ctrl+Q keys to exit Adobe Media Encoder.

6. After both files have finished encoding, close Adobe Media Encoder. The bunny.flv and kitten.flv files are stored in the Flash6\Tutorial folder included with your Data Files, ready to be imported into your Flash document.

Each converted file is placed in the same location as the original file unless you specify a different location by clicking the file's path link in the Output File column. The encoding process can be time consuming, depending on the size of the video files and the capabilities of the computer. If you have multiple files to encode, you can encode all the files in a batch mode by adding them to the queue, setting the export settings for each file, and then starting the encode process. Adobe Media Encoder encodes each file in turn until all the files in the queue are converted.

Delivering Video

For video to be available as part of a Web site, it must be uploaded to a Web server, just like the site's Web pages and SWF files. When you import video into Flash, you need to know the type of Web server to which the video will be uploaded and how the video will be delivered to a client computer. You can deliver video using Flash in three ways: Stream the video using Adobe Flash Media Server, progressively download the video from a Web server, or embed the video in a Flash document.

Video streaming requires that the video file be uploaded to a Web server running **Adobe Flash Media Server**, the server software that provides Web developers features to add interactive audio and video to Web sites. With video streaming, only the part of the video file to be viewed, not the entire video file, is downloaded to the user's computer. This also enables the user to select any part of the video to view without having to wait for the entire video to be downloaded.

Progressive downloading downloads the entire video file, which is stored on a Web server, to the user's computer for viewing. This method is best for shorter videos that are accessed infrequently or by only a few users at the same time. With video streaming and progressive downloading, the video file is saved separately from the Flash SWF file you create to play the video. This makes it easier to change video content without having to change or republish the SWF file.

Embedded video places the entire video in the Flash document, similar to the way that bitmaps are imported and become part of the document. When you publish the Flash file, the video is published as part of the SWF file and can significantly increase the size of the published file. Embedding video is recommended only when you are targeting site visitors with slow Internet connections or visitors using older versions of Flash Player, or when the video clip is fewer than 10 seconds in length. Embedded video must be in the FLV format, not in the F4V format.

Using the Import Video Wizard

After you convert videos into the FLV or F4V format using Adobe Media Encoder, you can use the Import Video Wizard in Flash to embed or link the video in the Flash document. The Import Video Wizard presents a series of dialog boxes that guide you through the import process. You first select the video file, and then you choose if the video is to be loaded externally during playback or if it will be embedded in the Flash document. If the video is to be loaded externally during playback using video streaming or progressive downloading, Flash creates an instance of the FLVPlayback component on the Stage that serves as the video player. If you are using embedding, the video can be embedded directly on the Stage or within a movie clip symbol. By default, the Timeline expands to match the number of frames in the video.

You will use the Import Video Wizard to create an instance of the FLVPlayback component, which will serve as the video player for the pet video clips in the Katie's Pet Shop banner. You will then modify the FLVPlayback parameters and add two Button components to enable playing the two video clips in the same player, as shown in Figure 6-32. Finally, you will add the necessary ActionScript code to make the buttons operational.

Figure 6-32	Videos section

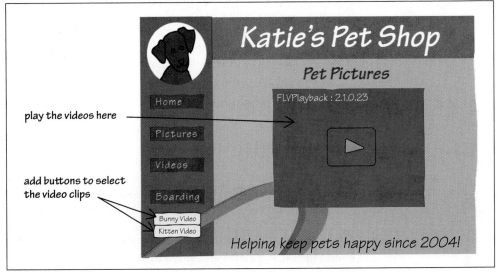

© 2013 Cengage Learning

You will start by adding the bunny.flv video to the Videos section of the banner.

To import the bunny.flv video clip using the Import Video Wizard:

1. In the Timeline, select **Frame 30** of the content layer. The Videos content starts in this frame.

2. On the menu bar, click **File**, point to **Import**, and then click **Import Video** to start the Import Video Wizard. The Select Video dialog box opens, prompting you to specify the location of the video file to be imported, which is on your computer or on a Web server. In this case, the video file is located on your computer.

Be sure to select the FLV file, which you previously encoded with the Adobe Media Encoder, and not the MOV file.

3. Click the **Browse** button, navigate to the **Flash6\Tutorial** folder included with your Data Files, and then double-click **bunny.flv**. The video file is selected.

4. Click the **Load external video with playback component** option button, if necessary, to select it. See Figure 6-33.

Figure 6-33   **Select Video dialog box in the Import Video Wizard**

FLV video file selected to import

option to load playback component

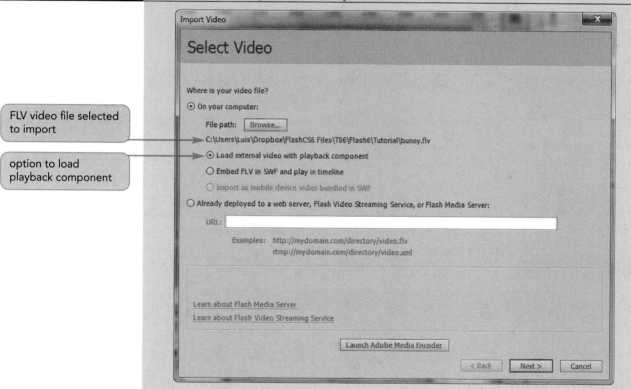

5. Click the **Next** button. The Skinning dialog box opens, so you can select the type of playback controls to add to the Flash file.

TIP

You can change the FLVPlayback component's skin at any time by changing its skin parameter in the Component Parameters section of the Property inspector.

6. Click the **Skin** button, and then click **SkinUnderPlayStopSeekMuteVol.swf**. The skin is applied to the video component in the preview area. See Figure 6-34.

Figure 6-34   **Skin applied to the video component**

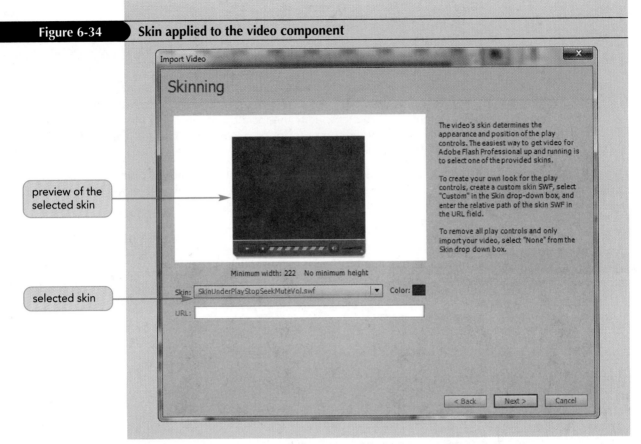

After you select a skin, the final dialog box in the wizard shows a summary of your selections and indicates what will be done when you click the Finish button. When you use progressive download or video streaming, an FLV file is created and an instance of the FLVPlayback component with the selected playback controls is added to the Stage. The FLVPlayback component provides the display area in which the video is viewed.

To complete the import process for the bunny.flv video clip:

1. Click the **Next** button. The Finish Video Import dialog box displays a summary of the import process, including the location of the bunny.flv file.

2. Click the **After importing video, view video topics in Flash Help** check box, if necessary, to remove the check mark.

3. Click the **Finish** button. A Getting metadata dialog box opens, showing the importing progress of the video. When the process is complete, an instance of the FLVPlayback component is placed on the Stage. You will resize the component instance on the Stage.

4. On the Stage, select the FLVPlayback component instance, if necessary.

5. In the Property inspector, click the **Lock width and height values together** button to select it, if necessary, and then change the width to **250**. The component instance is proportionally resized.

6. Reposition the FLVPlayback instance to **100** pixels from the top of the Stage and **170** pixels from the left of the Stage. See Figure 6-35.

| Figure 6-35 | FLVPlayback instance resized and positioned on the Stage |

iStockphoto.com/PK-Photos; istockphoto.com/Chanyut Sribua-rawd

You will save and test the FLVPlayback component instance you added to the Videos section of the banner.

To test the FLVPlayback component instance in the Videos section:

1. Save the petBanner.fla document, and then test the movie. The home section opens in Flash Player.

2. In the Flash Player window, click the **Videos** button to advance to the Videos section. The Videos section appears and the video clip starts to play.

3. After the video stops playing, on the video controls click the **Play/Pause** button to play the video again, and then click the **Play/Pause** button to pause the video. As the video plays, the small triangle under the seek bar moves to indicate the progress of the video. See Figure 6-36.

Figure 6-36   **Video playing in the Videos section of the banner**

Play/Pause button controls the playing of the video

seek bar shows the video's progress as it plays

iStockphoto.com/PK-Photos; iStockphoto.com/Chanyut Sribua-rawd

4. Close the Flash Player window to return to the Flash document.

The Videos section displays the bunny.flv video clip and includes controls to play, pause, and mute the video. To enable the FLVPlayback component to also play the kitten.flv video, you will add two buttons and ActionScript code so that when each button is clicked, a different video plays, enabling users to choose between the two videos. Because the video you added to the page uses the FLVPlayback component, you can modify the component's parameters so that the video played is determined by ActionScript.

To modify the FLVPlayback's parameters:

1. On the Stage, select the **FLVPlayback** instance, if necessary, and then, in the Component Parameters section of the Property inspector, click the **Edit** button 📝 for the skin parameter. The Select Skin dialog box opens.

2. Click the **Skin** button, and then click **None** to remove the skin from the FLVPlayback instance. See Figure 6-37.

Figure 6-37   **Select Skin dialog box selection**

None selected for the skin

Edit button for the skin parameter

iStockphoto.com/PK-Photos; iStockphoto.com/Chanyut Sribua-rawd

▶ **3.** Click the **OK** button. The dialog box closes, and the skin with the player controls is removed from the Stage.

▶ **4.** In the Component Parameters section of the Property inspector, click the **Edit** button ✎ for the source parameter. The Content Path dialog box opens, and the bunny.flv filename is selected. See Figure 6-38.

Figure 6-38   **Content Path dialog box**

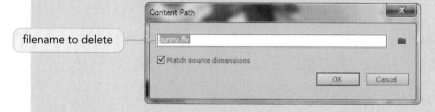

filename to delete

▶ **5.** Press the **Delete** key to delete the filename and path, and then click the **OK** button. The source file is removed.

▶ **6.** In the Property inspector, name the FLVPlayback instance **videoPlayer**. The name assigned to the FLVPlayback instance can be referenced with ActionScript.

Because you previously added an instance of the Button component to the document, the Button component is already in the document's library. You can add instances of the same Button component by dragging them from the Library panel.

To add Button instances to the Videos section:

▶ **1.** Drag an instance of the **Button** component from the Library panel to the Stage, and then position the instance below the Boarding button on the left side of the Stage.

▶ **2.** On the Stage, select the **Button** instance, if necessary, and then, in the Property inspector, name the instance **videoButton1_btn** and set its width to **80** but do not change its height.

▶ **3.** In the Component Parameters section of the Property inspector, type **Bunny Video** in the label box, and then press the **Enter** key. The videoButton1_btn instance on the Stage is relabeled as Bunny Video.

▶ **4.** Repeat Steps 1 through 3 to create a second Button instance positioned below the videoButton1_btn instance and assign the instance name **videoButton2_btn** and the label **Kitten Video**. The videoButton2_btn instance on the Stage is relabeled as Kitten Video. See Figure 6-39.

Figure 6-39   **Buttons added to the Videos section**

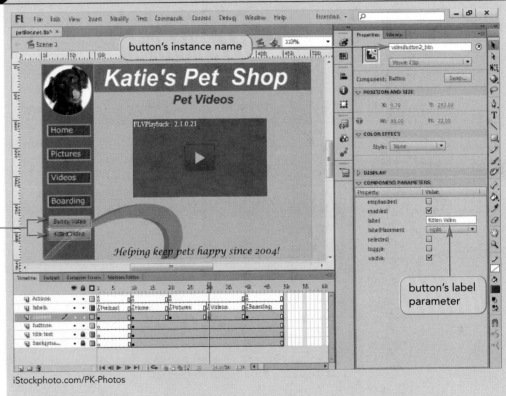

iStockphoto.com/PK-Photos

Next, you will add the ActionScript code that controls the loading of the video clips into the FLVPlayback component. The code will include two functions, one for each video. Each function will assign the name of the video clip to the source parameter of the FLVPlayback instance, and it will assign SkinUnderPlaySeekMute.swf to the skin parameter. Event listeners will be added so that when a button is clicked, the associated function will run.

You will add ActionScript code to make the video clip buttons operational.

To add ActionScript code to play the two videos in the Videos section:

1. In the Timeline, select **Frame 30** of the Actions layer, insert a keyframe, and then open the Actions panel.

2. In the Script pane, type the following lines of code to define the functions that load a video clip file and a skin into the FLVPlayback instance:

```
// Functions to add video clips and skin to FLVPlayback
component
videoButton1_btn.addEventListener(MouseEvent.CLICK, playVideo1);
function playVideo1(event:MouseEvent):void
{
    videoPlayer.source = "bunny.flv";
    videoPlayer.skin = "SkinUnderPlayStopSeekMuteVol.swf";
}
videoButton2_btn.addEventListener(MouseEvent.CLICK, playVideo2);
function playVideo2(event:MouseEvent):void
{
    videoPlayer.source = "kitten.flv";
    videoPlayer.skin = "SkinUnderPlayStopSeekMuteVol.swf";
}
```

3. In the Actions panel, click the **Check syntax** button ✔ to check for syntax errors in the code. The script is checked. If no errors are displayed in the Compiler Errors panel, the script is correct.

   Trouble? If your code contains errors, the errors will be listed in the Compiler Errors panel at the bottom of the screen. Review your script to compare it with the code you modified in the previous steps, make any necessary corrections, and then repeat Step 3 until no errors are encountered.

4. Close the Actions panel, save the document, and then test the movie.

5. In the Home section of the banner, click the **Videos** button to advance to the Videos section, and then click the **Bunny Video** button to play the first video clip. The video plays in the FLVPlayback instance, and the video controls appear under the video. See Figure 6-40.

Figure 6-40   Buttons and video player in Flash Player

video plays in the FLVPlayback instance

click a button to play a video

video controls appear under the video

iStockphoto.com/PK-Photos; iStockphoto.com/Chanyut Sribua-rawd

▶ **6.** Click the **Kitten Video** button to play the second video.

▶ **7.** Close the Flash Player window to return to the Flash document. The Videos section is complete, and the banner can showcase video clips of pets.

In this session, you learned basic concepts involved in using video and importing it into Flash. You reviewed the video formats you can use with Flash and different types of compression techniques. You encoded videos using the Adobe Media Encoder, and then you imported a video file using the Import Video Wizard in Flash. Finally, you modified the parameters of the FLVPlayback component and added ActionScript code to play two videos.

Session 6.3 Quick Check

REVIEW

1. List three video formats that can be imported into a Flash document.
2. Why is it important to compress video files?
3. _____ video places the video in the Flash document, similar to the way that bitmaps are imported and become part of the document.
4. What is a codec?
5. Which codecs are used by Flash?
6. _____ are markers you can set in the video to synchronize the video with animation, graphics, or text in the document.
7. Which option in the Import Video Wizard creates an instance of the FLVPlayback component on the Stage?

PRACTICE

Review Assignments

Data Files needed for the Review Assignments: kpsDraft.fla, Pic1.jpg, Pic2.jpg, petVideo.mov

Aly wants you to complete a new version of the banner she started for Katie's Pet Shop. You will need to add Web links to the banner's Welcome section in the form of a drop-down list. You will also add a Photos page with pet pictures and a Video section to showcase a pet video. You will add feedback to the movie's preloader and add a preloader for the pictures that load in the Photos section.

1. Open the **kpsDraft.fla** file located in the Flash6\Review folder included with your Data Files, and then save the file as **kpsBanner.fla** in the same folder.
2. In the Timeline, select Frame 1 of the content layer and add a dynamic text block on the Stage to the left of the % text. Type **preloaderValue** as the instance name for the dynamic text block, and make the text block 30 pixels wide and 26 pixels high.
3. In the Timeline, select Frame 1 of the actions layer, and in the Script pane of the Actions panel, type the following lines of code in the line before the conditional if statement:

```
var percent:int = amtLoaded*100;
preloaderValue.text = String(percent);
```

4. In the Timeline, move the playhead to Frame 10. On the Stage, select the Welcome button and then in the Property inspector, type **welcome_btn** for the instance name. Select the Photos button and type **photos_btn** for the instance name, and then select the Video button and type **video_btn** for the instance name.
5. In the Timeline, select Frame 10 of the content layer, drag an instance of the ComboBox component from the Components panel to the Stage, change the width of the instance to 150 pixels, do not change its height, position the ComboBox instance 270 pixels from the left of the Stage and 230 pixels from the top of the Stage, and then name the instance **webLinks_mc**.
6. With the ComboBox instance selected, in the Component Parameters section of the Property inspector, enter **Pet Resources** for the prompt parameter, and then enter the following label/data value pairs in the dataProvider parameter: **Best Friend Pet Adoption**, 1; **Adopt a Pet**, 2; and, **SPCA of Texas**, 3.
7. In the Timeline, select Frame 10 of the actions layer, place the insertion point after the last line of the existing code in the Actions panel, and then type the following lines of code to make the Web links operational:

```
// Function to open Web site based on selection
webLinks_mc.addEventListener(Event.CHANGE, gotoWebsite);
function gotoWebsite(event:Event):void
{
    // String variable that will hold the URL
    var weblink:String;
    // Switch statement determines which URL to assign to weblink
    switch (webLinks_mc.value)
    {
        case "1" :
            weblink = "http://www.bfpa.org";
            break;
        case "2" :
            weblink = "http://www.adoptapet.com";
            break;
        case "3" :
            weblink = "http://www.spca.org";
            break;
        }
```

```
//Open Web site using the selected URL
navigateToURL(new URLRequest(weblink), "blank");

//Reset the ComboBox instance to display the prompt, Web Links
webLinks_mc.selectedIndex = -1;
}
```

8. In the Timeline, select Frame 20 of the content layer, and then drag one instance of the UILoader component and two instances of the Button component from the Components panel to the Stage. Position the UILoader instance 230 pixels from the left of the Stage and 100 pixels from the top of the Stage. Position the first Button instance 230 pixels from the left of the Stage and 270 pixels from the top of the Stage, and then position the second Button instance 370 pixels from the left of the Stage and 270 pixels from the top of the Stage.

9. Name the first Button instance **petPic1_btn**, name the second Button instance **petPic2_btn**, name the UILoader instance **pictureLoader_mc**, and then change the dimensions of the UILoader instance to 240 pixels wide by 160 pixels high.

10. In the Component Parameters section of the Property inspector, change the label parameter of the first Button instance to **Picture 1** and change the label parameter of the second Button instance to **Picture 2**.

11. Drag an instance of the ProgressBar component from the Components panel to the Stage and place it at the center of the UILoader instance. In the Property inspector, type **progressBar_mc** for the instance name, and in the Components Parameters section of the Property inspector, type **pictureLoader_mc** for the source.

12. In the Timeline, insert a keyframe at Frame 20 of the actions layer, and then, in the Actions panel, type the following lines of code so that when a button is clicked, the corresponding pet picture will load into the UILoader instance:

```
//Hide the ProgressBar instance
progressBar_mc.visible = false;
// Function to load the first picture
petPic1_btn.addEventListener(MouseEvent.CLICK, loadPicture1);

function loadPicture1(event:MouseEvent):void
{
progressBar_mc.visible = true;
pictureLoader_mc.load(new URLRequest("Pic1.jpg"));
}
// Function to load the second picture;
petPic2_btn.addEventListener(MouseEvent.CLICK, loadPicture2);

function loadPicture2(event:MouseEvent):void
{
    progressBar_mc.visible = true;
    pictureLoader_mc.load(new URLRequest("Pic2.jpg"));
}
// When the loading is complete, hide the ProgressBar instance
pictureLoader_mc.addEventListener(Event.COMPLETE, hideBar);
function hideBar(event:Event)
{
    progressBar_mc.visible = false;
}
```

13. In the Timeline, insert a keyframe at Frame 30 of the labels layer and type **Video** for the Frame label.

14. In Adobe Media Encoder, add the **petVideo.mov** file located in the Flash6\Review folder included with your Data Files to the queue.

15. Select FLV as the format, Web - 256×144, 16×9, Project Framerate, 300kbps as the preset, and then encode the file.

16. In Flash, select Frame 30 of the content layer, and use the Import Video Wizard to import the **petVideo.flv** video file. For the delivery option, select Load external video with playback component. In the Skinning dialog box, select SkinUnderPlaySeekMute.swf for the skin.

17. On the Stage, position the FLVPlayback instance about 230 pixels from the left of the Stage and 100 pixels from the top of the Stage. In the Component Parameters section of the Property inspector, deselect the autoPlay check box.

18. Save the kpsBanner.fla file and test the banner to make sure the Web links work, the pictures load, and the video plays. (If the Web site links do not work, the URLs for the sites might have changed since the printing of this book.)

19. Submit the finished files to your instructor.

Add input and dynamic text blocks, Web links, and ActionScript code for a sports store's Web site.

APPLY

Case Problem 1

Data File needed for this Case Problem: softballDraft.fla

Jackson's Sports Store   Dan asks Chris about creating a new Flash document to use on the Jackson's Sports Web site to promote the store's softball services. You will create the advertisement based on a document Chris has developed. You will add links to the Web links section, input and dynamic text blocks to the Player Trophy Cost section, and the ActionScript code to make the Web links and the Trophy cost calculate button operational. You will also need to complete the preloader animation and code. The finished advertisement is shown in Figure 6-41.

Figure 6-41	Completed advertisement for Jackson's Sports

iStockphoto.com/Shaun Lowe

1. Open the **softballDraft.fla** file located in the Flash6\Case1 folder included with your Data Files, and then save the file as **jsSoftball.fla** in the same folder.

2. In the labels layer, insert keyframes at Frame 20 and Frame 30, and then add the label **Preload** at Frame 1, the label **Weblinks** at Frame 20, and the label **Trophies** at Frame 30.

3. On the Stage, select the Web Links button instance, and then, in the Property inspector, name the instance **weblinks_btn**, and then name the Trophies button instance as **trophies_btn**.

4. In the Timeline, select Frame 20 of the content layer, drag an instance of the ComboBox component from the Components panel to the Stage, position the ComboBox instance 200 pixels from the left of the Stage and 150 pixels from the top of the Stage, name the instance **softballLinks_mc**, and then change the width of the instance to 150 pixels. Do not change its height.

5. With the ComboBox instance selected, in the Component Parameters section of the Property inspector, enter **Softball Links** for the prompt parameter, and then enter the following label/data value pairs in the dataProvider parameter: **ASA Youth Softball**, **1**; **USA Softball**, **2**; and, **Softball Team Web Sites**, **3**.

6. In the Timeline, select Frame 20 of the actions layer, and then type the following lines of code in the Actions panel to make the Web links operational:

```
// Function to open Web site based on selection
softballLinks_mc.addEventListener(Event.CHANGE, gotoWebsite);
function gotoWebsite(event:Event):void
{
    // String variable that will hold the URL
    var weblink:String;
    // Switch statement determines which URL to assign to weblink
    switch (softballLinks_mc.value)
    {
        case "1" :
            weblink = "http://www.softball.org/youth/";
            break;
        case "2" :
            weblink = "http://www.usasoftball.com";
            break;
        case "3" :
            weblink = "http://www.eteamz.com/websites/softball/";
            break;
    }

    //Open Web site using the selected URL
    navigateToURL(new URLRequest(weblink), "blank");

    //Reset the ComboBox instance to display the prompt, Web Links
    softballLinks_mc.selectedIndex = -1;
}
```

7. Collapse the Actions panel, select Frame 30 of the content layer, and create an input text block to the right of the Add individual names (Enter Y or N) text block. Select Arial for the font family, Regular for the font style, black for the text color, 16 for the point size, and right align for the paragraph format. Make the text block 50 pixels wide and 20 pixels high, set the line type to Single line, show the border around text, set the maximum characters to 1, set the font rendering method to Use device fonts, and then name the input text block instance as **playerNames**.

8. Create an input text block to the right of the Number of players text block using the same dimensions and properties as the playerNames text block, except set the maximum characters to 0 and name the input text block instance as **numberOfPlayers**.

9. Create a dynamic text block to the right of the Total cost (w/o tax) = text block using the same dimensions and properties as the playerNames text block, except name the dynamic text block instance **total**.

10. Align the text blocks vertically by their left edges.

11. In the Timeline, select Frame 30 of the actions layer, and then, in the Actions panel, type the following code after the last line, check the code for syntax errors, and make any necessary corrections:

```
if (trophyType.text == "1") {
    price = 5.95;
}
if (trophyType.text == "2") {
    price = 8.95;
}
if (playerNames.text =="Y" || playerNames.text == "y") {
    price += .50;
}
totalCost = int(numberOfPlayers.text)*price;
total.text = String(totalCost);
}
```

12. In the Actions panel, check the code for syntax errors, and make any necessary corrections.

13. Collapse the Actions panel, select Frame 1 of the content layer, deselect all the contents on the Stage, and select the rectangle's orange fill but not its stroke. Convert the rectangle's fill to a movie clip symbol named **Rectangle** with the upper-left registration point selected. In the Property inspector, name the Rectangle instance **loadBar_mc**.

14. On the Stage, create a dynamic text block to the left of the % text block, set the font family to Arial, set the font style to regular, set the point size to 20, set the text color to black, set the paragraph format to align right, deselect the Show border around text button, make the dimensions of the text block 50 pixels wide and 20 pixels high, and then name the text block instance **percent_txt**.

15. In the Timeline, select Frame 1 of the actions layer, and then, in the Actions panel, type the following code after the last line, check the code for syntax errors, and make any necessary corrections:

```
loadBar_mc.scaleX = amtLoaded;
var percent:int = amtLoaded*100;
percent_txt.text = String(percent);

if (loadedBytes == totalBytes)
{
    gotoAndPlay("Home");
}
else
{
    gotoAndPlay("Preload");
}
```

16. Save the jsSoftball.fla document, and then test it. In Flash Player, use the Simulate Download command to test the preloader. Click the Web Links button to go to the Web Links section. In the Web Links section, click each Web link to open its linked Web site in a browser window. (If an error message appears indicating an error opening the Web pages, the URLs for these Web sites might have changed since this tutorial was published. See your instructor or technical support person for assistance.)

17. Click the Trophies button to go to the Player Trophy Cost page. In the Type of Trophy text block, type **1**. In the Add individual names (Enter Y or N) text block, type **Y**. In the Number of players text block, type **11**. Click the Calculate button to display 70.95 for the total cost.

18. Submit the finished files to your instructor.

Add photos, a video clip, and input and dynamic text blocks.

APPLY

Case Problem 2

Data Files needed for this Case Problem: aczDraft.fla, elephant.jpg, loadPics.as, rhino.jpg, zooClip1.avi

Alamo City Zoo Janet requests a new banner for the zoo's Web site that includes photos of some of the animal exhibits, a video clip to show an example of the animals, and a tour calculator so visitors can plan the cost of tours ahead of time. Alex instructs you to complete a draft banner he has created by adding zoo animal pictures to the Photos section, adding a video clip to the Video section, and completing the tour calculator on the Tour section. You will encode the video clip and then import it into the document so it loads as external FLV files and is displayed on the Video section. Then you will create the photos section and then add the text blocks to complete the calculator. Figure 6-42 shows the completed banner.

| Figure 6-42 | Completed banner for the Alamo City Zoo |

© Luis A. Lopez

1. Open the **aczDraft.fla** file located in the Flash6\Case2 folder included with your Data Files, and then save the file as **aczBanner.fla** in the same folder.

2. In the Timeline, insert a layer above the content layer and name it **labels**. In the labels layer, insert keyframes at Frame 10, Frame 20, and Frame 30, and then add the label **Home** to Frame 1, the label **Photos** to Frame 10, the label **Video** to Frame 20, and the label **Tours** to Frame 30. In the actions layer, insert blank keyframes at Frame 10 and Frame 30.

3. On the Stage, name the Home button instance **home_btn**, name the Photos button instance **photos_btn**, name the Video button instance **video_btn**, and then name the Tours button instance **tours_btn**.

4. In the document's main Timeline, select Frame 10 in the content layer, and then drag an instance of the UILoader component from the Components panel to the center of the Stage. Resize the UILoader instance to 200 pixels wide by 200 pixels high. Name the instance **picLoader_mc** and reposition the instance 110 pixels from the top of the Stage and 180 pixels from the left of the Stage.

5. Drag an instance of the Button component from the Components panel to the lower left of the UILoader instance on the Stage. Position the instance 80 pixels from the left of the Stage and 260 pixels from the top of the Stage. Drag a second instance of the Button component and place it below the first Button instance. Position the second instance 80 pixels from the left of the Stage and 285 pixels from the top of the Stage. Name the first Button instance **pic1_btn** and the second

Button instance **pic2_btn**. Change the label parameter in the Property inspector to **Photo1** for the first instance and **Photo2** for the second instance.

6. Drag an instance of the ProgressBar component from the Components panel to the Stage and place it in the center of the UILoader instance. Name the ProgressBar instance **progressBar_mc** and change its height to 10. Do not change its width. In the Component Parameters section of the Property inspector, change the source parameter to **picLoader_mc**.

🛟 EXPLORE

7. In the Library panel, open the ProgressBar component symbol in symbol-editing mode, double-click the small rectangle to the left of the Bar Skin label to edit the ProgressBar_barSkin symbol, and then increase the zoom level to 800%. Double-click the blue stroke of the rectangle to edit it, and then change its color to maroon (#660000). On the Edit bar, click ProgressBar_barSkin, double-click the fill of the rectangle, and then change the fill color to orange (#FFCC00). Exit symbol-editing mode.

🛟 EXPLORE

8. Select Frame 10 of the actions layer, open the Actions panel, click the Actions panel options menu, and click Import Script. Open the **loadPics.as** file located in the Flash6\Case2 folder included with your Data Files to add its code to the Script pane.

9. In the Script pane of the Actions panel, type the following lines of code after the last line to complete the script and make the picture buttons operational. Clicking a picture button loads the corresponding picture into the UILoader instance. The ProgressBar instance appears temporarily, indicating the picture is loading.

```
// When the loading is complete, hide the ProgressBar instance
picLoader_mc.addEventListener(Event.COMPLETE, hideBar);
function hideBar(event:Event) {
        progressBar_mc.visible = false;
}
```

10. In Adobe Media Encoder, add the **zooClip1.avi** file located in the Flash6\Case2 folder included with your Data Files to the queue.

11. Select FLV for the format and Web - 320×240, 4×3, Project Framerate, 500kbps as the preset, and then encode the file.

12. In Flash, select Frame 20 of the content layer. Use the Import Video Wizard to import the **zooClip1.flv** video file. For the delivery option, select Load external video with playback component.

🛟 EXPLORE

13. In the Skinning dialog box, select SkinUnderPlayStopSeekMuteVol.swf for the skin, and then change the skin color to tan (#FFCC66) with an alpha amount of 50%.

🛟 EXPLORE

14. After you import the video, center the FLVPlayback instance below the Animal Video text block on the Stage. In the Property inspector, in the Component Parameters section, deselect the autoPlay check box and select skinAutoHide.

15. Use the Transform panel to resize the FLVPlayback instance to 80% of its original size.

16. In Frame 30 of the content layer, create an input text block to the right of the Type of Tour text block, select Arial for the font family, Regular for the font style, black for the text color, 16 for the point size, and right align for the paragraph format. Make the text block 50 pixels wide and 22 pixels high, set the line type to Single line, show the border around text, set the maximum characters to 1, set the font rendering method to Use device fonts, and then name the input text block instance as **tourType**.

17. Create an input text block to the right of the Number of people text block using the same dimensions and properties as the tourType text block, except set the maximum characters to 0 and name the input text block instance as **numberOfPeople**.

18. Create an input text block to the right of the Include T-Shirts (Enter Y or N) text block using the same dimensions and properties as the tourType text block, and name the input text block instance as **shirts**.

19. Create a dynamic text block to the right of the Total cost (w/o tax) = text block using the same dimensions and properties as the tourType text block, except name the dynamic text block instance **total**.

20. Align the text blocks vertically by their left edges.

21. Save the aczBanner.fla document and then test it. Click the Photos button to go to the Photos section, and then click each photo button to load their respective pictures. Click the Video button to go to the Video section and play the video.

22. Click the Tours button to go to the Zoo Tours Calculator section. In the Type of Tour text block, type **2**. In the Number of people text block, type **4**. In the Include T-Shirts (Enter Y or N) text block, type **N**. Click the Calculate button to display 159.8 for the total cost.

23. Submit the finished files to your instructor.

Add pictures and buttons, and import a video to complete a nursery Web site banner.

CHALLENGE

Case Problem 3

Data Files needed for this Case Problem: glDraft.fla, flower1.jpg, flower2.jpg, flower3.jpg, loadPics.as, glLandscape.avi

G&L Nursery   Alice requests a new banner for the nursery's Web site. The banner will include a section with photos of plants that are on sale. Each photo will be displayed when its respective button is clicked. The banner will also include a landscaping section with a short video clip of a sample landscape to give potential customers an idea of the nursery's landscaping work. Amanda asks you to import the short video and to complete the new banner. Figure 6-43 shows the completed banner.

Figure 6-43	Completed banner for G&L Nursery

1. Open the **glDraft.fla** file located in the Flash6\Case3 folder included with your Data Files, and then save the file as **glBanner.fla** in the same folder.

2. In the Library, make a duplicate of the Home button and name it **Landscaping button**. Edit the Landscaping button by changing the Home text to **Landscaping** in both the Up and Over frames. Exit symbol-editing mode.

3. In the main Timeline, select Frame 10 of the buttons layer, and then drag an instance of the Landscaping button to the Stage and place it below the Photos button.

4. On the Stage, name the Home button instance **home_btn**, name the Photos button instance **photos_btn**, and then name the Landscaping button instance **landscaping_btn**.

5. In the Timeline, in the labels layer, insert keyframes at Frame 20 and Frame 30, and then add the label **Preload** to Frame 1, the label **Photos** to Frame 20, and the label **Landscaping** to Frame 30.

6. In the Timeline, select Frame 20 of the content layer, and then drag one instance of the UILoader component and one instance of the Button component from the Components panel to the Stage. Position the UILoader instance 150 pixels from the left of the Stage and 70 pixels from the top of the Stage. Position the Button instance to the right of the UILoader instance 370 pixels from the left of the Stage and 80 pixels from the top of the Stage.

7. Resize the Button instance so that its width is 50 pixels. Do not change its height. Make two copies of the Button instance on the Stage and place the copies below the first instance and align them vertically. On the Component Parameters section of the Property inspector, change the label parameter of each Button instance to **Pic 1**, **Pic 2**, and **Pic 3**, respectively.

8. Name the first Button instance **pic1_btn**, name the second Button instance **pic2_btn**, the third Button instance **pic3_btn** and then name the UILoader instance **picLoader_mc**.

9. Drag an instance of the ProgressBar component from the Components panel to the Stage and place it at the center of the UILoader instance. In the Property inspector, type **progress_mc** for the instance name and change its height to **8** pixels. Do not change its width.

EXPLORE 10. On the Stage, double-click the ProgressBar component to edit it in symbol-editing mode. Double-click the striped Indeterminate Pattern to edit it. Change the fill color of each of the blue stripes in the pattern to green (#336600). Exit symbol-editing mode. In the Component Parameters section of the Property inspector, change the source parameter to **picLoader_mc**.

EXPLORE 11. Select Frame 20 of the actions layer, insert a keyframe, open the Actions panel, click the Actions panel options menu, and click Import Script. Open the **loadPics. as** file located in the Flash6\Case3 folder included with your Data Files to add its code to the Script pane.

12. In the Script pane of the Actions panel, type the following lines of code after the last line to complete the script and make the picture buttons operational. Clicking a picture button loads the corresponding picture into the picLoader instance. The ProgressBar instance appears temporarily, indicating the picture is loading.

```
// Function to load the third picture;
pic3_btn.addEventListener(MouseEvent.CLICK, loadPicture3);

function loadPicture3(event:MouseEvent):void
{
    progress_mc.visible = true;
    picLoader_mc.load(new URLRequest("flower3.jpg"));
}
```

13. In Adobe Media Encoder, add the **glLandscape.avi** file located in the Flash6\Case3 folder included with your Data Files to the queue.

14. Select FLV for the format and Web - 320×240, 4×3, Project Framerate, 500kbps as the preset, and then encode the file to output the glLandscape.flv file.

15. Select Frame 30 of the content layer, and then use the Import Video Wizard to import the **glLandscape.flv** video file located in the Flash6/Case3 folder. For the delivery option, select Load external video with playback component.

EXPLORE 16. In the Skinning dialog box, select SkinOverPlaySeekStop.swf for the skin, and then change the skin color to blue (#0099CC) with an alpha amount of 70%.

17. After you import the video, open the Transform panel, select the Constrain button, if necessary, and change the width of the FLVPlayback component instance to 70%. Reposition the FLVPlayback instance in the center of the Stage above the FLOWERS text. In the Component Parameters section of the Property inspector, click the skinAutoHide check box to select it.

18. In the Timeline, select Frame 1 of the actions layer, open the Actions panel, and in the Script pane of the Actions panel, type the following lines of code to create the preloader animation:

```
loaderInfo.addEventListener(ProgressEvent.PROGRESS, preloader);
function preloader(event:ProgressEvent):void {
var totalBytes:Number = event.bytesTotal;
var loadedBytes:Number = event.bytesLoaded;
var amtLoaded:Number = loadedBytes/totalBytes;
loadBar_mc.scaleX = amtLoaded;
if (loadedBytes == totalBytes) {
     gotoAndPlay("Home");
   } else {
     gotoAndPlay("Preload");
   }
}
```

⊕ EXPLORE   19. Save and test the glBanner.fla file. Use the Simulate Download command with a download setting of DSL (32.6 KB/s) to test the pictures' ProgressBar. Click each picture thumbnail to display the ProgressBar. After a picture loads, the ProgressBar instance is hidden. Also, make sure the video clip plays in the Landscaping section.

20. Submit the finished files to your instructor.

Add pictures, Web links, and a calculation to a banner for a Web site.

CREATE

Case Problem 4

Data Files needed for this Case Problem: rccsDraft.fla, building1.jpg, building2.jpg

River City Conservation Society   Brittany wants a new banner developed that includes a section with links to sites related to the other preservation organizations, as well as a section that displays pictures of some of the reserved buildings. She also wants to include a section where visitors can select the type of tour and enter the number of people in the tour to calculate the cost of a tour. Anissa developed a draft banner that you will complete by adding Web links, pictures, and a tour cost calculator. Figure 6-44 shows one possible solution for the Pictures and Tour cost sections of the banner.

Figure 6-44   **Sample Pictures and Tour cost sections of the banner**

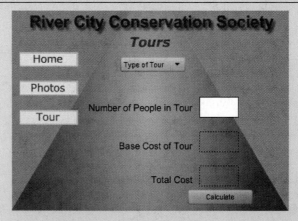

1. Open the **rccsDraft.fla** file located in the Flash6\Case4 folder included with your Data Files, and then save the file as **rccsBanner.fla** in the same folder.

2. In the Timeline, add a layer with descriptive labels in Frames 1, 10, 20, and 30 to correspond to the preloader, Home, Photos, and Tour sections of the banner.

3. In the Timeline, add a layer for the content, and add keyframes in Frames 10, 20, and 30 to correspond to the sections of the banner.

4. In Frame 1 of the content layer, add a rectangle to represent the preloader bar and add a text block describing the loading process.

5. In the Timeline, add a layer for the actions, and in Frame 1 of this layer add the ActionScript code to make the preloader animation operational.

6. In the Timeline, select Frame 10 of the actions layer and add the ActionScript code to make the navigational buttons operational.

7. In the Timeline, select Frame 10 of the content layer, and add a welcome title for the Home section. Repeat to add appropriate titles for each of the other sections in their respective frames in the content layer.

8. In the Timeline, select Frame 10 of the content layer for the home section, and then use a ComboBox component to provide a list of three URL links. (*Hint:* You can use the San Antonio Office of Historic Preservation Web site, **http://www. sanantonio.gov/historic/**, plus two other links from within the same site or other preservation-related sites.)

9. In the corresponding frame of the actions layer, add code in the Script pane to make the ComboBox instance operational so that selecting an item in the ComboBox list opens the corresponding Web link.

10. In the Timeline, select the frame in the content layer for the photos section, and then drag two instances of the Button component and one instance of the UILoader component to the Stage. Use the UILoader to display the **building1.jpg** (300×225) picture when the first Button instance is clicked and the **building2.jpg** (300×225) picture when the second Button instance is clicked. Add an instance of the ProgressBar component to the UILoader instance so that the progress bar is displayed as the pictures are being loaded.

11. In the corresponding frame of the actions layer, add code in the Script pane to make the Button instances operational so that clicking a button displays the corresponding picture in the UILoader instance. The ProgressBar component instance should not be displayed until a picture is loading and it should not be displayed after a picture has completely loaded.

12. In the Timeline, select the frame in the content layer for the tour calculator section, and then use the ComboBox component to list the type of tours (30-Minute Tour, 1-Hour Tour, Bus Tour). Create an input text block for the number of people in the group, create a dynamic text block for the base cost of the tour, and create another dynamic text block for the total cost of the tour. Add an instance of the Button component to use as a Calculate button. Name all of the instances.

13. In the corresponding frame of the actions layer, add code in the Script pane to make the ComboBox instance and Button instance operational so that when a visitor selects a type of tour, enters the number of people in the group, and clicks the Calculate button, the base cost of the tour and total cost will be displayed. Assign a base cost to each type of tour and a cost for each person in the tour. (*Hint:* You can use the formula, *group tour cost = base cost of tour × cost per person × number of people*, where the base cost of the tour is a cost assigned to each type of tour such as $20 for a 30-minute tour, $30 for a one-hour tour, and $40 for a two-hour bus tour, plus $10 cost per person.)

14. Save and test the rccsBanner.fla file. Make sure the navigational buttons are operational. Also, use the Simulate Download command to test the pictures and the ProgressBar. Make sure the Web links work and the tour calculator calculates the correct cost.

15. Submit the finished files to your instructor.

ENDING DATA FILES

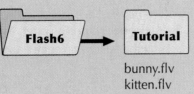

Flash6 → **Tutorial**

bunny.flv
kitten.flv
petBanner.fla
petBanner.swf
picture1.jpg
picture2.jpg
picture3.jpg
SkinUnderPlayStop
  SeekMuteVol.swf

Review

kpsBanner.fla
kpsBanner.swf
petVideo.flv
Pic1.jpg
Pic2.jpg
SkinUnderPlay
  SeekMute.swf

Case1

jsSoftball.fla
jsSoftball.swf

Case2

aczBanner.fla
aczBanner.swf
elephant.jpg
rhino.jpg
SkinUnderPlayStop
  SeekMuteVol.swf
zooClip1.flv

Case3

flower1.jpg
flower2.jpg
flower3.jpg
glBanner.fla
glBanner.swf
glLandscape.flv
SkinOverPlay
  SeekStop.swf

Case4

building1.jpg
building2.jpg
rccsBanner.fla
rccsBanner.swf

FLASH

OBJECTIVES

- Insert layers and enter frame labels
- Create and edit button symbols
- Add and edit code snippets
- Use ActionScript to insert actions, functions, and event listeners
- Create static, dynamic, and input text blocks
- Use Adobe Media Encoder to add video
- Add the UILoader, ProgressBar, and Button components

Creating an Interactive Banner for a Web Site

Case | *Metro Children's Museum*

The Metro Children's Museum is a nonprofit organization dedicated to providing information and exhibits of special interest to children. The museum has been in operation for more than 15 years and is accredited by the American Museum Association. The museum is open year-round and has recently redesigned its Web site. Cecilia Fuentes, museum director, wants to add a new banner to the Web site to promote an upcoming space shuttle exhibit at the museum. The banner will display a video and several pictures related to the space shuttle program. It will also allow visitors to determine the cost of group tickets based on the size of the group.

1. Open the **museumDraft.fla** file located in the AddCases\Case1 folder included with your Data Files, and then save the file as **mcmBanner.fla** in the same folder.
2. In the Timeline, insert a new layer above the content layer and name it **labels**. In the labels layer, add the frame label **preload** at Frame 1, add the frame label **welcome** at Frame 10, add the frame label **photos** at Frame 20, and add the frame label **tickets** at Frame 30.
3. In the library, make two duplicates of the Welcome button and name one duplicate **Photos** and name the other duplicate **Tickets**. Edit the Photos button and change the Welcome text to **Photos**. Edit the Tickets button and change the Welcome text to **Tickets**.
4. In the Timeline, select Frame 10 of the buttons layer. Drag an instance of the Photos button to the Stage and place it below the Welcome button instance. Drag an instance of the Tickets

STARTING DATA FILES

museumDraft.fla
preloaderCode.as
shuttle1.jpg
shuttle2.jpg
shuttle3.jpg
shuttle4.jpg
shuttlemedia.mp4

button to the Stage and place it below the Photos button instance. Align the button instances by their left edges and space them evenly.

5. Assign the instance name **welcome_btn** to the Welcome button instance, assign the instance name **photos_btn** to the Photos button instance, and then assign the instance name **tickets_btn** to the Tickets button instance.

6. On the Stage, select the Welcome button instance. From the Code Snippets panel, insert the Click to Go to Frame and Stop code snippet. In the Actions panel, delete the multiline comment and then type the following code starting at Line 1:

```
stop();

// Event listeners and functions for navigational buttons
```

7. In the Actions panel, change the number 5 in the `gotoAndStop(5);` function to **"welcome"**.

8. On the Stage, select the Photos button instance. From the Code Snippets panel, insert the Click to Go to Frame and Stop code snippet. In the Actions panel, delete the multiline comment. In the Actions panel, change the number 5 in the `gotoAndStop(5);` function to **"photos"**.

9. Repeat Step 8 for the Tickets button instance, changing the number 5 in the `gotoAndStop(5);` function to **"tickets"**.

10. In the Timeline, select Frame 1 of the content layer. On the Stage, above the Loading text block, draw a rectangle with a blue (#0000FF) fill and no stroke that is 300 pixels wide and 10 pixels high.

11. Convert the rectangle to a movie clip symbol named **preloader bar** with the upper-left registration point selected. In the Property inspector, type **loadBar_mc** for the instance name.

12. On the Stage, to the left of the % text block, create a dynamic text block, set the font family to Arial, set the font style to Regular, set the point size to 18, set the font rendering method to Use device fonts, set the text color to black, set the paragraph format to Align right, and then deselect the Show border around text button, if necessary.

13. In the Property inspector, set the text block's dimensions to 40 pixels wide and 26 pixels high, and then enter **percent_txt** as the instance name of the text block instance.

14. In the Timeline, select Frame 1 of the Actions layer. Open the Actions panel, click the Actions panel options menu, and click Import Script. Open the **preloaderCode.as** file located in the AddCases\Case1 folder included with your Data Files to add its code to the Script pane.

15. In Adobe Media Encoder, add the **shuttlemedia.mp4** file located in the AddCases\Case1 folder included with your Data Files to the queue. Select FLV for the format and Web - 256×144, 16×9, Project Framerate, 300kbps as the preset and then encode the file to output the shuttlemedia.flv file.

16. In Flash, select Frame 10 of the content layer, and then use the Import Video Wizard to import the **shuttlemedia.flv** video file located in the AddCases\Case1 folder. For the delivery option, select Load external video with playback component.

17. In the Skinning dialog box, select SkinUnderPlayMute.swf for the skin. After the video is imported, position the FLVPlayback component 120 pixels from the left of the Stage instance and 90 pixels from the top of the Stage. In the Component Parameters section of the Property inspector, click the skinAutoHide check box to select it, and then click the autoPlay check box to deselect it.

18. On the Stage, above the video, create a static text block, set the font family to Arial, set the font style to Bold, set the point size to 20, set the font rendering method to Anti-alias for readability, set the text color to black, and set the paragraph format to Align center. Type **Space Shuttle Exhibit** in the text block.

19. In the Timeline, select Frame 20 of the content layer, and then add an instance of the UILoader component to the Stage. Resize the UILoader instance so that it is 240 pixels wide and 180 pixels high, and then position the UILoader instance

140 pixels from the left of the Stage and 70 pixels from the top of the Stage. Assign the instance name **photoLoader_mc** to the UILoader instance.

20. Add an instance of the Button component to the Stage and center it immediately below the UILoader instance. Assign the instance name **next_btn** to the Button instance, and in the Component Parameters section of the Property inspector, type **Next Photo** for the label property.

21. Drag an instance of the progressBar component from the Components panel to the Stage and place it at the center of the UILoader instance. In the Property inspector, type **progress_mc** for the instance name.

22. Insert a keyframe at Frame 20 of the Actions layer. In the Actions panel, type the following code:

```
// Code to load photos; set initial value of num to 1

var num:Number = 1;

// Hide the ProgressBar instance

progress_mc.visible = false;


// Load photos function

function loadPics(eventObj:MouseEvent):void

{

   progress_mc.visible = true;


// Create the photo filename using the value in num

   var pic:String = "shuttle"+num+".jpg";

   // Load the photo into the Loader instance

   var picURLReq:URLRequest = new URLRequest(pic);

   photoLoader_mc.load(picURLReq);

   // Increment the value in num

   num += 1;

   // If num is greater than 4, set it back to 1

   if (num > 4){

      num = 1;

   }

}


// When the loading is complete, hide the ProgressBar instance

function hideBar(eventObj:Event) {

   progress_mc.visible = false;

}


next_btn.addEventListener(MouseEvent.CLICK, loadPics);

photoLoader_mc.addEventListener(Event.COMPLETE, hideBar);
```

23. In the Timeline, select Frame 30 of the content layer. On the Stage, centered toward the top, create a static text block, set the font family to Arial, set the font style to Bold, set the point size to 20, set the font rendering method to Anti-alias for readability, set the text color to black, and set the paragraph format to Align center. Type Museum Group Tickets in the text block.

24. Create three more static text blocks using the font family and point size of your choice. Type **Group size** for the first text block. For the second text block, type **Include lunch($5)?**, press the Enter key, and then type **y=yes, n=no**. Select the y=yes, n=no text and reduce its font size. For the third text block, type **Total**. Align the text blocks vertically by their right edges and space them evenly.

25. Create an input text block to the right of the Group size text block. Make the text block 50 pixels wide and 25 pixels high. In the Property inspector, select the Show border around text option, select black (#000000) for the text color, select Use device fonts for the font rendering method, and select Align right for the paragraph format. Name the text block instance **groupSize_txt**.

26. Create an input text block to the right of the Include lunch($5)? text block with the same properties as the groupSize_txt block. In the Property inspector, name the text block instance **lunch_txt**.

27. Create a dynamic text block to the right of the Total text block. Make the text block 50 pixels wide and 25 pixels high. In the Property inspector, deselect the Show border around text option, select black (#000000) for the text color, select Use device fonts for the font rendering method, and select Align right for the paragraph format. Name the text block instance **ticketTotal_txt**.

28. Add an instance of a Button component to the bottom of the Stage, assign the name **calc_btn** to the instance, and change its width to 100 pixels. In the Component Parameters section of the Property inspector, type **Calculate Cost** for the label parameter.

29. In the Timeline, insert a keyframe in Frame 30 of the Actions layer. In the Script pane of the Actions panel, type the following code:

```
// Function to determine the ticket cost

function calculateCost(evt:MouseEvent):void

{

  var costPerGuest:Number;

  var size:Number = int(groupSize_txt.text);

  if(size > 20)

  {

    costPerGuest = 6;

  } else

  if(size > 10)

  {

    costPerGuest = 8;

  } else

  if(size > 0)

  {

    costPerGuest = 10;

  }
```

```
// Check if lunch will be included

if (lunch_txt.text =="Y" || lunch_txt.text == "y") {

    costPerGuest += 5;

}


// Determine the total cost

var totalCost:Number = costPerGuest * size;

// Display the results

ticketTotal_txt.text = String(totalCost);

}


//Event listener

calc_btn.addEventListener(MouseEvent.CLICK, calculateCost);
```

30. Save the banner, and then test it in Flash Player.
31. Submit the finished files to your instructor.

ENDING DATA FILES

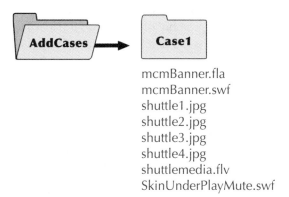

mcmBanner.fla
mcmBanner.swf
shuttle1.jpg
shuttle2.jpg
shuttle3.jpg
shuttle4.jpg
shuttlemedia.flv
SkinUnderPlayMute.swf

OBJECTIVES

- Insert layers and enter frame labels
- Duplicate and edit button symbols
- Add and edit code snippets
- Use ActionScript to insert actions, functions, and event listeners
- Create movie clip symbols
- Create a custom gradient
- Create a text animation
- Create a mask effect
- Add the UILoader, ProgressBar, and Button components
- Use Adobe Media Encoder to add video
- Create input and dynamic text blocks
- Add the ComboBox component

Creating an Interactive Banner for a Car Seller's Web Site

Case | *Discount Autos*

Discount Autos of San Antonio has been providing quality used vehicles to local residents for more than 15 years. Located on the corner of Highway 151 and Alamo Parkway, Discount Autos' sales have been steadily increasing. To continue this trend in sales, owner Allen Bidwell has developed a new marketing campaign. As part of this new campaign, Allen wants to improve the company's Web site by adding a new banner as well as a tool that potential customers can use to calculate their monthly loan payments based on a loan amount, the number of months for the loan, and the interest rate. He also wants the banner to include an area to showcase auto specials, using pictures of vehicles and a section to display a video of vehicles for sale.

1. Open the **autoDraft.fla** file located in the AddCases\Case2 folder included with your Data Files, and save the file as **autoBanner.fla** in the same folder.
2. In the Timeline, add a new layer above the content layer and name it **labels**. In the labels layer, add the frame label **Welcome** at Frame 1, the frame label **Photos** at Frame 10, the frame label **Video** at Frame 20, and the frame label **Calculator** at Frame 30.
3. Create three duplicates of the Start button symbol and name them **Photos**, **Videos**, and **Calculator**, respectively. Change the text in the text layer of the Photos button to **Photos**. Change the text in the text layer of the Video button to **Video**. Change the text in the text layer of the Calculator button to **Calc**.

STARTING DATA FILES

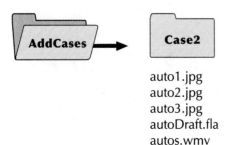

auto1.jpg
auto2.jpg
auto3.jpg
autoDraft.fla
autos.wmv

4. In the document's main Timeline, select the buttons layer. On the Stage, place an instance of the Photos button to the right of the Start button, place an instance of the Video button to the right of the Photos button, and place an instance of the Calculator button to the right of the Video button. Name the Start button instance **start_btn**, name the Photos button instance **photos_btn**, name the Video button instance **video_btn**, and name the Calculator button instance **calc_btn**. Horizontally align and evenly space the four button instances on the Stage.

5. On the Stage, select the Start button instance, and then from the Code Snippets panel, insert the Click to Go to Frame and Stop code snippet. In the Actions panel, delete the multiline comment and then type the following code starting at Line 1:

```
stop();

// Event listeners and functions for navigational buttons
```

6. In the Actions panel, change the number 5 in the `gotoAndStop(5);` function to **"Welcome"**.

7. On the Stage, select the Photos button instance. From the Code Snippets panel, insert the Click to Go to Frame and Stop code snippet. In the Actions panel, delete the multiline comment, and then change the number 5 in the `gotoAndStop(5);` function to **"Photos"**.

8. Repeat Step 7 for the Video button instance, changing the number 5 in the `gotoAndStop(5);` function to **"Video"**.

9. Repeat Step 7 for the Calculator button instance, changing the number 5 in the `gotoAndStop(5);` function to **"Calculator"**.

10. Test the movie in Flash Player, clicking each button to make sure it displays its associated section.

11. Create a new movie clip symbol named **autoBanner**. Rename Layer 1 as **background**, and add a regular frame at Frame 60 to extend the layer.

12. Use the Color panel to create a linear gradient. Set the color of the left gradient pointer to light maroon (#663333) and the right gradient pointer to white. Create a rectangle 450 pixels wide and 60 pixels high using the new gradient as its fill and no stroke. The rectangle will serve as a background for the banner. If necessary, reposition the rectangle so it is centered on the editing window.

13. Create a new layer named **title** for the title text block. Select a font family such as Impact, a text color such as maroon (#660000), and a large point size, and then type **DI$COUNT AUTO$** in the text block. Increase the letter spacing slightly for the text, and then center the text within the background rectangle. The text should extend the width of the rectangle.

14. Create a text animation with the dollar sign so that it alternately increases and then decreases in size for a pulsating effect. Start by breaking the title text block into its individual letters and then converting the left $ character into a graphic symbol named **dollar sign**.

15. Edit the dollar sign graphic symbol in symbol-editing mode and create a motion tween. Extend the tween through Frame 60. In Frame 10, use the Transform panel to increase the size of the dollar sign to 110% of its original size, being sure to constrain its width and height. In Frame 20, decrease the size of the dollar sign to 100%. In Frame 30, increase its size to 110%. In Frame 40, decrease its size to 100%. In Frame 50, increase its size to 110%. In Frame 60, decrease its size to 100% so that the dollar sign exhibits a pulsating effect throughout the motion tween.

16. Edit the autoBanner symbol, select the title layer, delete both $ text blocks, and then create a new layer and name it **dollar signs**. In the dollar signs layer, insert an instance of the dollar sign graphic symbol between the letters I and C on the banner, being sure to align the $ with the rest of the letters.

17. In the dollar signs layer, insert another instance of the dollar sign graphic after the letter O in AUTO, being sure to align the $ with the rest of the letters in AUTO. In the Looping section of the Property inspector, change the first frame of the instance to 10.

18. Add a mask effect to the banner using a gradient that moves horizontally across the text. First select all the letters in the title layer (the $ symbols should not be selected) at the same time, and then convert the letters to fills. Copy all the letters at the same time and paste the copies in a new layer above the title layer in the same relative position as the original letters and name the new layer **title2**.

19. Insert a new layer between the title and the title2 layers and name the layer **gradient**. In this layer, draw a rectangle that is 450 pixels wide and 60 pixels high. The rectangle should have a linear gradient as its fill and no stroke. The linear gradient should be black on the ends and have a narrow white strip in the middle.

20. Convert the rectangle into a movie clip symbol, and then move the rectangle to the left of the letter D. Create a motion tween in Frame 1 of the gradient layer, and in Frame 30, move the rectangle to the right of the $ in AUTO. In Frame 60, move the rectangle back to the left of the letter D. The rectangle should move from the left side of the title text horizontally across to the right side of the title text for 30 frames and then back to the left side of the title text for the next 30 frames.

21. Convert the title2 layer into a mask layer. The gradient layer with the rectangle should be masked. Press the Enter key to test the banner animation. The animation creates a highlight effect on the title text in which the highlight moves across the text and back.

22. Return to the document's main Timeline, and in Frame 1 of the heading layer, delete the title text block. Add an instance of the autoBanner to the top of the Stage and align the instance with the left and top sides of the Stage.

23. In the Timeline, select Frame 10 of the content layer and add an instance of the UILoader component to the center of the Stage. Name the instance **photos_mc** and set its width at 251 pixels and its height at 167 pixels. This is where the auto photos will be loaded.

24. Add a Button component instance to the left of the UILoader instance and aligned with its lower edge. Name the button instance **next_btn** and change its label parameter to **Next Picture**.

25. Insert a keyframe at Frame 10 of the Actions layer. In the Script pane of the Actions panel, add the following code. When the Next button is clicked, a photo will be loaded into the UILoader instance. The photo filenames used are auto1.jpg, auto2.jpg, and auto3.jpg. The code uses the variable num for the value (1, 2, 3) in the filename.

```
// Code to load photos; set initial value of num to 1

var num:Number = 1;

// Load photos function

next_btn.addEventListener(MouseEvent.CLICK, loadPics);

function loadPics(event:MouseEvent):void

{

    // Create the photo filename using the value in num

    var pic:String = "auto"+num+".jpg";

    // Load the photo into the Loader instance

    photos_mc.load(new URLRequest(pic));

    // Increment the value in num

    num += 1;

    // If num is greater than 3, set it back to 1
```

```
    if (num > 3)
    {
        num = 1;
    }
}
```

26. Test the movie. In the Photos page, click the Next Picture button three times to display each of the three auto pictures.

27. In Adobe Media Encoder, add the **autos.wmv** file located in the AddCases\Case2 folder included with your Data Files to the queue. Select FLV for the format and the Web - 256×144, 16×9, Project Framerate, 300kbps as the preset, and then encode the file.

28. In Flash, in the Timeline, select Frame 20 of the content layer, and use the Import Video Wizard to import the **autos.flv** video file. For the delivery option, select Load external video with playback component. In the Skinning dialog box, select SkinUnderPlaySeekMute.swf for the skin, and change the skin color to maroon (#660000).

29. On the Stage, center the FLVPlayback instance on the Stage below the Car Lot Video text block and reduce the size of the instance to 240 pixels wide and 135 pixels high. In the Component Parameters section of the Property inspector, deselect the autoPlay value, and select the skinAutoHide check box.

30. Test the movie. Click the Video button to display the autos.flv video. Click the video's Play button to play the video.

31. In the Timeline, select Frame 30 of the content layer. Create four text blocks using the font family of your choice and a small point size. Type **Loan Amount** for the first text block, **Length of Loan** for the second text block, **Interest Rate** for the third text block, and **Monthly Payment** for the fourth text block. Align the text blocks vertically by their right edges and space them evenly.

32. Create an input text block to the right of the Loan Amount text to be used to enter the amount of the loan. Create another input text block to the right of the Interest Rate text block to be used to enter a rate. Make each input text block 60 pixels wide and 20 pixels high. In the Property inspector, for each text block, select the Show border around text option, select black (#000000) for the text color, select Use device fonts for the font rendering method, and select Align right for the paragraph format. Name the first input text block instance **loanAmount_txt** and name the second input text block instance **interestRate_txt**.

33. Add an instance of the ComboBox component to the right of the Length of Loan text block to be used to select the number of months for the loan. Name the ComboBox instance **lengthOfLoan_mc** and make the instance 100 pixels wide. In the Component Parameters section of the Property inspector, enter **No. of Months** for the prompt parameter. Add the following labels and data value pairs for the dataProvider parameter: label:**36 mo.**, data:**1**, label:**48 mo.**, data:**2**, label:**60 mo.**, and data:**3**.

34. Create a dynamic text block to the right of the Monthly Payment text block. Make the text block 60 pixels wide and 20 pixels high. In the Property inspector, deselect the Show border around text option, select white (#FFFFFF) for the text color, select Use device fonts for the font rendering method, and select Align right for the paragraph format. Name the text block instance **monthlyPayment_txt**.

35. Add an instance of a Button component to the right of the dynamic text block and assign the name **payment_btn** to the instance and change its width to 110 pixels. In the Component Parameters section of the Property inspector, type **Calculate Payment** for the label parameter.

36. In the Timeline, insert a keyframe in Frame 30 of the Actions layer. In the Script pane of the Actions panel, type the following ActionScript code to calculate the monthly payment and place the result in the Monthly Payment dynamic text block:

```
// Function to calculate the monthly payment
payment_btn.addEventListener(MouseEvent.CLICK, calculatePayment);
function calculatePayment(event:MouseEvent):void
{
  var numberOfMonths:Number;
  switch (lengthOfLoan_mc.value)
  {
    case "1" :
      numberOfMonths = 36;
      break;
    case "2" :
      numberOfMonths = 48;
      break;
    case "3" :
      numberOfMonths = 60;
      break;
  }


  // Convert input values into Integer numbers
  var Loan:Number = int(loanAmount_txt.text);
  var Rate:Number = int(interestRate_txt.text);
  // Determine the monthly interest rate
  var monthlyRate:Number = (Rate/12)/100;
  // Calculate part of the formula using the Math power function
  var factor:Number = 1 - Math.pow(1 + monthlyRate,
-  numberOfMonths);
  // Calculate the payment; round to the nearest dollar
  var payment:Number = Math.round((monthlyRate/factor)*Loan);
  // Display the resulting monthly payment
  monthlyPayment_txt.text = String(payment);
  //Set ComboBox to display the initial prompt, No. of Months
  lengthOfLoan_mc.selectedIndex = -1;


}
```

37. Save the document, and then test the monthly payment calculator in Flash Player. Enter **20000** for the loan amount, select 48 mo. for the No. of Months, and enter **5** for the interest rate. Click the Calculate Payment button. The Monthly Payment amount is 461.

38. Submit the finished files to your instructor.

ENDING DATA FILES

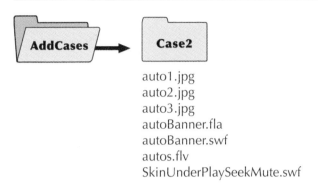

auto1.jpg
auto2.jpg
auto3.jpg
autoBanner.fla
autoBanner.swf
autos.flv
SkinUnderPlaySeekMute.swf

GLOSSARY/INDEX

C

call To execute a function from within a script in which it is defined. FL 271

Check Spelling command, FL 95–98

Check Spelling dialog box, FL 97–98

child movie clip A nested movie clip instance. FL 221

class A blueprint for an object that describes the properties, methods, and events for the object; all objects in ActionScript are defined by classes. FL 268

Classic Text engine The text engine that can create static, dynamic, or input text blocks. FL 92

closing a document, FL 53

code

    entering accurately, FL 340
    syntax, FL 272
    testing, FL 340

codec A video coder/decoder program. FL 353

Code Snippets panel, FL 274–276

color

    strokes and fills, FL 34–36
    Web-safe, FL 34–35

ComboBox component, FL 336–342

comment A note in ActionScript code that explains what is happening but does not cause any action to be performed and is not required for the actions to work. FL 267, FL 281–282

comparison operator An operator used in conditional statements; for example, ==, , , and !=, which are used to test for equality, greater than, less than, and not equal to, respectively. FL 319

component A prebuilt movie clip installed with Flash that includes a set of user interface and video components with parameters that can be changed in the Components panel. FL 334, FL 336–349

    adding, FL 336
    ComboBox, FL 336–342
    displaying pictures using UILoader component, FL 342–345
    downloading, FL 336
    ProgressBar, FL 346–349

compression The process of taking away some of a file's data to reduce its size. FL 85

compressor An encoder program that uses compression. FL 353

conditional statement A statement in which one value is compared to another. FL 319

Connect Path dialog box, FL 363

Convert to Symbol dialog box, FL 99, FL 198

copying

    custom buttons, FL 261–262
    frames, FL 129–130
    layers, FL 129–130

cue point A marker set in a video to synchronize the video with animation, graphics, or text in a Flash document. FL 350

custom button

    copying and editing, FL 261–263
    creating, FL 256–261

D

decompressor A decoder program that uses decompression. FL 353

Deco tool, FL 14

displaying

    pictures, using UILoader component, FL 342–345
    rulers and guides, FL 28–30

Distort modifier, Free Transform tool, FL 79

dock A collection of individual panels or panel groups. FL 3

document A Web medium created in Flash; can include text, static images, sound, video, and animation.

    adding sounds, FL 291–299
    changing settings, FL 30–31
    closing, FL 53
    previewing, FL 8–11

document-level undo The undo mode in which the steps being reversed affect the entire document. FL 49

Document Settings dialog box, FL 30–31

Document window The main work area that consists of the pasteboard and the Stage. FL 2

dot notation A dot (.) is used to link an object name to its properties and methods. FL 266, FL 269, FL 271

Down frame The frame in a button symbol that shows what the button looks like as the user clicks it. FL 248

downloading Flash components, FL 336

drawing

    lines and shapes, FL 62–75
    objects, FL 32

dynamic text Text in the form of characters or numbers received from a Web server or from an expression in ActionScript that can be displayed on a Web page in Flash Player. FL 321–323

dynamic text field A field that contains text that can be updated as a result of actions within the SWF file or with information from a Web server when the document is published and displayed in a Web browser. FL 92

E

easing The control for how fast or slow an object moves throughout an animation, which can create a more natural appearance of movement. FL 137

Editable text block A text block whose text can be selected and changed by the user. FL 92

Edit bar A toolbar that displays the current scene number, the Edit Scene button, the Edit Symbols button, and the Zoom control. FL 2

editing

    bitmap graphics, FL 83
    custom buttons, FL 262–263
    instances of symbols, FL 103–104
    symbols, FL 101–102

else keyword, FL 319

embedded video An encoding method that places an entire video in a Flash document, similar to the way that bitmaps are imported and become part of the document. FL 358

Envelope modifier, Free Transform tool, FL 79

equal sign (=), comparison operator, FL 319

Eraser tool, FL 14

event Something that happens when a movie is playing, such as when the user clicks a button or presses a key. FL 277

motion preset A prebuilt motion tween anima-tion that is applied to an object selected on the Stage. FL 136, FL 145–150

applying, FL 146–150
default, FL 146

motion tween An animation applied to instances of symbols or text blocks where an object changes position, size, or color; rotates; or fades in or out. FL 137, FL 138–145, FL 184–190

changing properties in Motion Editor, FL 184–190
creating, FL 138–141
modifying, FL 141–145
modifying path, FL 142

movie clip A symbol that contains its own Timeline and operates independently of the Timeline of the movie in which it appears. FL 91

child, FL 221
nested movie clip symbols, FL 222–223
parent, FL 221

Movie Explorer A panel that displays a hierar-chical view of all the elements in a document, making it simpler to manage and locate individ-ual elements. FL 221, FL 232–236

MP3 format, FL 291

N

naming

conventions, ActionScript, FL 273
scenes, FL 131

nested symbol A symbol that contains instances of other symbols within its Timeline. FL 221, FL 222–223

numeric data A number or numbers in an expression that are not enclosed in quotation marks. FL 329

numeric data, converting values to, FL 330

O

object An element in Flash that has properties, or characteristics, that can be examined or changed with ActionScript, such as a button. FL 31–36, FL 266

ActionScript, FL 268–271
aligning on Stage, FL 263–264
color controls, FL 34–36
controlling speed in animations, FL 143
drawing, FL 32

fills, FL 31, FL 34–36
grouping, FL 32–34
selecting. See selecting objects
strokes, FL 31, FL 34–36
target, FL 182
transforming precisely, FL 82

object-based animation An animation that can be modified as one entity just like any other object; called a motion tween in Flash. FL 138

Object Drawing mode The drawing mode in which drawn shapes are treated as separate objects and do not merge with or alter other objects in the same layer. FL 32

object-level undo The undo mode in which steps performed on individual objects are reversed without affecting the steps performed on other objects. FL 49

object-oriented programming (OOP), FL 268

onion skinning The display of more than one frame at a time on the Stage; the content of the current frame, indicated by the position of the playhead, appears in full color and the contents of the frames before and after the current frame appear dimmed. FL 220, FL 223–229

locking layers, FL 223

OOP (object-oriented programming), FL 268

operator, input forms, FL 329–333

Oval Primitive tool The tool used to create ovals that are treated as separate objects whose characteristics can be modified using the Property inspector without having to redraw the shape from scratch. FL 61

Oval tool The tool used to draw ovals of differ-ent sizes and colors. FL 61, FL 63–64, FL 69–70, FL 71–72

Over frame The frame in a button symbol that contains the content displayed when the pointer is over the button. FL 248

P

page tab A tab that identifies the open docu-ment and is used to navigate among open docu-ments. FL 2

Paint Bucket tool The tool used to fill to an enclosed area of a drawing with color or change the color of an existing fill. FL 14, FL 61, FL 76–77

panel An area that contains controls for viewing and changing the properties of objects. FL 3, FL 17–20

organizing, FL 18

panel group Two or more panels displayed together. FL 3

organizing, FL 18

parameter An additional setting added to an action or a value sent to a function; also called an argument or a property. FL 267

parent movie clip The movie clip in which a child movie clip is nested. FL 221

pasteboard The gray area surrounding the Stage that holds objects that are not part of the viewable Stage and that move onto or off the Stage as part of the animation. FL 2, FL 11–12

Pencil tool The tool used to draw free-form lines and shapes, like using an actual pencil to draw on paper. FL 14, FL 73–75

Pen tool The tool used to draw free-form lines or curves. FL 14, FL 61

pixel The smallest picture element on a monitor screen that can be controlled by a computer; short for picture element. FL 4

measuring using, FL 28

playhead A marker that indicates which frame is currently selected in the Timeline. FL 2

PNG (Portable Network Graphics) format, FL 4

exporting graphics, FL 46

pose layer The layer in which a symbol instance or shape and its armature are moved when bones are added to that symbol instance or shape. FL 220

precision, transforming objects, FL 82

preloader A short animation or a message such as the word "Loading" located in the first few frames of a Flash file to indicate that the Web site is loading while the frames of the SWF file continue to download. FL 312, FL 314–323

code, FL 319–321
creating, FL 315–317
creating animation, FL 317–319
dynamic text, FL 321–323

previewing documents, FL 8–11

ProgressBar component, FL 346–349

TASK REFERENCE

TASK	PAGE #	RECOMMENDED METHOD
Actions, check for syntax errors	FL 320	In Actions panel, click ✔, check errors in Compiler Errors panel
ActionScript code, add using Code Snippets panel	FL 274	In docked panel group, click ⊞, expand folder, click snippet, click { }, click Insert
Adobe Media Encoder, start program	FL 354	Click Start button, click All Programs, click Adobe folder, click Adobe Media Encoder CS6
Animation, test	FL 151	*See* Reference box: Testing a Document's Animation
Bitmap, change properties	FL 86	In Library panel, select bitmap, click 🅸
Bitmap, import to library or Stage	FL 83	*See* Reference box: Importing a Bitmap
Bone, add to an instance or shape	FL 229	In Tools panel, click 🦴, click and drag to connect instance or object on Stage
Button, add from Buttons library	FL 251	Click Window, point to Common Libraries, click Buttons, expand button category, drag button from Buttons Library panel to Stage or library
Button, create	FL 256	*See* Reference box: Creating a Custom Button
Button, test within program window	FL 252	Click Control, click Enable Simple Buttons, click button on Stage
Code, check for syntax errors	FL 280	In Actions panel, click ✔, click OK, check errors in Compiler Errors panel
Code snippet, add using Code Snippets panel	FL 274	In docked panel group, click ⊞, expand folder, click snippet, click { }, click Insert
Code snippet, edit	FL 278	Open Actions panel, edit code as needed in Script pane
Color, select	FL 35	Click 🖊 ▮ or 🪣 ▮ in Property inspector, or click 🖊 or 🪣 in Tools panel, click color swatch in colors palette
Comment, add multiple lines to ActionScript code	FL 281	In Actions panel, type /* followed by comment text and then type */
Comment, add single line to ActionScript code	FL 281	In Actions panel, type // followed by comment text
Component, create instance	FL 336	*See* Reference box: Adding a Flash Component
Component, set parameters	FL 338	Select component on Stage, in Component Parameters section of Property inspector, set parameter values
Document, close	FL 53	Click File, click Close; or click ✖ in page tab
Document settings, modify	FL 30	Click Modify, click Document
Dynamic text box, create	FL 328	In Tools panel, click **T**; in Property inspector, click Text type button, click Dynamic Text, create text block on Stage, set properties
Fill, apply with Paint Bucket tool	FL 76	Click 🪣 in Tools panel, select fill properties, click modifier, click object on Stage
Filter, apply to object	FL 105	In Filters section of Property inspector, click 🔲, click filter, set properties

TASK	PAGE #	RECOMMENDED METHOD
Filter, copy and paste	FL 106	In Filters section of Property inspector, click ▣, click Copy All, select object to apply filter to, click ▣, click Paste
Flash, exit program	FL 53	Click File, click Exit; or click ✕ on menu bar
Flash, start program	FL 7	Click Start button, click all Programs, click Adobe folder, click Adobe Flash Professional CS6
Flash document, close	FL 23	Click File, click Close
Flash document, open	FL 8	Click File, click Open, select file, click Open
Flash document, preview by scrubbing	FL 13	Drag playhead in Timeline header
Flash document, preview in Flash Player	FL 9	Click Control, point to Test Movie, click in Flash Professional; or press Ctrl+Enter
Flash document, preview in Flash program window	FL 9	Click Control, click Play; or press Enter
Flash document, preview in Web browser	FL 10	Click File, point to Publish Preview, click HTML
Flash document, save with current name	FL 23	Click File, click Save
Flash document, save with new name	FL 8	Click File, click Save As, select folder, type filename, click Save
Flash document, test download in different settings	FL 320	Test movie in Flash Player, click View, point to Download Settings, click setting, click View, click Simulate Download
Frame, make Frame 1 current	FL 21	Click Control, click Rewind
Frame, make last current	FL 22	Click Control, click Go To End
Frame-by-frame animation, create	FL 165	Insert graphic object in initial frame, add keyframe and new content or properties at each place the object changes
Frame label, add	FL 270	Select keyframe in Timeline, type label in Name box of Property inspector, press Enter
Gradient fill, transform	FL 111	In Tools panel, click ▣; click object with gradient on Stage, adjust gradient
Graphic, convert to symbol	FL 104	Select instance, click Modify, click Convert to Symbol, set options, click OK
Graphic, export	FL 46	Click File, point to Export, click Export Image
Grouped object, edit	FL 35	Double-click grouped object
Grouped object, exit group-editing mode	FL 36	Click scene name on Edit bar; or double-click blank area of Stage
Guide, create	FL 29	Display rulers, drag guide from a ruler to Stage
Guides, clear	FL 70	Click View, point to Guides, click Clear Guides
Guides, hide	FL 31	Click View, point to Guides, click Show Guides
Guides, modify appearance	FL 29	Click View, point to Guides, click Edit Guides
Help system, use	FL 51	*See* Reference box: Using the Flash Help System
History panel, open	FL 47	Click Window, point to Other Panels, click History
Input text box, create	FL 326	In Tools panel, click **T**; in Property inspector, click Text type button, click Input Text, create text block on Stage, set properties

TASK	PAGE #	RECOMMENDED METHOD
Instance name, add	FL 269	Select instance on Stage, type name in Instance name box in Property inspector, press Enter
Keyframe, insert	FL 167	Select frame in Timeline, click Insert on menu bar, point to Timeline, click Keyframe; or click F6
Layer, copy	FL 129	In Timeline, right-click layer name, click Copy Layers
Layer, move into layer folder	FL 128	In Timeline, drag layer over the layer folder
Layer, paste	FL 129	In Timeline, right-click layer name that you want to paste above, click Paste Layers
Layer, rename	FL 129	In Timeline, double-click layer name, type new name, press Enter
Layer, select	FL 128	In Timeline, click layer name
Layer folder, insert	FL 128	In Timeline, click
Layer folder, rename	FL 130	In Timeline, double-click folder name, type new name, press Enter
Letter animations, create	FL 213	*See* Reference box: Animating Individual Letters
Library panel, open	FL 100	Click Window, click Library or click Library tab
Lines, draw with Pencil tool	FL 73	Click in Tools panel, click modifier, set stroke properties, draw on Stage
Mask layer, create	FL 192	*See* Reference box: Creating a Mask Layer Animation
Merge Drawing mode, select or deselect	FL 69	Click in Tools panel
Motion path, add to motion tween	FL 140	Drag instance to new location
Motion path, modify	FL 142	*See* Reference box: Modifying a Tween's Motion Path
Motion preset, apply	FL 146	Select symbol instance on Stage, click desired motion preset in Motion Presets panel, click Apply
Motion tween, create	FL 139	Add instance of a symbol or text block in beginning frame, right-click frame, click Create Motion Tween, modify instance in ending frame
Motion tween, modify motion path	FL 142	*See* Reference box: Modifying a Tween's Motion Path
Motion tween, modify properties	FL 143	Select tweened object on Stage, change settings in Property inspector
Motion tween, modify properties in Motion Editor	FL 185	Select motion tween on Stage, click Motion Editor tab, modify tween's properties
Movie Explorer, use	FL 233	Click Window, click Movie Explorer, click Show buttons to select and deselect as needed
Object, change orientation	FL 232	Click Modify, point to Transform, click option
Object, copy and paste	FL 81	Select object, click Edit, click Copy, click Edit, click a paste command
Object, flip horizontally	FL 169	Select object on Stage, click Modify on menu bar, point to Transform, click Flip Horizontal
Object, manipulate in 3D	FL 218	Select frame with object, in Tools panel, click , drag red line to rotate x axis, drag green line to rotate y axis, drag blue circle to change z axis, drag orange circle to change all axes
Object, modify anchor points	FL 40	*See* Reference box: Using the Subselection Tool
Object, modify with Selection tool	FL 37	Click in Tools panel, drag a line or a corner of the object to change its shape

TASK	PAGE #	RECOMMENDED METHOD
Object, modify with Subselection tool	FL 40	Click [icon] in Tools panel, click object's stroke or fill, drag an anchor point to change its shape
Object, move	FL 37	Click [icon] in Tools panel, click object, drag object
Object, orient to path	FL 145	Select layer with object in Timeline, click Orient to path check box in Rotation section of Property inspector
Object, reposition on Stage	FL 16, 21	Drag object with Selection tool; or change object's X and Y values in Property inspector
Object, scale on Stage	FL 22	Select object on Stage, change object's W and H values in Property inspector
Object, select one or more with Selection tool	FL 37	Click [icon] in Tools panel, click object or draw selection marquee around objects
Object, transform	FL 79	*See* Reference box: Transforming an Object Using the Free Transform Tool
Object Drawing mode, select or deselect	FL 69	Click [icon] in Tools panel
Objects, align on Stage	FL 263	Select several objects at one time, open Align panel, click align button(s)
Objects, distribute to layers	FL 216	Select objects, click Modify, point to Timeline, click Distribute to Layers
Objects, group	FL 34	Select objects, click Modify, click Group
Objects, select with Lasso tool	FL 41	Click [icon] in Tools panel, drag to select objects
Onion marker, set number of frames	FL 224	In Timeline, click [icon], click option
Onion skinning, toggle on or off	FL 224	In Timeline, click [icon]
Oval, draw	FL 69	Click [icon] in Tools panel, set stroke and fill properties, click and drag pointer on Stage
Panel, close panel group	FL 26	Click panel's title bar, click panel menu button [icon], click Close Group
Panel, collapse to icons	FL 19	Click Collapse to Icons button [icon]
Panel, display	FL 18	Click Window, click panel name
Panels and panel groups, organize	FL 18	*See* Reference box: Organizing Panels and Panel Groups
Rectangle, draw	FL 65	Click [icon] in Tools panel, set stroke and fill properties, click and drag pointer on Stage
Rectangle, set corners	FL 65	Click [icon] in Tools panel, enter Rectangle corner radius values in Property inspector
Regular frame, insert	FL 140	Select frame in Timeline, click Insert on menu bar, point to Timeline, click Frame
Rulers, display or hide	FL 29	Click View, click Rulers
Scene, duplicate	FL 134	In Scene panel, select scene, click [icon]
Scene, rename	FL 132	In Scene panel, double-click scene, type new name, press Enter
Scene, select	FL 133	On Edit bar, click [icon], select scene
Scenes, reorder	FL 133	In Scene panel, drag scene to new location
Shape tween, apply to text	FL 211	*See* Reference box: Creating Text Shape Tweens

TASK	PAGE #	RECOMMENDED METHOD
Snap to Objects, select or deselect	FL 69	Click 🧲 in Tools panel
Sound, add effect	FL 298	Select keyframe with sound, click Effect button in Property inspector, click sound effect
Sound, add to background	FL 295	Select Frame 1 of sound layer, click Name button in Property inspector, click sound file
Sound, add to button	FL 293	See Reference box: Adding a Sound to a Button
Sound, add to document	FL 292	Click Window, point to Common Libraries, click Sounds, select file, drag to library or Stage
Sound, change Sync setting	FL 297	Select keyframe with sound, click Sync button in Property inspector, click setting, click Sound loop button, click option, set number of times to repeat
Sound, import to library	FL 295	Click File, point to Import, click Import to Library, select file, click Open
Spelling checker, set options	FL 96	Click Text, click Spelling Setup
Stage, change view	FL 26	See Reference box: Changing the View of the Stage
Stage, move its view	FL 27	Click ✋ in Tools panel, drag Stage to new position
Static text box, create	FL 93	Click T in Tools panel; in Property inspector, click Text engine button, click Classic Text, click Text type button, click Static Text, set text properties, create text block on Stage
Steps, replay	FL 48	Select steps in History panel, select object on Stage, click Replay button in History panel
Steps, undo	FL 50	Click Edit, click Undo; or move slider to previous steps in History panel
Stroke or fill properties, copy	FL 78	See Reference box: Using the Eyedropper Tool
Symbol, change type	FL 100	In Library panel, select symbol, click ⓘ, click Type button, select type, click OK
Symbol, create	FL 98	See Reference box: Creating a Symbol
Symbol, create duplicate	FL 101	In Library panel, select symbol, click 📋, click Duplicate, type name, click OK
Symbol, edit	FL 102	See Reference box: Editing a Symbol
Symbol instance, create	FL 103	Drag copy of symbol from Library panel to Stage
Symbol instance, swap	FL 162	Select symbol instance on Stage, click Swap button in Property inspector, select symbol, click OK
Text, create	FL 93	Click T in Tools panel, set text properties in Property inspector, click or click and drag on Stage to create text block, type text
Text, spell check	FL 97	Click Text, click Check Spelling
Text, split letters into individual text blocks	FL 216	Select text block, click Modify, click Break Apart
Text animations, create	FL 154	See Reference box: Creating Text Animations
Text box, set type	FL 322	In Tools panel, click T; in Property inspector, click Text type button, click Input Text or Dynamic Text or Static Text, create text block on Stage
Timeline, change view	FL 127	In Timeline, click 📋, click desired view

TASK	PAGE #	RECOMMENDED METHOD
Tool, select	FL 15	Click tool's button in Tools panel; or press tool's shortcut key
Toolbar, open or close	FL 8	Click Window, point to Toolbars, click toolbar name
Tween span, extend or reduce	FL 144	In Timeline, drag right side of tween span right or left
Tween span, move	FL 163	In Timeline, drag selected frames within tween span right or left
Video, encode	FL 354	In Adobe Media Encoder, click File, click Add Source, select file, click Open; set export settings, click Start Queue (Return) button
Video, import	FL 359	Click File, point to Import, click Import Video, follow steps in Import Video Wizard
Workspace, show frame	FL 9	Click View, point to Magnification, click Show Frame
Workspace, switch or reset layout	FL 8	Click workspace switcher button, click layout or click Reset layout
Zoom level, change	FL 27	On Edit bar, click Zoom control arrow, click setting; or click 🔍 and click 🔍 or 🔍 in Tools panel, click specific area of Stage